THE JEWS IN AMERICA: A HISTORY

Books by RUFUS LEARSI

ISRAEL: A HISTORY OF THE JEWISH PEOPLE

FULFILLMENT: THE EPIC STORY OF ZIONISM

THE JEWS IN AMERICA: A HISTORY

THE JEWS IN AMERICA: A HISTORY

by RUFUS LEARSI

EPILOGUE

AMERICAN JEWRY 1954-1971

by

ABRAHAM J. KARP

KTAV PUBLISHING HOUSE, INC.

NEW YORK

1972

LIBRARY OF CONGRESS CATALOG CARD NUMBER: 54-5347

NEW MATTER

KTAV PUBLISHING HOUSE, INC.

SBN 87068-177-X

REPRINTED BY SPECIAL ARRANGEMENT WITH
WORLD PUBLISHING COMPANY

In a special way this book
is for
DAVIDIE, J. *and* J. *and* ARTLEE

Foreword

WITH ALL their distinctness and "high visibility" the Jews in America are not, of course, the compact body which the anti-Semite professes to see in them. They are instead a highly diversified group, socially and ideologically, and their character and destiny as a community are envisioned by them in a variety of ways. They have, for example, their extreme "isolationists," who contend that the Jews in America can and should follow their own course, unaffected by the lot of their coreligionists in other lands, and, on the other hand, those who see no future for the community in America apart from those in other lands—from the one that constitutes the state of Israel, in particular.

The present writer advocates neither of those extremes. But every story, as is well known, is tinged by the prepossessions of the storyteller, and the author's outlook, which he has been at no pains to conceal, emerges clearly at various stages of the book. His most pervasive assumption, perhaps, is that the story of the Jews in America must embrace the historic heritage and concurrent fortunes of their people the world over, in addition, of course, to their life as an integral part of the American nation.

The author is persuaded that his general outlook is shared by the great majority of his fellow Jews in America, but in no sense is this narrative a reflection of the "official" attitude of any group in the community, large or small. No such group has engaged him to write this book, and he has not sought or followed the advice of any before, during or after its composition. And if at times he has shown himself partisan, he has not, he trusts, failed to present other viewpoints fairly and fully.

For help in the writing of this book I am particularly indebted to Professor Joshua H. Neumann of Brooklyn College, whose competence in matters of style is as thorough as his acquaintance with the subject matter; to Sundel Doniger, who has had personal contact with many of the events of the last four decades with which the book deals; and to her whose help has never failed me in this as in other tasks—my wife. Others supplied me with information, material or specially prepared reports. The list includes Rabbi Isidore S. Meyer of the American Jewish Historical Society; Mark Uveeler and Dr. Shlomo Noble of the Yiddish Scientific Institute (YIVO); Harry J. Alderman, Morris Fine, Dr. Simon Segal and George Kellman of the American Jewish Committee; Samuel Caplan, editor of *Congress Weekly*; Ann S. Mazer and Allen Lesser of B'nai B'rith; Dr. Alfred Jospe of the B'nai B'rith Hillel Foundation; Jacob Pat of the Jewish Labor Committee; Bernard Postal of the National Jewish Welfare Board and Arnold Isreeli of the American Zionist Council.

The list includes also Saul Bernstein of the Union of Orthodox Jewish Congregations of America, Dr. Emil Lehman of the United Synagogue of America, Rabbi Louis I. Egelson of the Union of American Hebrew Congregations, William Wolpert of the United Hebrew Trades, Mark Starr of the International Ladies Garment Workers' Union, Richard Rohman of the Amalgamated Clothing Workers, Julius G. Feit of the Galician Farband, Tamar Neumann of the Zionist Archives and Library, Bernard G. Richards of the Jewish Information Bureau, Dr. H. S. Linfield of the Jewish Statistical Bureau, Dr. Theodore Norman of the Jewish Agricultural Society, Akiva Skidell of the Jewish Agency, Moshe Rivlin of the General Consulate of Israel, Dr. Israel S. Chipkin of the Jewish Education Committee of New York and Dr. Uriah Z. Engelman of the American Association for Jewish Education.

I have also had the advice of a number of men with expert knowledge in specialized fields, among them Dr. Israel S. Wechsler and Dr. Maurice Goldberg for medicine, Dr. Mordecai Soltes for the Yiddish press, Professor Abraham W. Binder for music, Dr. Noah Goldberg for crime statistics and Harold U. Ribalow for literature and sports. And my secretary, Mrs. Janet Gendelman, deserves my thanks for competent service.

Among the numerous sources I have consulted I name the following four to which I am especially indebted: *Early American Jewry* by Jacob Rader Marcus (Philadelphia, The Jewish Publication Society of America; vol. 1, 1951; vol. 2, 1953); *American Jewry and the Civil War* by Bertram Wallace Korn (Philadelphia, The Jewish Publication Society of America, 1951); *The Needle Trades* by Joel Seidman (New York, Farrar & Rinehart, 1942) and *The Price of Liberty* by Nathan Schachner (New York, The American Jewish Committee, 1948).

With regard to Jewish population statistics there are no accurate figures and those given are the best available estimates. The reader is also asked to note that in the transliteration of Hebrew words considerable diversity existed and still exists (e.g. *Shalom, Sholom, Shalome, Sholem*), and in proper nouns the style used by the person or institution in question has been followed.

RUFUS LEARSI

Table of Contents

List of Illustrations

Maps

THE JEWS IN AMERICA: A HISTORY

CHAPTER 1

Overture in Minor

1

IN 1654 THE STATELY METROPOLIS OF AMSTERDAM STOOD where the River Amstel flows into an inlet of the Zuyder Zee; and in the New World, on the tip of Manhattan Island where the North and East Rivers mingle with the Bay, lay the rude settlement of New Amsterdam. The ancient city in the Old World was the busiest port in Europe and the chief city of the United Provinces, or the Netherlands, a country better known as Holland, whose independence had been recognized by the rest of Europe only six years earlier. The bleak village on Manhattan was the center and capital of New Netherland, a large and vaguely defined region, which Holland claimed as her share of the New World.

In 1654 thirty years had passed since the first Dutch settlers had set up their huts on Manhattan Island but the situation of New Netherland, administered under government charter by the West India Company of Amsterdam, was still precarious, the chief peril stemming from the English possessions north and south, which the Dutch colony divided and menaced. In 1626 the Company's director-general, Peter Minuit, after concluding the most famous bargain in history by acquiring Manhattan Island from the Indians for beads and calico worth twenty-four dollars, had erected Fort Amsterdam on the Island's tip; and far up the Hudson River, on the present site of Albany, stood a fortified trading post named Fort Orange. The name was in honor of William the Silent, Prince of Orange, who had liberated the Protestant Netherland provinces from the bloody yoke of Philip II of Spain.

Most of the Dutch settlers were attracted by the quick profits of the fur trade, and the liberal inducements which the Company offered them to go into farming, the only sound economic basis of a colonizing enterprise, failed to lure them. And the Dutch governors, harassed by pirate depredations, Indian raids and English encroachments, turned a deaf ear on the demands of the settlers for self-government, another essential for successful colonization.

Now in 1654, the month being September, the vexations of Peter Stuyvesant, director-general of New Netherland, were aggravated by a new and unexpected visitation. A French privateer, the *St. Charles*, had tied up at the wharf with twenty-three passengers—men, women and children—who petitioned for asylum and residence in New Amsterdam. They were not Dutch, nor did they belong to any of the nations with whom the Dutch were contending for their place in the sun of the New World: French, English, Spanish, Portuguese or Swedish. They did not, of course, belong to the Reformed Church of the Dutch settlers, a form of Protestantism that adhered to the austere creed of John Calvin; and they were not Lutherans or Quakers or Catholics, all of whom the Dutch disliked and did their best to exclude. The newcomers, in fact, were not even Christians; they were Jews, members of a race and faith whom Europe for more than a thousand years had been taught to shun and suspect. They were the first group of this people to land on the soil of what is now the United States of America, the tiny vanguard of its largest aggregation in four millenia of history.

2

The baggage this group of fugitives brought with them on the *St. Charles* was pitifully small, most of it, it is thought, having been pilfered by pirates on the way, and what there was of it had to be auctioned off to pay the captain for their passage. But they carried a spiritual baggage which must be entered in any inventory of their resources. For nearly sixteen centuries they and their forebears had been wanderers and outcasts in the Old World, but imbedded in their consciousness and faith were memories of a precious and glorious past. The story of the Jews in any land cannot be divorced from their story in many other lands, and in particular from the little land along the eastern Mediterranean where it began and reached its apogee.

In the prayers those fugitives recited in all their sojournings and wanderings, in the fasts and feasts they observed and in the Sacred Scriptures they read and studied, they saw that past in an aura of holiness and divine purpose. They were the descendants of the Patriarch Abraham whose covenant with the One God controlled their destiny. They were the bondsmen whom Moses led forth from Egypt and brought to the foot of Sinai for the most sublime experience in the spiritual journey of man. They had sinned and suffered, rebelled and repented, and fought victoriously under Joshua for the land they were promised. They struggled for generations against a ring of enemies and rose to glory with David the King, whose psalms illumined their prayers, and with his son Solomon, who built the Temple that epitomized their pride and faith. Every Sabbath these fugitives still read the stern and tender words of their great prophets. Every year they observed glad or solemn festivals that made the past live again, and on the ninth day of the month of Ab they gathered to lament the fall of Kingdom and Temple, destroyed by Nebuchadnezzar the Babylonian. The same ill-starred day marked also the destruction of a Second Commonwealth and Temple at the hands of the ruthless Romans six and a half centuries later. Some sixteen hundred years had now passed since that disaster, but to the refugees seeking asylum in New Amsterdam and their coreligionists across the world, that event and the others, happy or sad, were not mere entries in a record, but present realities that shaped their inner life.

The centuries that followed were studded with less vivid memories; by and large they made up a somber stretch which they called the *Galuth* or "Exile." Now the nation was dispersed—for the most part over Europe and North Africa—aliens in every land and often segregated outcasts, forced to live on the margin of its economy and on the ragged fringe of its tolerance. But even across this forest-dark Dispersion there were occasional clearings that glowed with a strange brilliance, the most significant being a period of five centuries in Babylonia that produced the Talmud, the most normative book in the life of any people, and a longer period in Spain, where a large, affluent, and proud Jewish concentration created a religious and secular culture of astonishing variety and splendor.

A little more should be told about the Spanish period because those exiles who arrived in New Amsterdam in 1654 were descended from those who lived it. The efflorescence began in the tenth century when the Moslems, who conquered Spain in 711, still ruled the country; and it continued for at least three centuries after 1085, when the Christians, in their efforts to recover the land, achieved a great triumph by capturing the city of Toledo. Across those centuries moves an imposing procession of Jewish genius: soldiers and statesmen, scholars and scientists, philosophers and poets, moralists and mystics. The mention of only a few of them—Shmuel Ha-Nagid, Solomon ibn Gabirol, Yehudah Halevi, Moses Maimonides, Abraham ibn Ezra—suffices to evoke the grandeur of this episode in the long story of the Jewish people.

Some of the *St. Charles'* passengers may themselves have been born on the Iberian peninsula, if not in Spain, then in Portugal; and the ancestors of all of them were certainly born there. Their origins, in other words, were in the country called in Hebrew *Sepharad*, and they were known therefore as Sephardim. The name distinguished them from their coreligionists in Central and Eastern Europe, the Ashkenazim, who either lived in, or hailed from, *Ashkenaz*, or Germany.

3

What had befallen the proud community of Spain that drove these Sephardim to the shores of Manhattan and had driven scores of thousands before them through dire perils to many other shores? In 1492 they suffered an overwhelming disaster. In March of that year King Ferdinand of Aragon and his wife Queen Isabella of Castile, whose realms comprised much the greater part of Spain, decreed that any Jew found within their borders after July of that year must accept baptism or suffer death. The 300,000 Jews of Spain became a horde of fugitives, seeking haven in all the other lands washed by the Mediterranean. Many of them perished in storm, wreck and pestilence, or were sold as slaves by the captains of their ships or by pirates who captured them. Most of them got across into Portugal. They paid a handsome price for permission to stay there for eight months, but when the term expired they were prevented by a variety of chicaneries from leaving the country and were sold into slavery or baptized by force. Children under fourteen were torn from their parents, and many fathers and mothers, to save their children from baptism, slew them and then themselves.

4

The edict of expulsion of 1492, which liquidated the Jewry of Spain, had been the last of a series of measures which the clergy, nobility and populace of Spain had for more than a century employed to solve their "Jewish Question." Among the other methods the most important were mob violence and legal extrusion and pauperization, the same devices, in fact, which Nazi Germany applied before resorting to the more efficacious method of systematic large-scale extermination. In Spain, however, the combination of massive pogroms and legal degradation had a peculiar consequence. It compelled many Jews to accept baptism, producing a large number of New Christians or Conversos, many of whom—called Marranos, or "the accursed"—remained loyal to the faith they had been forced to renounce and continued to practice it in secret. And since, after receiving baptism, a relapse of this sort constituted heresy, the Marranos became eligible for the ministrations of an imposing and appalling system of "correction" known as the Inquisition.

A place in this chronicle may fairly be claimed by the Inquisition, or Holy Office as it is also called, not only because, as we shall see, it followed the New Christians and Marranos into the Spanish possessions of the New World, but because the hope of escaping from its clutches was a powerful motive impelling Jews to seek a new life in the Western Hemisphere or, as in the case of those we left on the wharf of New Amsterdam, to flee from one part of the Hemisphere to another. The Spanish Inquisition, as it flourished in the realms of Ferdinand and Isabella, was a model of its kind. It attained its peak of efficiency under Thomas de Torquemada, a Dominican monk of ferocious zeal and rare ingenuity, who still held the office of Inquisitor-General in 1492. He was also confessor to the royal couple and the chief instigator of the expulsion decree of that year.

"The Inquisition," writes the eminent historian John Lothrop Motley,* "was a bench of monks without appeal, having its familiars in every house, diving into the secrets of every fireside, judging and executing its horrible decrees without responsibility . . . It arrested on suspicion, tortured till confession, and then punished by fire . . . The torture took place at midnight, in a gloomy dungeon, dimly lighted by torches. The victim—whether man, matron or tender virgin—was stripped naked, and stretched upon the wooden bench. Water, weights, fire, pulleys, screws—all the apparatus by which the sinews could be strained without cracking, the bones crushed without breaking, and the body wracked exquisitely without giving up its ghost, was now put into operation. The executioner, enveloped in a black robe from head to foot, with his eyes glaring at his victim through holes cut in the hood which muffled his face, practiced successively all the forms of torture which the devilish ingenuity of the monks had invented."

The crowning glory of the Inquisition was the auto-da-fé, the "act of faith," when a sizable number of those from whom confessions had been extorted were consigned to the holy flames. It was a solemn and festive occasion, marked by pageantry and pomp, and attended by royalty, nobility, clergy, and the populace who, says Motley, "regarded

* *The Rise of the Dutch Republic;* v. 1, p. 323, New York, Harper Brothers, 1885.

it as an inspiring and delightful recreation." After a program of pious exercises, including the preaching of a sermon and the mass singing of the Miserere, the victims, attired in grotesque penitential robes called Sanbenitos, were handed over to the executioner. But the Inquisition was not wholly without mercy: if the victim, facing the stake, renounced his heresy, he was strangled before being thrown to the flames.

Such was the Spanish Inquisition which flourished in the kingdom of Ferdinand and Isabella, and which was later established in Portugal also to minister to the large body of Marranos to which the forced conversions in Spain had given rise.

5

On the sounding board of world history the year 1492 "rings a bell" much louder than the expulsion of the Jews from Spain. But strangely enough, in the ears of the man in whose honor the bell rings the expulsion sounded very loud indeed. In his diary Columbus links that event with his momentous voyage. "After the Spanish monarchs had banished all the Jews from their kingdoms and territories," the diary begins, "in the same month they gave me the order to undertake with sufficient men my voyage of discovery to the Indies." Was it because the expulsion was the news sensation of the year? But in January, 1492, the Spaniards conquered Granada, the last Moslem stronghold in the Iberian peninsula, and for a pious Christian that event should have taken precedence. All Christendom, in fact, was profoundly stirred by it: in London Henry VII ordered a special thanksgiving service in St. Paul's cathedral.

It is believed by many, among them the distinguished Spanish scholar and historian Salvador de Madariaga, that there was a peculiar and secret reason why Columbus was so sensitive to the plight of the Jews. Columbus, they assert, was himself of Jewish descent. He belonged, says Madariaga, to a Spanish-Jewish family that bore the name Colom or Colon, a common name among Jews in Spain: not a few Colons, in fact, were burned by the Inquisition. To escape persecution, the family, about the year 1390, had fled to Italy and settled in Genoa, where some sixty years later, the inspired navigator was born. The Spanish-Jewish or Marrano descent of Columbus has not been proved beyond doubt, and perhaps it never will be. But on no other hypothesis can certain puzzling facts about him, in addition to his odd preoccupation with the tragedy of Spanish Jewry, be explained: among them his greater facility with the Spanish language than the Italian; the frequent mention in his writings of characters in the Hebrew Scriptures and events in the ancient history of the Jews; his apparent preference for Jews and Marranos in his quest not only for financial, but for diplomatic and scientific assistance as well.

It was a costly enterprise Columbus proposed, and if the popular legend that the Queen sold her jewels to finance it is true, those jewels must in large part have come from Marranos, victims of the Inquisition who, of course, forfeited their possessions along with life and liberty. Large means were provided also by the exiles who had sold their property for a song—"a house for a cart and a vineyard for a donkey." It is certain that the property of the exiles provided the funds for the second and much larger expedition of Columbus in 1493.

But, the legend notwithstanding, the money for the first voyage also appears to have been furnished by certain Jews and Marranos directly: by Abraham Senior and Isaac Abarbanel, the chief commissaries of the Spanish army; by the Marrano Gabriel Sanchez, the treasurer of Aragon; and especially by Luis de Santangel, farmer of taxes and customs and a man of great influence with the monarchs. Santangel too had had a narrow escape from the toils of the Inquisition, and obtained a royal exemption from charges of heresy for himself and his descendants. It was Santangel who was instrumental in retaining the disgruntled Columbus in Spain when early in 1492 he was setting out to solicit the support of France, and he advanced the considerable sum of 17,000 florins for the voyage. The first report of his discoveries that Columbus wrote he addressed to Gabriel Sanchez and Santangel.

There were numerous Jews in Spain possessed of wealth and power, and even more New Christians—a state of affairs that produced even more resentment against them than the religion they professed openly or in secret. It was a resentment compounded by envy and cupidity, and the lure of despoiling them was at least as strong a motive as religious zeal for banishing Jews and burning Marranos. New Christians stood high in the government, in the army, the universities—in the church itself! And as a result of intermarriage there were few noble families in Spain without an admixture of Jewish blood. It was, indeed, inevitable that Jews and Marranos should play a prominent part in promoting an enterprise so significant as the first voyage of the great discoverer. It is not a far-fetched surmise that many of them hoped it would produce a haven from the Inquisition; and apart from anything else, it held out great promise for the expansion of international trade, in which they were particularly prominent.

Nor is it surprising that they made important contributions to the scientific aspects of the undertaking also. For generations they had been cultivating not only the vast lore of their faith, but the secular disciplines also, especially medicine, astronomy and mathematics. Nor did they play a minor role in the science and art of navigation, including the development of nautical instruments like the astrolabe and quadrant, the preparation of astronomical tables, and the art of cartography. Yehudah Cresques, who was born on the island of Majorca, where in 1391 he survived a bloody pogrom, eventually became the director of a nautical school established by the famous Prince Henry the Navigator of Portugal. Cresques was known as "the map Jew" and the "compass Jew." Of more direct help to Columbus was the astronomer and mathematician Abraham Zacuto of Salamanaca, whose perpetual almanac and astronomical tables were used by the discoverer. Zacuto recommended Columbus to the Spanish monarchs, but he himself, after a sojourn in Portugal, died an exile in Turkey.

A distinguished pupil of Zacuto, however, the physician and nautical expert Joseph Vecinho, found no merit in the mariner's plans, and the king of Portugal, his patron, rejected them. Vecinho's repudiation of Columbus led to the greater glory of Spain; it compelled the future discoverer to seek help from Ferdinand and Isabella. But Portugal's glory was also advanced by Zacuto. The redoubtable voyager Vasco da Gama, who sailed for the monarch of Portugal and in 1497 reached India by way of the Cape of Good Hope, obtained endorsement and considerable help from Zacuto, who had taken refuge in Portugal after the Great Expulsion.

But the part played by sons of this hounded people in the great adventure was not confined to providing money and scientific knowledge; they were present in the crews of the vessels that sailed the uncharted ocean, and they were among the first who trod the soil of the New World. In fact, the first European to set foot on the first island which Columbus reached and called San Salvador, was Luis de Torres, his interpreter. Torres would naturally be required to hasten and parley with the natives; he knew Hebrew, Aramaic and Arabic, and surely one or another of those tongues should be intelligible to inhabitants of India! But though Torres must have failed to impress the copper-colored natives with his palaver, the country impressed him greatly, for he decided to stay there: he settled in Cuba, the second island touched by Columbus. And there were other Jews in the crew besides the eager interpreter. Among them were two, Bernal and Marco, who were doctors, and Rodrigo Sanchez, who was a relative of Gabriel Sanchez, the Admiral's benefactor.

All of them, of course, had been baptized; for on the second of August, which happened to fall on the calamitous Ninth of Ab, the last Jewish exiles had departed from Spain, and the following day the Admiral's little argosy had glided out of the port of Palos; and how could a Jewish foot defile its decks, representing as they did the sacred soil of Spain? But is it too hard to believe that when, in the course of that seven weeks voyage, the little caravels were lashed by wind and wave, Maestre Bernal the doctor, who had once suffered public penance for practicing Judaism in secret, or Luis de Torres, who could chant the psalms in Hebrew, prayed silently but fervently to the God of Abraham, Isaac and Jacob?

6

It was not long before the mariners of the Old World realized that the islet on which Columbus knelt and planted the Spanish ensign was not one of the coveted Spice Islands of the East, and that the name he gave the timid and astonished natives was a misnomer. San Salvador was only a crumb of an immense new world that lay between Europe and those opulent islands, and a long contest began among the European monarchs for its possession and exploitation, the chief contenders being Spain, Portugal, France, Holland and England, with Spain far in the lead.

Gold, slaves and souls were the three objectives of the Spanish discoverers and conquistadors. When Columbus returned from his first voyage the gifts he brought his sovereigns included some gold and a number of Indians, who were duly baptized. On his second voyage he took along twelve missionaries and returned with five shiploads of Indians to be sold as slaves. By that time he had discovered the biggest islands of the West Indies: Cuba, Jamaica, Puerto Rico and Haiti. The Spaniards pushed on and by 1540 Spain laid claim to Central America, the southern reaches of North America and nearly all of South America. Brazil, however, where a number of settlements along the coast, including Recife or Pernambuco, were already established, was held by Portugal. Hernando Cortez had overthrown the Aztec Kingdom of Montezuma in Mexico, and Francisco Pizarro had devastated the realms of the Incas in Peru, the two regions where the civilization of the natives, ruthlessly extinguished by the Spaniards, had reached its peak. The invaders enjoyed advantages over the natives that proved decisive: metal tunics that made arrows harmless, thundersticks that vomited death and terror, ferocious dogs that slew and devoured, and strange monsters consisting of huge animals with projections on their backs that looked like men.

But perhaps the Spanish conquerors possessed an even greater advantage in their ferocity and cruelty. They exterminated the natives by working them to death in the fields and mines. To punish them they fed them to their dogs or burned them, wrapped in wet straw, on slow fires. In Mexico the entire population of many villages preferred to die by their own hands as the conquerors approached. Cuba, Haiti and Puerto Rico were practically depopulated, and in Central and South America cities were obliterated and every man, woman and child slain. The missionary, Bartolome de Las Casas, estimated the number of natives who perished at the hands of his countrymen at 20,000,000.

The havoc wrought by the seekers after gold and slaves was completed by the hunters of souls: the Inquisitors came and mopped up after the conquistadors. A great many natives, baptized by force, naturally reverted at the first opportunity to their own immemorial rites. They became Indian Marranos, and as early as 1511 the daughter and successor of Queen Isabella ordered the Inquisition into the New World to deal with the "heretics" in its own fashion. "The Inquisition," says Motley, "taught the savages of . . . America to shudder at the name of Christianity."

7

The primary aim of the Holy Office in the Spanish Americas, it appears, was to "correct" Jewish rather than Indian heretics. For it was natural for Marranos to venture forth into the New World, to hope that in its wide primeval spaces they would be safer from detection in the practice of the faith they loved. In addition, the economic opportunities which the new discoveries presented appealed to the spirit of enterprise for which the Spanish Jews were noted. The first grant of a license to trade in the newly discovered islands, in fact, was issued by Isabella in 1502 to Juan Sanchez, whose father had been immolated by the Inquisition.

Over the years the rulers tried hard to stop the migration of New Christians into the New World, issuing edicts against it that exhibit the usual combination of piety and greed. Philip III of Spain, for example, who reigned from 1598 to 1621, decreed that "no one recently converted to our holy faith," or his offspring, "should settle in our Indies without our distinct permission." Even more drastic was the prohibition against the "child or grandchild of any person who has ever worn the *sanbenito* in public . . . or was burnt as a heretic or otherwise punished for the crime of heresy." The penalty for disobedience was confiscation of the culprit's property for the benefit of the royal treasury; but lest poverty should provide immunity, the decree ordained that "whoever does not possess personal effects should atone for his transgression by the public infliction of one hundred lashes."

The harsh decree failed to halt the migrations, but the zeal of the Inquisition in America did not go unrewarded. Its tentacles had become numerous and prehensile in the reign of the gloomy fanatic, Philip II (1556-1598). A new codification of its laws and regulations was sent to America and its human ferrets were carefully briefed in what to look for in a suspect. Did he move his lips in a benediction before drinking wine or tasting food? Did he look worn or hungry on the Day of Atonement? Did he wear neat clothes and a clean shirt on Saturday? Was the chimney on his roof smokeless on that day? If so, he qualified for the Inquisition. The grisly apparatus of the all-powerful tribunal: dungeons, torture chambers, autos-da-fé, was set up in the New World, although many of the prisoners, especially those apprehended in the Portuguese possessions, were deported for trial and punishment to Portugal or Spain. Over the years its victims must have been many, although no reliable estimate of the number can be given. Some incidents, however, may be cited which will reveal the shadow that lay for centuries on the Jews who hoped to find respite in the New World.

In Mexico the Holy Office was officially established in 1570, but there were executions for Jewish heresy as early as 1528, when one of the victims was Hernando Alanso, who had been a conquistador under Cortes. At an auto-da-fé in Mexico City which took place in February, 1590, the family of Francisca de Carabajal, after having been duly tortured, confessed they had practiced Jewish rites. Nearly six years later, after a long imprisonment, the mother and four of her children were consigned to the flames: they were found guilty of having relapsed. Francisca's brother was Luis de Carabajal, a New Christian who was governor of a district in Mexico, but he was powerless to avert his sister's fate; had he tried to do so his own might have been equally tragic. From 1642 to 1645, the teen-age Marrano, Gabriel de Granada, was held and harried by the Inquisition in a Mexico City prison until he implicated many members of his family, including his mother, in the crime of practicing Jewish rites in secret. Several of them suffered the extreme penalty, but Gabriel's mother foiled the executioner by starving herself to death. The Inquisition in Mexico was not abolished until 1820!

In Peru the Holy Office was particularly zealous, no doubt because the Marranos in that country were numerous and wealthy. Dozens of autos-da-fé were celebrated, at which Jews, Moors, Lutherans and Calvinists were degraded or burnt with exemplary impartiality. The biggest and proudest of them took place in Lima in 1639. Sixty-three of the victims, of whom eleven died at the stake, were Jews. Among them was the physician Francisco Maldonado de Silva, the most famous of the "Judaisers" who fell into the clutches of the Inquisition in America. He had been arrested twelve years earlier in Chile on a denunciation lodged by his own sister at the insistence of her father confessor. Maldonado de Silva was the stuff that saints and martyrs are made of. His father, a Marrano, had brought him up as a Catholic, but the son, deeply religious and convinced by study and meditation, returned to Judaism. During the terrible years of his incarceration he bore his sufferings heroically, stood his ground against the priests, who made special efforts to convert him, and inspired his fellow-prisoners also to stand firm. He fasted a great deal, especially towards the end, and the executioner had little more than a skeleton to bind to the stake.

In Brazil the first European settlement was planted by the Portuguese in 1532, and until 1654 the history of that broad and rich portion of America is highlighted by the struggle for its possession between Portugal and Holland, a struggle in which the Jews had a vital stake and played an important part. Marranos who came to Brazil early and in large numbers were prominent in the commercial, industrial and professional life of the country, especially in Bahia and Recife. Sugar growing, the leading industry, was brought to Brazil as early as 1548 by Jewish planters from Madeira.

But the secret Jews lived in constant dread of the Inquisition. In Bahia, for example, Jewish physicians took care to prescribe plenty of pork to their patients so as not to be suspected of leaning towards Judaism. The Inquisition itself was not set up in Brazil, but its long arm reached them all the way from Portugal; those suspected of Jewish heresies were arrested and sent for trial and punishment to the homeland. From 1580 to 1640, the period of the "Spanish Captivity," when

Portugal was kept in forced union with her stronger neighbor, they might be sent to the more efficient Holy Office in Spain.

8

To the rulers of Spain and Portugal the prospect of possessing the entire Western Hemisphere was more than a rosy dream. Had not Pope Alexander VI, famous in history as the father of the perfidious Cesare Borgia, drawn a line of demarcation dividing the new discoveries between them to the exclusion of all others? Had the line been respected by the other European powers, as the Pope no doubt expected it would be, it is doubtful that a wholesome Jewish life would have found a place in the New World. At best some scattered Marranos, singly or in small groups, like those discovered shortly after the First World War in Oporto, Braganza and other cities of northern Portugal, would have continued a furtive and sterile existence. But three other European nations—France, Holland and England—came forward and challenged the Papal Line, the last two after turning Protestant and repudiating the authority of the Pope not only in the political, but in the religious sphere—a revolutionary act in which lay the seeds of ultimate religious freedom.

In the race for the New World, Holland was more than a century behind Spain and Portugal: the Dutch had a tremendous preliminary to dispose of before their sturdy seamen could turn their ships' prows towards America. In 1555, as a result of marriage and bequest, the Dutch became subjects of Philip II of Spain, and when he moved to make their country a Spanish province, complete with the Inquisition, they revolted. A long and bitter struggle followed, comparable in heroism and endurance as well as in objective—national independence and religious freedom—to the Maccabaean war of the Jews against Antiochus and his successors. In 1581 the seven northern provinces declared their independence, and although it was not until 1648, when the Peace of Westphalia ended the bloody Thirty Years' War, that the independence of the United Provinces, or the Netherlands, was recognized, Dutch prosperity and maritime power grew and reached out to the New World. In 1621, the Dutch West India Company was founded, and Amsterdam became the leading port of Europe.

Long before the Peace of Westphalia, Marranos from Portugal had made their way to Amsterdam, where they returned openly to the faith from which they had been torn. It is related that in 1596 Amsterdam burghers became aware of a strange worship being conducted in their city, and when the magistrates appeared on the scene, the worshipers managed to explain that they were Marranos who had fled from Portugal and that they were observing the Day of Atonement. They were permitted to remain, and as the years passed more Marranos came to join them. Later came refugees from the ghettos of Germany who sought escape from the terrors of the Thirty Years' War, and fugitives from Poland fleeing from the fury of the Cossacks, who in 1648 rose up against their Polish overlords and massacred the Jews. Nor did the Dutch regret their hospitality, for the enterprise and commercial skill and connections of the Jews played an important part in making Holland one of the great powers of Europe. The three Jewish groups, Sephardic, German and Polish, each established its own synagogue and other institutions, and only gradually overcame their mutual aloofness. For it seems to lie deep in human conceit that those who arrive earlier should distrust and snub those who come later, and it is worthy of note that in the United States the same aloofness prevailed for a long time among the same groups who arrived very much in the same order.

The Jews of Amsterdam were not admitted to civil and religious equality—the concept of equality had hardly been born. They were subject to a variety of disabilities: they could not engage in handicrafts, for example, or in retail trade. But under the rights and privileges which they were granted they enjoyed religious freedom and prospered. It was natural that they should not be absent from among the stockholders of the Dutch West India Company, and they were even present among its directors. They made up the most important Jewish community in the world, and people spoke of Amsterdam as the New Jerusalem.

The life of the community did not, of course, flow in halcyon tranquillity. It had its problems, tensions and crises. In 1640 came the tragedy of the restless and disaffected Uriel Acosta, who ended his own life after undergoing the ordeal of a public recantation. Sixteen years later the community pronounced the ban of excommunication on a more important dissident, Baruch Spinoza, an act which had no tragic consequences, but which many Jews are still unable to forgive. In 1666 the Amsterdam community, like every other in Europe, Asia and Africa, was rent by the passions and dissensions which were roused by the false Messiah, Sabbatai Zevi of Smyrna.

And in 1654, when that little group of Jewish pilgrims was heading for New Amsterdam, Menasseh ben Israel, a distinguished member of the Amsterdam community, had agents in London on a brave and important mission. He was bent on convincing the Lord Protector, Oliver Cromwell, that England should rescind the ban against the Jews, which had been enacted in 1290, and permit them to return. England, he urged, would benefit from their presence, as had Holland, her rival. During those centuries, it is true, Jews had not been altogether absent from England: a few Marranos, keeping their identity as secret as they could, managed to sojourn there, and in Menasseh's day a number of wealthy Jewish merchants were residing in London, some of them, like Antonio Carvajal and Simon de Caceres, conducting global commercial operations and enjoying special protection. But the ban of 1290 was still the law of the land, and Jews dared not come in sizable numbers, nor could they hope to establish a dignified communal life of their own. Menasseh encountered formidable obstacles: the English clerics wanted no infidels, and the English merchants no competitors. But his mission was not unsuccessful. The Jews were not readmitted by formal fiat, but more and more of them came and they were not molested.

Menasseh was that paradoxical combination of man of affairs and mystic, not uncommon in our own days but more common in his. He looked fervently forward to the coming of the Messiah who would redeem his people from exile, but in his view, shared by many Christians, his people must dwell in every land of the earth, including of course England, before the great ingathering could take place. And what of the New World and its many lands? The question had been answered to Menasseh's satisfaction. A certain Antonio Montezinos, a Marrano who had traveled widely in South America, had convinced him that the New World natives were descended from the Lost Ten Tribes. "I think," wrote Menasseh, "that the Ten Tribes live not only there, but also in other lands." The theory that the Indians were of Jewish descent found many Christian supporters and not a few opponents, and the controversy on the subject, which continued well on into the nineteenth century, was lively and sometimes acrimonious.

9

In 1621 the Dutch were again at war with Spain, and since the "Spanish Captivity" still bound Portugal to her neighbor, the newly formed Dutch West India Company looked upon the Portuguese settlements in Brazil as fair game. It goes without saying that the Marranos in those settlements, living in the red shadow of the Inquisition—a shadow which had deepened when Portugal was taken over by Spain—

and aware of the fortunate lot of their coreligionists under the Dutch, scanned the horizon eagerly for their coming. They came in 1624 and seized Bahia, but were forced out a few months later; some 200 Marranos who had welcomed them and thrown off the mask of Christianity, were given good cause by the Portuguese to rue their too hasty rejoicing. But in 1630 the Dutch conquered a more important prize, the town of Recife, better known as Pernambuco. They held it for twenty-four years, and a vigorous Jewish community, the first in the Western Hemisphere, came to life there and flourished.

Recife and the settlements north and south, as well as the vast hinterland which the Dutch took over, prospered under the able administration of the Stadholder, Maurice of Nassau. Marranos from other parts flocked at once to Recife and joined their coreligionists in free and open profession of their faith. They overestimated, it appears, the tolerance of their neighbors, Protestant as well as Catholic; they were directed to worship with less exuberance. But they grew in wealth and numbers: one observer, in fact, relates that among the free inhabitants of Brazil the Jews were the most considerable in number. The report of their good fortune reached their people in Holland and other lands, and many of them took ship and joined them. A larger contingent than usual, numbering about six hundred, arrived in 1642, and among them were Isaac Aboab da Fonseca, who became the Chacham, or Rabbi, of the community, and Moses Raphael de Aguilar, who was chosen reader or cantor.

Three years later the Portuguese moved to reconquer Brazil, directing their main efforts to the recapture of Recife. "That city," their leader told them, "is chiefly inhabited by Jews . . . They have their open synagogues there to the scandal of Christianity. For the honor of the faith, therefore, the Portuguese ought to risk their lives and property in putting down such an abomination." The struggle continued for nine years, and after a long and devastating siege Recife was starved into surrender. Jews and Dutch fought desperately to hold off the enemy, but their government across the ocean, hard pressed by a war with England, was unable to help them. In January 1654 Recife and the neighboring settlements were surrendered to the Portuguese, and the proud and prosperous Jewish Community of Brazil came to a swift end.

It was a repetition in miniature of the expulsions from Spain and Portugal a century and a half earlier. But there were differences. The terms of capitulation under which the Dutch handed Brazil back to Portugal permitted the Jews to remain, but few of them cared to go

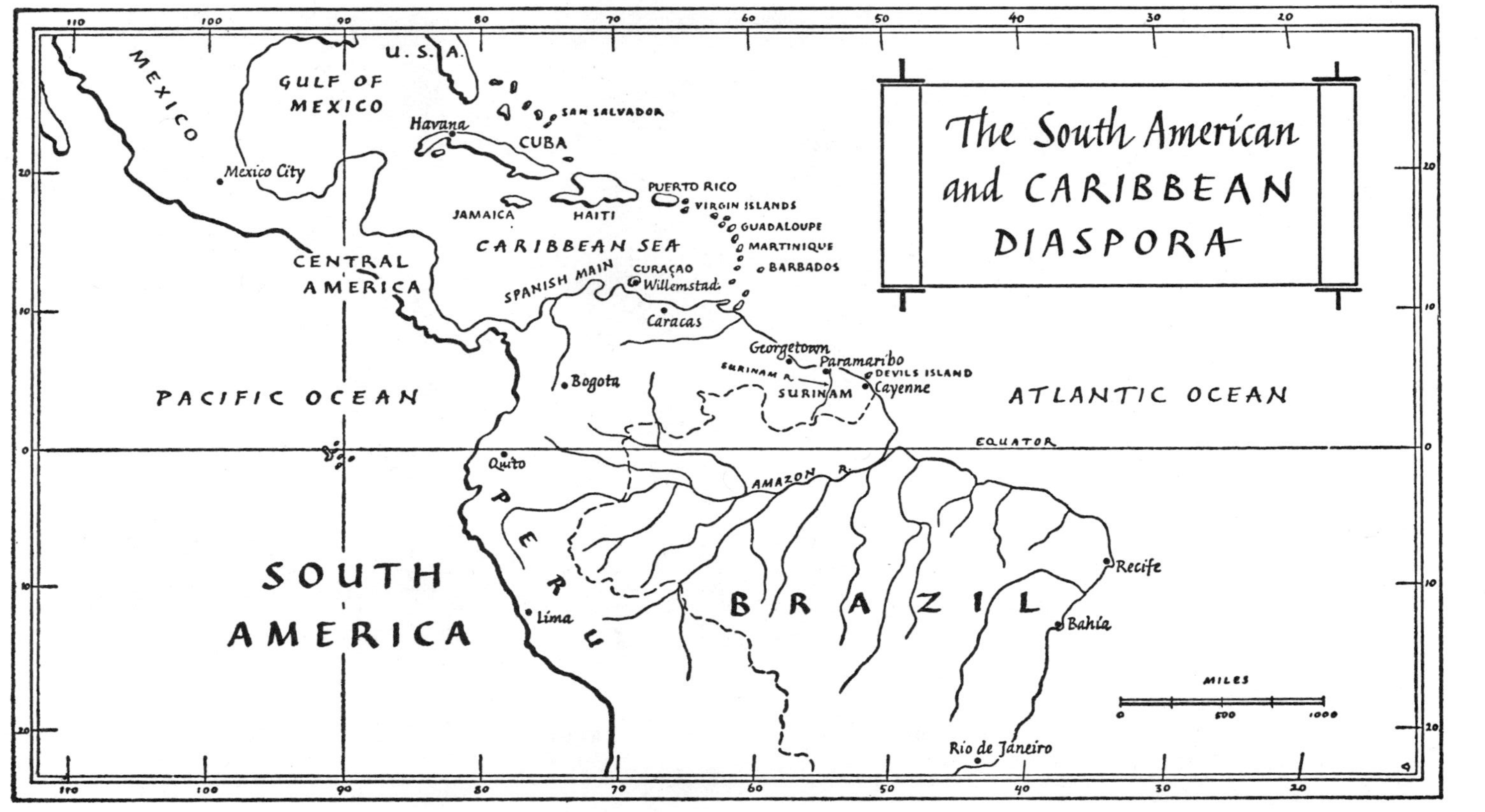
The South American and CARIBBEAN DIASPORA
MEXICO
GULF OF MEXICO
U.S.A.
Mexico City
Havana
CUBA
SAN SALVADOR
JAMAICA
HAITI
PUERTO RICO
VIRGIN ISLANDS
GUADALOUPE
MARTINIQUE
BARBADOS
CARIBBEAN SEA
CENTRAL AMERICA
SPANISH MAIN
CURAÇAO
Willemstad
Caracas
Georgetown
Paramaribo
DEVILS ISLAND
Cayenne
SURINAM R.
SURINAM
Bogota
PACIFIC OCEAN
ATLANTIC OCEAN
EQUATOR
Quito
AMAZON R.
PERU
SOUTH AMERICA
Lima
BRAZIL
Recife
Bahia
Rio de Janeiro
MILES
0
500
1000

underground again, with the specter of the Inquisition continually stalking them. This time, moreover, there were places where they could expect to find haven. So the Portuguese governor who, of course, was glad to be rid of heretics and infidels, assembled sixteen ships, which carried almost all the Jews of Brazil to various destinations.

Almost, but not quite all; and in later years the small number that remained was augmented by New Christians who had incurred suspicion in Portugal and were exiled to Brazil. And from time to time Marranos in Brazil were taken to Portugal to be dealt with by the Inquisition. As late as 1739 the most illustrious of these victims was delivered to the flames in Lisbon. He was the brilliant Antonio Jose da Silva, born thirty-four years earlier in Rio de Janeiro, who in his brief span had time to become one of Portugal's foremost dramatists. Da Silva was found guilty of being secretly loyal to Judaism; in the history of Portuguese literature he is usually called "the Jew."

10

They produced a diaspora within the greater diaspora of their people, those refugees from Brazil of the year 1654. Many of them, including Isaac Aboab and Moses Aguilar, returned to Holland, and it may be noted that twelve years later, both were numbered among the adherents of Sabbatai Zevi in the excitement and strife which that Messianic pretender provoked among the Jews of the Old World. A few, it is thought, found their way to London where they joined the small group of Sephardim who managed to live there even before the new toleration which the efforts of Menasseh ben Israel produced. But most of them sailed to Jewish communities which had sprung up in other parts of the New World.

The most important of these settlements and the one to which many of the exiles from Brazil sailed, had arisen in Surinam, better known as Dutch Guiana. A number of times Surinam changed hands between the Dutch and the English. The latter, having found "that the Hebrew nation, now already resident here, have, with their person and property, proved themselves useful and beneficial for the colony," enacted a generous charter of privileges for the "Hebrew nation," granting them unrestricted religious freedom and a large measure of judicial autonomy. That was in 1665, more than a quarter-century after the first Jews arrived in the colony; and two years later, when the Treaty of Breda awarded Surinam to the Dutch, those rights were confirmed.

Jews were among the leading planters of the colony, and in 1682 the wealthiest of them, Samuel Nassi, made over a large island on the Surinam River for colonization by his coreligionists, a little "Jewish homeland", as it were, which became known as the "Savannah of the Jews." A similar project had been launched earlier in Dutch Cayenne by David Nassi, probably a kinsman of Samuel. In 1654 some of the exiles from Brazil had found refuge in Cayenne, and six years later a sizeable group of Jews arrived from Italy, they too, no doubt, fugitives from the Inquisition. David Nassi's project of establishing a Jewish settlement was making good progress when in 1664 the French captured Cayenne and the Jews had to go: the French monarchs, instructed by the Jesuits, could not tolerate the presence of infidels in their possessions. And it is tempting to mention still another Nassi who was inspired by the same vision of creating a distinctly Jewish settlement, though to meet him we must go back a whole century to Constantinople, capital of the expanding Ottoman Empire. He was Joseph Nassi, the most illustrious bearer of the name, also a Marrano refugee from Portugal. He rose to power and splendor under Suleiman the Magnificent (1520-1566), and made a bold but unsuccessful attempt to provide a refuge for his persecuted people by settling them in and around the city of Tiberias in Palestine.

Unlike the other two "Zionist" Nassis, Samuel of Surinam was fairly successful. Most of the Surinam Jews settled on the "Savannah" and prospered. In 1785 the handsome synagogue they had built there celebrated its hundredth anniversary. But by that time the settlement was already declining, its career bedeviled by the slave economy on which all the plantations of the New World rested. From time to time the Negro slaves revolted and escaped to the jungles, whence they descended on their masters. For nearly a century the "Savannah" suffered from these depredations, and to fight them off the Jewish planters had only themselves to depend on. They were also active in repelling French attempts to seize the colony.

Today the "Savannah of the Jews" is only an interesting ruin, but there is still a Jewish community in Dutch Guiana, concentrated in Paramaribo. In time Ashkenazim from Germany were added to the original Sephardim, but even as in other parts of the world, the former established institutions of their own. The Surinam community is able to boast of a brave, honorable and distinguished career, the longest of any Jewish community in the Western Hemisphere.

A career of almost equal length may be claimed by the Jewish community on the island of Curaçao, which the Dutch took away from the Spaniards in 1634, and which also received a considerable influx from

Brazil twenty years later. The trade between Curaçao and New Amsterdam was largely in Jewish hands, a state of affairs that Peter Stuyvesant found most deplorable. The community, most of it dwelling in Willemstad, the capital, continued to prosper, erected impressive synagogues, established philanthropic and other communal institutions, but seems to have had a rather heavy load of internal tensions and conflicts. In 1693 there was a substantial Jewish emigration from Curaçao to the continent, many of the emigrants settling in Newport, Rhode Island, among them members of the Touro family. The Jews of Curaçao rose to leading positions not only in the economic and professional, but also in the political and military affairs of the colony.

11

The large island of Jamaica, held by the Spaniards since its discovery by Columbus on his second voyage, was seized by the British in 1655 and has been theirs ever since. A goodly number of Marranos, or "Portugals," as the English called them, were living their clandestine Jewish life on the island, and shortly afterwards they were joined by others who came from Brazil. The island's history has not been a happy one, what with natural disasters like earthquakes and hurricanes, and social disturbances, including slave revolts and unemployment riots. The British allowed the Jews to stay, but taxed them heavily and "by the lump." In 1700 they petitioned for relief, and in his reply the governor maintained that they monopolized "the keeping of the shops and merchandise," and that by "their parsimonious living" they were underselling the English. But mindful that frugality is a sterling British virtue, the governor hastened to add that their "parsimonious living" was not being charged "as a fault in them." They petitioned also against being forced to bear arms on the Sabbath "without any necessity or urgent occasion," and the governor admitted that "when any public occasion has happened or an enemy appeared, they have been ready and behaved themselves very well."

Disabilities against the Jews in Jamaica, like their exclusion from positions in the civil service, were not removed until 1831. Four years later Alexander Bravo became the first Jewish member of the Jamaica assembly, and fourteen years later eight of the forty-seven members were Jews. In fact, the large number of Jews who held political and military posts on the island was cited in 1838 by Sir Francis Goldsmid in his valiant struggle for the emancipation of the Jews in England. That struggle, it may be added, was not won until twenty years afterwards, when Lionel Rothschild, having been elected to Parliament, was permitted to take the oath with head covered in Orthodox fashion, and to substitute "so help me God" for the formula "upon the true faith of a Christian."

The small British island of Barbados, with its fine soil for sugar growing, also received a number of refugees from Brazil in 1654. Jewish traders are believed to have come there as early as 1628, but they were not accorded formal toleration until 1656: the local planters favored their admission, but the merchants in London opposed it. In 1674 their oath taken on the Five Books of Moses was validated for testimony in a court of law, but it was only in 1820 that Parliament granted them political equality. After a devastating hurricane in 1831 the community in Barbados, never large, gradually dispersed, most of its members migrating to other American colonies under the British flag, and to the United States.

12

Large numbers of refugees from Brazil sought asylum also in the French possessions of the West Indies, especially in Guadaloupe and Martinique. For many years the Jews in those islands were the stakes in a stubborn contest between the Jesuits, who wanted them degraded and expelled, and the local authorities to whom it was clear that the prosperity of the islands depended on them. Almost all trade, in fact, was in their hands. The contest reached out to the court in Versailles, where the Jews had a powerful friend in the chief minister of Louis XIV, the great statesman Jean Baptiste Colbert. But Colbert died in 1683, and two years later *le grand monarque* extended the Black Code, applying to the French West Indies the edict of expulsion which Louis XIII had issued against the Jews of France in 1615. In Jesuit phrasing, the Code provided that all Jews, "as declared enemies of the Christian faith," were to leave the islands in three months "upon penalty of the confiscation of their bodies and property." The island officials in many instances managed to circumvent the edict, and years later Jews again resided on the islands, their position of course always precarious. It took the revolution of 1789, which emancipated all Jews under French jurisdiction, to bring them civil and religious equality.

13

In this Caribbean world of immense spaces and countless islands nature was both bountiful and cruel. The coasts and islands had rich resources, mineral and agricultural, but they were not seldom visited by destructive hurricanes, volcanic eruptions and tidal waves. The Europeans who descended on them were a greedy swarm, goaded by a lust for quick gain, and the greediest of all were the Spaniards: they sometimes abandoned islands to their rivals because they failed to find in them the gold and gems they sought. By the middle of the seventeenth century, moreover, the Caribbean had become a pirates' paradise. They belonged to all the contending nations, but the English were the boldest and most successful. English buccaneers based on the islands preyed on the treasure ships of Spain as they sailed along the Spanish Main, or plundered Spanish settlements on the coast, reaping rich harvests for themselves and their sovereigns. With the spread of sugar, cotton, cacao, and other plantations the slave ships began to plow those waters, nor can it be said that Jewish traders were absent from the hideous traffic.

In the development of its resources the Jews who entered this world played a leading part, though it was not primarily the hope of gain that impelled them to seek its shores, but rather the longing to find a place where they could live by the faith of their fathers. For nearly three centuries after the Great Discovery, however, it appeared as if the noisome brood of prejudices that made the Jew an outcast in Europe would establish itself firmly in America. In the vast regions controlled by Spain and Portugal the Inquisition with all its horrors lowered over them. In the French they were hounded by the Jesuits and the Black Code of Louis XIII. The Dutch and the English permitted them to stay, and Jewish communities arose and flourished under their aegis. But with all the rights and privileges they were granted in consideration of their usefulness, they were still not recognized as equal members of the colonies of which they were part. The legal discriminations against them which existed in Holland and England accompanied them to the New World.

Such was the Caribbean diaspora into which most of the Jews who fled from Brazil in 1654 became absorbed. But our chief concern is with the tiny group that ventured out beyond it to the Dutch settlement on Manhattan where we left them.

CHAPTER 2

In Colonial America

1

VIEWED IN LONG PERSPECTIVE, THE ASSOCIATION OF JEWS and Dutch in North America was but for a day; the growth and maturation of American Jewry proceeded in the framework of a civilization that was dominantly Anglo-Saxon. The Dutch period involved only one community and it lasted only ten of the three hundred years that have elapsed since the arrival of that group in New Amsterdam, thirty decades that divide conveniently into the twelve that preceded the Declaration of Independence and the eighteen that have followed it. The Dutch decade, however, exhibits more than its share of the anomalies that marked the civil status of the Jew in the colonial period and the struggles which enabled him to live and thrive in spite of them.

To Peter Stuyvesant and his Council the twenty-three *St. Charles* passengers were heartily unwelcome. It was bad enough that they were insolvent: the proceeds from the sale of their belongings did not suffice to pay the master of the vessel for their passage, and three of them were held in custody for several weeks as security for the balance. It was worse that their religion was not Dutch Reformed: the Director General had no use for other kinds of Protestants, let alone Papists. But it was worst of all that they were Jews, members of "a deceitful race," who professed "an abominable religion," to quote Stuyvesant's own rhetoric. He wrote his employers in Amsterdam urging that "the Jewish nation" be banned from their domains, but the instructions he got from the board of the West India Company forced him to let the newcomers stay. The instructions were based on two considerations: first, that the Jews had suffered grievously in the war with the Portuguese; second, that the Jews in Amsterdam had large holdings in the shares of the Company. They were also among the Company's directors, and they probably had a share in drafting the instructions, for in answer to Stuyvesant's warning that if he admitted the Jews he would have to admit Lutherans and Papists also, he was told he must "not force people's consciences, but allow everyone to have his own belief, as long as he behaves quietly and legally." This simple formulation of the principle of religious freedom seems to echo with the experience of those who had suffered from its violation. It is clear, at any rate, that the refugees who knocked on the gate of New Amsterdam that day in September 1654 owed their admittance to the influence of "their nation" in old Amsterdam.

There was another statement in the correspondence between Stuyvesant and his masters in Holland that meant much to the refugees and their successors. "The poor among them," Stuyvesant was told, "shall not become a burden to the Company or community, but be supported by their own nation." That stipulation has frequently been cited by Jewish philanthropic leaders in America as imposing a sacred and eternal obligation. On closer examination it seems to cut across the principle of equality, but the motives, chiefly religious, for providing for their own poor and unfortunate are too cogent for Jewish communities not to honor it.

2

It is not easy for a faraway master to control a balky servant, even if the master is always clear and consistent as to his wishes. The directors of the Dutch West India Company were not always explicit as to the rights they desired the Jews in New Netherland to have, and Stuyvesant and his Council were able to indulge their ill will. Those rights could not, of course, include what was denied "their nation" in Amsterdam; they could not, in other words, engage in retail trade, practice a handicraft, hold a public post, or serve in the trainbands or militia. The directors, moreover, denied them the right of "exercising their religion in a synagogue or a gathering." Their tax bills were high enough: to build a rampart against Indian raids, for example, the Jewish taxpayers who numbered about 3 per cent of the total, paid 8 per cent of the cost, but they could not own real estate, or trade in Fort Orange and along the Delaware River. The rampart, it appears, was the stockade or "waal" along which ran a path that eventually became the celebrated and symbolic Wall Street.

In all their wanderings the Jews have looked upon the synagogue and "the house of life," or burial ground, as the two essentials for their collective life: they transformed an aggregation into a community. The synagogue was not only the house of prayer, but the school, and the center of their social life and works of charity. The "house of life" was the focal point of their dearest memories; by reason of it they felt their community to be not for a day but for eternity. Ten months after their arrival the Jews of New Amsterdam petitioned for the right to purchase a burial plot; the request was turned down because "as yet there was no need." They obtained the plot a year later: the need must now have arisen; but a synagogue was something which Stuyvesant never permitted the Jews to have. They held their religious services in their homes.

But most significant in the career of this tiny group under the grumpy Dutchman was the gallant struggle they waged against him for the vindication and extension of their rights. They obtained a document from the Company in Amsterdam affirming their rights to own real property and to trade on the Hudson and Delaware, and compelled the Director General and his Council to honor it. In a firm and dignified petition, dated March 14, 1656 and signed by Abraham de Lucena, Jacob Cohen Henricques, Salvador Dandrada, Joseph d'Acosta, and David Frera, the five largest taxpayers, the Jews of New Amsterdam "humbly request that your Honors permit them, if, like other burghers, they must and shall contribute, to enjoy the same liberty allowed to other burghers, as well in trading to all places within the jurisdiction of this government as in the purchase of real estate."

But even more important was the campaign they waged for the right to serve in the militia, and "like other burghers, to enjoy the burgher's right," and obtain "the customary burgher certificate." In this effort the outstanding figures were Jacob Barsimson and Asser Levy. They pleaded inability to pay the tax imposed on them for exemption from military service, and insisted on their right to "keep guard with other burghers." Their petition was denied, and with heavy sarcasm the denial added that "since the petitioners are of opinion that the result of this will be injurious to them, consent is hereby given to them to depart whenever and whither it pleases them." But later the demand was granted; Asser Levy was a man of resolution, and Barsimson too belonged to the stiff-necked race. Levy, in fact, went further. He thought he should be recognized as a burgher, and when he was joined in this demand by the men of substance of the community, who pointed out that "our nation enjoys in the city of Amsterdam in Holland the burgher rights," all the Jews of New Amsterdam were admitted to burghership.

In the meantime more came to New Amsterdam from other Dutch possessions in the Caribbean and from across the ocean, though some of them, and some of the original arrivals also, left for other parts. At the end of the decade the community on Manhattan was still a diminutive body, its growth hampered by the ill will of the officials and by the legal restrictions that bore down on it, of which the prohibition against erecting a house of worship was the most galling.

In London, in the meantime, Charles II had disposed of the future of New Netherland, and prepared a new sovereignty for the little group on Manhattan Island. With royal aplomb he made over the entire region between the Connecticut and Delaware Rivers to his brother, the Duke of York: the Dutch must not be allowed to divide his colonial empire in America. In August 1664 four English men-of-war appeared in the harbor and demanded the capitulation of the fort. Early the following month the doughty but helpless Stuyvesant surrendered. His burghers saw no hope in offering resistance. "Whether we turn us for assistance to the north or to the south, to the east or the west, 'tis all in vain," they said in a remonstrance addressed to him and his Council. The English permitted the garrison of the fort to leave with full military honors, and New Amsterdam became New York.

3

For the future of American Jewry and the whole Jewish people that surrender was a momentous decision. It meant the beginning of the largest community under one sovereignty in the history of that people, the strongest and freest in the two millennia of the Dispersion.

As one decade followed another to the fateful year 1776 the community grew, but it was a slow and unpromising growth, lagging far behind the general growth of the colonies. In 1664 there were probably some 300 Jews in North America and by the outbreak of the Revolution they had grown eight or nine fold. But in the same period the general population had grown nearly eighty fold. Not that a scarcity existed in the Old World of Jews who yearned for a life free from brutal persecution and grinding poverty; such a scarcity, alas, has not been known in the millennia of the Dispersion. But comparatively few of the two million Jews of the world during the period had the means to undertake the costly and hazardous voyage. To most of them, perhaps, America was only a vague echo, and there were no Jewish West India Companies to spur them with promises and subsidies. It was those who lived in Western Europe, in lands where they saw men and merchandise go down to the sea in ships, and to some from Central and Eastern Europe who made their way to those lands, to whom

America was a reality. That is why during the colonial period most of those who took the journey were Sephardim, descendants of Portuguese and Spanish Marranos dwelling for the most part in Holland, France and England, international traders to whom the ocean was not so much a terror as a highway.

By 1776 there were Jews in all thirteen colonies, but in only five of them were there organized Jewish communities: in Rhode Island, New York, Pennsylvania, North Carolina and Georgia. And first we note briefly the further fortunes of the community in New York which has been holding our attention.

4

Whatever rights the Dutch, willingly or otherwise, had granted the "Jewish nation" in Amsterdam, the new master allowed them to retain; and in some respects their rights exceeded those enjoyed by Jews in other English colonies. The ban against public worship remained, but was not, it appears, strictly enforced. By the end of the century a place on Beaver Street was known as "the Jewish Synagogue," though it was probably not a distinctive structure; and in 1730 the Congregation *Shearith Israel* (Remnant of Israel) dedicated a place of worship on Mill Street. Neither street nor synagogue has withstood the growth of the expanding city.

Remnant of Israel was the wistful name they chose for their congregation, the oldest in the United States, and it still lives and thrives, though it is better known today as the Spanish and Portuguese Synagogue. But the membership lists that have come down to us indicate that the Sephardic majority was being whittled down by Ashkenazim hailing from Germany, Poland and other countries. By 1754, in fact, most of the first-grade members of *Shearith Israel* were Ashkenazim, although its worship followed the Sephardic ritual. In 1776 its minister was Gershom Mendes Seixas,* who left the city when the English captured it in September of that year.

Unobtrusively the Jews of the growing town disregarded the disabilities, like the prohibition to engage in handicrafts or retail trade, that still lay upon them. In 1737, however, the General Assembly, or Legislature, denied them the right to vote for members of that body on the ground that their coreligionists in England did not have the right to vote for members of Parliament. Nevertheless, a list of voters dated

* Pronounced *Say-shus.*

twenty-four years later contains the names of a number of Jews, and long before that time the Assembly had made it possible for them to be naturalized by allowing them to omit from the oath the words "upon the true faith of a Christian." But it was only in the State Constitution of 1776 that the Jews of New York were granted complete equality.

5

North of New York, in the colony of Rhode Island, founded by Roger Williams as a haven for religious dissenters, rose the town of Newport, which in 1776 had the largest Jewish community on the Continent. It numbered nearly 1200 souls, by some estimates about half of the total number of Jews in the thirteen colonies. The Newport of that day surpassed New York as a port and commercial center, and the Jews played a leading role in it as merchants, manufacturers and shippers. They were prominent also in the social life of the town, and their generosity attracted emissaries from impoverished Jewish communities across the ocean. In 1768 their congregation, *Jeshuat Israel* (Salvation of Israel), erected a beautiful synagogue, designed by the distinguished architect Peter Harrison. Today the commercial eminence of Newport is a thing of the past and its thriving Jewish community a nostalgic memory, made more poignant by the poems which Longfellow and Emma Lazarus indited—to its cemetery! "Gone are the living but the dead remain," Longfellow sang, and of their sorrows in the lands they came from he wrote:

Pride and humiliation hand in hand
Walked with them through the world where'er they went;
Trampled and beaten were they as the sand
And yet unshaken as the continent.

A few Jews from New Amsterdam and Curaçao may have found their way to Newport only a year or two after the *St. Charles* docked at Manhattan, but the definite beginning of the Newport community is traced to the arrival of fifteen families from Holland in 1658. More came from the West Indies, and about the middle of the eighteenth century, especially after the disastrous earthquake at Lisbon in 1755, came a group of daring Marrano merchants who founded the prosperity of the community and, it is believed, of the town in general.

In the two decades before the Revolution Newport seems to have been a sort of rabbinical center. The minister of its own congregation was Isaac Touro, who arrived in 1760 from Jamaica, but visiting rabbis came from other lands, including Poland and Hungary, and from Jerusalem and Hebron in Palestine. They came, of course, to seek help for their people from the more fortunate Americans. The visitor from Hebron was Raphael Chaim Isaac Corregal; he was there in 1773, and seems to have made quite an impression, especially on Pastor Ezra Stiles, later president of Yale who, as his diary reveals, established a warm friendship with the exotic and learned rabbi.

Newport was captured by the British in 1776, and the ships of the Jewish merchants, nearly all of whom espoused the colonial cause, were confiscated. The community went into exile, most of its members taking refuge in Leicester, Massachusetts. After the war some of them returned, but the only highlight in the subsequent annals of the community is a famous letter it received from President Washington in 1790. The Revolution and the British occupation had ended the commercial importance of the town. New York's supremacy became established and most of the merchants settled there, though Philadelphia, Charleston and Savannah also received some members of the scattered community.

But on August 31, 1947 the congregation of two centuries ago was vividly recalled when, in the presence of a distinguished gathering of notables, its house of worship was formally dedicated as one of the national historic shrines of America. It is now known as the Touro Synagogue in honor of Judah Touro and his brother Abraham, sons of Isaac Touro, whose generosity had preserved the structure. It is the oldest synagogue building in the United States still standing.

6

The Philadelphia community had its start with Jewish traders who operated in southeastern Pennsylvania even before the arrival of William Penn in 1682, but its first congregation, *Mikveh Israel* (Hope of Israel) was not established until the middle forties of the following century. The community was substantially increased by the arrival of a large number of Jewish patriots from New York, who would not remain in that city after its capture by the English. Mikveh Israel's place of worship became too small and a new synagogue was erected and dedicated, with the governor of the state attending the exercises, in September 1782. Gershom Mendes Seixas, still a refugee from New York, became its first minister.

Some sixty miles west of Philadelphia lay the frontier trading post of Lancaster. A Jewish burial plot had been set aside there as early as 1747, and Jewish religious services were conducted in the home of Joseph Simon, father-in-law of Michael Gratz of Philadelphia, and one of the biggest landholders in the colonies. Simon was also one of the foremost Indian traders and furnished large quantities of rifles, ammunition and other supplies to the Continental Army. But Lancaster was only an offshoot of Philadelphia, and at the beginning of the nineteenth century its Jewish inhabitants moved east to that city. Their number was exaggerated by the curious fact that the Pennsylvania Dutch, who settled in Lancaster and its neighborhood, appeared to observers to practice Jewish rites. The language of the Jews, which was Yiddish, sounded also like the German of the Pennsylvania Dutch.

Jewish merchants had established themselves elsewhere in Pennsylvania also: in Easton, where in 1780 Myer Hart and his son Michael headed the list of taxpayers in the county; and probably also in Schafferstown. In Center County lies the town of Aaronsburg, named for Aaron Levy, who founded it in 1786. Some years later Levy donated a tract of land to the Salem Lutheran Church for a house of worship and school, and today Aaronsburg has become a symbol and gathering place for those "seeking a formula for national serenity and world peace through brotherhood and understanding." In the summer of 1953 a three day conference of the Aaronsburg Assembly, which is dedicated to that aim, brought together a group of men and women of outstanding prominence in the political and religious life of the country. Aaron Levy, now playing this handsome posthumous role, had migrated from Holland, engaged in many bold trading enterprises and numbered among his partners Joseph Simon of Lancaster and Robert Morris, the financier of the Revolution.

7

South Carolina began its colonial career by entrusting the great liberal philosopher John Locke with the task of framing its constitution, in which freedom of conscience was guaranteed to everybody, including "Jews, heathens and dissenters." As early as 1702 Jews voted in the colony in a general election, but it was only in 1750 that the congregation in Charleston, which called itself *Beth Elohim* (House of God), built the first synagogue. Most of its members were Sephardim, but some thirty years later the Ashkenazim were numerous enough to establish a congregation of their own. The community had many wealthy and prominent members, the most distinguished being Francis Salvador, who served in the General Assembly and the Provincial Congress of the colony that met in 1775.

In July 1733, a month after Georgia was founded by James Oglethorpe, forty Sephardic Jews arrived in Savannah and the following year came a group of German Jews. The trustees of the colony were not happy to see them, especially not the later arrivals, but their wish that the Jews "be given no encouragement" was ignored by the founder. They promptly established a congregation, which they named *Mikveh Israel* (Hope of Israel). There is peculiar interest in an observation recorded by John Wesley the founder of Methodism, who visited Georgia in 1737 and became acquainted with the Jews of Savannah. He studied Spanish in order to converse with them and, says his diary, some of them "seem nearer the mind that was in Christ than many of those who called Him Lord."

8

To the five or six centers of organized Jewish life in the colonies which were to constitute the United States of America should be added one that arose in Canada. In 1768 a congregation was established in Montreal by a group consisting largely of Sephardim who hailed from England. They called it *Shearith Israel*, the name their fellow Sephardim of New York had adopted more than a century before. With this Montreal group, which built its first synagogue in 1777, the history of the Jews of Canada is associated for the greater part of the next century. They were a sturdy and venturesome lot, who carried their trading westward and into the region of Hudson Bay.

9

In each of the five towns in the original thirteen colonies—Newport, New York, Philadelphia, Charleston and Savannah—where organized Jewish communities existed in 1776, the Jews were only a small fraction of the population; but in the economic life of each, especially in maritime commerce, their share was considerable. There were, of course, many among them who followed other occupations. There were skilled craftsmen working in wood and metal; tailors, shoemakers and saddlers; bakers, butchers and candlemakers. In the south there were a few Jewish plantation owners, but by and large they were an urban people, as they had been in the Old World, where for centuries they had been legally divorced from the soil.

Nor, in the field of commerce, were they all merchant princes with ships that sailed the seven seas. Most of them were storekeepers and peddlers, who followed hard upon the new settlements that rose on navigable rivers and on trails that were broadening into roads. A few were large scale purveyors who supplied the armies, but more of them followed the soldiers on their marches as sutlers. There were Jewish fur-traders who reached out to the outermost trading posts to obtain pelts from the Indians in exchange for trinkets, firearms and firewater.

But it was their place in shipping and ocean commerce that made the Jews a factor in the economic growth of colonial America. Their ships carried the yield of American fields and forests to Europe and brought back to the colonies the textiles, implements and luxuries of the Old World. The complicated steps involved in disposing of cargoes abroad and obtaining return cargoes were greatly facilitated by their friends and relatives in Amsterdam, London, Lisbon and other European ports, who served as their partners and agents—an advantage which an international people would naturally enjoy. A few ventured into the hazards of preying on enemy merchant ships as licensed privateers; and to some extent the importation of Negro slaves, nearly all of whom were sold in the West Indies, figured in their transactions. The unspeakable traffic, alas, was not in disrepute: the royalty and nobility of England amassed fortunes from it.

Not all the Jewish merchants in colonial America who traded at home or overseas achieved wealth and distinction. Most of them remained in the low-income brackets, and they were all exposed to the much greater risks and perils which the entrepreneur faced in those days than he does today. There were some, however, in New York, Newport and Philadelphia who might well be called merchant princes. In New York there was Lewis Moses Gomez, a refugee from Spain and later from France, and his six sons. There was Moses Levy, whose descendants achieved even greater prominence than he: his son Hayman was a leading fur trader and at one time the employer of John Jacob Astor. Finally, there was Jacob Franks, son-in-law of Moses Levy, who became one of the wealthiest men in the country; he was one of the chief purveyors to the English during the French and Indian War. Jacob's son David became one of the leading merchants and politicians of Philadelphia; his attachment to his faith was tenuous, he was a staunch supporter of George III, and his vivacious daughter Rebecca had no scruples about marrying an English officer who was afterwards knighted. Lady Rebecca became a source of dubious pride to some American Jews.

Even more prominent was the Gratz family of Philadelphia, which began its career with the two brothers and partners, Barnard and Michael. Four of Michael's twelve children rose to distinction: Simon and Hayman, partners in commerce and philanthropy, the latter being the founder of Gratz College; Benjamin, lawyer and soldier, who moved on to Kentucky; Jacob, who served in the Pennsylvania legislature; and Rebecca, the best known of them all, a pioneer in education and social service, a woman of charm and attainments, and, it has been said, the model of her namesake, the daughter of Isaac of York, heroine of Walter Scott's *Ivanhoe*.

Especially distinguished was the Seixas family, with members in New York, Newport and Philadelphia. Its founder was Isaac Mendes Seixas, a refugee from Portugal and France, and it included not only merchants like Isaac and Benjamin, the latter a founder of the New York stock exchange, but religious leaders. Its most famous member was Benjamin's brother Gershom Mendes (1745-1816), who at different times was, as we have seen, the religious head of the two leading congregations in colonial times, *Shearith Israel* in New York and *Mikveh Israel* in Philadelphia. And Philadelphia was the principal home of Haym Salomon, the financier who became posthumously famous for his services to the Revolution.

In the Newport community the leading merchants were Jacob Rivera and his son-in-law, Aaron Lopez. Jacob's father, Abraham, was a Marrano refugee who, when he came to New York with his wife and three children, followed the Marrano custom and married his wife over again, this time "according to the law of Moses and Israel," and the entire family adopted first names that were Jewish. In time Abraham Rivera and his son Jacob moved on to Newport. His son-in-law, Aaron Lopez, was, it appears, among the foremost merchants in colonial America. The famous diary of Ezra Stiles describes him as "a Merchant of First Eminence: for Honor & Extent of Commerce probably surpassed by no Merchant of America."

An important contribution to the industrial growth of the whole of colonial New England was made by Jacob Rivera when he introduced the manufacture of spermaceti candles. Some years later the United Company of Spermaceti Candlers was formed with the avowed aim of checking competition among its members by fixing the maximum price they would pay for the "brown oyl" and the minimum price at which they would sell their product, and adjusting their output "to the needs of the time." About half the firms who made up the Company were Jewish, among them those of Jacob Rivera, Aaron Lopez, Moses Lopez and Isaac Hart.

10

Of all pursuits commerce, large-scale or small, creates the widest social contacts, and Jews in colonial America mingled with their non-Jewish neighbors in social, philanthropic and political endeavors also. Large numbers of Christians now made their first acquaintance with Jews and learned for the first time that they were neither Biblical patriarchs nor mysterious ogres. Concerning Joseph Jonas, the first Jew to come to Cincinnati, the story is often told that people in the settlement came to look at him, and among them a Quaker woman eager to see "one of God's chosen people." She scrutinized him and circled around him and said finally with evident disappointment, "Thee art no different to other people."

The Jews adopted readily the language, the dress, and the political opinions and passions of their Christian neighbors. The principal problem was the language. Immigrants who arrive in adulthood cling to their mother tongue, for a language is more than a means of communication: it becomes charged with memories and emotions, a friend and familiar to which not only the ears and vocal organs are attuned, but the inner being also. Unlike other immigrant groups the Jews came to America with a number of languages: Spanish, Portuguese, German, Yiddish and others. Hebrew, the language they had in common, was confined to sacred uses and never became a vernacular, except in small circles dedicated to that purpose.

The Sephardim who arrived in the seventeenth and eighteenth centuries labored, of course, to acquire the dominant tongue: it was essential for success in the daily struggle. But at home and among themselves they spoke Spanish or Portuguese; congregational affairs were conducted and recorded in those languages, and the occasional sermon of the *hazzan*, or minister, was preached in Spanish. Connected with each synagogue was a school for the children with a curriculum of religious and secular studies, one of the latter being Spanish.

Gradually, however, English won an equal place and then quickly gained the upper hand. Its victory was no doubt accelerated by the large number of Ashkenazim who became members of the Sephardic congregations and whose language was German or Yiddish: a common language became a necessity and the logical one was English. In the sixties of the eighteenth century there appeared English translations of the prayerbooks, and even earlier English was accorded a place beside Portuguese in the recorded proceedings of *Shearith Israel* in New York.

11

Every community, through the synagogue directly or through an agency operating under its sponsorship, fulfilled the solemn obligation of caring for its distressed and needy. The awareness that "all Israel is responsible one for another" had its roots in the Old World and in the immemorial past, and the reasons—religious, social and, in a sense, political—why the Jews should care for their own were too strong to require external sanctions. And they aided not only their own members, but those of other communities, in America and other lands, being particularly sensitive to the appeal of the emissaries who sought help for the Jews in Palestine.

For the great majority the adoption of the language and other modes of the environment did not mean a weakening of their attachment to Judaism. They retained intact the traditional religious forms they or their forebears had brought to America. There were some defections, of course, especially among those who found themselves isolated in the inland outposts: they took wives who were and remained Christian, and the children, as is usual in such cases, were brought up in the faith of the mother. But the seaboard communities, to which the great majority belonged, held the individual to the group, satisfying alike his social and spiritual wants. The effective centripetal force, as in all lands and eras, was the synagogue.

CHAPTER 3

Revolution and Emancipation

1

THE SURRENDER OF NEW AMSTERDAM TO THE ENGLISH IN 1664 brought the Jews of America into a political system that was further advanced than any other on the road to personal liberty and representative government. The surrender of Cornwallis at Yorktown in 1781 and the Treaty of Paris two years later made them part and parcel of a new nation, "conceived in liberty and dedicated to the proposition that all men are created equal," to use the words of the peerless statesman who sealed them with his life.

The new nation was born defending the heritage of personal liberty it received in the land of its origin—from the Magna Carta of 1215, the Petition of Right of 1628, the Habeas Corpus Act of 1679, and other precious checks on despotism—but extended this heritage to include the principle of equality. Political rights, therefore, were not, as in England, limited to the well-heeled and wellborn, but reached out to all men, who were deemed to have been "created equal" because they were all created in the image of God.

For the destiny of the American Jewish community that heritage of liberty, and its momentous extensions in the Declaration of Independence and the Federal and State Constitutions, were of decisive importance. For one of the lessons which the history of the Jewish Dispersion points up is that the best chance for a Jewish community to thrive and survive is offered by a democratic political system, of which an essential ingredient is religious equality or freedom. The reason is not far to seek. To survive in a non-Jewish civilization a Jewish community must have the right to be "different," and that right is more likely to be honored in a political democracy, where the social order can endure without conformity or uniformity, than in any other system.

2

In the ferment that preceded and accompanied the Revolution, the rights and immunities guaranteed by the great constitutional landmarks of English history played, of course, a major role, as the merciless indictment of "the present King of Great Britain" in the Declaration of Independence attests. But strange as it may sound, the Jews also provided a leaven that played a major role, and not only in the agitation that preceded the Revolution, but in the keen political debates that followed it. And if the Jewish leaven did not come directly from the Riveras of Newport, the Gratzes of Philadelphia or the Salvadors of Charleston, it came from their remote ancestors, whose words and deeds stand recorded in the Bible.

In New England, where the psychological climate was created by Puritanism, it was natural that the Hebrew Scriptures should become the intellectual arsenal of the Revolution. Concerning the Puritans the historian James Truslow Adams states that "in spirit they may be considered as Jews and not Christians. Their God was the God of the Old Testament, their laws were the laws of the Old Testament, their guides to conduct were the characters of the Old Testament." The constitutions and laws of the Plymouth Colony, the Massachusetts Bay Colony and Connecticut leaned heavily on the Hebrew Scriptures. The legal code of New Haven, founded in 1638 as a separate colony, contained scores of references to the same source; John Davenport and Theophilus Eaton, its Puritan founders, even precribed the teaching of Hebrew in its first public school.

In the Hebrew Scriptures, also, the apostles of rebellion found precedent and inspiration, and the pulpits of the land, where public opinion was molded, resounded with their revolutionary summonses. The exodus from Egypt was the classic example of liberation from tyranny: the colonies of America should also make their exodus. The ten tribes of Israel defied the arrogant son of Solomon and established their own government: the thirteen colonies should do likewise. The Hebrew prophets denounced kings and potentates, and God-fearing Americans may do the same. Even the call engraved on the Liberty Bell: "Proclaim liberty throughout the land unto all the inhabitants thereof" was found in that Book (Leviticus 25:10). Revolutionary doctrine became crystallized in the slogan "Rebellion to tyrants is obedience to God." Indeed, those were the words which Franklin, Jefferson and John Adams proposed for the seal of the United States: they were to be inscribed around a picture of the children of Israel crossing the Red Sea. The New Testament, on the other hand, provided no fuel for the flames of revolution: its spirit was one of resignation and submission. In it, in fact, those who defended the king found justification. They could always cite the injunction of the Nazarene: "Render to Caesar the things that are Caesar's and to God the things that are God's."

Not less potent was the influence of the Hebrew Scriptures in determining the basic political system of the new society that emerged from the War of Independence. To discredit the monarchy, preachers like the bold and brilliant Jonathan Mayhew of Boston held up the warning of the prophet Samuel against royalty. Samuel Langdon, the president of Harvard, considered the Jewish government "a perfect republic," and Ezra Stiles, the president of Yale, found in the American government the fulfillment of Biblical prophecy. In his classic work, *History of the Rise and Influence of the Spirit of Rationalism in Europe*, the eminent nineteenth century historian William Edward Lecky, declares that "the Hebraic mortar cemented the foundations of American democracy," and the statesman, diplomat and scholar Oscar S. Straus, in his *Origin of the Republican Form of Government in the United States*, concludes that "in the spirit and essence of our Constitution, the influence of the Hebrew Commonwealth was paramount."

Engrossed in their daily struggles, the Jewish merchants, peddlers and craftsmen in the colonies were probably less aware of the immediate relevance of their ancient heritage than many of their Christian neighbors, and the latter identified their Jewish neighbors only vaguely with the men and women of the Bible. But the Book of Books was a normative force in the great crisis, and its contribution to the shaping of events was a Jewish contribution.

3

In the immediate issue of submission or rebellion, however, the Jews were as much divided as their neighbors. There were rebels among them—or patriots, as we prefer to call them—and loyalists or Tories, and in what proportion the two groups stood to each other is as difficult to determine with precision in their case as in that of the population at large.

From all the indications, however, it is clear that the great majority in every Jewish community threw in their lot with the Revolution. That they did so is made more significant by the large proportion among them who engaged in commerce and were well-to-do, for it is well known that men in those circumstances oppose radical change. We have already noted that the Newport community, the largest of the five, preferred to depart and disperse rather than continue under British occupation. The same cause disrupted the New York community also, although in its case a fair proportion remained: the congregation *Shearith Israel* was torn by dissension over the great question of the day. Many of those who left Newport and New York took refuge in Philadelphia, where they added to the large patriot majority of the community in that city. As for the Jews of Charleston and Savannah, their patriot sympathies were never in doubt, although in the South as a whole the proportion of Tories was larger than in the North.

In fact, beside the list of Jews who are known to have served in the armed forces of the Revolution, or assisted it with their means, the number of known Jewish Tories is remarkably small. The most distinguished of them was David Franks of Philadelphia. In October 1765 Franks had signed a Non-Importation Resolution which pledged the citizens of Philadelphia to boycott British goods "until after the repeal of the Stamp Act." Seven other Philadelphia Jews had signed the Resolution, among them Barnard Gratz and his brother Michael. At the outbreak of the war, however, Franks chose to remain loyal to King George. He employed his business talents "for victualing the troups of the King of Great Britain," was imprisoned by the Colonial Government and finally expelled from Philadelphia. A more tragic fate befell Isaac Hart of Newport; he was mobbed to death for his Tory sympathies. And there were other Jewish Tories, one of them Mordecai Levy of Philadelphia who, however, recanted in a public declaration that his conduct "proceeded from the most contracted notions of the British Constitution and the rights of human nature," a quaint formulation which testifies, however, to the high level of education in political science conducted by the patriots.

4

Among the Jews who fought in the armies of the Revolution the number of officers is strikingly high, and naturally so, because they belonged to a group that was on the whole educated and well-to-do. Not a few of the officers, however, had been promoted from the ranks for gallantry in action.

In the South the most distinguished Jewish patriots were Francis

Salvador of South Carolina and Mordecai Sheftall of Georgia. Salvador, scion of a prominent and wealthy family in London, was a typical southern planter and slave-owner. He played a leading part in the Revolutionary politics of his colony and state, and lost his scalp and his life defending the frontier against an attack by the Cherokee Indians, who had been incited by the British. Mordecai Sheftall, the leading member of the Savannah community, was equally prominent in the Revolutionary affairs of Georgia. One of his posts was that of Commissary-General to the troops of his state, and he was known to the British as "a very great rebel." In 1778 they took Savannah, and Mordecai and his son were captured and held for several years, first on a prison ship and later in the West Indies. After the war he received a grant of land for his services, and three years later he was one of the incorporators of the Union Society of Savannah, which appears to have been the first interfaith venture in America.

Three of the Jewish soldiers of the Revolution—David Salisbury Franks, Isaac Franks and Solomon Bush—rose to the rank of lieutenant-colonel, the career of the first being the most eventful. David S. Franks had settled in Montreal, where he was arrested for his rebel sympathies even before the outbreak of hostilities. He enlisted in a Massachusetts regiment and later served as aide-de-camp to Benedict Arnold, stood trial as a result of his chief's treason and was promptly acquitted. But the terms of the acquittal did not satisfy him and he applied to the commander in chief for a special court of inquiry, which cleared him completely. After the war he accomplished a number of diplomatic missions and received a large grant of land for his services.

Isaac Franks of New York, probably a relation of David Franks, fought in the Battle of Long Island, was taken prisoner and escaped. He was no doubt a brave soldier, but he is best remembered for the fact that in 1793 he was host to President Washington in Germantown: Washington went there to escape an epidemic of yellow fever in Philadelphia, then the national capital.

Solomon Bush of Philadelphia, the third Jewish soldier of that rank, held the post of Deputy Adjutant-General of the State Militia. He was severely wounded in action, and when the British seized Philadelphia in 1777 he was taken prisoner. After the war Bush tried hard to obtain a post in the diplomatic service; he failed, but he seems to have found consolation in being elevated to the office of Grand Master of the Masonic Lodge of his State; Freemasonry appears to have had a strong appeal for the Jews in colonial America.

Among the Jewish soldiers in the Continental Army who earned the rank of major were two brothers named Bush—cousins, probably, of Solomon Bush. They were George and Lewis of whom the latter died of wounds he received at the Battle of Brandywine. But perhaps the most picturesque Jewish soldier was Major Benjamin Nones. He was born in Bordeaux, France, and when he arrived in Philadelphia in 1777 he promptly volunteered for military service, took part in the defense of Savannah, and was cited for conspicuous gallantry in action. Major Nones commanded a unit that included a sizable number of his coreligionists. He was at the Battle of Camden, South Carolina, under Baron de Kalb, together with Captain Jacob de la Motta and Captain Jacob de Leon. De Kalb was mortally wounded in that battle, and the three Jewish officers are reported to have carried their commander from the field. Nones was a proud and militant Jew. "I am a Jew. I glory in belonging to that persuasion," he wrote the Philadelphia *Gazette of the United States* in a letter dated August 11, 1800, in which he denounced aspersions against him which had appeared in that publication. After the war Nones was for many years the *parnas*, or president, of the Congregation *Mikveh Israel* of Philadelphia.

There were other Jewish soldiers of officer rank in the Continental Army, Solomon Pinto, for example, who was wounded in action; he belonged to a Connecticut family that gave four of its men to the armed forces. This abridged roster cannot include them all, but it is tempting to name two more. One was Asser Levy, a descendant of his doughty namesake whom we met in the early story of the little community in New Amsterdam. The other was Manuel Noah, whose son, Mordecai Manuel Noah, we shall meet in the pages that follow.

5

Financing the Revolutionary War was, if possible, an even more formidable task than raising armies, and the two problems were, of course, closely related. A goodly number of Jewish patriots, among them Manuel Noah, Mordecai Sheftall and the Minis family of Savannah, made loans or gifts to the Continental Congress, and though the halo of glory rarely descends on the heads of financiers, it did come to rest on one who was a Jewish immigrant from Poland. He became posthumously famous as one who "gave great assistance to the government by loans of money and by advancing liberally of his means to sustain the men engaged in the struggle for independence." The words just quoted are from a report which a Committee of the United States Senate adopted in 1850 on the services to the cause of the Revolution rendered by Haym Salomon of New York and Philadelphia. But Salomon was not just a hero of the counting-house; he was more than a broker who negotiated bills of exchange and foreign loans for Robert Morris, the "financier of the American Revolution." In 1776 the British arrested him in New York, and after a term in prison he was rearrested and sentenced to death as a spy. With the help of patriot friends he managed to escape, having previously assisted a number of other prisoners to escape also.

Salomon was born in Leszno, Poland, about 1740 and traveled a good deal in Europe, acquiring a number of its languages, before he came to America. After his escape from prison in 1778 Salomon got to Philadelphia penniless, but when he died there seven years later he had been the principal depositor in the Bank of North America, which Morris had founded, and head of a far-flung business with agents in America and Europe. His money, as the Senate Committee reported, was advanced not only to the Government, but to the leaders of the Revolution; among those who found him a friend in need were Jefferson, Madison, Monroe, Edmund Randolph and the Pennsylvania scientist and political leader, David Rittenhouse. Salomon was actively devoted also to the welfare of the Philadelphia Jewish community. He was one of the first members of *Mikveh Israel* and served on its Board of Trustees. He took a prominent part in its charities and in the struggle for Jewish rights.

Salomon's patriotic services received warm commendation, but he died insolvent, and the efforts of his heirs to recover the loans he made to the Government were not successful. In December 1941, however, he won more concrete, if belated, recognition than mere words of praise: a monument was unveiled to his memory in Chicago the cost defrayed by numerous contributors. The central figure of the monument is General Washington, who is clasping the hand of Robert Morris on his left and that of the immigrant from Poland on his right.

6

On the pedestal of this monument are inscribed the following words from a letter which President Washington addressed to the Jewish Congregation of Newport when he visited that city in the summer of

1790: "The Government of the United States which gives to bigotry no sanction, to persecution no assistance, requires only that they who live under its protection should demean themselves as good citizens in giving it on all occasions their effectual support."

Washington's letter was in reply to one which Moses Seixas wrote him on behalf of the Newport community, and it also contains the sonorous and significant phrase, "a government which gives no sanction to bigotry and no assistance to persecution." When the British had evacuated Newport in 1779 they demolished its docks and ramparts, and left the city a shell of its former self. Some of the Jewish exiles had come back, but only a few remained. The General Assembly of Rhode Island, on its return to Newport, had convened in the Synagogue, and the last important act of the community was the letter it sent to Washington which evoked the famous reply.

The Congregation's letter was in magniloquent style but not the less sincere on that account, as the following paragraph attests:

> "For all the blessings of civil and religious liberty which we enjoy under an equal and benign administration, we desire to send up thanks to the Ancient of Days, the great Preserver of men, beseeching him that the angel who conducted our forefathers through the wilderness into the promised land may graciously conduct you through all the difficulties and dangers of this mortal life; and when, like Joshua, full of days and honors, you are gathered to your fathers, may you be admitted into the heavenly paradise to partake of the water of life and the tree of immortality."

Washington's reply was more than a perfunctory acknowledgment. It expresses gratification, of course, "with your favorable opinion of my administration and fervent wishes for my felicity," but it affirms political doctrines which are clearly traceable to the influence of Jefferson and Madison. This is its important paragraph:

> "The Citizens of the United States of America have a right to applaud themselves for having given to mankind examples of an enlarged and liberal policy: a policy worthy of imitation. All possess alike liberty of conscience and immunities of citizenship. It is now no more that toleration is spoken of as if it was by the indulgence of one class of people that another enjoyed the exercise of their inherent natural rights. For happily the Government of the United States, which gives to bigotry no sanction, to persecution no assistance, requires only that they who live under its pro-

tection should demean themselves as good citizens in giving it on all occasions their effectual support."

The Savannah community also received a letter from Washington in response to an address on its behalf signed by Levi Sheftall, brother of the famous patriot. Washington's reply, couched in gracious and flowing diction, does not add substance to the one received by the Newport Congregation, and the same is true of still another letter to the remaining Jewish congregations in America. That one, however, deserves notice because it came in reply to a joint address by the congregations of Charleston, Philadelphia, New York and Richmond, the last, bearing the name *Beth Shalome* (House of Peace), having come into existence in 1789. The joint address was signed for all four by Manuel Josephson, leader of the Philadelphia community and a man distinguished for learning. Josephson had tried to bring the six communities into his démarche, but succeeded with only four of them, and some have conjectured that Josephson's lineage—he was not of Sephardic descent—may account for the rejection of his overtures by the Newport and Savannah congregations. It was not, however, a bad start, this first attempt to secure common action in a matter that concerned the whole of American Jewry.

7

In his reply to the Jews of Newport Washington had written that "all possess alike liberty of conscience and immunities of citizenship." But that statement was not yet in complete accord with the facts. In most of the states of the Union the Jews were not yet fully emancipated.

In American thinking and parlance Emancipation is primarily associated with Negro slavery and its abolition: its application to Jews and other religious groups in the fabric of American society may strike many Americans, including members of those groups themselves, as somewhat bizarre. But if the word connotes full legal equality—civil, political and religious—the Jews who lived in the colonies in the year of decision 1776 were not emancipated. Restrictions in the exercise of their religion and the pursuit of their callings had by that year practically disappeared, but the fence around political rights was still high and firm. There were laws providing for naturalization and a subordinate form of it called "endenization," but they excluded the right to vote or hold public office.

The Jews in the colonies had not chafed under their political disabilities. They belonged to a people whom the Christian world had always kept in a state of legal inferiority; they knew that in the lands they or their forebears came from the status of their coreligionists was greatly inferior to their own, that in central and eastern Europe they were social outcasts. Even in England, where many Jews had already achieved wealth and influence, they were still aliens, or without political rights. So for a century and a quarter the Jews of Colonial America were content with civil and religious rights which gave them freedom to promote their economic welfare and remain loyal to the faith of their fathers.

The Revolution, however, widened the horizon of their civic demands. To its triumph they had contributed their share of blood and treasure. They had fought and died on its battlefields, and being an urban people, had suffered proportionately more than the rest of the population from enemy action, as the fate of the New York and Newport communities proved. They had grown in civic stature and they were no longer satisfied with the status of second grade citizens.

8

Many of the Jews expected that the full equality they now desired would be guaranteed them by the Federal Constitution. Unfortunately, however, the two provisions of the original Constitution that dealt with political and religious rights failed to provide such guarantees. The first, which occurs in Article One, provides that the electors, or voters, who choose members of the House of Representatives "shall have the qualifications requisite for electors of the most numerous branch of the State Legislature." The second, which occurs in Article Six, states that "no religious test shall ever be required as a qualification to any office or public trust under the United States." The right of suffrage, in other words, was left in the gift of the separate states, which could also, if they chose, disqualify on religious grounds a seeker of "any office or public trust" of their own. Nor did the First of the Ten Amendments, which are known as the Bill of Rights and became part of the Constitution in 1791, improve the situation. The Amendment which provides that "Congress shall make no law respecting an establishment of religion, or prohibiting the free exercise thereof," did not prevent the State Legislatures from dealing with those matters as they might see fit.

Thus the federal character of the new government, based as it was on the principle of delegated rights, threw the struggle for political equality back into each of the thirteen states. It was another matter in the case of the states that were later admitted into the Union: their admission depended upon an act of Congress and their constitutions had to satisfy the standards established by Congress. Those standards were set by the Ordinance of 1787, frequently called the Northwest Ordinance. It was adopted by the Continental Congress to govern the region between the Great Lakes and the Ohio River, which ultimately yielded five new states and part of a sixth, and it guaranteed political and religious liberty to all its inhabitants. But as for the original thirteen states, the framers of the Constitution found it hard enough to allay their fears, jealousies and deep-seated separatism without tampering with their precious religious prejudices. In a centralized political unit like France the process of emancipation could be much simpler. When in September 1791 the French National Assembly voted "that the Jews in France enjoy the rights of full citizens," the decree extended to the entire country. In the new-born United States of America every state called itself—and still calls itself—sovereign.

The struggle for political equality converged, therefore, upon the discriminations that all the states, with the exception of New York and Virginia, still retained in their constitutions when the Federal Government was established. In Virginia a formidable attempt, made in 1784, to establish Christianity as the state religion had been defeated largely through the efforts of James Madison. The victory for religious freedom, wrote Thomas Jefferson, then minister to France, "has been received with infinite approbation in Europe." Two years later he joined Madison and Mason to secure the passage of a law which removed religious discrimination in Virginia. Georgia followed suit in 1789 and Pennsylvania and South Carolina a year later. It is significant that in the five states where vigorous Jewish communities existed political equality had by 1790 been achieved.

In the other states, except Delaware, where religious tests were abolished in 1792, the process moved more slowly. In Rhode Island, with the community of Newport liquidated by the Revolution and the great legacy of Roger Williams abandoned, it was only in 1842 that full equality was established. The other states—New Hampshire, Massachusetts, Connecticut, New Jersey, Maryland and North Carolina—also carried their discriminations into the nineteenth century; they were not abolished in North Carolina until 1868 and in New Hampshire until 1876.

9

In Maryland, whose constitution required public officers to declare their belief in the Christian religion, the struggle was particularly intense. In 1649, fifteen years after it was founded, Maryland had adopted a "Toleration Act," but the religious freedom it provided was for Christians only; those who denied the divinity of Jesus were guilty of blasphemy for which the penalty was death. Ten years later, in fact, the "Jew doctor" Jacob Lumbrozo, who had settled in Maryland, was charged with that crime. He was imprisoned and was only saved by a general amnesty. The intolerance of Maryland's "Toleration Act," entrenched for a century and a half, would not be easily expunged.

The first petition for the removal of the religious test from the Maryland Constitution was laid before its General Assembly in 1797 and was squashed in committee on a technicality. Petitions were again submitted in 1802, in 1803, and in 1804, but they were all rejected. The leaders of the struggle became disheartened and it was not resumed until 1816. From that year until 1826 every session of the General Assembly was confronted with a demand for the removal of the disabling provision. The effort, which aroused nation-wide interest, was led by Solomon Etting and the influential banker Jacob I. Cohen, with the assistance of a group of prominent Christians, headed by Thomas Kennedy. The question before the Legislature was "to consider the justice and expediency of extending to those persons professing the Jewish religion the same privileges that are enjoyed by Christians."

Finally, in 1825, the "Jew Bill," as it was popularly called, went through the Legislature, the vote in the Lower House being 26 to 25. The following year a confirmatory act was adopted, which provided that a citizen of the state could qualify for any office of profit or trust by declaring "his belief in a future state of rewards and punishments." It was still a religious test of a sort, but its specific target was no longer the Jew.

It should be noted that the religious test, even when still spread upon the statutes, was sometimes connived at or circumvented in practice. A notable case was that of Jacob Henry of North Carolina. In 1809 Henry was elected to the legislature of his State, but his right to be seated was challenged on the ground that he was a Jew. Henry delivered a stirring defense of liberty and equality, which was widely circulated and became something of a classic. He retained his seat: the ground on which he was allowed to do so was a dubious distinction between those who make laws and those who execute them, a distinction which would permit a Jew to be a member of the legislature but not a constable. In general the current of American opinion ran strong against perpetuating the union of church and state "after so many ages during which the human mind has been held in vassalage by kings, priests and nobles," as Jefferson put it. In America history was on the side of the Jews.

10

It was different in the lands across the ocean, which in later decades were to furnish huge increments to their numbers. True, the French National Assembly in its revolutionary élan had emancipated them, an act which appeared Messianic to its overjoyed beneficiaries. And it is worthy of note that in their struggle to win emancipation the Jews of France had pointed to the progress which the cause had made in America. "America has rejected the word toleration from its code," they said in a petition they addressed to the National Assembly in January 1790. "To tolerate is, in fact, to suffer that which you could, if you wished, prevent and prohibit." And when the armies of the French Republic swept across the frontiers, marching not only as conquerors but as liberators, they brought emancipation to the Jews of the cities and countries they occupied. When, early in 1798, they took Rome and made Pope Pius VI a prisoner of war, the Jews of that city broke down the gates of their foul ghetto and tore the yellow patch from their garments. And wherever else the French established themselves and exercised direct control the Jews were emancipated as a matter of course. In Central Europe, however, and in the lands further east which lay under the scepter of the czars, untouched by the leaven of the Revolution, the masses of the Jewish people were still deprived of elementary human rights, victimized by cynical governments and their brutal minions, and exposed to mob violence which governments and minions could either incite or decline to suppress.

But even in the states of Germany the gains which the French Revolution had brought the Jews were soon lost. They were erased in 1815 by the reactionary Congress of Vienna, which was charged with the task of "restoring" Europe. And to disfranchise the Jews in those states, now united in the German Confederation, all that was necessary was to substitute one preposition for another in the text of a resolution which the Congress adopted. The original text read: "The rights already conceded to them [the Jews] in the several federated states will be continued." An amendment was accepted to replace *in* with *by*. Those rights had been granted the Jews *in* the states but not *by* them, and so did not have to "be continued."

The Jews of Maryland and the other states of the Union struggled to remove the vestiges of discrimination against them, but compared to the status of their coreligionists in Europe, theirs was already one of dignity and freedom. The legal emancipation of the Jews of England, Germany, Italy and Austria was still decades away, and it was not to be accomplished without an intense struggle and in the wake of wars and political upheavals. In Russia it was a whole century away and it came only after the First World War and the cataclysmic revolution that followed. And the dire events on the European continent between 1933 and 1945 proved that this emancipation was only a fragile reed after all. It had no solid support in the will and convictions of the peoples among whom the Jews lived and could be swept away overnight.

In America the prospects of genuine and enduring equality were brighter. The land had become the home of diverse religions, making the elevation of one of them to the position of a state church a practical impossibility and compelling a status of legal equality for all of them. And in America men felt that humanity should make a fresh start, unshackled by the hates and prejudices that bedeviled the nations of Europe.

CHAPTER 4

In War and Peace

1

THERE IS A SPAN OF A QUARTER-CENTURY BETWEEN THE first inauguration of the first President of the new Republic and the Treaty of Ghent, which brought to a formal end the War of 1812, the Second War of Independence, as it has been called. The year of that inauguration, 1789, was the year of the outbreak of the French Revolution, and in 1814, when the Treaty of Ghent was signed, the Congress of Vienna had already begun its task of "restoring" Europe. The affairs of the new-born nation in that quarter-century were disturbed by the cataclysmic events in Europe, and the tiny Jewish group in America, its source of replenishment cut off by the same events, remained stationary in size and importance, and may even have declined in both as a result of departures from the country and the faith. From the standpoint of numbers the group was barely in evidence. In 1787 the population of the country must have been well over 4,000,000, while the number of Jews still hovered around 2,500. Most of them, of course, were concentrated in the six cities on the seaboard where they were organized in congregations, and the population of those cities was a very small fraction of what it is today: New York, for example, had only 30,000 inhabitants. The 500 Jews in Philadelphia made up less than 1 per cent of the total, and the proportion in New York was even smaller.

By 1821 eleven new states had been admitted into the Union, beginning with Vermont in 1791 and ending with Missouri in 1821. The other nine in the order of their admission were Kentucky, Tennessee, Ohio, Louisiana, Indiana, Mississippi, Illinois, Alabama and Maine. But in some of those states no Jews are known to have resided at the time, and in the others, like Kentucky and Ohio, they were still too few to establish communal life. It was only after the fall of Napoleon, when Europe was no longer trampled by armed hosts and ships on the high seas were exposed to the dangers of the elements only, that a new migration movement began from the Old World to the New. And many of the Jewish newcomers joined the westward surge that seized upon the entire country, and laid the foundations for Jewish communal life in those as well as in other new states of the Union.

2

The warning against "entangling alliances" which Washington directed to his countrymen in his Farewell Address has been fervently echoed by American isolationists. It was, no doubt, a timely warning, evoked by the clumsy attempts of the French to compel the infant Republic to adhere to the military alliance of 1778. But if the admonition is taken to mean that America can go its way in halcyon aloofness from Europe, the seventeen years that followed may well be cited as a warning against the warning. For apart from the vise in which the great and growing American shipping industry was caught and nearly destroyed by the implacable feud between France and England, and apart from the undeclared war against France which ended in 1801 and the declared war against England which ended in 1814, the most momentous event of the period, the purchase of Louisiana in 1803, also stemmed from the situation in Europe. It became possible only as a result of Napoleon's engrossing ambitions and preoccupations on that continent.

In its results the "Second War of Independence" was much less decisive than the first: in the Treaty of Ghent the most popular American grievance, the impressment of seamen from American ships on the high seas by British men-of-war, was not even mentioned. But on land and sea the war was fought with keen ferocity, and in both fields of operation the tiny Jewish group furnished soldiers and sailors who added their meed of luster to American arms. Of the sailors two stand out conspicuously: the privateersman John Ordronaux and Uriah P. Levy who, when he died nearly fifty years later, held the rank of Commodore, the highest in the American Navy at the time.

Captain Ordronaux was described by a subordinate, who did not apparently overflow with affection for his superior, as "a Jew by persuasion, a Frenchman by birth, and an American for convenience." He was in his early thirties when he began scouring the seas for British prizes, a man of diminutive stature, indomitable will, and great daring. In one month of the war he hauled in nine prizes, evading his pursuers with uncanny skill or fighting them off with desperate courage when brought to bay. He performed his chief exploit when, as captain of the privateer *Prince de Neufchatel*, he captured the British frigate *Endymion*. When a boarding party from the frigate began forcing his men back he stopped the retreat by threatening to blow up the magazine: the lighted match was in his hand and his men knew he meant it.

In the War of 1812, the career of Uriah Philip Levy was undistinguished: he served as sailing master on the *Argus*, was put in command of one of the prizes his ship captured, was captured in turn and remained a prisoner in England until the end of the war. But afterwards and until 1855, when he was already well over sixty, Uriah was a veritable storm center. He owed his difficulties to three circumstances. The first was his appointment as lieutenant and later as captain, a rise from the ranks not likely to make him popular with his brother officers, who were graduates of the Naval Academy. The second was his race and religion, of which he was militantly proud; Levy was a charter member of the Washington Hebrew Congregation. The third was a fiery temperament and a passion for equality and justice with which many of his coreligionists have been known to be "afflicted." Levy, in fact, was a keen admirer of Thomas Jefferson; in 1833 he presented the government with a bronze statue of the great equalitarian, whose home, Monticello, was purchased by him and later became a Jefferson memorial.

Levy's difficulties with his fellow officers involved him in a duel, in which he killed his man, but it brought him a series of courts-martial and demotions. But Levy was not of those who accept injustice tamely. In 1855 Congress ordered a special court of inquiry, which vindicated him and restored him to rank, and some years later he achieved the rank of Commodore. The cause that was dearest to his heart, but also involved him in controversy, was the abolition of corporal punishment in the Navy. This aim he carried far forward; at his desire, the inscription on his tombstone reads: "He was the father of the law for abolition of the barbarous practice of corporal punishment in the United States Navy."

In the land operations of the War of 1812 the number of Jews who took part, as well as the proportion of officers among them, is impressive. Some of the names are familiar to us from the records of the Revolutionary War, among them those of several grandsons of Mordecai Sheftall of Georgia and a son of Haym Salomon. There were thirty Jews in the garrison of Fort McHenry when its famous defense inspired the composition of "The Star-Spangled Banner." Conspicuous in the record are Captain Mordecai Myers and Major Abraham Massias. The first saved many lives during rescue operations on Lake Ontario; the second had an important share in foiling British attempts to invade Georgia from the sea.

3

There was another American Jewish soldier who fought in the War of 1812, but his title to a place in this chronicle does not rest primarily on military prowess. He was Judah Touro, son of Isaac Touro, the first minister of the Newport synagogue. Judah was brought up by Moses Michael Hays, his rich Boston uncle, and in 1802 established a business of his own in New Orleans, which grew and prospered. Twelve years later he enlisted in the army of Andrew Jackson for the defense of his adopted city against an onslaught by the British. In the course of a hazardous mission, for which he had volunteered, Touro was severely wounded and taken from the field by a devoted comrade. That was in the glorious but superfluous Battle of New Orleans, the most important American victory in the War of 1812, fought on January 8, 1815, two weeks after the treaty of peace had been signed in Ghent. The news had not yet reached the New World.

Touro returned to his business and accumulated considerable wealth which, however, he did not hoard. He dispensed it liberally for many causes, mainly charitable: for hospitals, synagogues, schools, libraries and orphan homes. He contributed $10,000, a large sum in those days, for the erection of the Bunker Hill Monument. He gave $50,000 to establish colonies for Jews in Palestine. That princely gift he remitted to Moses Montefiore of England, the greatest Jewish philanthropist and champion of the period.

For forty years Touro lived with Rezon Davis Shepherd, the friend who had taken him to safety when he was wounded in battle. He obtained the manumission of the household slaves who served him and freed the only slave he owned, after making provision for their future. He supported but did not join the Ashkenazic congregation of New Orleans, which was founded in 1826; twenty years later a Sephardic congregation was established and he joined it. Such was Judah Touro, an able man of business, big hearted and open handed, brave, humane and modest, but not without the prejudices of his lineage and upbringing.

4

By 1815 the tumult and the shouting that began in Europe in 1789 had died down, and the Holy Alliance of Prussia, Russia and Austria—with the pious and gullible Alexander I of Russia mouthing its "noble" aims while the crafty and ruthless Prince Metternich of Austria fixed its policies—had solemnly resolved to permit no more revolutions. Europe sank into a torpor, and the stalwart young nation on the other side of the Atlantic was free at last to pursue its own destiny. For a whole century, until the First World War drew it again into the European vortex, America indulged in the luxury of isolation, following its own course as determined by its geography, moving westward in pursuit of its vanishing frontier and out of its seemingly inexhaustible resources, natural and human, building up a nation of unprecedented power. And to make sure that Europe and its holy alliances would not stretch out their unholy hands to stifle this growth, a "No Trespassing" sign was set up in 1823, known as the Monroe Doctrine.

The governments of Europe were warned not to extend their holdings in the New World, but the men and women of Europe were welcomed by the growing nation: the immense areas it possessed in the Northwest Territory between the Great Lakes and Ohio River, augmented by cessions south of the river, and the vast region between the Mississippi and the Rocky Mountains known as Louisiana, were in desperate need of settlers.

The despotism which the Holy Alliance imposed on the European continent sent thousands of immigrants flocking to the New World, now that the sea lanes were again open to peaceful traffic; in 1817 alone not less than 20,000 were estimated to have landed in the United States. Among them there was no doubt a substantial proportion of Jews, most of them from the German states where, as we saw, the Congress of Vienna had put an end to the brief interval of freedom and equality they had enjoyed under the French.

It was the beginning of what is usually called the "German period" in the annals of Jewish immigration to America, to distinguish it from the preceding "Spanish period" and from the one that began in the eighties of the nineteenth century, called the "Russian period." These designations have their uses, but they also have their limitations. For among the Sephardim of the first period there were, as we had occasion to note, many Ashkenazim, and among those who came from the Germanies in the second period there were many who hailed from the lands to the east—Austria, Hungary, Poland and even Russia. The newcomers, on the whole, lacked the wealth and outward graces of their Sephardic predecessors. They came from countries where centuries of legal degradation had kept them in dire poverty and made them socially timorous and ill at ease. Tradition and wealth had enabled many of the Sephardim to rise quickly in the economic and social scale. The later arrivals will find it harder and it will take them longer, but their influence on the growth of the Jewish community in America, if only by reason of their larger numbers, will be greater.

5

Among the Jews who served in the war with Mexico the newcomers already predominated. The war, which extended the boundaries of the Republic from the Gulf of Mexico to the Pacific, was declared in May 1846, and it ended with the signing of the Treaty of Guadalupe Hidalgo in February 1848; but in a real sense it began in March 1836, when Texas declared her independence from Mexico and Sam Houston established it by his victory at the San Jacinto River a month later.

Among the 750 men in Houston's force at the San Jacinto was Albert Emanuel who had migrated from Germany only two years earlier. Houston's surgeon-general was Moses Albert Levy, and Isaac Lyons was surgeon-general in the command of Tom Green. There was at least one Jew, Abraham Wolf, who died at the Alamo, and another was among those who were massacred after their surrender to the Mexicans at Goliad, the two events that fired the wrath of the Texans and gave them their battle cry. Other Jews who served in the Texan forces were Major Leon Dyer, Levi Myers Harby and Lieutenant Henry Seligson.

Among those who held political office in the Republic of Texas were Adolphus Stern and David Kaufman. Stern had taken part in the premature and ill-starred attempt in 1826 to make Texas independent, known as the Fredonian Rebellion, and later served in both houses of the Texas Congress. Kaufman was wounded in the Battle of Neches. He was later chosen speaker of the Lower House and served also in the Senate of the Texas Republic. When Texas joined the Union, Kaufman represented his state in Congress, and later gave his name to one of its counties and to the city which became the county seat.

In the Texas Senate Kaufman was an ardent advocate of joining the United States; and when in December 1845 the annexation of Texas was accomplished, war with Mexico became inevitable. Several scores of Jews who served in this unpopular war have been identified, including some like Dyer, Seligson and Harby, who had fought in the earlier struggles of Texas against her neighbor. In Baltimore a company was organized that consisted largely of recent Jewish immigrants from Germany; among its officers were Levi Benjamin, Joseph Simpson and Samuel Goldsmith. A news item in the *New York Herald* reported that this company, "formed . . . for the most part of Jews, attracts particular attention."

But the most picturesque Jewish soldier of the Mexican War was the surgeon David Camden de Leon of South Carolina, who had already served as surgeon in the bloody war against the Seminoles ten years earlier. When need arose the doctor laid down the scalpel and took up the sword. At the Battle of Chapultepec in September 1847, which preceded the occupation of Mexico City by the American forces under General Winfield Scott, de Leon twice led a cavalry charge after the officers in command of the unit had been put out of action. "The fighting doctor" was the name by which he was known, and special note of his gallantry was taken by Congress. In 1861 de Leon resigned his commission in the United States Army and became Surgeon-General of the Confederate forces.

6

In addition to the soldiers and sailors in the War of 1812 and the Mexican War, certain men and women of the still tiny Jewish community who achieved distinction in other ways must be noted in this chronicle. The Charleston community seems to have furnished more than its share of them, with the Harby and Moise families in the lead.

The most distinguished Harby was Isaac, educator, journalist and dramatist, brother of the soldier Levi Myers Harby. Solomon Harby, the founder of the family in America, had come to Charleston from England via Jamaica, and Isaac Harby was born in that city in 1788. Isaac established a boys academy in South Carolina and later in New York, edited newspapers in his native city and wrote essays and criticism in addition to plays. He also took a leading part in the first movement for Reform Judaism in America. His brother, Washington Harby also won recognition as a playwright, and many years later his granddaughter Leah Cohen Harby wrote fiction, history and verse.

The chief ornament of the Moise family was the poetess Penina. The family, as its name indicates, was of French origin: Penina's father, Abraham, hailed from Alsace and settled in the West Indies, whence he fled to Charleston to escape the perils of a slave insurrection. The Moise family included other distinguished members. Penina's nephew Edwin Warren Moise, who died in 1868, won success in a number of careers—as physician, lawyer, jurist and political leader. Another nephew of the same name, who died in 1902, fought gallantly for the South all through the Civil War, and after the war played a prominent part in the political affairs of South Carolina.

Penina Moise earned her livelihood by teaching, was active in the affairs of her congregation in Charleston, serving as superintendent of its Sabbath School, and contributed prose and verse to many periodicals of her day. Her poetic gifts were widely recognized, especially in the South, and her native city regarded her as its poet laureate. She was a spinster of 83 when she died in 1880. She had borne poverty and ill health with fortitude, and in the last twenty-five years of her life she was blind. Penina found solace in the hymns she wrote, and they bring solace to the many who still sing them. Her natural piety found support in the philosophy of her faith, to which she was no stranger. The lines that follow are from her hymn *Man, the Image of God*:

Exult my soul in consciousness proud,
That I in God's image was made:
That 'mid nature's irrational crowd,
Moral light to me was conveyed;
When dust, by His pure breath refined,
In flesh the vital spark enshrined.

How glorious this filiation
Between the Lord of worlds and me!
Oh! how shall I deserve the station,
Next to the angels in degree?
Like these, by walking in His ways;
Like these, by singing e'er His praise.

In vivid contrast to the long and demure life of Penina Moise was the brief but fabulous career of her contemporary Adah Isaacs Menken, who was born near New Orleans and died in 1868 in her early thirties in Paris. Adah too wrote poetry; two volumes of it appeared and evoked praise from noted critics and literati. But her fame rested chiefly not on her brilliant mind, but her dazzling beauty and her sensational performances as an actress. For a decade audiences in America and Europe acclaimed her, the high and mighty danced attendance on her, and the conventional were scandalized by her. Her parentage has been disputed, but she herself insisted it was Jewish. She kept the name of her first husband, son of a Cincinnati Jewish merchant, whom she met in Texas, and she died with a rabbi at her bedside.

7

But the most conspicuous figure in the American Jewish community in the period between the War of 1812 and the Mexican War was the versatile and quixotic Mordecai Manuel Noah. His colorful career linked him closely to many interests of his day: its theater, journalism, diplomacy and politics; but to these he added another interest, which linked him to the ancient past of the Jewish people and its not so distant future. Mordecai Manuel Noah made a spectacular Zionist gesture in the New World three quarters of a century before Theodor Herzl launched the modern Zionist movement in Europe. He attempted to establish a Jewish colony in America as a preliminary to the return of the Jews to Palestine.

Now, as a colonizer Noah was far behind another American Jew who from 1843 to 1846 promoted a colonization project at the behest of Sam Houston, then president of the Republic of Texas. He was Henry Castro, scion of a Marrano family which had found refuge in France, who preferred to call himself Henri comte de Castro. Some 5,000 Germans migrated to Texas and settled there as a result of his efforts. Castro County and the quaint little town of Castroville west of San Antonio preserve his memory. As colonizer, Castro was a success and Noah was a failure. Nevertheless the muse of history smiles graciously on Noah and has all but forgotten the "Comte de Castro."

Mordecai Manuel Noah was born in Philadelphia in 1785, both his parents ardent patriots, his father, as we saw, having supported the Revolution with money and arms. Early in life Noah evinced an enthusiasm for the theater, which was destined to find expression not only in the authorship of successful stage plays, but in other aspects of his dramatic and varied career. At twenty-four he became editor of a newspaper in Charleston and won a place among the "young war hawks," as those who advocated hostilities against England were called. He also won enemies, fought a number of duels and in one of them he killed his opponent.

In 1813 President Madison appointed Noah consul to Tunis in the Barbary States, where he obtained the release of Americans who had been captured and sold into slavery by the Barbary pirates. It was a difficult task requiring considerable adroitness, but he spent more than his allotment for the purpose and his commission was revoked, the letter of recall affirming that his religion was deemed to disqualify him for the post. Apparently, some of his enemies had been at work in Washington. In time, however, he got a clean bill of health in the conduct of his mission, and the sums he advanced in performing it were reimbursed.

Noah returned to his country and became prominent in the public life of New York, where he established himself. He founded and edited a number of papers, entered with zest into the rough-and-tumble of local and national politics, served as High Sheriff of New York, Surveyor of the Port and Judge of the Court of Sessions and continued writing plays that attracted large audiences. "What a pity," wrote an outraged citizen concerning Sheriff Noah, "that Christians are to be hung by a Jew." "What a pity," replied the Sheriff, "that Christians should have to be hung."

Finally in 1825 Modecai Manuel Noah played out the most spectacular drama of his career. It had its origin in reflections which had engrossed him for years and became crystallized in the conviction that the time had come to restore his scattered people to its ancient homeland. In his travels in Europe on the way to Barbary he became acquainted with the plight of his coreligionists on the continent, and his conviction was deepened. One of his reasons for going to Tunis, in fact, was to inform himself on the "situation, character, resources and numerical forces of the Jews in Barbary." He was apparently toying with the idea of raising a Jewish army to wrest Palestine from the Turks. The final redemption, Noah believed, would be accomplished by the Messiah, but the Jews must collaborate in the task.

But to attain his objective Noah determined upon a rather strange detour. With the help of a friend he acquired a tract of some 17,000 acres on Grand Island in the Niagara River northwest of Buffalo, as the site for a Jewish settlement. Other religious groups had established their own settlements in America; why not the Jews? The place, he decided, should be called "Ararat, a City of Refuge for the Jews," in memory of the first dry spot where the Ark of his Biblical namesake rested during the Great Flood. Ararat, situated near the Great Lakes and the outlet of the Erie Canal, would become an important commercial center, and serve as a pilot project for the restoration to Palestine, a curtain raiser for the great drama to follow.

On September 2, 1825 imposing dedication ceremonies took place in Buffalo, of which Noah of course was the central figure. As "Governor and Judge of Israel," he wore a robe of crimson trimmed with ermine and marched in a procession that included military units, state and federal officials, clergymen and Masonic dignitaries. There were Indians also in the procession, for Noah was one of those who were convinced that the American aborigines were descended from the Lost Ten Tribes of Israel. The concluding exercises were held in the Episcopal Church of the city, and in his address Noah said: "In calling the Jews together under the protection of the American Constitution and laws . . . it is proper for me to state that the asylum is temporary and provisionary. The Jews never should and never will relinquish the just hope of regaining possession of their ancient heritage."

Noah issued a grandiloquent manifesto to his coreligionists over the world, inviting them to come and settle in Ararat, but his exhortations were either ignored or ridiculed. The dedication in Buffalo was the beginning and the end of the enterprise. All that remained of it was the cornerstone on which the inscription, except for the date, is no longer legible. But Noah remained firmly convinced that the Land of Israel would once more pass "into the possession of the descendants of Abraham," and that the Jews would take "their rank once more among the nations of the earth." In 1844, nearly twenty years after his superb gesture in Buffalo, he delivered his most notable plea for Jewish national restoration before a Protestant congregation in Philadelphia. Under the title of "Discourse on the Restoration of the Jews," the address was printed and widely circulated. It was a moving utterance. "The time will come," he declared, "the promise will be fulfilled."

Among his coreligionists in America the response to Noah's summons was less than apathetic: the Protestants, in fact, many of whom held that the conversion of the Jews would follow or accompany their return to Palestine, evinced more interest than did the Jews. Some years before the Grand Island flourish, Noah had informed two former Presidents of his country, John Adams and Thomas Jefferson, of his hopes and convictions. Adams wrote him: "I really wish the Jews again in Judea an independent nation," and the sage of Monticello also commended the aims of the young enthusiast. In Jewish quarters there was either indifference or levity, or a reminder that the Great Return must be left to God's will and the advent of His Messiah. One objection, however, appears to have been unspoken: Noah was not charged with dual allegiance or lack of patriotism. That was the charge which, many years later, when the movement to establish a Jewish state in Palestine had assumed world proportions, was freely made and vehemently denied.

CHAPTER 5

Across the Continent

1

IN THE MEANTIME THE FLOW OF JEWISH MIGRATION FROM Europe continued and rose higher. In 1820 there were probably some 4,000 Jews in the country, and in 1850 they numbered not more than 50,000 in a population of 23,000,000. By the end of the next decade, however, when the nation was approaching its supreme crisis, their number had risen to 150,000.

It was the sorry aftermath of the revolutionary outbreaks in Europe in 1848 and 1849 that was chiefly responsible for the accelerated flow. The eruptions began in Paris in February 1848—when the sham liberal, Louis Philippe, was overthrown—and spread rapidly to Germany, Austria and Italy. The following month there were riots in Vienna, and Count Metternich whose Holy Alliance had forbidden all revolutions, fled for his life to England. The same month there was a bloody outbreak in Berlin; the king of Prussia promised a constitution, and the hope for equality rose high in the hearts of the Jews in Germany. Leopold Zunz, the leading Jewish scholar of his time, saw the dawn of a new day, with the "recognition of Man unclouded by distinctions of sect or class," and Gabriel Riesser, who led the Jews of Germany in their struggle for emancipation, was an outstanding member of the Frankfort Assembly. That over-optimistic body tried but failed to unify Germany under a democratic constitution: its offer of the imperial German crown on those terms to the king of Prussia was met with the "Great Refusal." Nor did the revolutions in Austria, Hungary and Italy fare better. Republican uprisings in those countries, as well as in Germany, were crushed.

The tide of emigration from the Germanies, Bohemia and other lands mounted; the disillusioned "forty-eighters" were on the way to the New World. America became the lodestar of the oppressed and disinherited of the Old World: between 1850 and 1860 nearly 2,000,000 of them entered the United States. Naturally those who pulled up their roots and braved the hazards of a new world were in the main the young and the strong; among the Jewish immigrants were many youths and maidens from European lands where the number of Jewish marriages was severely restricted by law. The proportion of Jews in the total was only about 5 per cent, but they were able not only to add considerably to the existing communities on the Atlantic seaboard, but to found new ones in the Atlantic States, the Middle West, the Southwest, and further on to the Pacific.

In this movement the Jews became an integral part of the great American tide that rose and flowed west, following the courses of the great rivers, toiling over the mountain trails, and conquering the prairies and forests. With remarkable speed they threw off the yoke which the ghettos of Europe had laid upon their bodies and souls and joined in the American Adventure. In the new outposts that sprang up along the vanishing frontier individual Jews made their appearance, and as more of them came they found each other and formed small groups. The traditions and institutions of the ancient faith held them together, in addition to what the social scientists call "the consciousness of kind." At the same time they reached out to the civic and cultural life of the larger communities in which they moved and had their being.

The central religious bond was of course the synagogue, an institution taken so much for granted by themselves as well as their neighbors, who had its analogue in the church, that though its vital function was never doubted, its antiquity and historic role were scarcely realized. The synagogue was the vehicle of religious expression which had sprung up some 2,500 years earlier, when the need arose for a substitute to take the place of the Temple in Jerusalem, destroyed by the Babylonians. It was among the captives in Babylonia, whom the conquerors had taken with them from Judea and Jerusalem, that this product of the Jewish religious genius seems to have arisen. It accompanied them back to their own land when their captivity was ended, it traveled with them in all their later wanderings, and it served as a model for the Christian church and the Mohammedan mosque. From earliest times the synagogue was not only a House of Prayer; it was also a House of Study, or school, and a House of Assembly, or communal center.

The establishment of a congregation by a Jewish group came promptly, though collective worship began in quarters not specifically built for the purpose. Delay was often occasioned by the requirement that such worship must be conducted with at least ten male participants, the *minyan*, as this quorum is called, and it is easy to imagine scattered groups in frontier outposts short of the quorum looking out for the arrival of another member of their faith, or for a boy in their midst to reach the age of thirteen, when he attained his religious majority and was qualified to be counted towards the *minyan*. The erection of a synagogue structure was often beyond the means of the small initial groups; they waited for reinforcements and sometimes they appealed to older and more prosperous congregations for assistance. For the immigrants from Germany, unlike many of their Sephardic predecessors, did not arrive with wealth and commercial connections. Their road to economic independence was rough and laborious.

Nor is it surprising that the well-established and cultured Sephardim, most of them now native born and nurtured in what is complacently called "gracious living," often looked upon the inelegant newcomers with condescension or irritation. They could not ignore or deny their kinship with them; their own conscience and their Christian neighbors would not allow them to do so. But for the first time, perhaps, many of them became aware that they belonged to a much larger fraternity than they had realized, a world people, whom history had broken into disparate and unhappy segments, who challenged not only their basic humanity, but the obligations they owed to their common past.

As we approach the bitter and tragic conflict on which the destiny of the American Adventure depended, it seems fitting to turn for a rapid survey of the new centers of Jewish life which by 1860 had sprung up across the continent.

2

In that year the two largest Jewish aggregations were located in New York and Philadelphia, with some 40,000 in the first and about half that number in the second. In the South the old communities in Charleston and Savannah showed no such growth: other northern communities in fact had already overtaken them. New York and Philadelphia were the leading commercial and industrial centers of the country, and New York was the principal port of entry for the new arrivals, many of whom found employment there and went no further. And many of those who were inclined to seek new pastures were not attracted by the prospect of competing with the slave labor on which the economy of the South was based. North and south of the two largest centers many smaller ones had by 1860 grown up in the Atlantic states. In Boston the first congregation was launched in 1842, the second, *Adath Israel* (Community of Israel) in 1853. In the Empire State congregations had been organized in Albany, Syracuse, Rochester and Buffalo; it was in 1846, as rabbi of *Beth El* in Albany, that Isaac Mayer Wise began his career as the leader of Reform Judaism in America. In Connecticut the cities of New Haven and Hartford had established congregations in the early forties. In New Jersey Paterson, the great silk manufacturing center, launched a congregation in the late forties, and in Elizabeth a little group of Jews first met for worship in 1857.

Philadelphia, of course, was not the only city in Pennsylvania where Jewish communal life existed. In Easton *Brith Shalom* (Covenant of Peace) was formed in 1839, and in Pittsburgh *Etz Chaim* (Tree of Life) in 1846. There were congregations in Wilkes-Barre and Harrisburg also: in the former *B'nai B'rith* was established in 1848, in the latter *Ohav Sholom* three years later. In Lancaster, where the tiny pre-Revolutionary community had, as we saw, gone out of existence, the new immigrants established a new congregation in 1856.

Even before their long and hard struggle for emancipation in Maryland, which ended in 1826, the Jews of Baltimore had begun to organize their collective life, and by 1838 there were two congregations in the city, *Nidche Israel* (Fugitives of Israel) and the Fell Street Congregation. By 1853 there were several others, the two most important being *Har Sinai* and *Oheb Shalom*. Both had their origin in a desire to "modernize" the worship, the first moving much further towards Reform than the second. In 1855 David Einhorn became rabbi of the first, and four years later Benjamin Szold was rabbi of the second: both men will figure prominently in the religious controversies that troubled American Jewry.

In Virginia *Beth Shalom* of Richmond began its career before 1790: in that year, as we saw, it joined the congregations in New York, Philadelphia and Charleston in their formal address to the first President of the Republic. Among those who occupied its pulpit was Isaac Leeser, who was to stand forth later as the foremost champion of the traditional faith. Two more congregations arose in Richmond before the Civil War: *Beth Ahabah* (House of Love) established in 1839 by new arrivals from Germany, and *Kenesseth Israel* (Assembly of Israel), launched in 1856 by immigrants from Poland.

In North Carolina the purchase of a burial plot, often the preliminary to the establishment of communal life, was made in Wilmington in 1852, though the congregation was not established until fifteen years later. Besides Charleston the only other city in South Carolina where a congregation existed in 1860 was Columbia. The career of *Beth Elohim* in Charleston had been a rather checkered one. In 1824 a group calling itself the "Reform Society of Israelites" separated from it and set up a congregation of its own. It was the first secession of its kind in America. In Georgia there were, in addition to Savannah, three other cities where collective Jewish life existed by 1860. In Augusta the Sons of Israel was organized in 1850; in Columbus one bearing the same name in 1854, and in Macon the House of Israel was set up in 1859.

Jews held public office in Georgia even before the revision of the oath which included the words "upon the faith of a Christian." David Emanuel, who was a soldier of the Revolution, became Governor of Georgia in 1801. Emanuel has excited curiosity among those who are intrigued by historic "firsts." The prevailing opinion is that he was a Jew, and therefore the first Jewish governor of a state of the Union, although he may, by the time he reached that elevation, have denied the faith of his fathers.

3

In the Ohio Valley the first congregation, Sons of Israel, was organized in 1824 in Cincinnati, but it was not until 1836 that it was able to erect a synagogue building. Its twenty-four members lacked the means and they circulated an appeal for help to the older congregations. "We are scattered through the wilds of America as children of the same family and faith," they declared, "and we consider it our duty to apply to you for assistance in the creation of a House to worship the God of our forefathers." The appeal, which did not remain unanswered, went on to assert that "there is not a congregation within 500 miles of this city" and that "for the last four or five years . . . nothing was heard but the howling of wild beasts and the more hideous cry of savage men."

But the Jews who came to Cincinnati from Germany in the forties did not feel drawn to the existing congregation and formed their own, calling it Sons of Jeshurum; and before the Civil War still other congregations were established in the city. Special importance, however, attaches to the first two, because in 1854 Max Lilienthal became rabbi of the first and Isaac Mayer Wise of the second, and as we shall see, both men exerted an influence which extended beyond their own

Jewish Communities in AMERICA in 1860
· LEGEND ·
Cities with Jewish Communities
OTHER PLACES mentioned in text
Portland
Sacramento
San Francisco
UNITED STATES
CASTROVILLE
San Antonio
MEXICO

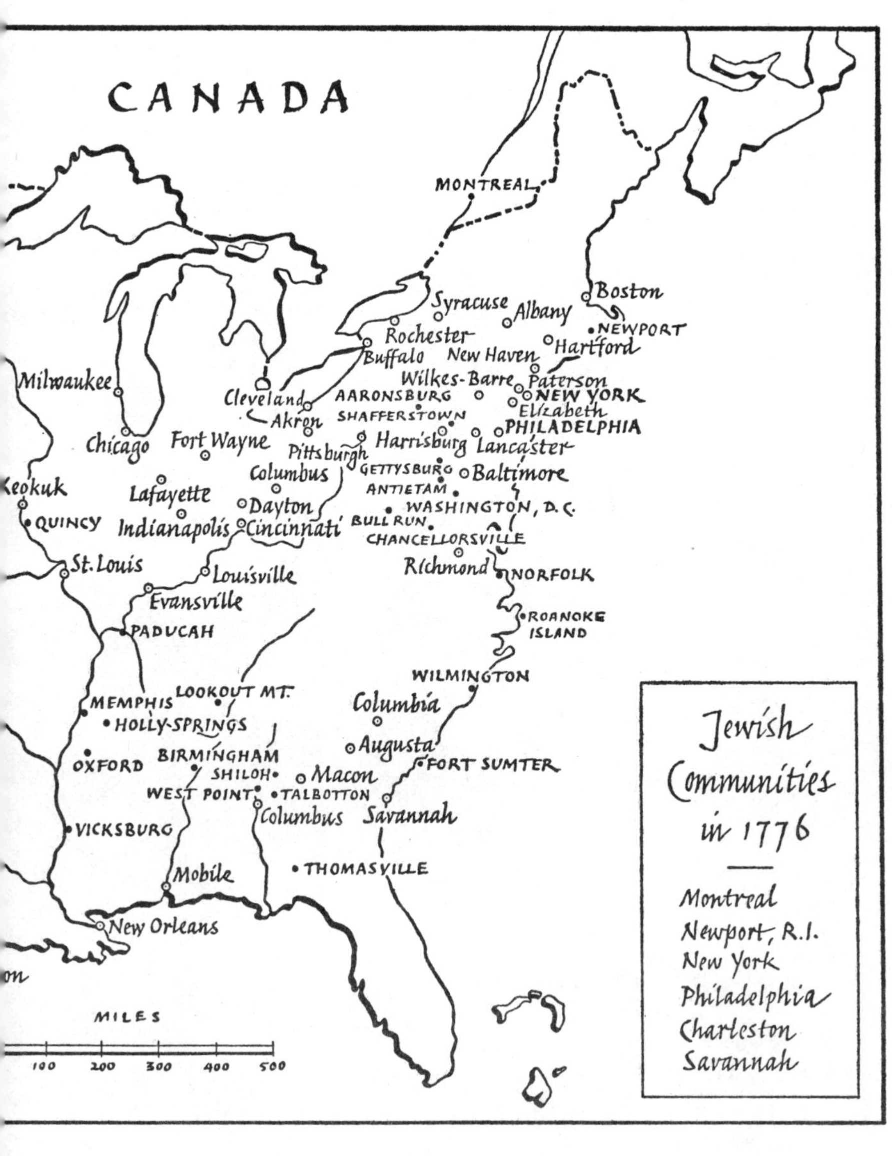
CANADA
MONTREAL
Boston
Syracuse
Albany
NEWPORT
Rochester
Hartford
Buffalo
New Haven
Wilkes-Barre
Paterson
Milwaukee
Cleveland
AARONSBURG
NEW YORK
Elizabeth
Akron
SHAFFERSTOWN
PHILADELPHIA
Chicago
Fort Wayne
Pittsburgh
Harrisburg
Lancaster
Columbus
GETTYSBURG
Baltimore
ANTIETAM
Keokuk
Lafayette
Dayton
WASHINGTON, D.C.
QUINCY
Indianapolis
Cincinnati
BULL RUN
CHANCELLORSVILLE
St. Louis
Louisville
Richmond
NORFOLK
Evansville
ROANOKE ISLAND
PADUCAH
WILMINGTON
MEMPHIS
LOOKOUT MT.
Columbia
HOLLY-SPRINGS
Augusta
OXFORD
BIRMINGHAM
FORT SUMTER
SHILOH
Macon
WEST POINT
TALBOTTON
Columbus
Savannah
VICKSBURG
THOMASVILLE
Mobile
New Orleans
MILES
100
200
300
400
500
Jewish Communities in 1776
Montreal
Newport, R.I.
New York
Philadelphia
Charleston
Savannah

congregations and made Cincinnati the citadel of Reform Judaism in America. In Cleveland the Israelitish Society was formed in 1839 and *Anshe Chesed* (Men of Good Deeds) in 1842. Eight years later those who found its worship too Orthodox seceded and formed a congregation of their own. By 1860 there were congregations in half a dozen other Ohio cities also, among them Columbus, Dayton and Akron.

Jews worshipped together for the first time in St. Louis in a rented room on the Rosh Hashanah festival of 1836. Three years later they organized a congregation, but its first house of worship was not dedicated until 1859. Their members, it should be noted, were not the first Jews to settle in St. Louis, but most of the earlier arrivals, isolated and deprived of a collective life of their own, had intermarried and were lost to the faith.

In Louisville, Kentucky, the first congregation, *Adath Israel*, was incorporated in 1842, but its synagogue was not erected until eight years later. Most of its members were from Germany, but by 1856 another congregation had been founded by Jews who had come from Poland. There were differences in the mode of worship, the immigrants from Germany bringing with them a partiality for Reform, and those from Poland clinging to Orthodoxy. But another impulse also asserted itself in these divisions: the deep-seated desire to associate with those they knew and understood best.

One of the first Jewish pioneers in Alabama was Abram Mordecai. He came there in 1785 and has been credited with being the founder of Montgomery, the state capital. A local historian described him as "an intelligent Jew who lived fifty years in the Creek nation." Mordecai traded with the Indians, studied their customs, married a squaw, and found evidence that satisfied him that the Indians were descended from the Jews. The oldest congregation in the state was organized in Mobile in 1844, and eight years later one was established in Montgomery. Even before the Civil War, Jews in Alabama rose to importance in public affairs.

In New Orleans community life began in the 1820's with the purchase of a burial plot by a society that called itself Gates of Loving Kindness. A house of prayer, now known as the Touro Synagogue, soon followed, and by 1850 still another congregation existed in the city. In Texas three congregations managed to establish themselves in the decade before the Civil War: in Houston, Galveston and San Antonio. In each the acquisition of a burial ground preceded by many years the erection of the first synagogue: death, it would seem, is a stronger summons to faith than life.

4

The first Jewish pioneer in Illinois was John Hays, who served as county sheriff and collector of internal revenue before the territory became a state in 1818. Chicago, which became the metropolis of the Middle West, was incorporated in 1837, and by 1845 enough Jews, most of them immigrants from Germany, had settled there for a burial plot to be purchased. Two years later the Congregation Men of the West (*Anshe Maarab*) was organized, and in 1851 its first house of worship was dedicated. Immigrants from Poland followed with a congregation of their own. Towards the end of the decade a young teacher named Bernhard Felsenthal launched a movement for Reform, which led to the secession of enough members from the Men of the West to establish the Sinai Congregation.

In Indiana, towards the end of the forties, there were small organized communities in Fort Wayne, Lafayette and Evansville, and in 1856 the first congregation was formed in Indianapolis. Iowa, which was admitted to the Union in 1846, is reported to have suffered an "invasion" of Jewish peddlers: about a hundred of them arrived there in the first decade of its statehood. The peddlers who hailed from Eastern Europe had one center, those from Germany another. The first congregation arose in 1855 in Keokuk, the "East European" center.

There was no Jewish community in Wisconsin when it became a state in 1848, but not long afterwards the Forty-eighters began to arrive and a congregation was organized in Milwaukee. The same is true of Michigan, where *Bet El* was formed in Detroit in 1850. A decade later changes were introduced in its Orthodox ritual, which led to a division and the establishment of another congregation.

When the gold rush descended on California in 1849 many of the Forty-eighters joined it and became Forty-niners. On the Day of Atonement of that year they held religious services in San Francisco. The place of worship was a tent, and one of the men who made up the quorum was a brother of the famous Mordecai Manuel Noah. Before the Civil War ten congregations had arisen in San Francisco and one in Sacramento, and in the ephemeral mining towns a dozen others had appeared and vanished. During those years Solomon Heydenfeldt and Henry Lyons were Associate Justices of the Supreme Court of the state, and Heydenfeldt's brother Elkan was a member of the legislature. There were other Jews in San Francisco who in later years achieved national prominence, particularly in finance, among them the Seligman and Lazard brothers.

The community that arose in Portland, Oregon, also produced an impressive number of members who rose to high station in public service. Its first congregation was launched in 1858, a year before Oregon was admitted to statehood.

5

Nearly every synagogue maintained a school for the young, with a curriculum that usually included secular as well as religious subjects. Some of the schools maintained good standards; the one attached to the *Beth Ahabah* congregation in Richmond, for example, attracted Christian pupils also. But on the whole they suffered from untrained teachers and poor text books. With the spread of the public school system there was a tendency for congregations to be satisfied with a Sunday School only, and the problem of an adequate religious education for the children was even more grave than it is today.

In the larger centers like New York, Philadelphia, Baltimore, Cincinnati and Chicago, the synagogue was no longer the only source and receptacle of communal life. Societies for charity, mutual help, good fellowship, and the cultivation of literary, musical and other cultural interests now existed that were independent of the synagogue. By 1860 five national fraternal orders had been established, among them the Independent Order Sons of Abraham, Free Sons of Israel, and Sons of the Covenant (B'nai B'rith), the latter already having more than fifty lodges.

The separation from the synagogue was especially marked in the sphere of philanthropy. In the decade before the Civil War the unprecedented influx of immigrants, of whom many were destitute, created problems of relief with which the synagogue charities were unable to cope, and in which, moreover, those who were unaffiliated with synagogues were willing to share. In the smaller centers a single body, usually called Hebrew Benevolent Society, performed a variety of charitable functions, but in the larger ones, in addition to the fraternal and mutual benefit groups, numerous independent charitable societies arose, each devoted to a special field, like the care of orphans, providing food, fuel and clothing, finding employment and visiting the sick. Free burial societies saw to it that indigence did not deprive the dead of consecrated ground. Free loan societies helped the needy towards self-support by advancing loans without interest. There were societies that distributed unleavened bread and other necessities for Passover, a festival which from time immemorial has made special demands on the family budget. And in New York and Cincinnati, Jewish hospitals had already been established.

Palestine continued to exert its unique appeal, notwithstanding the greater distance that now separated them from the ancient homeland. There were destitute scholars and saints in Jerusalem—and also in Hebron, Safed and Tiberias, the other three "holy cities" of the land —who spent their lives in sacred study, pious acts and cabbalistic meditation. Many had gone there in their old age to die and be laid in the holy soil. Their only support came from what was known as the *Chalukah,* the word meaning "distribution," and emissaries from Palestine visited the Jewries of the world on their behalf. America, of course, had won an honored place on their itineraries, and their appeals did not remain unanswered, although some of their coreligionists, conditioned by the American spirit of self-reliance and enterprise, referred to the Chalukah pensioners as indolent rather than indigent.

The practice of charity was an obligation imposed by their faith, which equates charity with justice, using the same word, *zedakah,* for both, and the modes it followed in the New World were those which the immigrants knew in the communities of the Old. It was not an integrated system of philanthropy, it suffered from overlapping, duplication and competition. But, in the opinion of many, the warmth of human contact and sympathy it created between benefactor and beneficiary went a long way to compensate for its defects.

6

Wherever a group of immigrant Jews established itself, it became the target of one complex of forces that made for disintegration and of another that promoted cohesion. In the first, the gravitational pull of the majority culture was certainly the most powerful. The immediate problem of every immigrant was to strike root in the economic soil to which he was transplanted, and his success in finding a livelihood depended largely on what may be called cultural adjustment, including the acquisition of the language, manners and general outlook of the majority. Then came the desire "to belong," and it seemed capable of fulfillment only by shedding as many differences as possible, by being as much as possible like the rest. In a later decade the process was summed up in the word "Americanization," and agencies were created by the native born and less recent arrivals to accelerate it among the great masses of East Europeans who began flocking to America in the early eighties. In 1860 the process was allowed to take its own course, and it operated quite efficiently on its own. For unwittingly a majority may exercise as much tyranny as an autocrat, and this velvet pressure was no doubt responsible for the defection and absorption of a large number of Jews, especially in the smaller centers.

But even in the larger ones it made heavy inroads into the ancestral way of life. That way was summed up in the phrase "Torah and Commandments." Torah meant primarily the study of the sacred lore, and Commandments meant ritual observance and the fulfillment of the ethical precepts. With regard to the last there was apparently no backsliding among the Jews of America, a conclusion borne out not only by their devotion to charity, but by the low incidence of crime among them, with crimes of violence practically unknown. But Jewish learning, or Torah, was at a low ebb, and ritual observance declined, especially the observance of the Sabbath. This cornerstone of Judaism was shaken by what was called economic necessity.

Nevertheless religion was still the principal cohesive force in the community. The ancient citadel was assailed but not overthrown. A great many still clung to all its rites, and all adhered to some of them. The climactic events in the life of the individual were still religious occasions. Circumcision brought the infant into "the Covenant of Abraham," confirmation was a happy and solemn event in the life of the boy, marriage was a holy rite; and most potent was the desire to be buried in consecrated ground. The solemn days of the year, Rosh Hashanah and Yom Kippur, brought practically all Jews to the house of worship. By their mere size the larger concentrations also acted as a centripetal force. It was natural for the members of the group to live in quarters of their own; they had to be near their synagogues and to satisfy the human need to be near each other. The term "ghetto" came to be applied to these quarters, but they were ghettos of their own making. And wherever such quarters existed they neutralized to an extent the powerful and incessant pull of the majority culture.

The communities that resulted were far from being the well-knit organisms that existed in the Old World. They lacked a central authority for either legislative, executive or judicial functions. To the naked eye the fragmentation was far-reaching and alarming, aided and abetted as it was by the personal liberty and religious freedom which the newcomers found in America and which they embraced with enthusiasm. Every synagogue was an independent entity, and within each of them dissident groups could secede and establish new ones without a by-your-leave to anyone. Such secessions might proceed from disagreements as to modes of worship or from less venial and purely personal rivalries. In philanthropy the fragmentation, as we have noted, was equally marked; the urge to bring help to the needy was often mixed with the all too human weakness for recognition and prominence. And in the social sphere the cleavage between Sephardim and Ashkenazim, and among the latter between those who hailed from Germany and those who hailed from Eastern Europe, remained unhealed.

On the surface there was much to justify those who held that the Jews of America did not really constitute a community—but on the surface only. The influence of the common faith could not be suppressed; the past, ancient and more proximate, could not be effaced; nor could the verdict of the Gentile majority, which pronounced the Jews a distinct ethnic and religious group, be brushed aside. A family may show strains and divisions and still be a family, nor is uniformity a necessary condition of unity. The country at large had for its motto *E pluribus unum.*

CHAPTER 6

Old World Sorrows

1

OCCASIONS AROSE WHEN THE BASIC SOLIDARITY OF THE diverse Jewish groups in America bestirred itself. The situation stemmed from the ancient animosity that harried the Jews in the Old World, but they imperiled the good name and interests of these denizens of the New World also, confirming their identity not only with each other, but with a people that lay scattered across the globe.

There were three such occasions in the two decades before the Civil War. The first was the Damascus blood libel in 1840. The second was the struggle to prevent Switzerland from treating Americans of the Jewish faith, traveling or sojourning within her borders, as inferior to Americans of other faiths. The third, which occurred in 1858, was the abduction by papal decree of a Jewish child in Italy named Edgar Mortara. In each of these episodes the honor and interests of the Jews in America were clearly challenged: in the first and third the challenge was directed with equal force to them and to all their people the world over; in the second it concerned primarily themselves.

2

Well-read persons are familiar with "The Prioress's Tale," the famous ballad by Chaucer, in which, as rendered by William Wordsworth into modern English, little Hugh of Lincoln was "laid low by cursèd Jews," but perhaps not many of them know that the Jews in the case were actually charged with ritual murder and eighteen of them were put to death. That was in the medieval year 1255, and in 1840, half a century after the glorious French Revolution, the Jews of the world, and certainly the emancipated Jews of America, must have been confident that the weird slander that charged the Jews with mixing their Passover bread with Christian blood would never again raise its ugly head. But in February of that year news reached them from the ancient city of Damascus in Syria that the medieval legend had come to life and was being written again not with Christian blood, but as so often in the past with the innocent blood of their fellow Jews.

This Damascus Affair, which consisted of a series of brutal and sordid events that continued for eight months, can only be understood against the background of the international configuration of the hour. The Turkish question had reached an acute stage, and Mehemet Ali, the sultan's governor in Egypt, had rebelled against his master and possessed himself of Palestine and Syria. France, ruled by Louis Philippe and governed by the famous historian Adolphe Thiers as chief minister, sided with the rebel, while the other European powers supported the sultan. The policy of France, which the Catholic institutions in Syria were to promote, was, of course, to make the Near East a French sphere of influence.

Now it happened that on February 5, 1840 the head of a Franciscan monastery in Damascus disappeared, and when the monks raised the cry that the Jews had murdered him for ritual purposes the French consul decided that his country's interests required that the accusation should be sustained. He took charge of the case, and since he represented the only friendly foreign power, Mehemet's governor in Damascus collaborated with him. Thirteen Jews, including three rabbis and other community leaders, were arrested and tortured, and sixty Jewish children were locked in a pen and starved to wring confessions from their parents. A few "confessed" and were prepared for execution, but repudiated their confessions when the torture was relaxed. The French consul in the meantime did not neglect to incite the Moslems against the Jews and his zeal was rewarded with anti-Jewish outbreaks in different parts of Turkey and another blood accusation on the island of Rhodes. The contagion reached Europe, and the reactionary and clerical press of France, Belgium and Italy indulged in a violent campaign of defamation against the Jews.

But other actors came upon the stage to halt the carnival of torture and slander. The British foreign minister, Lord Palmerston, intervened with Mehemet Ali and so did Prince Metternich for Austria; their motives were not purely humanitarian: French ambitions in the Near East had to be checked. And the Jews of the world came forward, and for the first time in the somber history of the Dispersion enlisted the public opinion of the nations against their persecutors.

The lead was taken by the brilliant lawyer and orator Adolphe Crémieux of France, who was courageous enough to defy his own government, and the president of the Board of Deputies of British Jews, the philanthropist and indefatigable Jewish champion Moses

Montefiore. At the call of the Lord Mayor of London an imposing indignation meeting took place on July 3, 1840 in the famous Mansion House, and the following month a deputation representing British and French Jewry and headed by Montefiore, Crémieux and the eminent Orientalist Solomon Munk, was received by Mehemet Ali in Cairo. The shrewd old Pasha, caught between France and nine other European powers, lost no time in ordering the pardon and release of the prisoners in Damascus and, on the insistence of the deputation, changed "pardon" to "acquittal."

Thus came to an end the infamous Damascus Affair, and decent men the world over rejoiced. But of the thirteen who had been imprisoned and tortured only nine survived to be released, and there was food for sober thought in the spectacle of a government representing a great and liberal European nation countenancing the vilest barbarities in the name of its "national interests." For Jews throughout the world the Affair carried still another moral. They became aware for the first time of the strength a righteous cause may gain from an appeal to the decent opinion of mankind.

3

In 1840 American Jewry was still a diminutive group, numbering some 40,000 in a population of more than 17,000,000, its congregations recognizing no single authority, its capacity for united action weakened by divisions stemming from differences in countries of origin, social cleavages and religious dissensions. In the face of the sinister events in Damascus, however, they could not remain passive. Unlike their British and French coreligionists they did not act as a single body, but in New York, Philadelphia and Richmond, the cities which must have contained more than half their number, there were public meetings of indignation and protest, and the Administration in Washington was besought to intervene on behalf of the victims.

In New York the meeting took place August 19, 1840 in the Bnai Jeshurun Synagogue after a request to permit its holding in Shearith Israel had been denied by the trustees of the premier Jewish congregation in the New World. "No benefit can arise from such a course," was the verdict of the trustees, and the statement is significant, because it represents a sentiment that asserted itself time and again in the career of American Jewry when a decision for or against public action on behalf of Jewish interests had to be made: there was always a body of opinion that frowned upon the public airing of Jewish issues.

Bnai Jeshurun did not share those well-bred misgivings; Bnai Jeshurun, in fact, had been established as the result of a secession from Shearith Israel fifteen years earlier, of which the basic cause was the impatience of the newly arrived Ashkenazim with the Sephardic patricians of the original congregation. The principal address at the meeting was delivered by Mordecai Manuel Noah, who was generally regarded as the ranking American Jew and who never hesitated to exhibit the hopes and wrongs of his people to the gaze of the world. The chairman of the meeting and leader of the movement in New York was Israel Baer Kursheedt, an immigrant from Germany who had breached the Sephardic citadel by marrying a daughter of Gershom Mendes Seixas. A week later a public meeting, in which several Protestant clergymen participated, took place in Philadelphia with Isaac Leeser as principal speaker.

Both meetings adopted resolutions calling on President Martin Van Buren for diplomatic intervention in Damascus, and the committees in charge were surprised to learn from Secretary of State John Forsyth that such intervention had already taken place. Instructions had gone out shortly before to John Gliddon, the American Consul at Alexandria, and to David Porter, the chargé d'affaires at Constantinople, to extend "the active sympathy and generous interposition of the Government of the United States" on behalf of "an oppressed and persecuted race, among whose kindred are found some of the most worthy and patriotic of our citizens."

In his letter Forsyth informed the New York Committee that "the heart-rending scenes which took place at Damascus had previously been brought to the notice of the President by a communication from our Consul at that place." There are passages, however, in the instructions to the Consul and chargé d'affaires, which reveal so authentic a knowledge of the blood libel and its motives as to suggest that Jewish sources may have been consulted by the Secretary of State in framing them. He calls the charges "extravagant and strikingly similar to those which, in less enlightened ages, were made pretexts for the persecution and spoliation of these unfortunate people." And today, more than a century later, another passage in the Secretary's letter to the American representative in Constantinople invites rather rueful reflections. The chargé d'affaires is instructed to endeavor "to prevent or mitigate these horrors, the bare recital of which has caused a shudder throughout the civilized world." Recent and much greater horrors, including the systematic annihilation of six million European Jews by Nazi Germany failed to produce a palpable shudder throughout the civilized world. The capacity of the world to shudder at horrors appeared to have definitely declined.

4

The immediate victims of the libel in Damascus were the lowly Jews of an ancient Levantine city, but every other Jewish community in the world felt that it too was its target. A decade later an issue arose that affected the American Jews only, but it also brought vividly home to them their kinship with a world people that the world still treated with contumely and disdain. In November 1850 the American Minister to Switzerland signed a general treaty with the Swiss Confederation establishing the rights of the citizens of each country to travel and sojourn in the other. Now, the Swiss Confederation consisted of a number of Cantons each governed by its own constitution; and in some of them, notably the important Canton of Basel, Jews were subjected to severe restrictions and disabilities. The treaty, which President Millard Fillmore laid before the Senate in February 1851, conceded to those Cantons the right to impose the same restrictions on American Jewish citizens within their borders. "On account of the tenor of the Federal Constitution of Switzerland," said the first article of the treaty, "Christians alone are entitled to the enjoyment of the privileges guaranteed by the present Article in the Swiss Cantons." A grave question now faced American citizens of the Jewish faith: Will their government enter into a treaty with another placing them on a different and lower footing than citizens of other faiths?

President Fillmore in a message to the Senate declared that clause to be "a decisive objection." And he went on to say that "neither by law, nor by treaty, nor by any other official proceeding is it competent for the Government of the United States to establish any distinction between its citizens founded on differences in religious beliefs." Secretary of State Daniel Webster and Senator Henry Clay, who wielded commanding influence, also disapproved of the treaty, and the Senate refused to ratify it. The refusal, it should be noted, was rendered easier by a vigorous agitation current at the time which aimed to secure for Protestant citizens the right to free worship in Catholic countries.

Shortly afterwards, however, something happened which will only surprise those who are unfamiliar with the wonderland of politics. A second treaty was negotiated by the American minister to Switzerland, and it stipulated that citizens of both countries "shall be admitted and treated upon a footing of reciprocal equality," but it hastened to add "that such admission and treatment shall not conflict with the constitutional or legal provisions, Federal as well as State and Cantonal, of the contracting parties." So the word "Christian," which underscored the invidious distinction, was omitted, but the artfully artless statement carried the same discrimination, and even added insult to injury by intimating that similar disabilities existed in American law also. Nevertheless, in November 1855 the new treaty was ratified by the Senate and three days later President Franklin Pierce declared it in force.

The following year the restrictions which Swiss laws imposed on American Jews, and which the treaty sanctioned, were highlighted by the case of A. H. Gootman, an American Jewish citizen, who was threatened with expulsion by the Canton of Neufchatel. He appealed to Theodore Fay, the American Minister to Switzerland, who found himself powerless under the treaty to be of help. The facts of the case became known, and the fast-growing community in America was stirred to action. All the apparatus for influencing public opinion in a democracy was resorted to, though not without misgivings in some quarters. There were meetings of protest against the treaty in Baltimore, Cleveland, Chicago and Cincinnati; petitions were prepared and sent to Washington, and the press of the country denounced an affront of which not the Jews alone, but every American citizen was the target. In Baltimore a conference was held on the issue, and notwithstanding certain frictions which developed in the course of its proceedings, a committee headed by Isaac Wise was set up and in October 1857 it was received by President James Buchanan. The President assured the committee that the wrong would be righted.

The committee went away satisfied that its mission was accomplished, but it was many years before the wrong was righted. From the exchanges between the two governments that followed, it was clear that the offending Swiss cantons would have to amend their basic laws if American Jews were to have the same rights within their borders as other Americans. The Federal Council of Switzerland would have welcomed such changes, for not only the United States, but Britain and France also were insisting upon equal treatment for their Jewish citizens. But the cantons were obdurate and the Canton of Basel, in particular, was hard-set in its anti-Jewish policy. Its contention was that if it relented in favor of American Jews, it would have to admit "the usurious Israelitish population" of the contiguous French province of Alsace.

This tocsin against the Alsatian Jews had been sounded before; it was heard in 1791 in the French National Assembly when the emancipation of the Jews of France was debated by that body; it was a pious cloak which covered the ancient fear of Jewish competition. But, as Fay wrote to Secretary of State Lewis Cass, this warning against the Alsatian Jews had closed "the mouths of all foreign governments and preceding treaty makers." The American minister, however, refused to accept the warning at its face value. He investigated the charges against the "Israelitish population" of Alsace, and in November 1858 he informed the Secretary of State that as a result of the information he had gathered "no Swiss authority will ever dare to advance that objection against us as an argument." In a document known as the "Israelite Note," the information was transmitted to the Swiss Federal Council which helped to circulate it. The "Note" played its part in the eventual emancipation of the Jews of Switzerland and appears to have exerted influence in neighboring countries also.

But the complete emancipation of the Swiss Jews, on which the settlement of the controversy hinged, did not come until sixteen years later. During those years the cantons individually accorded Jews equal rights, even Basel falling in line in 1872, and two years later the Swiss Confederation adopted a new constitution, which placed the rights of aliens under federal instead of cantonal jurisdiction, and erased all distinctions based on religion. The American government in the interval kept the issue more or less alive. The most emphatic gesture was made by President Lincoln when he appointed a Jew as Consul in Zurich: he could not have made his attitude plainer both to the Swiss and the Jews of America. Among the latter, however, the agitation eventually came down to a simmer. Other and more anxious issues absorbed their attention.

5

The case of the little boy in Bologna, Italy, whom the Catholic Church tore from his parents in 1858, administered an even greater shock to the Jews of the world—and to countless thousands of Christians also—than did the atrocities against the victims of the blood libel in Damascus. A whole generation was to pass and the Dreyfus Affair to emerge from the dark recesses of reaction and bigotry in France before the Jewish world was so deeply outraged and distressed. Nor could the broad ocean immunize the Jews of America from the shock and the pain.

In 1858 Bologna, the capital of the Emilia region in central Italy, was part of the Papal States whose ruler, Pius IX, did not overflow with benevolence towards the Jews. A decade earlier, the Italian *Risorgimento*, led by the illustrious Mazzini, had forced him to flee from Rome, and the Jews of the city had torn down the gates of the foul ghetto, but with the help of Napoleon III he returned the following year and deprived them of the civic equality they had won. The two outstanding events in his long pontificate were the promulgation of the dogma of papal infallibility and the end of the temporal power of the papacy.

Now, on June 23, 1858, a troop of Papal guards broke into the home of the Mortaras in Bologna and took the six-year-old Edgar away from his parents to be placed in a convent and brought up as a Catholic. The order to do so had come from the Holy Office of the Inquisition in Rome, and the ground for it was a confession by the boy's nurse that four years earlier, when the boy was seriously ill, she had secretly baptized him. Papal doctrine, it is true, did not favor the baptism of children without the consent of the parents, but it also held that once the sacrament had been administered, the child no longer belonged to his parents but to the Church. The same principle, as we saw, prevailed in the case of adults who had been forced into baptism; the Church frowned upon forcible conversion, but once baptized the adult, too, belonged to the Church, and was eligible for all its spiritual gifts in return for obedience and all its penalties for deviation or heresy. In the mundane affairs of men it is considered reprehensible to retain something obtained by reprehensible means, but apparently a different order may prevail in the sphere of religious dogma.

The parents of little Edgar, however, were unable to appreciate the dogmatic niceties. Their cry of anguish echoed across Europe, and Jewish communities roused themselves to action. In every land they called upon their governments for aid, and the sovereigns, Catholic as well as Protestant, responded: Napoleon III of France and Francis Joseph of Austria appealed personally to the Pope, and Protestant rulers expressed their sympathy. Other Christian leaders throughout the world made plain their sense of outrage, but in Rome Pius IX remained unmoved. He made no reply to a petition which the rabbis of Germany sent him, and when Sir Moses Montefiore came to Rome to plead with him, he refused to see him. The turmoil which the boy's abduction created he regarded as a Jewish fabrication, and he vented his resentment upon the Jews in his domain. As for the boy, he was brought up a Catholic and remained one.

So dogma triumphed, but it is generally believed that the Mortara Affair contributed not a little to the reverses which the Pope suffered. They began in 1860 when the Emilia region joined the Kingdom of Sardinia, spearhead of the movement for the unification of Italy, and reached their climax in 1870 when Rome fell and the Papal States were no more. Today the Emilia region is still a stronghold of anti-clericalism in Italy.

6

In 1858 the majority of the Jews in America had arrived there in the course of the current decade; their memory of the cynical high-handedness with which the elementary rights of their people in Europe were flouted was still vivid, and the news of the Mortara scandal stirred them to prompt action. A number of congregations in the country received word of what had transpired from Montefiore himself, and the depth of feeling the news engendered may be measured by the fact that congregations like Shearith Israel, which had been opposed to public meetings in the Damascus Affair, joined with the others in sponsoring demonstrations of protest. The most impressive meeting took place in New York with an attendance of 2,000—a large number for those days—which included Protestants as well as Jews. The leading Protestant weekly, *The Independent*, called upon the Christians of the country to "make common cause with their Hebrew fellow-citizens in protesting against this Bologna outrage."

But the resolutions which the meeting adopted, calling for intervention by the President of the United States, remained unheeded. Secretary of State Cass took the position that the Government could not interfere in a matter where the rights of an American citizen were not affected. The Government, however, had intervened in the Damascus Affair in which no American citizens were involved, and one political cynic, or realist, ventured to explain the inconsistency by pointing to the absence of a Moslem vote in the country and the presence of a Catholic one. The American Catholics of course deplored the commotion that had been stirred up over something that happened in a distant Italian city. Their organ, *The New York Tablet*, pointed out that abolitionists in America were abducting Negro slaves from their owners without provoking the indignation of those who were so concerned about a little boy in Bologna.

7

When Montefiore appeared before the potentates of Egypt and Turkey to redress the wrongs inflicted upon the Jews in Damascus, he did not speak as an individual, eminent as he was in his own right. He spoke as President of the Board of Deputies of British Jews, a body founded in 1760 and representing all congregations, Sephardic and Ashkenazic, in Britain. It was, in fact, to this body that Mehemet Ali communicated his decree which brought release to the prisoners in Damascus. In the United States the British Board of Deputies stood out as an object lesson in the value of a similar body with authority to speak and act for the entire American Jewish community.

The first attempt to create such a body was initiated by Isaac Leeser of Philadelphia in 1841, shortly after the Damascus Affair, and it proved abortive. Eight years later he was joined by Isaac Mayer Wise in a second attempt, which also failed, and in 1855 a national rabbinical conference met in Cleveland with the same ultimate objective in view. But the conference included both Orthodox and Reform rabbis, and it foundered on the rock of doctrinal and ritual antagonisms; Leeser and Wise, the two foremost leaders of American Jewry, became estranged. Viewing those attempts at union after the lapse of a century, we are able to account for their failure by their commitment to a religious program: apparently both religious trends were under the illusion that they could compose their differences by a process of give and take, and perhaps each of them was so sure of the merits of its own case that it expected to take more than give. This religious approach was no doubt inevitable if only because the leaders of the movement were all rabbis; the laymen they enlisted in their efforts were followers, not leaders. American Jewry had not yet developed a lay leadership which, it is fair to assume, would have based its plan of union on what united the community, not on what divided it.

That basis of unity, the protection and promotion of Jewish rights and honor, was clearly indicated by the Damascus Affair, the discriminations legalized in the Treaty with Switzerland, and the Mortara scandal. In France, under the inspiration of Adolphe Crémieux, the Mortara case led to the establishment of the *Alliance Israélite Universelle*, "to defend the honor of the Jewish name wherever it is attacked," and "to work for the emancipation of our brethren who still suffer under the burden of exceptional legislation"; and in New York Samuel Meyer Isaacs, rabbi of the congregation Gates of Prayer, initiated the formation of the "Board of Delegates of American Israelites," the first body representing a sizable segment of American Jewry.

The convention at which the Board was founded met in New York in November 1859, with representatives of congregations located in thirteen cities, eleven of them in New York. But the important Reform congregations of the country were conspicuously absent: Isaac Wise saw in the effort a threat to Reform Judaism. Wise was a Democrat and a foe of abolitionism, and he accused the sponsors of the movement of planning to commit the Jews of America in the bitter political tensions that were rending the country. The charge was denied; the movement would eschew political and religious issues; its sole aim would be to protect Jewish rights wherever they might be assailed. But the leaders of Reform were not reconciled. Absent also were the two "aristocrats" among the congregations in the New World: Shearith Israel of New York and Mikveh Israel of Philadelphia. The two were not Reform, but how could they follow when for so many decades it had been their role to lead? How could they join a democratic body and expose themselves to the risk of being dominated by the newcomers from Germany and Poland? Besides, they were opposed to public protests and demonstrations, which the newcomers seemed to favor, as weapons against the infringement of Jewish rights; quiet intervention in the right quarters by the right people was, in their view, more advisable and likely to be more effective, a view which was largely shared by Reform groups throughout the country.

Though seriously handicapped by the noncooperation of the most influential segments of the community, the Board of Delegates of American Israelites was duly constituted and began a career which lasted from 1859 to 1878, when it surrendered its functions to the newly formed Union of American Hebrew Congregations and its name was changed to "Board of Delegates of Civil and Religious Rights." Henry I. Hart was its president, Samuel Meyer Isaacs its secretary, and until his death in 1868 Isaac Leeser was its vice-president. It was a difficult but not unfruitful career. The Board played a creditable part in the campaign against the discriminatory treaty with Switzerland, and asserted itself on a number of occasions during the Civil War when, as we shall see, issues arose that touched the fair name and welfare of American Jewry. But its authority was constantly challenged, nor did it always command the means required to meet the obligations it had to assume. It was the first approximation to a single authority representative of the entire community, which many American Jews still consider a necessity, and for which they are still waiting.

CHAPTER 7

Civil War

1

AMONG THE MOST IMPORTANT REVOLUTIONS ON RECORD should be included the one that took place in men's minds on the subject of human slavery. From the dawn of history until less than a century ago millions of people considered property in human beings as natural as in domestic animals. In 1834 John C. Calhoun, the foremost political philosopher and spokesman of the South, affirmed that "there cannot be a durable republic without slavery," and his millions of civilized constituents applauded. Today slavery is held in universal abhorrence and the enslavement of men, to which totalitarian regimes have more or less clandestinely resorted, is denounced as a throwback to barbarism. And in the making of this revolution a major role was played by the conflict between the States which from 1861 to 1865 tore the Republic apart and drenched it with blood and tears.

With respect to slavery the ancient tradition to which the Jews in America were the heirs marked an enormous advance not only over the age in which it originated, but even over the time in which they were living. Throughout the ancient world slavery was a fixed institution, and the Mosaic Code could no more undertake to abolish it among the children of Israel than it could abolish animal sacrifice. But just as it strove to spiritualize sacrifice, changing it from a crude act of propitiation to a vehicle for higher religious expression, so it strove to humanize slavery and prepare the ground for its eventual disappearance. In Babylonia it was a capital crime to shelter a fugitive slave. The Bible makes kidnapping a man and selling him into slavery a capital crime, and forbids the return of a fugitive slave to his master. The Babylonian code directed the ears of a slave to be cut off if he asked for freedom. The Mosaic Code required that a slave should be freed if he suffered bodily injury at the hands of his master.

In the Mosaic Code the slave is not "an animated tool," as Aristotle defined him: he is not a chattel but a person. In Greece slaves at work in the fields were chained, and if they multiplied to excess the surplus was exterminated. In Rome the master could mutilate or crucify a slave at his pleasure and abandon the sick among them to die of starvation. No such barbarities were practiced among the Hebrews. The Decalogue proclaims the Sabbath a day of rest not only for the master but for his bondsman. The Greeks and Romans, who had no day of rest, derided the Jewish Sabbath as the device of a lazy people; their slaves were doomed to incessant labor. Many a page of Greek and Roman history is red with slave uprisings; the history of the Jews in Palestine, which covers a much longer span, knows nothing of such eruptions. Greek and Roman economy, in fact, like that of the South before the Civil War, rested largely on slavery. The economy of the Hebrew Commonwealth was based on the small independent farmer and the free artisan.

It cannot, however, be said that this lofty tradition had an important part in determining the side which the Jews in America took in the conflict. They divided along sectional lines as did the rest of the population. Nor did it always mean in the case of the Jews who fought for the Confederacy, any more than it always meant in the case of their Christian comrades, that loyalty to the South meant approval of Negro slavery. The issue was not as simple as the extreme abolitionists in the North saw it. It was complicated by the doctrine of state sovereignty and the right of secession, and by the fear which haunted the Southern planters that the election of Lincoln in 1860 meant the immediate emancipation of their three million slaves, the destruction of their economy and way of life, and their subjugation to the Yankee traders, manufacturers and bankers. The Jewish planters naturally shared that fear. They were in the main native-born Sephardic Jews with a double dose of aristocracy: one derived from their Spanish or Portuguese origin, the other from their life as planters and country gentlemen. And as for the recent Ashkenazic immigrants who established themselves in the South, they were nearly all traders or peddlers, the South having few attractions or opportunities for craftsmen, and no trader can prosper who openly opposes the politics of his customers.

Without worshipping at the shrine of historical materialism, one may still admit the force of material advantage in shaping men's attitudes and judgments. The cotton planters of the South were themselves an egregious illustration of that truth. At the turn of the nineteenth century public opinion in the South held that slavery must in some way be abolished. But a decade or so earlier the steam-powered spinning jenny and the power loom had been installed in factories in England. The demand for cotton took a tremendous leap, and the planters were enabled to meet it by the cotton gin, the machine for separating the seed from the fiber which Eli Whitney invented in 1793. Those landmarks in the Industrial Revolution transformed the attitude of the planters towards slavery. The wealth which King Cotton showered down upon the South could not be renounced, and there was an enormous increase in the demand for slaves.

2

In the North the sentiment that sustained the long and bloody struggle was not so much the detestation of slavery as the resolve to preserve the Union, but the Jews of the North, especially the more recent arrivals, did have a deep aversion for the evil: in the Europe from which they hailed they had become imbued with libertarian ideals. Quite a number of them were attracted by the unpopular abolitionist movement, and some of them took an active part in it. According to Bernhard Felsenthal, himself an ardent abolitionist, the large majority of American Jews were "heart and soul dedicated to the anti-slavery movement." And no doubt more of them would have been active in it, but for the burdens of adjustment which handicapped every immigrant. They were not yet articulate enough in the new language to share in a cause that could only thrive on agitation.

Among the outstanding Jewish abolitionists was David Einhorn, rabbi of the Har Sinai Congregation in Baltimore, who had already achieved prominence as a militant advocate of Reform Judaism. His abolitionism was equally militant and it brought him into imminent personal danger. In April 1861, after four days of bloody rioting in Baltimore led by secessionists, Einhorn was with difficulty persuaded to leave the city. He was shown proof that the rioters had his name on their list, and prior to his departure his home and family were guarded by young men of his congregation. And there was another Jewish abolitionist in Baltimore, a member of Einhorn's congregation who, like his rabbi, had a narrow escape from the secessionist mob. He was Leopold Blumenberg, who had come to the United States from Prussia seven years earlier, and whom we shall meet again among the distinguished Jewish soldiers who fought for the Union.

Einhorn took refuge in Philadelphia but he was anxious to return promptly to his pulpit. He refused however to accept the condition laid down by his frightened trustees that he refrain from preaching on "the excitable issues of the time." There is a striking similarity between the warnings against slavery that came from Einhorn a century ago and those against the curtailment of civil rights that were heard in the mid-twentieth century. Einhorn held Negro slavery to be a menace to the rights of the Jews and all other minority groups in America. Only by extending democratic rights to all its people, he declared, could America take the lead in extending democracy throughout the world.

In Philadelphia Einhorn's most prominent colleague was also an ardent supporter of the Union cause. He was Sabato Morais, rabbi of the Mikveh Israel Congregation. Morais was so outspoken in praise of Lincoln, that his anti-Republican trustees tried to silence him, but the attempt was defeated by the congregation membership. He was a native of Italy and had known the leaders of the Italian *Risorgimento*. The disruption of the Union, he was sure, would be catastrophic for the cause of liberty not only in America, but throughout the world.

Another prominent Jewish abolitionist was Moritz Pinner, who had migrated from Germany, and in 1859, when he was about thirty, edited a German-language abolitionist paper in "Bleeding Kansas," where Free Soilers and pro-slavery "Border Ruffians" fought without quarter. There, in May 1856, the implacable John Brown had performed his first bloody exploit, and three of John Brown's followers have been identified as Jews: August Bondi, Jacob Benjamin and Theodore Weiner. Pinner was a delegate from Missouri to the 1860 convention of the Republican party in Chicago, which nominated Lincoln. His was the uncompromising brand of abolitionism. When the war broke out he declined an offer of a diplomatic post and enlisted in the army. A fellow delegate of Pinner's in Chicago, and one of the three who placed Lincoln in nomination, was Lewis Naphtali Dembitz, a forty-eighter who, at the age of twenty-eight, had already become a prominent lawyer and civic leader in Louisville, Kentucky. He was also a leader in Jewish communal and religious affairs. Dembitz was the pride of his family and in particular of his little nephew Louis Brandeis, born in Louisville four years before that epochal convention. The Electoral College, which sealed the popular vote of 1860, included Sigismund Kaufman of New York, also a forty-eighter and an active abolitionist.

Most of the prominent rabbis in the North also spoke out boldly against slavery and for the Union cause, among them Liebman Adler, a colleague of Felsenthal in Chicago, Max Lilienthal in Cincinnati and Samuel M. Isaacs in New York. Isaac Leeser had too many ties of friendship with the South and chose to be silent. Isaac M. Wise remained a staunch Democrat; he detested abolitionism, which he considered responsible for the war. Wise displayed no perception of

Lincoln's spiritual greatness except, to a degree, after his assassination, when he wrote of him as "an upright, honest unassuming man . . . forgiving in his nature, gentle as a child."

There was one rabbi in the North, however, who came out in defense of slavery. All its advocates were eager to find sanction for it in the Bible, and Morris Jacob Raphall, rabbi of B'nai Jeshurun of New York, came valiantly to their assistance. In January 1861, when South Carolina had already seceded and the six other leading states of the South were preparing to do likewise, Raphall chose to preach a sermon in which he maintained that the Decalogue approved of slavery. He charged abolitionist clergymen like Henry Ward Beecher with distorting the meaning of Holy Writ. He did distinguish between slavery among the Hebrews, who treated the slave as "a person in whom the dignity of human nature was to be respected," and the system in the South, "which reduces the slave to a thing," but he felt it his duty to brand the preaching against slavery in the South as a sin.

The sermon created something of a sensation; it appeared in the press, was reprinted as a pamphlet, and was pounced upon in the South as a treasure-trove. The good rabbi must have been gratified by the fame he won, but there is no reason to suppose that during the war his sympathies lay with the Copperheads. Both his son and son-in-law were in the armed forces of the Union, and he was once received by Lincoln when he came to Washington seeking promotion for his son from Second to First Lieutenant. The story has been set down by Adolphus Salomons, a member of the Executive Committee of the Board of Delegates of American Israelites, who accompanied Raphall to the President. It was one of the Days of Fasting and Prayer, which Lincoln had proclaimed, and the President asked the rabbi why he was not praying that day with his congregation. Raphall's answer was that his assistant was "doing that duty." Lincoln wrote out an order for the promotion and handing it to the rabbi, told him he could now go home and do his own praying.

The attempt of a rabbi to make the Bible testify in favor of human slavery did not, of course, remain unchallenged. The most effective reply came from Michael Heilprin, a recent immigrant whose love of liberty had been nurtured in comradeship with the Hungarian revolutionist Louis Kossuth. When Heilprin came to America in 1856 he did not have to learn English; it was one of more than a dozen languages he already knew. And his general knowledge was encyclopedic; shortly after his arrival, in fact, he became one of the editors of *Appleton's New American Encyclopedia*. His reply to Raphall, which appeared in

The New York Tribune, was both scholarly and scathing. He was, he declared, "outraged by the sacreligious words of the Rabbi . . . the Hebrew defamer of the law of his nation," and he went on to show that they were a "misinterpretation of Judaism . . . full of falsehood, nonsense and blasphemy." And shortly afterwards a work entitled *Slavery Among the Ancient Hebrews*, by Moses Mielziner, a Jewish scholar in Copenhagen, was translated and published in New York, the author's conclusions being that the aim of the biblical laws on slavery was to bring about its gradual disappearance.

3

The bombardment of Fort Sumter in Charleston Harbor on April 12, 1861 by order of the Confederate Government silenced all controversy in the North or reduced it to a mutter. Lincoln called on the states for 75,000 militiamen to put down rebellion, and the Confederacy set out to raise an army of 100,000 to vindicate the right of secession. Before the final decision four years later, these initial levies were to grow to over a million and a half men for the North and more than a million for the South. The bloodiest and most heartbreaking civil conflict in history had begun.

From the psychologic standpoint a remarkable aspect of it was the readiness of so many high-minded men and women to throw themselves heart and soul into a cause of which, after all, the fundamental aim was to preserve the evil and shame of slavery—the more remarkable since other Western nations had already abolished it in their homelands and colonies. The simple issue was, of course, obscured by other factors, among which the dread of "race pollution" and of the end of "white supremacy" were dominant. "We fight for our liberties, our altars, our firesides," was the simple formula in which the editor of one paper in the South summed up its case, and Southerners found the formula easy to accept because the South, which became the scene of most of the fighting, suffered much more grievously than the North.

The Jews of the South, especially the large proportion among them who were native to the soil and imbued with its traditions, embraced its cause promptly and enthusiastically. The simple formula proclaimed by that editor was echoed by leaders of Southern Jewry. Maximilian Michelbacher, the most prominent rabbi in the Confederate capital, composed and circulated a prayer for Jewish soldiers in the Confederate ranks. "Our firesides are threatened," declared the prayer, "the foe is before us, with declared intention to desecrate our soil, to murder our people, and deprive us of the glorious inheritance which was left to us by the immortal fathers of this once great Republic."

There were two Jewish Senators, David Levy Yulee of Florida and Judah Philip Benjamin of Louisiana, who joined the exodus of southern statesmen from Washington on the establishment of the Confederacy. They were both detached from Jewish community life, and both married outside the faith; but this narrative cannot ignore them, if only because their enemies refused to ignore their Jewish origin. David Yulee who, for the first thirty-six years of his life, called himself David Levy, was the first Jew to sit in the Senate of the United States. His father, Moses Levy, had come to Florida from St. Thomas in the West Indies where David was born, and the son became a planter, lawyer and politician. In 1845 when Florida was admitted into the Union, he was chosen to represent his State in the Senate, and after 1861 he was a member of the Confederate Congress. He spent a year in prison after the war when he was arrested on his way to Washington to secure the readmission of his state into the Union.

Judah P. Benjamin, also born in the West Indies, was a man of larger mold. In the cabinet of Jefferson Davis he served successively as Attorney-General, Secretary of War and Secretary of State, and so heavily did the Confederate President lean upon him in all matters, that Benjamin was called "the brains of the Confederacy."

Before his election to the Senate in 1858 he was a phenomenally successful lawyer in Louisiana. He served also in the State Legislature where he was responsible for a law that abolished imprisonment for debt. In the Senate he employed his keen mind and brilliant oratory in the defense of slavery, and one of his Northern colleagues called him "an Israelite with Egyptian principles," a paraphrase of the charge made against Martin Van Buren and other politicians that they were "Northern men with Southern principles." As Secretary of State he almost won recognition of the Confederacy from England and France: his failure was due mainly to the military reverses which his Government suffered. When Lee surrendered at Appomattox in April 1865 Benjamin knew that the cause of the South was lost, but he resolved not to be taken alive. He went through a series of breath-taking adventures on land and sea, and finally succeeded in reaching England by way of Nassau. After six months of study he was admitted to the British bar, quickly rose to the top level of the profession in Britain, and was the recipient of signal honors from Britain's leading men, including Disraeli, Lord Chief Justice Coleridge, Gladstone and Tennyson. Two mansions associated with his career, one on his estate in Louisiana, the other the house near Tampa, Florida, where he found refuge in 1865 during his flight from the country, have been converted into historic shrines.

Benjamin's enemies—and he seems to have had even more of them in the South than in the North—exploited his Jewish origin to the hilt: their favorite name for him was Judas Iscariot. But he seemed to know very little of the faith into which he was born. His eloquent defense of slavery in the Senate in March 1858 was based on the proposition that slaves, like plows and pitchforks, were property: to deprive people of their slaves was an act of spoliation. His moral judgment was equally obtuse in his confidence, which, of course, he shared with other Southern statesmen, that the textile workers of Britain would compel their government to support the Confederacy in order to insure the supply of cotton on which their livelihood depended. The British workers also proved willing to suffer in the cause of freedom. "I did not believe," said Benjamin to his new friends in England after the war, "that your Government would allow such mischief to your operators, such loss to your manufacturers, or that the people themselves would have borne it." With all his intellectual acumen Benjamin failed to appreciate the great moral advantage which the North possessed in this struggle of freedom against slavery.

4

The attempt to compile a full and accurate roster of the Jews who fought on both sides of the conflict comes upon serious obstacles: the official lists do not mention a man's religion and it is not always safe to assume that certain names belong to Jews and others do not. The effort to compute the proportion which the number of Jewish fighting men bore to the total number of Jews in the country is further complicated by divergencies in the estimates of the Jewish population of the time. The most thorough investigation was made by the Jewish leader Simon Wolf and published in 1895 in his book *The American Jew as Patriot, Soldier and Citizen*: it was a study undertaken to meet a statement in a letter, which appeared in *The North American Review* in 1891, that the writer had not met a single Jew in uniform during the Civil War. The book lists more than 6,000 Jews who fought for the Union and more than 1,000 who fought for the Confederacy. In all likelihood, however, Simon's findings are far below the number of Jewish soldiers and sailors in the Confederate forces, at least. In 1864 application was made to James A. Seddon, the Confederate

Secretary of War, to grant Jewish soldiers leave for the approaching High Holy Days. He denied the request on the ground that such leave might disrupt some commands, since there were ten to twelve thousand Jewish soldiers in the Confederate Armies.

It may also be assumed that the ratio of Jews who bore arms to defend the South was larger than the corresponding ratio in the North; there was a much larger proportion of native born among them, whose roots lay deep in the history and traditions of the land. That circumstance would account for the larger proportion of officers among them than in the North: the Southern staff officers alone, who have been identified as Jews, number twenty-four. It would also account for the more numerous instances of groups of brothers who took up arms together, like the five Moses brothers of South Carolina, the six Cohen brothers of North Carolina, the three Levy brothers from Louisiana, three more of the same name from Virginia, and still other "brothers in arms," as they have been called.

Orators and poets who assure the brave that their deeds will live forever—an assurance for which the brave seldom hanker—are often guilty of poetic license, a truth that is attested by the undoubtedly incomplete roster of Jews who distinguished themselves in the Confederate service. Some few have escaped oblivion, the most picturesque among them being Max Frauenthal. One witness described Frauenthal as "a little Jew . . . insignificant in appearance," who "had the heart of a lion." His name, which was corrupted to Fronthall, became a symbol: a soldier who displayed exceptional courage was described as "a regular Fronthall." Another gallant private was Max Ullman of Mississippi, who served all through the war, was twice wounded, and nearly thirty years later became rabbi of a congregation in Birmingham, Alabama. Captain Adolph Proskauer rose from the ranks after being wounded four times. Lieutenant Albert Luria died a hero's death in the Battle of Seven Pines and Marx Cohen Jr. in the Battle of Bentonville.

A few names may be added of those who belonged to the higher brackets of the service. The first surgeon-general was David Camden de Leon, whom we met as the "fighting doctor" of Chapultepec in the Mexican War. Lionel Levy was Judge Advocate of the Military Court. J. Randolph Mordecai was Assistant Adjutant-General, and A. C. Meyers was Quartermaster General. In the Confederate Navy the most prominent Jewish officer was Levi Meyers Harby, who had served in the War of 1812 and in the Mexican War. At the end of the Civil

War he was in command of Galveston Harbor, having previously distinguished himself in its defense as captain of the *Neptune*.

5

Only a few of the Jewish officers in the Confederate forces have been named, and whether or not they exceeded in number those who fought for the Union, the records concerning the latter are certainly more ample. Frederick Knefler, who migrated from Hungary in 1859, rose to the rank of major general; he took part in the main battles fought by the Army of the Cumberland and marched with General William T. Sherman through Georgia to the sea. Leopold Blumenberg who, as we saw, was almost lynched by a secessionist mob in Baltimore, took part in the Peninsular Campaign, was severely wounded in the Battle of Antietam and was finally breveted brigadier general. He had come to the United States in 1854, refusing to tolerate the anti-Semitism of Prussia after having fought with distinction in the Prussian army. Philip J. Joachimsen, who commanded a New York regiment, was also breveted brigadier general. As a United States Attorney in New York he had been the Nemesis of slave traders. After the war he played an important part in the establishment of a number of Jewish philanthropies, including the Hebrew Sheltering Guardian Society.

Still another Jewish soldier of the Union, also a breveted brigadier general, was Edward Solomon, who had previously been colonel of an Illinois regiment that included more than one hundred Jews. He fought with distinction at Chancellorsville, Lookout Mountain, Gettysburg and other battles. After the war he was four years governor of the Territory of Washington, and when he moved to San Francisco he served two terms in the California State Legislature. Marcus Spiegel was the son of a rabbi in Germany, and after enlisting in Ohio he gained one promotion after another until he became colonel of one of the regiments of his state. He was killed in battle after being recommended for promotion to brigadier general.

Max Einstein became a brigadier general in the Pennsylvania militia in 1860. The following year he organized an infantry regiment of which he became colonel, and in the first Battle of Bull Run, which proved so disastrous for Northern arms, he distinguished himself by covering the retreat of the Union Army. Leopold Newman, a lieutenant colonel in a New York regiment, was severely wounded in the Battle of

Chancellorsville, and before he died in Washington he was visited by President Lincoln, who brought him his commission of appointment as brigadier general. The record also speaks of General William Meyer, who tried to raise a predominantly Jewish regiment in New York, and during the draft riots in that city rendered valuable service, for which he received a letter of thanks from the President.

There was no predominantly Jewish regiment during the war. The Jews were in the main opposed to the organization of exclusively Jewish units: it smacked too much of segregation. Such units, of company strength, were, however, recruited in Syracuse and Chicago, and in the South one Jewish company was raised in Macon and another in West Point, both located in Georgia. In a number of Northern regiments, also, especially those recruited in New York and Philadelphia, Jews were prominently represented. The regiment commanded by Max Einstein, for example, included nearly one hundred Jews of whom thirty were above the rank of private. Another unit with a large proportion of Jews was a Pennsylvania cavalry regiment, known popularly as Cameron's Dragoons in honor of the Secretary of War, Simon Cameron, who authorized its recruitment. Its colonel was Max Friedman. Cameron's Dragoons will figure again in our story in connection with the controversy that arose over the appointment of Jewish chaplains in the Union Army. The number of Jewish fighting men furnished by different Northern states is a good index of the distribution of the Jewish population in that section of the country. New York furnished nearly 2,000, Ohio 1,134, Illinois 1,076, Pennsylvania and Indiana over 500 each, and Michigan over 200.

Seven of the Jewish soldiers in the ranks of the Union were awarded the Congressional Medal of Honor, the highest decoration for valor in battle. They were Abraham Cohen, Isaac Gans, Abraham Grunwalt, Henry Heller, Leopold Karpeles, Benjamin Levy and David Obranski. The exploits of these privates, corporals and sergeants are, of course, duly recorded. Karpeles, for example, is credited with having saved part of the army during a disorderly retreat in the Battle of the Wilderness by rallying troops around his colors, and Cohen performed a similar exploit in the same battle. Obranski displayed extraordinary courage under heavy fire at Shiloh and Vicksburg. Grunwalt captured the flag of Confederate Corps Headquarters at Franklin, Tennessee. Levy saved a Union ship from capture and performed other feats of valor. And there were Jewish commissioned officers who displayed comparable courage. To cite but one instance, Lieutenant Max Sachs, who was killed at Bowling Green, Kentucky, held the enemy at bay until enough support arrived to repel him. In the Union Navy, too, there were Jewish sailors who were conspicuous for gallantry, one of the best known being William Durst, who fought in the famous encounter between the *Monitor* and the *Merrimac* in March 1862.

6

The large number of fighting men contributed by the Jews of America in the war meant, of course, a proportionately large share in the suffering and bereavement which it brought. In the relative sense, however, the Jewish group was so small and the total suffering and bereavement so immense that the country at large was hardly aware of the Jewish contribution. And the group lacked the collective vision and organization to assemble the facts and publish them: in 1865 the Board of Delegates made a gesture in that direction but it remained only a gesture. There are those, of course, who do not relish such action, decrying it as apologetics, but a minority group may deplore the necessity for it, yet feel compelled to engage in it. This feeling is sure to be especially strong in a minority that has been for ages the favorite butt of calumny and prejudice.

The long and checkered history of this minority demonstrates that the tide of prejudice has a tendency to rise in times of crisis and distress, and the tragic years of the Civil War proved no exception to the rule. Additional impetus for such an upsurge was furnished by the Know-Nothing movement which had been making impressive progress since 1845 when it became a national political party; and although its avowed target was the Catholic immigrants, who formed large concentrations in the cities of the East, its nativism was directed against all "foreign" elements. The slavery issue had disrupted the Know-Nothing movement, and by 1860 it had ceased to be a factor in national politics, but the spirit which gave it birth was still very much alive.

In both sections of the torn land there were manifestations of anti-Jewish feeling, but although the gravest anti-Semitic incident, as we shall see, stemmed from the military command of the North, the animosity appears to have been more widespread and savage in the South. No attempt can here be made to unravel the tangled roots of this ancient antagonism, but it must be pointed out that the economic distress which the Civil War entailed stimulated the religious and nativist prejudices that were latent in large segments of the American people.

In war a country's industrial potential must be mobilized for the production of military goods, and without effective government controls the resulting scarcity of consumer goods is sure to bring inflation and distress. It is also sure to offer tempting opportunities to hoarders and speculators. The rise in the cost of basic necessities was hard enough on the North, it was calamitous for the South. Not only had the South plunged into war with a woefully inadequate industrial apparatus, but the flow of manufactures from England, on which its overconfident leaders relied, was drastically reduced by the Northern blockade. There was an alarming shortage of military supplies, let alone civilian goods. In Talbotton, Georgia, for example, a company was recruited of which Isidor Straus, a son of Lazarus Straus, the only Jewish merchant in the town, was elected first lieutenant; the company had to disband because there was no equipment for it. In 1862 Judah Benjamin, who was then Secretary of War, was censured by the Confederate Congress; he was charged with the loss of Roanoke Island off the coast of North Carolina, which fell to Union forces in January of that year; Benjamin had refused to send powder for its defense. If, however, he had done so, the city of Norfolk would have been left defenseless. Benjamin swallowed the censure without offering the explanation: he would not let it be known that the Confederacy was dangerously short of the vital stuff; the effect on Southern morale might have been serious.

The popular mind, impatient with involved explanations, has a simple one for rising prices: they are due to the rapacity and greed of merchants and storekeepers. And too many Jews, especially in the South, belonged to those occupations. And another inveterate habit of the popular mind went into operation, that of identifying the misdeeds of a single malefactor belonging to a minority with his entire group. That habit has been notably active in the case of a conspicuous minority like the Jews, and it was no doubt in recognition of its sinister importance that the ancient Jewish sages issued the warning that "all Israel is responsible one for another." It was, moreover, a great comfort to many Southern patriots, editors and journalists especially, convinced as they were that the South was infallible and invincible, to find so convenient a scapegoat for their miscalculations and misfortunes. The Jews became responsible for the economic woes of the South, and "Judas Iscariot" Benjamin for its military and diplomatic failures.

The agitation was particularly virulent in Georgia. In August 1862 the good people of Thomasville, near the Florida border, solemnly resolved to banish all its Jewish residents, an action which brought a spirited protest from the Jews of Savannah, who denounced it at a public meeting. In Talbotton a grand jury found the Jews guilty of "evil and unpatriotic conduct." Thereupon Lazarus Straus left the town and moved to Columbus; all the entreaties of his fellow townsmen, including the members of the jury, who had apparently undergone a profound change of heart, were unable to keep him. Nor were the other states of the Confederacy immune to the contagion. A special meeting of the venerable Beth Shalome Congregation in Richmond described the agitation as a "crusade against our people," and the *Richmond Examiner* printed so many calumnies against the Jews that Adolphus H. Adler, a colonel in the Confederate Army, challenged its editor to a duel. The arch enemy of the Jews in the South was Henry Stuart Foote, for four years a member of the Confederate Congress, who had previously been governor of Mississippi and had represented the state in the United States Senate. His position in the Confederate Congress was equivocal, to say the least: he is generally regarded as the Southern counterpart of Clement Vallandigham, the leading Copperhead in the North. His pet target was the Confederate Secretary of State, whom he accused of protecting the "foreign Jews" who were monopolizing the commerce of the South.

Of course, the Jews of the South had their defenders also, non-Jewish, as well as Jewish. Perhaps the most striking defense came from Maximilian Michelbacher, the rabbi of Beth Ahabah in Richmond. He boldly accused Christian merchants, who speculated in the basic commodities like grain, meat and fuel, from which Jewish merchants were absent, of deliberately diverting the wrath of the population from themselves to the eternal scapegoat.

In the North there was anti-Jewish agitation in the Union newspapers which the Jews found no less distressing. Isaac Leeser of Philadelphia described it as a "united onslaught." There were allusions in the press to the "accursed race who crucified the Savior," and the most popular accusations were that Jews were engaged in smuggling military and civilian goods into the Confederacy and destroying the national credit by speculating in gold. One of the favorite targets was the banker and diplomat August Belmont, who had once been an agent of the Frankfort Rothschilds and served as chargé d'affaires to Holland. Belmont raised and equipped a regiment for the Union Army and exerted his influence in European financial circles in behalf of the Union. But he was the Chairman of the National Democratic Committee and a Jew, and therefore presumed in certain quarters to be a Copperhead and traitor. The hue and cry against him "and the whole tribe of Jews" was especially venomous during the election campaign of 1864. It meant nothing to the agitators that another Jewish banking house had negotiated loans for the Union Government to the huge sum of $200,000,000. It was the firm of S. & W. Seligman and Company of New York, whose heads, Joseph and Jesse Seligman, were staunch Republicans and friends of Lincoln and Grant.

The most distinguished enemies of the Jews in the North were Major General Benjamin Franklin Butler, William Gannaway Brownlow of Tennessee, called "the fighting parson," and Senator Henry Wilson of Massachusetts. In 1855 Wilson was elected to the Senate as a Know-Nothing, then became a radical Republican. But his Know-Nothingism cropped out in Senate debate in his references to "Jew brokers" and to the race that "crucified the Redeemer of the world." The Methodist preacher from Tennessee was a violent hater and rabble-rouser, a past master in the art of vituperation. The Confederate Government kept him under guard for a brief period, and after his release he toured the North and attracted large audiences. Brownlow's aversion for Jews was only one in a long roster of hatreds: the Southern clergy, for example, was to him a most "unmitigated God-forsaken set of scoundrels." After the war "the fighting parson" was elected governor of Tennessee, and the rabid measures he applied for the reconstruction of that State nearly ruined it.

As a general Butler stood out by the number of times he was trounced by the Confederates; as the military governor of New Orleans, which was captured by the Union fleet under Admiral David Farragut in April 1862, the general won the sobriquet of "the beast": at the end of nine months he was removed from the post. As a politician, he was fairly successful: in 1882 he was elected governor of Massachusetts, and two years later the Greenback Party nominated him for President. As general and military governor Butler was a consistent and implacable Jew hater. In his view the Jews were all smugglers; they profited from the war and they supported the Confederacy. Meyer S. Isaacs, the Secretary of the Board of Delegates, tried in vain to enlighten the general: his prejudices were frozen hard. Nevertheless it is worthy of note that later, as a politician, the leopard did change his spots, or pretended to have done so.

It would, of course, be a distortion to suggest that the American people as a whole, in the North or South, were infected with this virus. Nathaniel Prentiss Banks, the general who replaced Butler in New Orleans, established most cordial relations with Bernard Illowy, the scholarly and eloquent rabbi of the Shaare Chesed Congregation, and Illowy succeeded in redressing the wrongs of many Jews who had been persecuted by Butler. There were newspapers in the North from coast to coast, and notably in California, who denounced the charges against the Jews, and if more of them failed to do so, it was in all likelihood not because they endorsed them but because they were too preoccupied with the general crisis, and the Jews were after all but a tiny minority in their midst. And finally the Jews had an unfailing friend in the President of the Union, the wise and simple man whose moral grandeur not many of his contemporaries seemed able to recognize.

7

On December 11, 1861 Lincoln received at the White House a representative of the Board of Delegates of American Israelites. He was Arnold Fischel, a young New York rabbi, who came to the President with a matter that was causing grave anxiety to the Jews of the North. In July and August of that year Congress had enacted laws which provided that a chaplain in the Union Army, "appointed by the vote of the field officers and the company commanders, must be a regular ordained minister of some Christian denomination." Under that provision Michael Allen of Philadelphia, who had been chosen chaplain of "Cameron's Dragoons," had been compelled to resign because he was a Jew, and the selection of Fischel himself to succeed him had been disallowed by the Secretary of War for the same reason. Obviously the laws in question invaded the constitutional rights of the Jews and menaced the rights of other minorities also. The issue was clearly expressed in a Memorial which the Board of Delegates had transmitted to the Senate and House of Representatives. It was dated December 6, 1861 and bore also the corresponding date of the Hebrew calendar, Tebeth 3, 5622. Those acts, said the Memorial, "are oppressive, inasmuch as they establish a prejudicial discrimination against a particular class of citizens, on account of their religious belief," and they violate the Constitution "inasmuch as they establish a religious test as a qualification for an office under the United States." Lincoln's response to Fischel's representations was prompt and sympathetic. Two days later he wrote to Fischel: "I shall try to have a new law broad enough to cover what is desired by you in behalf of the Israelites."

The intervention of the President, seconded by Fischel's vigilant and competent lobbying, and by numerous petitions sent to congressmen and senators in which Christians also joined, produced the desired change. In July 1862 the original Acts were amended and the phrase "some Christian denomination" was changed to "some religious denomination." It is probable, of course, that the original disqualifying phrase was inadvertent rather than deliberate, but once enacted, it had become a rallying point for hard-bitten bigots, and a strong and vigorous struggle was required to dislodge it. Under the amended law Jacob Frankel of Rodeph Shalom of Philadelphia and Bernhard Henry Gotthelf, rabbi of Adath Israel of Louisville, were commissioned as military hospital chaplains, and Ferdinand Leopold Sarner, who had previously served as rabbi of a congregation in Rochester, New York, was elected field chaplain by the officers of a New York regiment. Sarner's regiment took part in many actions, including the Battle of Gettysburg, where he himself was wounded.

8

Six months after the equality of the Jews, as an American "religious denomination," was vindicated in the amended Chaplaincy Act, a new and startling issue, more serious in import—the most serious, in fact, in the history of American Jewry—broke suddenly upon them. From the military headquarters of the Department of the Tennessee, located in Holly Springs, Mississippi, Order No. 11 was telegraphed on December 17, 1862 to all post commanders in the department, and it read as follows:

> The Jews, as a class violating every regulation of trade established by the Treasury Department and also department orders, are hereby expelled from the department within twenty-four hours from the receipt of this order.
>
> Post commanders will see that all of this class of people be furnished passes and required to leave, and anyone returning after such notification will be arrested and held in confinement until an opportunity occurs of sending them out as prisoners, unless furnished with permit from headquarters.
>
> No passes will be given these people to visit headquarters for the purpose of making personal application for trade permits.
>
> *By order of Maj. Gen. U. S. Grant*

The Department of the Tennessee, which took in the western part of the State of Tennessee, as well as southern Kentucky and northern Mississippi, had been the scene of the most important Union successes in 1862. It was the region that saw the rise of the star of Ulysses S. Grant. In February of that year Grant had captured Fort Donelson on the Cumberland River and Fort Henry on the Tennessee, and early in April, with the timely arrival of the army of General Buell, he had won the bloody Battle of Shiloh or Pittsburg Landing. The Mississippi was opened down to Vicksburg, and in June Memphis surrendered.

Following hard upon these victories, the rail and river transportation centers in the Department, with Memphis in the lead, became the scenes of an intense trading boom with the enemy. Some of the trade was illicit and some was not. That any part of it should have been legalized may appear rather strange; the generals in command were certainly opposed to such a policy: in July 1862 General William T. Sherman wrote from Memphis, "We cannot carry on war and trade with a people at the same time." But in the North men and women were idle because the mills had no cotton, and in the South planters could perhaps be weaned away from the Confederate cause by giving them a chance to repair their shattered fortunes. And the brood of speculators and profiteers, quite a number of them in positions of influence, which every war engenders, added their pressure in favor of a traffic that brought quick and handsome profits. They swarmed down into the Department, and many of the men in uniform, among them officers of high rank, were drawn into the operations, abusing their military authority for gain. And in addition to the cotton buyers came smugglers with military, medical and other goods of which the South was in sore need.

Of course there were Jews among the cotton buyers and also, no doubt, among the smugglers. The trade in cotton was approved by their Government and their right to share in it could not be questioned. And as for the other variety of trade, an examination of the available records has disclosed only a very tiny fraction of Jewish names among those who were apprehended for practicing it. Why, then, did Jews loom so large in Grant's field of vision and, it should be added, in Sherman's also? The answer to the question must be sought in the optical illusions which an aversion against people of different appearance and speech is able to produce, and in the recesses of rooted prejudice, which, like panic fear, can make a puppy look like a bear. To these atavistic aberrations should be added a feeling of special resentment against Jewish traders, because, as Grant wrote in a letter to the Assistant Secretary of War the same day that Order No. 11 was issued, they were more successful than others. "The Jews seem to be a privileged class that can travel everywhere," the letter complains. The very day after the Order was issued the price which buyers in the area paid for cotton fell from 40 to 25 cents a pound. Was the fall a mere coincidence? There were many who thought it was not. The Order, they asserted, was due in large part to the pressure which other traders, both civilian and military, brought to bear on Grant in order to rid themselves of formidable competitors.

For a moment the Old World specter of mass expulsions stood up and stared at the Jews of America, but for a moment only. In Holly Springs and in Oxford, both in Mississippi, and in Paducah, Kentucky, the Order was actually carried out. But in Paducah, there was a modest man named Cesar Kaskel, who met the emergency with remarkable resourcefulness and energy. He began by sending the President a telegram, and then proceeded to Washington. After sending out a general alarm to newspapers and influential Jews, he reached the capital armed with letters and other documents. On January 3, 1863 he was received by Lincoln who, after listening to him, wrote out a message to Henry W. Halleck, General-in-Chief of the Army, directing him to have the Order cancelled immediately. The following day Halleck carried out his Chief's instructions. The wording of the directive he addressed to Grant suggests that Halleck found it hard to believe that Order No. 11 had actually been issued:

War Department
Washington, January 4, 1863

MAJOR-GENERAL GRANT
Holly Springs, Miss.:

A paper purporting to be General Orders No. 11, issued by you December 17, has been presented here. By its terms, it expells all Jews from your department. If such an order has been issued, it will be immediately revoked.

H. W. HALLECK
General-in-Chief

But the storm the Order raised did not at once subside; it had many and prolonged repercussions. There were meetings of protest in New York, Philadelphia, Chicago and other cities which demanded Grant's dismissal, and Lincoln received a delegation of Jewish leaders who came to thank him for having acted so promptly. The *New York Times* called the Order "one of the deepest sensations of the war," and it was an important issue in the election campaign of 1868, when Grant was the presidential candidate of the Republican party. It was natural, of course, that political interests and passions should concentrate around the dismal Order: the Democrats found it a good stick with which to beat the Administration, and the Republicans felt compelled to extenuate and minimize it. Prominent Jewish Republicans tried hard to exonerate Grant from personal responsibility for it: it was unintentional; it had been foisted on him by subordinates. But although Grant gave assurances that he regretted the Order, those attempts at exculpation, especially one that was undertaken by Simon Wolf, were not convincing: the devil's tail of politics bulged out of them only too plainly.

9

In the midst of this storm, as in other and greater storms, Lincoln stood serene and irreproachable. His sense of justice was unerring, and he exercised it with a homely humor that purged it of solemnity or pose. "And so the children of Israel were driven from the happy land of Canaan," he said to Cesar Kaskel of Paducah just before writing out his directive to Halleck.

Lincoln had known a number of Jews before he became President and met more while in office. He was touched by a gift which came to him early in 1861 from Abraham Kohn, the City Clerk of Chicago, whom he had met after the nominating convention in that city. It was a painting of the flag on which Kohn inscribed certain verses from the Book of Joshua, including the verse: "Be strong and of good courage; be not affrighted, neither be thou dismayed; for the Lord thy God is with thee whithersoever thou goest." One of his "most valued friends" was Abraham Jonas of Quincy, Illinois, brother of Joseph Jonas, who was the first Jewish settler in Cincinnati. Like Lincoln, Abraham Jonas was an effective platform speaker and a successful politician, having served four years in the Kentucky legislature. In 1854 the two met, became close friends and Jonas remained one of Lincoln's staunchest supporters. In 1861 Lincoln appointed him postmaster of Quincy, and three years later he bestowed a final favor on his old friend. Four sons of Jonas were fighting—for the Confederacy! One of them had been captured and Jonas, who lay on his deathbed, had requested that the prisoner be permitted to visit him. Lincoln wrote out the permission in his own hand:

> Allow Charles H. Jonas, now a prisoner of war at Johnson's Island, a parole of three weeks to visit his dying father, Abraham Jonas, at Quincy, Illinois.
>
> A. LINCOLN

10

On April 15, 1865 the Union was shocked by the tragic death of its leader, and none were more deeply grieved than the Jews. They gathered for memorial services in their synagogues, and in New York they formed a large part of the imposing funeral parade held in that city. They had lost a matchless champion of freedom and equality for all men, boons of which they were still deprived in other lands, and which, therefore, they knew how to cherish.

But Lincoln's basic task was accomplished. He had saved America from the peril of fragmentation, for discerning men realized that if the principle of secession were established, the process of fission would not end with the Confederacy. America would become Balkanized. And as the decades of the nineteenth and twentieth centuries followed one another, Lincoln's accomplishment, not only for America but for the entire world, became more and more significant. It guaranteed the continued growth of a nation devoted to the principle of freedom and equality, and strong enough to determine the issue when that principle was faced with world challenge.

For American and world Jewry it was not less momentous. It made possible the rise of the largest single Jewish community in history, a vital part of the American nation, and possessed of the spirit and strength to play a signal role for the weal and future of the Jewish people as a whole.

CHAPTER 8

Religious Divisions

1

THE CAREER OF AMERICAN JEWRY, NUMBERING AT THE END of the Civil War some 200,000 and soon to be enormously increased, exhibits a polarity which certain elementary astronomical facts help us to visualize. For just as the earth revolves around the sun and spins at the same time on its own axis, the Jews in the United States have been part and parcel of the American nation and at the same time an increasingly important segment of a world-wide people and faith. Our story, therefore, moves forward, as it were, on two fronts, one oriented towards the spirit and aspirations of America, the other towards the problems of a distinctive group.

This polarity, of course, has not been confined to the Jews. In the huge throngs that flocked to America there may have been individuals who thought of themselves, in Walt Whitman's phrase, as "simple, separate Persons," but the vast majority identified themselves with a group—ethnic, religious, or both. And every group had a nostalgic longing to preserve its selfhood and, paradoxically, a driving urge to be absorbed in the majority, to belong to it by getting lost in it. The American majority exerted no legalized pressure on them to surrender their distinctiveness; what America demanded from all of them was stated succinctly and completely by Washington in his letter to the Hebrew Congregation in Newport: "The Government of the United States . . . requires only that they who live under its protection should demean themselves as good citizens by giving it on all occasions their effective support." But a majority may exercise pressure without legal sanctions; its gravitational pull may be more effective than police regulations; its rewards for conformity and its penalties for nonconformity may be uncodified but real and potent.

The story of every minority group in America is therefore one of polarity and ambivalence. Every ingredient in the vast melting pot was at once amenable and refractory. Some of the groups have gone far on the road to dissolution, others have to a greater or lesser degree maintained their group character. Will America continue to be "a nation of nations," as it has been called? There are those who say it should. Every group, they say, will adopt the language and basic culture of America: the educational, political and economic institutions of the land will see to that. But every ethnic group should be encouraged to conserve its own culture also, for its own weal and for the enrichment of the overall culture of America. Every group will then be bilingual and bicultural and for that reason higher in the cultural scale, and America will be a "symphony of cultures."

"Cultural pluralism," as this program has been called, envisions a future that can only be seen through the prism of longing and hope. The course it prescribes is at the mercy of numerous and unpredictable deflections, most of them involuntary and unconscious. In Central and Eastern Europe minority cultures have been the targets of official persecution. They have persisted in spite of it, more perhaps because of it. In America, where there has been no such hostility, minority cultures are undergoing rapid attenuation and their future is far from secure.

But the Jews, as they see themselves and as others see them, are both an ethnic and religious group; anthropologists may deny them ethnic distinctiveness, but history is made by convictions and passions, not by cephalic indexes. Protestants and Catholics find coreligionists in a large variety of ethnic groups; Jews find them only in their own; in their case alone ethnic identification and religious affiliation are practically coterminous. Their culture has been primarily religious, and one of the imperatives of their religion is the preservation of the group. The religious problems that have faced the Jews in the New World are, therefore, of vital importance in their story.

2

As a system of doctrine, ritual and law, the Judaism for which Marranos in the Old World and the New died at the stake, and which the Sephardim brought to America in the seventeenth century, had taken fairly definite shape some two thousand years earlier in the period of the Second Commonwealth in Palestine. For five centuries after the fall of that Commonwealth the system grew with the growth of the Oral Tradition, of which the Babylonian Talmud became the principal repository, and which served the double and seemingly paradoxical function of fixing its norms and providing a method for adapting them to new conditions. Ashkenazim and Sephardim alike accepted the authority of the Talmud; it became an object of passionate study and endless elucidation, and the summary of its vast legislation known as the *Shulchan Aruch* (Ready-set Table), which appeared in Palestine in the sixteenth century, became the guide to the pious in all things that touched their earthly life from the cradle to the grave. The only serious challenge to the Talmud had arisen in the eighth century and led to the formation of the sect known as Karaites,* which has persisted to our own day: before the Second World War there were still sizable Karaite communities in the Crimea and smaller ones in Lithuania and the Near East, and in 1942 about a hundred Karaite families were estimated to be living in the United States.

The second and greater challenge to the authority of the Talmud came more than a thousand years later and is known as Reform Judaism. Many impulses combined to produce it, ideological, aesthetic, social and political. Its advocates found that the ancient doctrines and practices had too long resisted the process of change to which, as taught by the widespread philosophy of Hegel, all human institutions, including religion, were subject. The views of the philosophers were reinforced by the "higher critics" of the Bible, who found that even the Sacred Scriptures had yielded to the same process, and by the Science of Judaism, essentially an inquiry into the historic origins of Jewish beliefs and practices, which a group of brilliant scholars headed by Leopold Zunz launched in the first quarter of the nineteenth century.

From this ideological base powerful political and social impulses, associated with the struggle for Emancipation, asserted themselves with confidence and boldness. It was imperative that the acceptance of the Jews as equal citizens should not be retarded or thwarted by religious dogmas and observances that emphasized their separateness. The dietary laws, for example, had a segregating effect and were ruled to be nonbinding, and even the immemorial rite of circumcision, the sign of the Great Covenant and affiliation with the community of Israel, was questioned by Reform leaders in Germany like Samuel Holdheim and Abraham Geiger. But above all, Reform felt it necessary to reject or reinterpret the doctrines which reflected the particularist character of the ancient faith and envisaged the national restoration of the Jewish people. Judaism, of course, was never an exclusively national religion; the *Alenu,* which concludes the daily morning,

* The name, derived from the Hebrew word meaning "Scripture," underscores the allegiance of the sectaries to the Written Tradition only.

afternoon and evening prayers, is only one of numerous expressions of its universal as well as particular aspects; its first paragraph gives thanks that the Lord of All "has not made us like the nations of the earth"; the second, in language of unsurpassed grandeur, prays "that the world will be made perfect under the kingship of the Almighty," and that all the inhabitants of the earth "will accept the yoke of Thy kingship." But the traditional faith did emphasize the selection of the Jewish people, regarded their dispersion among the nations as a punishment for their sins, and looked forward to the coming of the Messiah, who would not only fulfill the hope of the *Alenu* prayer for all mankind, but restore the Jewish people to their ancient land.

Those beliefs the exponents of Reform found incompatible with the obligations imposed upon the Jews by the grant of civil and political equality, and they proceeded to revise them. Divine selection was not repudiated, but the dispersion, far from being a punishment or exile, was a means for realizing its purpose: the Jews were scattered among the nations in order to bear witness among them to the Unity of God and His law of righteousness and purity. Thus Reform proclaimed the doctrine of the Mission of Israel, which became one of its cornerstones, especially in America, and over which its champions and opponents were to break many a lance. The notion of a personal Messiah was rejected and replaced by the hope for a Messianic Age, when the divine law of justice would be honored not in the breach but in universal observance. Its most determined opposition, however, Reform directed against the hope of Jewish national restoration: it clashed with the Mission of Israel, and it laid the Jews open to the charge that they looked upon the countries where they lived, and where they demanded or had already obtained equal status, as places of temporary sojourn only. In the first half of the nineteenth century, when Reform tried its wings, controversy over national restoration was more or less academic; towards the end of the century, however, and in the early decades of the twentieth, the issue became imminent, and throughout the world, and not least in America, the controversy became loud and bitter.

Such, in essence, were the basic affirmations and negations of Reform Judaism, and they were, of course, embodied in ritual changes, as in the omission from the prayers of all reference to exile and national redemption. But other changes were made which were defended on other grounds, chiefly aesthetic. Organs were installed in the Reform temples, as well as mixed choirs. Men and women sat together, the

Ewing Galloway

The Haym Salomon Monument
Unveiled in Chicago, December 1941

Frick Art Reference Library

Mordecai Manuel Noah

American Jewish Historical Society

Judah Touro

Frick Art Reference Library
Courtesy of Miss Henrietta Clay

Rebecca Gratz

American Jewish Historical Society

Uriah P. Levy

men with bared heads. The prayers were shortened and recited for the most part not in Hebrew, but in German. New hymns in the vernacular were introduced, and the sermon became the most important part of the service. The second days of the Feasts of Passover, Weeks, Tabernacles and New Year were abolished, and some of the Reform temples held services on Sundays. But perhaps the greatest stress was laid on what was called decorum: in the traditional houses of worship the services were found to lack that quality. For many centuries, of course, the synagogue had been more than the scene of a weekly religious service. Men worshipped in it three times daily, they came there for study and disputation, and they met there to deliberate on community affairs. At some stages in the long Sabbath and festival services, as during the reading of the Pentateuchal portions, the atmosphere relaxed and became informal; it was not like the hushed and solemn atmosphere of the Protestant services, for example; it lacked decorum. And this question of decorum assumed an inordinate place in the controversies to which Reform gave rise.

3

In Europe the first move in the direction of Reform took place in Amsterdam in 1796 when those who welcomed the emancipation which the French conquerors brought them, separated from those who were dubious about it, and established a synagogue of their own with changes in the traditional ritual. In America the first attempt at Reform was, as we have already seen, made in Charleston, South Carolina. In 1824 forty-seven members of the seventy-five-year-old Sephardic congregation Beth Elohim petitioned the trustees to shorten the services and introduce English into the liturgy as well as a sermon in that language. The trustees were not receptive, and, led by Isaac Harby, the petitioners seceded and organized the Reformed Society of Israelites. Eight years later they returned, but when a new house of prayer was erected in 1841, the Reform advocates, with the help of the rabbi Gustav Poznanski, whose education in Germany had made him a Reform partisan, overruled the trustees and installed an organ into the new edifice. The action tore the community apart; those who opposed it now seceded and they even challenged it in a lawsuit, which they lost; the organ had become the most provocative symbol of Reform. In America, of course, Reform did not, as in Germany, accompany the attainment of legal equality or the hope of attaining it. Nevertheless, the resolve to assert the total patriotism of the American Jew and reject any inference against it that might be drawn from traditional doctrines, was not absent from the mind of its leaders. In Charleston they declared: "This country is our Palestine, this city our Jerusalem, this House of God our Temple."

The foremost apostle and architect of Reform Judaism in America, Isaac Mayer Wise, was born in Bohemia in 1819, but even before his arrival in the United States in 1846 there were two other Reform congregations in the land besides the one in Charleston. In Baltimore Har Sinai was organized in 1842, and in New York Emanu-El, which eventually became the ranking Reform congregation in the country, came into existence three years later. Both were Reform from the start and were spared the pangs of dissension and parturition that afflicted other congregations. In 1855 David Einhorn became the rabbi of Har Sinai and, as we have seen, ministered there until 1861, when his ardor for Abolitionism forced him to flee for his life to Philadelphia. When he died in 1879 Einhorn was the rabbi of Temple Beth El in New York. As an advocate of Reform Einhorn was more radical than Wise, and he propagated his views not only in his eloquent sermons, but in his monthly magazine *Sinai* and in a Reform prayer book which he prepared for his congregation. It should be noted that his sermons, his periodical, as well as his translations of the old prayers and the new ones he added, were all in German: his flock had been borne in on the migration wave from the Germanies.

An even more radical proponent of Reform was Samuel Hirsch, who in 1866 succeeded Einhorn in the pulpit of Har Sinai in Baltimore; he was among the first to advocate supplementary religious services on Sundays. The two most distinguished rabbis of Emanu-El in New York were Samuel Adler, who retired in 1874, and his successor Gustave Gottheil, who occupied the post until 1899. Like Hirsch, both had participated in the Reform movement in Germany and held its standard high in America; but already in the case of Gottheil one of its basic tenets, the denial of a national destiny for the Jewish people, had begun to waver; Gottheil embraced the nascent Zionist movement. He even served as vice-president in 1898 of the newly formed Federation of American Zionists, and made brave but futile efforts to inspire his congregants with some of his enthusiasm for the cause launched by Theodor Herzl. It will be more than one decade before the ramparts of Reform will come tumbling down before the trumpets of the modern Joshua and his followers.

4

Not New York but Cincinnati was destined to become the citadel of Reform Judaism in America, and not the radical innovations of David Einhorn and Samuel Hirsch were destined to prevail in it, but the more moderate program of Isaac Mayer Wise and Max Lilienthal. The latter became rabbi of Bene Israel of Cincinnati in 1855, five years after Wise came there to be rabbi of Bene Jeshurun, and the two worked together to make the United States the most important center of Reform Judaism in the world.

In Germany the movement had fallen into the doldrums. On the one hand it failed to stem the tide of baptism which ran high among the German Jews—a baptism which meant not conversion, but the key to a successful career, or as the poet Heinrich Heine, the most famous of the baptized, mockingly called it, "a passport to European civilization." Reform, it was charged, had become a way station to the baptismal font. On the other hand two religious counter currents rose up to combat it. One was represented by middle-of-the-road advocates like Leopold Zunz, who once told Abraham Geiger, "We must reform ourselves, not our religion"; Zechariah Frankel, who headed a newly established theological seminary in Breslau; and Heinrich Graetz, who became the foremost historian of the Jews. This "golden mean," which Frankel described as "positive-historical," maintained that the antiquity of a religious institution and the devotion it commanded invested it with inviolate sanctity. The other and even bolder opponent of Reform was the ancient faith, militant and unapologetic, but furnished with the weapons of modern education and dialectics. It became known as Neo-Orthodoxy, and its champions were men like Isaac Bernays of Hamburg, who created a sensation by preaching Orthodox sermons in impeccable German; Samson Raphael Hirsch of Frankfort, who demanded loyalty to the *noblesse oblige* of the ancient Covenant; and Samuel David Luzzato of Padua, Italy, scholar, mystic, and intrepid defender of the traditional faith.

In America, too, Reform was to find itself challenged by two similar religious currents. But the challenge did not become formidable until the first decade of the twentieth century, and in the second half of the nineteenth Wise, Lilienthal and their colleagues in the East found the road fairly clear for the steady advance of Reform.

When Lilienthal landed in New York in 1845 at the age of thirty he had already had five years of experience trying to promote Reform in a community much larger and much less receptive to it. In 1840 the government of the "Iron Czar," Nicholas I, decreed a new system of elementary and secondary schools for the Jews of Russia with the aim of "reforming" the traditional system of Jewish education, and Sergius Uvarov, the Czar's Minister of Public Instruction, chose Lilienthal, who was conducting a modern Jewish school in Riga, to "sell" the new system to the Jews of Russia. Lilienthal undertook the mission, but it proved a failure: the Russian Jews saw in the new schools only a device of their ruthless government to wean their children away from their faith. In New York Lilienthal spent ten years as rabbi and head of a private school for boys, and in Cincinnati where, besides the rabbinate, he held a number of civic posts also, he worked closely with Isaac M. Wise. He was associate editor of Wise's publications and had an important share in setting up the institutions fathered by Wise for the advancement of Reform in America.

The man with whom Lilienthal collaborated was gifted with unusual tenacity and versatility. Isaac Mayer Wise was an impressive preacher, a careful scholar, a prolific writer, and a successful publisher and editor. In addition to works in theology and history he wrote a dozen novels, some of them in German, and two plays. To promote his convictions and projects Wise founded, edited and published two periodicals, *The Israelite* in English, and *Die Deborah* in German. He was active in the civic life of Cincinnati, where he ministered for forty-six years until his death in 1900, and as a Democrat and confirmed anti-abolitionist he took a hand in politics also. But his principal talent, and the one that produced his enduring achievements, was that of an organizer.

His first objective was to overcome the liturgic variations that existed among the congregations and the lack of a recognized authority in other matters also. Shortly after his arrival Wise compiled a revised order of prayers which he called *Minhag Amerika*, "The American Way." It was eventually adopted by many congregations and served as the foundation of the Union Prayer Book, which became standard for Reform worship in 1894. Wise aimed at a formal union of all congregations in the country, an aim which he accomplished in large measure in 1873, when the Union of American Hebrew Congregations came into existence. It was the Union which, as we saw, took over the functions of the Board of Delegates of American Israelites.

Two years later Wise saw the realization of another project which he deemed essential for the religious health of American Jewry: a theological school to furnish competent rabbis for its congregations.

He found only too many in the pulpits who lacked the necessary qualifications. In October 1875, after a struggle of two decades, the Hebrew Union College in Cincinnati, of which he became president, received its first group of students.

The third enterprise on which Wise set his heart, and which required an even longer and harder struggle, was to create a central religious authority, or synod, for American Jewry. Beginning with the first in 1855, Wise took the lead in convening a number of rabbinical gatherings, most of which suffered from dissensions which did more to retard his objective than to advance it. Finally, in 1889, the Central Conference of American Rabbis was organized on his initiative, and for the rest of his life he served as its president. Thus the three basic institutions of Reform in America: the Union of American Hebrew Congregations, the Hebrew Union College and the Central Conference of American Rabbis, the body that speaks the mind of Reform, or Liberal Judaism, as it now calls itself, became realities by the adamant persistence and organizing genius of Isaac Mayer Wise of Cincinnati.

5

Wise, of course, nourished the hope that American Judaism, for which he foresaw a glorious future, would be formed in the image he cherished, the image whose basic lineaments had been laid down by the Reform theologians in Germany, but with modifications which the American environment might necessitate. His *Minhag Amerika,* as its name indicates, was designed for all American Jews, and the synod he contemplated was to be the supreme religious authority for the entire community. There would thus arise a more or less monolithic structure, a goal dear to the heart of all stout believers.

There were two barriers, however, that made such a goal impossible to attain, one rising from the spirit and traditions of America, the other from the tenacious vitality of the traditional faith, which rejected Reform as a denial and perversion of the true character and meaning of Judaism. It was apparently written in the stars that American Judaism should not be a monolithic structure, a result which the divorce between religion and government as decreed in the basic law of the land and the consequent absence of a coercive authority in the sphere of religion would alone have guaranteed. America, with no established religion, had become not irreligious, but a land teeming with many religious enthusiasms and sects. In such an atmosphere demands for uniformity could not hope to be heeded. In such an atmosphere there was also bound to be a good deal of easygoing religious tolerance and religious indifferentism, which would blunt the sharp edges of whatever controversy might develop.

With the imposing gains which Reform garnered in the second half of the nineteenth century, it was natural for its leaders to expect it to become the American Judaism of the future, but the Orthodox faith was not to be so easily dislodged. Apart from the sanctity with which its millennial and heroic past invested it, the first congregations which the Sephardim established in the colonial period, most of which still flourished, were committed to the ancient doctrines and worship, and their leaders were scandalized by the innovations which Reform introduced in both spheres. The first rabbinical conference to convene in America was attended by Isaac Leeser, the foremost exponent of the traditional faith in the country. To placate him and his colleagues, the platform it adopted under Wise's prompting went so far as to accept the Talmud as "legal and obligatory," a concession which, it may be added, was vigorously denounced by the radical wing of Reform led by Einhorn. When, however, the Conference took steps to implement its own *Minhag Amerika,* Leeser would have nothing to do with it.

6

Nevertheless, Leeser's general position was closer to that of Zechariah Frankel and his disciples in Germany, the position known today as Conservative Judaism, than it was to Orthodoxy. That position lends itself less easily to definition than the other two. It stands midway between them; in theology and liturgy it is almost identical with Orthodoxy, but it is more responsive to the "demands of the environment," and resembles Reform in some of the innovations which its houses of worship have introduced.

In his capacity for work and organizing ability Isaac Leeser was not behind Wise, his colleague and rival. He arrived from Germany in 1824 at the age of eighteen, and five years later he was chosen preacher of Mikveh Israel in Philadelphia. In 1843 he launched his *Occident and Jewish Advocate,* a monthly journal which he made into a powerful weapon to defend the traditional faith and promote the educational and philanthropic projects of which he was the chief architect. They included institutions like the Jewish Hospital in Philadelphia and a variety of educational enterprises, among them the first Jewish congregational Sunday Schools, in which he had the ardent collaboration of Rebecca Gratz. They included the first American Jewish Publication Society, and Maimonides College, the first seminary in America for the training of rabbis, which opened in Philadelphia in October 1867 with himself as president. His life was crowded with many other labors and achievements. He produced Hebrew-English prayer books and a translation of the Hebrew Scriptures. For a long time it was the standard Jewish version in English, free from the errors and Christological renditions of the King James version. And he found time to combat the missionaries who were trying to convert Jews, to participate in the civic life of the city where he lived for nearly forty years, and to play a leading role in every effort to promote the unity of the American Jewish community and defend the good name and rights of his coreligionists the world over.

Among the other zealous defenders of the traditional faith, who collaborated with Leeser in many of his projects, was Sabato Morais, who came to America in 1851 from Italy by way of London. In London he spent five years adding a complete command of the English language to his many other attainments. The previous year Leeser had resigned his ministry in Mikveh Israel and Morais succeeded him. Maimonides College, on which both men laid so many hopes, was forced by lack of means to close in 1873, six years after it had opened; and when the Hebrew Union College opened its doors two years later, Morais hoped that the program of the new school would be broad enough to enable it to train teachers and preachers for all sections of American Israel. But the gulf between Reform and the religious outlook he cherished was too wide to be bridged by the school of which Wise was president. So Morais set about creating a new rabbinical school, and in January 1887 his efforts were rewarded with the formal opening of the Jewish Theological Seminary of America in New York. For the remaining years of his life Morais presided over the new school and taught in it. The Seminary became the key institution of Conservative Judaism in America.

There were other champions of the traditional faith in the later decades of the century who held the dikes against the rising tide of Reform. Samuel Meyer Isaacs of New York employed his pulpit and his *Jewish Messenger* not only to repel anti-Semitic attacks and promote the establishment of institutions like the Board of Delegates, Maimonides College, Mount Sinai Hospital and the United Hebrew Charities in New York, but also to oppose the new credos of Einhorn and Wise. For nearly four decades Isaacs ministered to Ashkenazic congregations in New York, and during the same period the minister of the Spanish and Portuguese Synagogue was Jacques Judah Lyons, who was equally resolute against those who sought to modify the ancient Sephardic ritual.

Still another opponent of Reform was Alexander Kohut, who did not enter the lists against it in America until 1885, when Isaacs and Lyons had been dead for nearly a decade. But Kohut's reputation as a prodigious scholar and leader of Conservative Judaism in Hungary had preceded him, and his arrival in New York provoked a new upsurge of activity in the Reform camp. In November of that year the Reform rabbis met in Pittsburgh and adopted a statement of principles, which came to be known as the Pittsburgh Platform. It was a bold and confident declaration of the religious and social ideals of Reform, its exuberant optimism reflected in the assertion that "we recognize in the modern era of universal culture of heart and intellect the approaching of the realization of Israel's great Messianic hope for the establishment of the Kingdom of Truth, justice and peace among all men." But the Platform minced no words on the negations and rejections of Reform, and it served as the clinching argument to Morais, Kohut and others that Conservative Judaism must go its own way. Kohut joined the faculty of the new seminary as professor of Talmud, a field in which his vast erudition was displayed in the nine-volume Talmudic dictionary which he authored. Another scholar who hailed from Hungary and took his stand with Conservatism was Benjamin Szold. He was rabbi of Oheb Shalom in Baltimore for thirty-three years, and the modified Orthodox prayer book which he prepared for his congregation was adopted by many other congregations over the country.

A close collaborator of Szold was Marcus Jastrow who, before he came to America, had been a rabbi and teacher in Germany and Poland. He was in Warsaw in 1861 when the Poles rose up in arms against Czar Alexander II. Jastrow called on his people in Poland to join the revolt, and after spending three months in a Russian prison, was expelled from the country. Five years later he was chosen rabbi of Rodeph Shalom in Philadelphia, and before he died in 1903 the Zionist movement had been launched and Jastrow was among the first in America to join it. With Leeser, Morais, Szold, Isaacs and Kohut he laid the groundwork of Conservative Judaism, and his adherence to Zionism underscored what was perhaps the most conspicuous divergence between Conservatism and the Reform of his day.

7

Orthodox

By the end of the century Reform stood dominant in the religious topography of American Jewry, and Conservative Judaism had emerged and begun to fashion its instruments and wrestle with its less precise philosophy and program. Ashkenazic Orthodoxy, the third and largest religious sector, was to have its era of expansion in later decades and it organized its forces much more slowly. It waited for the mass migration from Eastern Europe which began in the eighties, but already in 1852 immigrants from Russia and Poland had set up their first congregation in New York. Its rabbi was Abraham Joseph Ash, an accomplished Talmudist and militant foe of Reform who, in the course of his long association with his group, tried hard to heed the advice of the ancient sages not to "make the Torah a spade to dig with." Several times he ventured into business in order to be able to serve as rabbi without a salary. His congregation grew steadily and kept moving to larger quarters, nor was it spared dissension and secession. Finally in 1885 it emerged as the best known Ashkenazic synagogue in America, the *Beth Hamidrash Hagodol* (The Great Synagogue), formerly a Methodist Church on Norfolk Street. In the manner consecrated by hoary tradition it was not only a house of worship, but a house of study and a center of charitable works. One of those who assisted Ash was Judah David Eisenstein, a scholar of immense range and the author of many pious encyclopedic works.

Ash died in 1887 and by that time there were many more Orthodox congregations in New York and in other American cities. The mass migration from Eastern Europe was in full swing, bringing not only a huge increase in the size of American Jewry but a striking change in its religious configuration, its intellectual climate and its social and economic structure.

CHAPTER 9

1881

1

IN THE LONG AND EVENTFUL HISTORY OF THE JEWS THE YEAR 1881 is a year to remember. It marks a turning point not only in the career of American Jewry but in the Odyssey of the Jewish people as a whole.

The spring of that year saw an outburst of sanguinary fury against the Jews of Russia, the largest Jewish community in the world of that day—and the most vital, despite the official Pale of Settlement and other repressions from which it suffered. The orgy of violence began in April, a month after Alexander II was assassinated and his son Alexander III became Czar of "all of the Russias," and it continued for over a year. The first outbreak occurred in the city of Elisavetgrad, today called Kirovograd, in the Ukraine; and among the other cities where Jews were attacked were Kiev, the Ukrainian metropolis, Odessa, Berdichev, Pereyaslav, Nezhin, Balta and Warsaw. It was a large-scale performance, well planned and coordinated, and clearly directed from a central source; it could not otherwise have swept through scores of places at the same time, or been executed on the same pattern.

Pogroms, in fact, were part and parcel of the policy of the new regime. This policy the Czar's principal adviser, the Procurator of the Holy Synod of the Greek Orthodox Church, Constantine Pobyedonostzev, reduced to a simple formula: a third of the Jews in Russia would be forced to emigrate, a third would accept baptism and the remaining third would be starved to death. And the pogroms were in line with still another objective of the new ruler: to persuade the Russian people that the revolutionary movement, of which his father had been a victim, was a Jewish conspiracy against Holy Russia, and provide them with an outlet for their wretchedness and discontent. It was the old technique of the lightning rod and scapegoat.

In May 1882, when the violence had run its course, the Czar's government replaced it with a "cold pogrom," which had the merit of lasting longer and producing fewer repercussions in the world outside. It took the form of the infamous "May Laws," which barred Jews from the villages in the Pale of Settlement and forced Jewish traders in the towns to keep their shops closed on Sundays and Christian holidays. The congestion and destitution in the towns increased and Jewish tradesmen who competed with non-Jews received a staggering blow. And before very long the Czar's ministers found still another device for degrading and pauperizing his Jewish subjects. It was the *numerus clausus,* the "closed number," or school quota. In the cities inside the Pale, where Jews made up from 30 to 80 per cent of the population, this device limited the number of Jewish students in secondary schools and universities to 10 per cent of the total, in cities outside the Pale to 5 per cent, and in St. Petersburg and Moscow to 3 per cent. Young men and women eager for education flocked to the universities of Western Europe, but when they returned to their native land the wall of legal disabilities, especially the restrictions on domicile and movement, barred them from earning a livelihood.

The throwback to primitive savagery in Russia in the spring of 1881 did not, of course, escape the attention and condemnation of the western world. A public meeting of indignation and protest took place in Paris under the chairmanship of Victor Hugo, and a similar demonstration was held in London at the Mansion House with the Lord Mayor presiding. In America the repercussions were equally emphatic. On February 1, 1882 an impressive public protest was held in New York under the chairmanship of William R. Grace, the Mayor of the city; the call to the meeting had been issued over the signatures of nearly a hundred prominent Christians with ex-President Grant heading the list. Later that month an equally impressive demonstration took place in Philadelphia. Frederick T. Frelinghuysen, President Arthur's Secretary of State, expressed the hope "that the Imperial Government will find means to cause the persecution of these unfortunate beings to cease," and the House of Representatives adopted a resolution in less diplomatic terms.

2

Three separate areas, all of them important in the unfolding of the Jewish future, were deeply affected by the events that transpired in Russia in 1881: Russia itself, Palestine and America. In Russia they dealt a heavy blow at the hopes for emancipation cherished by increasing numbers of Jews who labored to make their people "deserve" the boon by urging them to shed their "separatism" and embrace the "enlightenment" which they offered them. The offer came from two sources. One was the "Society for the Diffusion of Enlightenment among the Jews of Russia," which had been organized in St. Petersburg in 1863, and had branches in Riga, Kiev, Odessa and other cities. Its leading patrons were the bankers Joseph Ginsburg and his son Horace, and its aim was to make Russian the language of the Jewish masses, to modernize Jewish education and to teach the young to be farmers and artisans. It also aimed to eradicate certain of their "peculiarities," which the Society held responsible for the disabilities under which they labored. The other source was the movement known as Haskalah, the Hebrew word meaning "enlightenment," whose votaries wrote in the ancient tongue and proclaimed the rebirth of Hebrew literature as their principal goal. But the Maskilim, or practitioners of Haskalah, among whom there were talented poets, essayists, and novelists, were also anxious to spread "modernism" among the Jews of Russia and to "Europeanize" them.

The bloody events that followed the accession of the new Czar had a profound effect on the advocates of both brands of enlightenment, especially the Maskilim. Haskalah changed its orientation: instead of worshipping at the shrine of European culture, it placed itself at the service of the national regeneration of the Jewish people, a change in which it was joined by many members of the "Society for the Diffusion of Enlightenment." Conspicuous among the latter was Leon Pinsker, an Odessa physician, who had been one of the Society's founders and had devoted long years to the goal of Russianization and emancipation. He now rejected that goal, and towards the end of 1882 he published a pamphlet with the bold title *Auto-Emancipation* in which he called for "the creation of a Jewish nationality . . . living on its own soil." The pamphlet was received with wide acclaim: the year 1881 had produced a new intellectual climate in Russian Jewry.

In his *Auto-Emancipation* Pinsker did not insist that the soil for a Jewish nationality must be Palestine, but those who were ready to heed his call could imagine no other land as the proper goal for such an effort. In fact, a movement to establish Jewish colonies in the ancient homeland, known as *Chibat Zion*, "Love of Zion," had already been launched in Russia, and two years after Pinsker issued his call the societies of which it was made up met and federated, and elected him their president. The impetus which the movement now received communicated itself to many of the young. Most of them were students preparing for professional careers, which they now renounced, and they chose instead to become pioneers in Palestine. They banded together under the name of BILU, a word compounded of the initials of the words in the second chapter of Isaiah meaning "House of Jacob, come and let us go." BILU wrote a heroic and important chapter in the story of the modern reclamation of Palestine.

3

But the most dramatic and far-reaching change which that year of sorrows produced, was upon the Jewish community in America. If the pogroms of 1881 were designed to implement that part of Pobyedonostzev's formula which called for the emigration of a third of the Russian Jews, they were to all appearances accomplishing their purpose. Shortly after the first outbreaks Jews in large numbers began streaming towards the borders. The government of Spain, anxious to atone for the expulsion of 1492, offered to receive the fugitives, but despite their distress, the offer failed to attract them. Those who turned their faces towards Palestine, however much their idealism and heroism signified for the future, were only a tiny minority. The great majority looked west towards the fabulous land across the ocean where, as they knew, many of their people had already found refuge and new life.

From 1881 to 1914 the salient fact in the story of American Jewry is its massive growth by immigration from Eastern Europe, principally from Russia and the regions of Poland that were ruled by the Czar. A large contingent came from Austria-Hungary, chiefly from the Polish province of Galicia, driven from its native soil by poverty, and a smaller one came from Rumania, where, as in the case of Russia, the impelling force was persecution. From 1915 to 1919 the flow was stemmed by the First World War, and after the war by the success of the anti-immigration agitation in the United States, whose crowning victory, as we shall see, came with the racist Johnson Immigration Act of 1924. From 1881 to 1914 some two millions were thus added to the American Jewish community from the lands that lay under the scepter of the czars, besides the several hundred thousand who hailed from Galicia and Rumania. For the sake of perspective, however, this influx must be seen against the background of the much greater flood of other nationalities and creeds that converged on America from the teeming and impoverished lands of the Old World. For the total number of immigrants who landed in the United States in the same period was over twenty-two million.

The statistics disclose significant differences between the Jewish and other immigrants. The proportion of women among the former was nearly twice as large as among the others, and of children under fourteen nearly two and a half times as large: the Jews came to stay and their families came with them. That conclusion is borne out by the record of immigrants who came and went. Between 1908 and 1914, when for every hundred of all who arrived nearly 31 departed, the number of Jews who left the country was only 7 out of every hundred. Between 1915 and 1920 the corresponding figures were respectively 56.6 and 4.3, and between 1925 and 1937 they were 40 and 3.8.

4

The year 1881 does not, of course, mark the beginning of Jewish immigration from Eastern Europe. There was a steady trickle of immigrants from those lands throughout the Colonial period; as we have seen, the outstanding member of the community in the Revolutionary years, Haym Salomon, was an immigrant from Poland. There was a fair admixture from Eastern Europe during the "German" period, especially from Russian Poland after 1845, when Nicholas I extended his barbarous conscription policy to the Jews of that province. There were crop failures and famines in Russia that propelled fugitives from the stricken areas, and besides, the pogrom wave of 1881 was not the first outbreak of anti-Jewish violence in Russia, Four years earlier a three-day pogrom had occurred in Odessa, the "Paris of Russia," and it also drove many Jews to seek asylum in western lands, especially America. And just as the pogroms of 1881 were not the first, they were not to be the last. Even more sanguinary outbreaks against the Jews were, as we shall see, staged in Russia during the first decade of the twentieth century, and after each eruption the tide of emigration rose higher and most of it flowed towards America, the world's City of Refuge.

But even in "tranquil" years the tide that began flowing in 1881 continued high, for the pogrom, as already noted, was not the only weapon in the anti-Jewish arsenal of the czars. Towards the end of 1890, for example, rumors reached the Jews in England and America that the ministers of Alexander III were preparing new blows against their favorite victims, and in both countries attempts were made to avert them. In December of that year a meeting of protest took place in London, and the Lord Mayor forwarded a memorial to the

Czar imploring him to "annul those special laws and disabilities that crush and cow your Hebrew subjects," and James G. Blaine, President Benjamin Harrison's Secretary of State, instructed the American minister to Russia to exert his influence against the threatened measures. But public protests, petitions and diplomacy were of no avail. In the spring of the following year the blow fell, and it took the form of mass expulsions of Jews who were residing in St. Petersburg, Kiev, and Moscow. Those cities were outside the Pale, but Alexander II, father of the reigning Czar, had opened them to Jewish artisans, intellectuals and first grade merchants. Now they were summarily and brutally rounded up and expelled. Needless to say, the number of Jewish fugitives who flocked to the United States that year rose to a new high.

The same year Baron Maurice de Hirsch, a great captain of industry and even greater philanthropist, laid before the Czar and his ministers an imposing plan for solving their Jewish problem. It proposed to transplant 3,000,000 Russian Jews over a period of twenty-five years and settle them in agricultural colonies in Argentina and other regions of the Western Hemisphere. To promote the project the Baron had established in London the Jewish Colonization Association, commonly known as ICA, with a capital of fifty million francs. The Czar and his ministers welcomed the proposal and the Baron went forward with it. But in the first ten years, instead of the expected million, only 10,000 were settled in Argentina. Not even the boldest and most affluent planners were able to fix the objective of the greatest migratory movement in Jewish history.

5

Fortunately, in the years since the end of the Civil War America had become ready to receive them. The depression which began with the panic on September 9, 1873, the day known as "Black Friday," had been overcome and was followed by a period of expansion and prosperity. The country offered the basic condition for the absorption of immense numbers of immigrants: the opportunity to earn a livelihood. There were roads and railroads to be laid down, mines to be dug, timber to be felled and sawed, and limitless acres to be cleared and ploughed. Old and new industries clamored for labor, skilled and unskilled, and immigrants were welcome guests, officially invited to become "members of our family." Poets and orators spoke proudly of

America as the City of Refuge for the oppressed of the earth, and a great many took the salvationist role of America very seriously, among them the choicest spirits of the land. Others found it easy to be idealists so long as they saw no clash between their interests and those of the impoverished and persecuted in the Old World.

Perhaps the most poignant expression of the concept of America as the "Mother of Exiles" came in 1883 from a young poetess of Sephardic ancestry. Emma Lazarus, a native and resident of New York, was thirty-four at the time and she was destined to live only four years longer. At twenty-two she had dedicated her first book of poems to Ralph Waldo Emerson, one of the many literary lights with whom she corresponded, some of the others being William Cullen Bryant, Edmund Stedman, James Russell Lowell and William Morris. In those poems and others that followed, her themes were not Jewish; she lived serenely in the ivory tower of classic poetry and resisted the efforts of some of her admirers to direct her to her own Hebraic sources. But contact with the refugees from Russia transformed her: she saw some of them on a visit to Ward's Island in the East River where women and children were being sheltered before admission. Thereafter she devoted not only her pen but all her energy in behalf of her persecuted people.

In 1883 Emma Lazarus wrote a sonnet, which was purchased for the impressive sum of $1,500 as her contribution to a fund that was being raised to provide a pedestal on Bedloe's Island for the Statue of Liberty, the colossal figure of "Liberty Enlightening the World," as it was called. Presented the following year by the people of France to the people of the United States, the statue has held its torch aloft in New York Harbor, a symbol of American liberty and idealism and a beacon of hope to the oppressed and homeless of the earth. In 1903 Emma's inspired lines were inscribed on a bronze tablet and placed inside the pedestal. The imposing statue recalled one of the seven wonders of the ancient world, the famous Colossus of Rhodes, so she called her sonnet *The New Colossus*.

Not like the brazen giant of Greek fame,
With conquering limbs astride from land to land,
Here at our sea-washed sunset gates shall stand,
A mighty woman with a torch, whose flame
Is the imprisoned lightning, and her name
Mother of Exiles. From her beacon hand
Glows world-wide welcome; her mild eyes command
The air-bridged harbor that twin cities frame.

"Keep, ancient lands, your storied pomp!" cries she,
With silent lips. "Give me your tired, your poor,
Your huddled masses yearning to breathe free,
The wretched refuse of your teeming shore,
Send these, the homeless, tempest-tost to me.
I lift my lamp beside the golden door!"

6

There were many other Jews in America whom the pogroms of 1881 and the sight of the fugitives roused to wrath and compassion. It was one of those not infrequent occasions of distress when the community became aware of the bonds that made it one—occasions that have proved more potent in producing common action than some of its basic but less spectacular needs. It was fortunate for the new arrivals that they found a body of their coreligionists, now numbering approximately a quarter-million, who had since the Civil War made remarkable economic progress and were not only eager but able to help them.

In the decades that followed the Civil War Jewish emigration from Germany had practically ceased. The Prussian constitution of 1850 had granted civil equality to the Jews, their rights in Bavaria and other German states were gradually extended, and in 1871 full emancipation was enacted for the whole of Germany which, after a series of wars in which Denmark, Austria, and France were successively defeated by Prussia, was unified into a powerful empire. With the removal of the disabilities which had driven the German Jews from their native land to America their exodus had come to an end.

The forty-eighters and their more numerous followers in the decade between 1850 and 1860 had become thoroughly adjusted and Americanized. They might still speak English with a German accent, but the former pack-peddlers and small storekeepers had now risen high in the industry and commerce of the country, and their sons were entering the liberal professions. They displayed a marked talent for organization and large-scale enterprise. In 1868 a writer on the merchants of New York stated that "it is the high standard of excellence of the old Israelite merchant of 1800 that has made the race occupy the proud position it now holds in this city and in the nation."

In 1880 the number of Jews in that city alone could not have been far below 100,000. Throughout the country their congregations, most of them Reform, were building bigger and more splendid temples, and in the larger centers Jewish hospitals, orphanages and agencies for the relief of the needy were created or strengthened. The first steps had been taken towards the integration of these enterprises into the city-wide networks which have given Jewish philanthropy in America its deservedly high repute. In Philadelphia a federation of the existing agencies, calling itself the United Hebrew Charities, was formed in 1869, and five years later the United Hebrew Charities of New York came into existence. Even earlier, Jewish hospitals had been established in those two cities as well as in Chicago and Cincinnati.

A marked feature of this period of consolidation was the expansion of the fraternal orders, especially of the Independent Order B'nai B'rith. This versatile and far-flung organization had been launched in New York in 1843 as a mutual aid and insurance project, but by 1868 its original purpose began to be overshadowed by a program of philanthropy and political action for the protection of Jewish rights at home and abroad. That year Julius Bien of New York, one of the leading engravers and cartographers of America, was chosen president and held the office until 1900. By 1890 B'nai B'rith had founded orphan homes and other philanthropies in New Orleans, Cleveland, Atlanta and Yonkers, established cooperative relations with the *Alliance Israélite Universelle*, and intervened against the discriminatory treaty with Switzerland. In the following decade the Order abandoned its secret ritual and mutual benefit program altogether. It extended its philanthropic and political interests, made an outstanding contribution through its Hillel foundation to the Jewish education of the student youth in the colleges and universities of the country, and through its Anti-Defamation League became a potent force against the perennial menace of anti-Semitism. The Order had also become international in scope: its first foreign unit was established in Berlin in 1882, its second in Rumania in 1889.

The Free Sons of Israel was founded in New York in 1849 primarily as a fraternal and mutual benefit order, but in time it, too, enlarged its program along the lines followed by B'nai B'rith. Ten years later came the Order Brith Abraham, and a secession that occurred in 1887 resulted in the Independent Order Brith Abraham, which invited Jews of Russian and Polish origin to join its lodges. The second had a phenomenal growth, reaching a peak of 200,000 members in 1917; the first began to decline after 1913 and was dissolved fourteen years later.

Thus on the eve of the large and sudden increment which came to American Jewry, its life was already set on strong foundations. Economically it was well entrenched and politically it was alert and resourceful in maintaining its rights. Its congregations flourished and its philanthropies were manifold and efficient.

7

The weak link in its collective life was the meager religious education it provided for its young. By 1870 the public schools had become firmly established, and the all-day schools which were attached to congregations and taught secular as well as religious subjects, had become a thing of the past. Jewish education became supplementary to the public schools, and congregations began by establishing religious afternoon schools. German was the language of instruction, but gradually it yielded to English, even as it did in the pulpits. The schools, however, shrank until their pupils met for instruction only once a week on Sunday morning. The three religious trends agreed that unless the young were taught the tenets and practices of their faith and imbued with devotion to it, Jewish life would go glimmering. Defections would multiply and the sense of solidarity would depend for nourishment on the antagonism of the non-Jewish environment rather than on loyalty to the ancient heritage. But was it possible for the Sunday school to provide more than a transient smattering of Jewish knowledge and attachment? The Orthodox said no, and in the face of formidable obstacles—pedagogic, financial and organizational—they strove to give their children a more adequate grounding in the faith and traditions of their people.

The earliest venture in adult Jewish education was a by-product of the Young Men's Hebrew Associations, whose primary aims were first social and recreational, then cultural in the general sense. The first Association appeared in Baltimore in 1854, but not until 1874, when one was founded in New York, and another in Philadelphia a year later, did the movement take root. By 1880 about fifty Associations were in existence, but only in 1902 was the first separate Young Women's Hebrew Association, also in New York, established. The movement took for its model the Protestant Young Men's Christian Associations, which started in Britain in 1844 and reached America seven years later. Their Jewish counterparts were from the start faced with the problem of including Jewish values in their educational program, and it was many decades later when, as we shall see, the Jewish Community Center movement showed the way to the earlier Associations, and both were federated and stimulated by the National Jewish Welfare Board, that this problem moved towards solution.

8

Many of the fugitives of 1881 were destitute and required help even before they reached their goal. In Austria, Germany, France, Holland and England committees were organized to assist them when they came to the border towns, and as early as 1882 an international meeting to regulate assistance for the migrants took place in Berlin. Most of their leaders in Russia, however, took no action to aid the emigrants: they feared they would be charged with encouraging Jews to desert "the fatherland"! Their attitude changed in 1891 when the Czar's government permitted Baron de Hirsch's ICA to operate in "the fatherland" and hundreds of ICA offices were established in Russia. In Germany, the principal country of transit for the migrants, they were aided by local committees until the *Hilfsverein der Deutschen Juden*, created in 1901 for the purpose, took over the task. The *Verein* became a powerful organization and for three decades performed outstanding political and educational service, but after 1933 its beneficiaries were no longer *Ostjuden*, but German Jews fleeing from the claws of the Nazi monster. The British Mansion House Committee helped those who were stranded in England to obtain transportation to the New World.

Many of those who landed in America were, as might have been expected, destitute and helpless. Their appearance was no doubt something of a shock to their Sephardic and German predecessors: the newcomers reminded them of the past they had forgotten or were anxious to forget when they or their ancestors were themselves fugitives from persecution. But not for a moment did they repudiate the duty of helping the "poor relations" that descended upon them. The existing philanthropic agencies applied their resources without stint, and new ones appeared on the scene. Among the latter were the Hebrew Sheltering Society, popularly known by its tradition-laden Hebrew name of *Hachnosas Orchim* (hospitality for wayfarers), the Hebrew Immigrant Aid Society, the American Committee for Ameliorating the Conditions of the Russian Exiles, and the Baron de Hirsch Fund. Years later, in 1909 to be exact, the first two organizations amalgamated into the Hebrew Sheltering and Immigrant Aid Society, better known as HIAS, which has steadily extended its program for aid to Jewish migrants at home and abroad. The Baron de Hirsch Fund was established by the munificent patron of the ICA in 1891, when the persecutions of that year sent a fresh flood of refugees to America.

In addition to the first and elementary task of providing temporary shelter and sustenance to the destitute, immigrants were helped to locate friends and relatives, find employment, learn trades and establish themselves in the less congested sections of the country. In 1900 the ICA and the Baron de Hirsch Fund established the Jewish Agricultural and Industrial Aid Society, which the following year set up the Industrial Removal Office "to relieve the prevailing conditions in our ghettos." The Office functioned until 1922, encouraging and assisting immigrants to go west and south, and for some years attempted to divert them from the Atlantic seaboard by routing them to the port of Galveston, Texas, and sending them on into the interior. Some 5,000 of them landed in Galveston and, under the able direction of David M. Bressler, a great many more were helped out of the congestion in New York and Philadelphia. In 1903 the National Council of Jewish Women, formed a decade earlier, joined in the work of aiding immigrants, with emphasis on helping unaccompanied Jewish girls and women to meet the problems they faced in a new world. The Council's work in this field was directed by Sadie American, one of its founders and a prominent civic leader. Almost from the start the different agencies added to their programs the work of inducting the new arrivals into a knowledge of America, its language, institutions and way of life, and aiding them to win the coveted prize of American citizenship.

The impression must not, however, be left that the majority, or even a large minority, of the newcomers required or received aid from communal agencies. Indeed, the number of those who received such aid made up only a small fraction, perhaps not more than 5 per cent, of the new arrivals. Three causes operated to keep the proportion low and, as time went on, to make it still lower. First and foremost was the fact that the country as a whole was in a period of industrial expansion and employment was not hard to find. Second was the uncommon adaptiveness of these newcomers. "Making a living" called for grueling toil, but they were industrious, frugal, and quick to abandon old occupations for which there was no demand and learn new ones. Third was the constantly growing number of immigrants who on their arrival found relatives and *landsleit* who had preceded them and were now able to help them. Hosts of husbands and grown children came out first, and after establishing themselves, lost no time in sending for the other members of the family. And very promptly the remarkable relationship implicit in the nostalgic word *landsman* (plural, *landsleit*) began to operate and, it may be safely presumed, provided more aid to the newcomers than the agencies. The *landsleit* were those who hailed from the same city or town in "the old country," and the warmth of the relationship that existed among them in the new country can only be known by those who have experienced it or observed it closely. The claim of the needy immigrant was almost as sacred to the *landsman* as that of his own flesh and blood. And that relationship, as we shall see, found expression also on a wider front in the organizations it engendered: congregations, societies for mutual aid, and eventually federations for political and other action on behalf of their kin who were still deprived of human rights in the lands from which they hailed.

CHAPTER 10

Cultural Roots

1

THE IMMIGRANTS FROM EASTERN EUROPE HAILED FROM three political jurisdictions, Russia, Austria-Hungary and Rumania, but their major cultural possessions, the Orthodox faith and the Yiddish language, were common to all of them. In Galicia, the Polish province of Austria-Hungary, Yiddish was spoken with a marked dialectal difference, and Chassidism, the pietist movement launched a century earlier by the saintly Israel Baal Shem Tov (Besht), the "Good Master of the Name," was more widespread there than in Lithuania and White Russia; it was a cult that banished gloom as sin, put fervor and joy in worship above learning, and exalted the religious leader, or "rebbe," who was often credited with miraculous powers. But these differences did not negate their basic religious and linguistic unity.

Economically their life was hemmed in by legal restrictions, and even where, as in Galicia, these had already been relaxed, the hostility of their neighbors and the systematic boycotts to which it gave rise destroyed the livelihood of a great many of them. In all those lands they were an urban people, practicing the handicrafts—tailoring, shoemaking, carpentry, blacksmithing and others—but too many of them were engaged in trade, too much of which was petty, casual and unstable. The policy in Russia, as we saw, was to bar them from the villages even of the Pale, and to crowd them into the cities, where craftsmen and traders competed with each other or their Christian neighbors, and destitution ran high. And along with the formal restrictions they were encompassed by a wall of inveterate hostility, compounded of religious antagonism, economic rivalry, and the distrust that is always generated by what is different and unfamiliar.

The question of daily bread was a daily problem to these millions. The Sabbath being the festive day of the week and demanding a less meager board, the uncertainty found proverbial expression in the half-anxious, half-humorous query *"Vu nemt men af Shabbes?"*—"How will

I provide for the Sabbath?"—and poverty bred congestion which, as is well known, is an effectual check on the graces and amenities of life. In strange contrast with this poverty was the illusion which prevailed in the world around them that every Jew was a Croesus, an illusion fed by the scant contact that existed between the two worlds and by the circumstance that a large portion of whatever contact did exist was between the Christian peasant and the Jewish trader.

2

What with penury and congestion, and the physical insecurity always latent and sometimes in eruption, the conclusion might be drawn that the life these millions led was depressed and ruled by chronic anxiety. Such a conclusion would be far from the truth. Their life was anything but drab and joyless: it offered proof that "man doth not live by bread only, but by everything that proceedeth out of the mouth of the Lord doth man live." The spiritual resources they possessed in the ancient faith and its institutions gave them not only the power to suffer and endure, but produced a way of life that was full of color and vitality, a civilization *sui generis*, integrated and self-contained.

The First World War dealt this way of life a staggering blow, not only by the ravages the war itself inflicted upon it, but by the political changes that followed, in particular the ruthless revolution in Russia, which doomed it for millions of its practitioners. In the Second World War the Nazi murder-machine, as the world at length discovered, erased it completely. But in the three decades after 1881 during which the massive East European immigration to America proceeded, the unique life of these multitudes was in full vigor, in spite of certain influences which began to impinge upon it and which will be noted shortly. And no adequate appraisal of the Jewish experience in America can ignore this life which the immigrants left behind them, their profound attachment to it, their struggle to sustain it in the New World, and the tensions and wounds this struggle entailed. For it serves no useful purpose to echo the smug assertions that the transplantation of these millions was all gain and no loss: fidelity to the truth forbids it and loyalty to America does not demand it.

3

The large cities of the Pale and of Galicia were, of course, the first to feel the impact of the new intellectual and social forces that came to challenge the established life-pattern of East European Jewry; the small town, or *shtetl*, was its natural home and citadel. The *shtetl* has had the attention of social analysts; it has been the theme of novelists, dramatists and poets; it has been dissected, satirized and bewailed; it has also been extolled and idealized. But the immigrant whose roots were nourished in it looked back on it with poignant nostalgia. Life in it was beset by poverty and anxiety, but it was also whole-souled and serene, founded in a faith that no vicissitudes could shake, and heightened with Sabbaths and festivals whose authentic color and flavor were lost in the New World and could not be recaptured. He could not and would not return to the *shtetl*, but he could dream of it and long for it. And in the cramped tenements where he lived, and even after he moved into handsome apartments, he sang about *mein shtetele Belz*, or *mein shtetele Slutzk*, the word *shtetele* being one of the endearing diminutives in which the Yiddish language is so exceptionally rich.

In the workshop and market place there was toil and care, and penury might dwell in the home as a familiar, but on Sabbaths and festivals the poorest home became the abode of peace and rest. The study of the sacred lore, which was not restricted to a learned caste, brought a peculiar joy. Study was not so much an intellectual exercise or a cultural pursuit, as a religious experience. The synagogue was the *Bet Hamidrash* or House of Study, every home had its library, large or small, of sacred tomes, and men studied alone or more often in groups that met in the synagogue. Exceptional learning was exceptional excellence: the only aristocrats were the men of great learning. Modern educators might judge this learning narrow and medieval: it was deficient in the secular disciplines, though less so than is generally supposed. But if the Talmudic scholar was unfamiliar with the sonnets of Petrarch or the love songs of Heine and Burns, he read every Friday the incomparable "Song of Songs Which Is Solomon's," and the allegoric meaning he ascribed to it only enhanced its beauty.

The *cheder*, or "room," where the young were schooled, has been the target of ruthless criticism, much of it deserved. It was physically cramped and unattractive and pedagogically primitive. It excluded half the child population, the pupils being the boys only; the girls were taught their prayers only, and at home. But it met the crucial test by which any system of education should be judged: it produced a literate people and transmitted to the new generation the ideals and way of life that were precious to the old. For the rest, even physically and pedagogically the *cheder* was not behind the elementary education which enlightened countries like Britain, for example, provided for their young in the nineteenth century, as the novels of Dickens and other sources attest. The *cheder* was supported by the parents, tuition having first call on the budget even of the poorest, and for orphans and children of paupers the community maintained a school called *Talmud Torah.* In the New World perhaps the most difficult problem of the immigrants would be the creation of a system of religious education that would maintain the spiritual level of their life in the Old.

It is doubtful if the sober language of exposition can convey the significance of the year-round festivals in the life of these millions, and it certainly cannot communicate their diverse aspects and color. For depth and variety they stand unique in the spiritual experiences of mankind. The Sabbath was not merely a day of rest from physical toil and week-day cares, but a *nachas ruach*, a day of peace and spiritual renewal. With the lighting of the Sabbath candles on Friday night the "angels of peace" entered into every home and hovered over the entire *shtetl.*

The eight days of Chanukah brought homely cheer, Purim was marked by a licensed hilarity, and Simchas Torah was a day of high gladness. Passover, Weeks and Tabernacles, and three "pilgrimage festivals," were "the appointed time for gladness, festivals and seasons for joy;" each had its own flavor and ceremonial, and the special synagogue rituals had their counterparts in the home. The awe and exaltation of Rosh Hashanah and Yom Kippur brought the year to its spiritual peak. And even the fast of the Ninth of Ab brought a species of consolation, for they who observed it never doubted that the past they mourned would live again. And only in collective observance, of course, could the Sabbaths, feasts and fasts have their authentic quality.

The community was organized around the synagogue, with the rabbi as its ex-officio head, assisted by a group of officials, elected or appointed. These included the *gabbai,* or lay head of the community; the *dayyan*, or head of the rabbinical court; the *shochet*, or ritual slaughterer; the *mohel*, or circumciser; the cantor, and the *shammas*, or sexton, who was also the general factotum. Some of the professional functionaries were not salaried and were dependent on fees: the income of the community, derived from an excise tax called *korobka*[*] and usually levied on meat and candles, was rarely sufficient to meet even its minimum needs. But the spirit of communal responsibility found its fullest expression in charitable works, concentrated in special societies,

[*] The word is Russian and means "basket." The reference may be to the contents of the housewife's shopping basket, but other explanations have also been offered.

as indicated in a passage from the Talmud, which is part of the morning prayers:

> These are the things of which the yield nourishes a man in this world, while the principal remains to his credit in the world to come; and they are these: honoring father and mother, doing deeds of kindness, repairing betimes morning and evening to the *Bet Hamidrash*, hospitality to wayfarers, visiting the sick, dowering the poor bride, following the dead to burial, devoutness in prayer, and making peace between man and man. But the study of Torah is as great as all of them.

The entire life of the community as such revolved around the *Bet Hamidrash.* It was the house of prayer and house of study, but it was also the place where the people met to transact communal business and share their joys and sorrows. A man with a grievance came there and demanded redress: he could forbid the scrolls to be taken from the Ark for the reading of the Sabbath portion until his grievance was heard. The bridegroom came to be congratulated and the mourner to be consoled. The *Bet Hamidrash* was the mold and repository of the people's soul. Chaim Nachman Bialik, by common consent the foremost Hebrew poet of modern times, has protrayed its role in a famous poem, *And Would You Know*, of which the following lines are a part:

> *And would you know the mighty wellspring whence*
> *Your brothers, doomed in evil days to die,*
> *The strength and valor drew to haste and meet*
> *Their death rejoicing, and freely stretch the neck*
> *To every knife and every lifted ax, and cry*
> *"The Lord is One!" and die a martyr's death?*
> *Then step into the* Bet Hamidrash, *the worn*
> *And ancient, on some desolate winter night,*
> *Or on a hot and blazing summer day,*
> *At dawn, or noon, or in the evening dusk.*
> *And if the Lord has still preserved alive*
> *His Remnant, you will behold even today,*
> *In the shadow of the beams, or in the gloom*
> *Of some dark nook, or seated round the stove,*
> *Like ears of corn ungleaned, or ghosts of things*
> *That are no more, sons of your people, gaunt,*
> *Harassed and somber, dragging the weary yoke*

Of Exile; in the yellowed Talmud page
Forgetting grinding toil, beguiling want
In oft repeated tales of ancient days,
Stilling the voice of care in the chant of Psalms.
(Alas, how mean and trivial the scene
To alien eyes and blind!) Then will your heart
Confess that o'er the threshold of our House
Of Life your feet have trod, and that your eyes
Have looked upon the Stronghold of our Soul.

* * *

Such in brief outline was the world in its varied aspects—economic, social, intellectual and spiritual—from which the Jews of Eastern Europe, propelled by a sudden exacerbation of persecution, now flocked to America. It will be more than a struggle for livelihood that will confront them in the New World. They will struggle to keep this heritage alive—under conditions not conducive to victory.

4

But the traditional or religious way of life, which the bulk of the immigrants from Eastern Europe carried with them to America, was no longer unchallenged even in their homelands. Intellectual and social movements were already afoot in all of them, whose basic character was secular. The first and the oldest was Haskalah, which traced its origin back to Moses Mendelssohn, the frail and gentle sage of Berlin, who died three years before the outbreak of the French Revolution. Under his inspiration Jews in Germany had begun to speak German in place of their Judeo-German or Yiddish, and established "modern" or secular schools for their children. Mendelssohn himself remained a devout Jew, but many of his disciples, including most of his children, went the whole way and became baptized. In the Austro-Hungarian Empire his influence was strong in Vienna and Prague, but the Chassidic masses in Galicia were impervious and hostile to it. In Russia, where Haskalah expressed itself in a Hebrew literary revival, it also moved generally in the direction of secularism. Haskalah produced poetry like the poignant lyrics of Micah Joseph Lebensohn and the satires and sermons of Judah Leib Gordon, who lived to see the pogroms of 1881 and learned to change his tune. It included novelists like Abraham Mapu, whose *Love of Zion*, a glowing picture of life in

Judah in biblical times, had an extraordinary effect on the youth of his generation, and essayists like Isaac Baer Levinson, called the "Russian Mendelssohn," and Moses Leib Lilienblum who, like Gordon, lived to see his ideals shattered by the iron fist of Alexander III. Haskalah and its twin brother, Russianization, reared disciples who, as in Germany, became estranged from the ancestral faith and sought the ultimate solution in the baptismal font, but the masses of the people held firm against it, their suspicions of its basic tendency confirmed by the encouragement it received from the czars and their minions.

Ultimately Haskalah merged with the second movement among the Jews of Eastern Europe that was essentially secular, the Jewish national movement. Among the fugitives who streamed to America in the eighties there were few who carried with them the ideal of national redemption. But in the succeeding decades their numbers steadily grew, and it was they, as we shall see, who made the American Jewish community a tower of strength to the Zionist cause. But while by and large a secular force, Jewish nationalism, it must be emphasized, was not anti-religious. It included from the start a large and militant religious wing, and even among the secularists it stimulated rather than weakened loyalty to the ancient faith.

But still a third force, radical socialism, had begun to impinge on the Jewries of Eastern Europe, especially in Russia, which was secularist *par excellence*, and if it did not lead its adherents to baptism it was because its hostility embraced all religions. In Russia socialism became the spearhead of the movement for the overthrow of the autocracy, and it would have been strange indeed if the youth of the most oppressed nationality in the country had been absent from it. In the eighties they were of small account in it, both in numbers and influence, although it suited the purpose of the Czar's government to exaggerate their importance, but in the succeeding decades it attracted more and more of them. In 1897, they organized the General Jewish Workers Alliance (*Arbeiterbund*) of Lithuania, Poland and Russia, which became known as the Bund, and soon it added a Jewish cultural program, strictly secular of course, to its revolutionary objective. And many of those who adhered to its ideology joined the throngs who flocked to America until they became an important component of the American Jewish community, determined, articulate and vocal; they left their impress especially in journalism, literature and the labor movement. But their indifference or hostility to religion was not as deep-seated as they themselves thought; in the new environment they often "backslided" to the ancient practices, especially when they attained parenthood and it became important to establish a bond between themselves and their offspring.

5

There was one cultural possession, however, which all the Jewish immigrants from Eastern Europe, regardless of ideological differences, had in common: the Yiddish language they spoke and loved.

In respect of language, as indeed in most other respects, the history of the Jews across the millennia is unique. Hebrew, the tongue with which they began their historic career and in which they expressed their deepest insights and left the most enduring monuments of their genius, never lost its pristine place in their allegiance and affection. Wherever the vagaries of fortune drove them—in ancient, medieval or modern times—Hebrew remained their Holy Tongue, the language of their prayers, the vehicle of their scholarship, the medium of their solemn pronouncements. At the same time, however, they appropriated and utilized other languages, those of nations contiguous to themselves or among whom they dwelt.

During the Second Commonwealth and succeeding centuries, Aramaic, a cousin of Hebrew, became current among them and vied with Hebrew not only in their daily speech, but in their literary output, especially in the Talmud. And, of course, they adopted the languages of the nations among whom their wanderings brought them. In a number of instances they incorporated Hebrew and other elements into them until they became distinct dialects, and when they wrote them they used their own Hebrew characters. Among them were Judeo-Greek, Judeo-Persian and Judeo-Italian. Judeo-Spanish, better known as Ladino or Judismo, is almost a distinct language. It is spoken and written by Sephardim in the Balkan countries and North Africa, and by emigrants from those regions in the Americas. In New York City some 50,000 of them were estimated to employ that medium in 1940, and in 1953 the Ladino newspaper, *La Vara*, printed of course in Hebrew characters, was still being published.

But among all these dialects the one based on Medieval High German with a large admixture of Hebrew and Aramaic words, achieved the position of a separate and important language. It arrived in the countries of Eastern Europe with the fugitives from the fury of the Crusaders, who rehearsed for their mission against the Saracen infidels by massacring Jews in Germany; in the middle of the fourteenth century, when the Black Death ravaged Europe, an even larger stream of refugees is believed to have flowed eastward: the populace was persuaded that the Jews were responsible for the plague. In its new abode the language these fugitives brought with them absorbed a fairly large number of Slavonic words and experienced a vigorous growth. In the middle of the seventeenth century, when Jewish community life was already sprouting in America, the refugee stream in Europe was reversed; it flowed from east to west; Jews were fleeing from the frenzy of the Cossacks that was unleashed against them in the Ukraine and Poland. But when they got to the Germanies the language of their coreligionists in those lands already sounded strange in their ears.

So Judeo-German, as Yiddish was for a long time called, was spoken in East Europe only until it was carried to the Americas, South Africa and other parts of the world. The idiom, when it arrived in America, was estimated to consist of 70 per cent of words of German origin, 20 per cent of Hebrew and Aramaic, and 10 per cent of Slavonic. But for a long time even the people who spoke it and loved it as their *mame-loshn*, or "mother tongue," looked upon it as something inferior. It was a strange attitude, partaking of the irrational that seems to underlie all life. Yiddish was the tongue of the home, the street and the market place. It was the language of instruction in the *cheder* and of Talmudic disputation in the synagogue. The roaming *maggid*, or preacher, held forth in Yiddish; he found it a matchless medium for his quaint parables and picturesque fulminations against sin. As a literary medium, however, it was held in disdain, fit only for writings intended for the ignorant: folk tales and prayers to be recited by women. The language of literature and correspondence for the educated had to be Hebrew. Even the early apostles of socialism among the Jews, like Aron Lieberman, who has been called "the father of Jewish socialism," and the poet Morris Winchevsky edited socialist periodicals in Hebrew. The Maskilim maintained the same attitude towards the tongue, which they called Zhagón (jargon), because in their view Yiddish was only a corruption of German with an admixture of distorted Hebrew. The name stuck, and for many decades Jews called their own language Zhagón.

By the middle of the nineteenth century, however, the attitude towards Yiddish had begun to change. Certain writers, who had begun their work in Hebrew, felt they had a message for the multitude which, of course, could only be conveyed in Yiddish. So they stooped to conquer, and wrote in the vernacular also. And as they did so they made a discovery. They found the "uncouth" Zhagón a remarkably flexible instrument, capable of expressing delicate nuances, and particularly adapted for depicting the many moods of the people who spoke it. A language, they and others came to realize, is not just a mass of words; the spirit that informs the mass is more important, and the spirit is created by the people whose ethos comes to dwell in it. Judged by its lexicon, there is hardly a language that is not a mixture and a "corruption." What is English but a mixture of the Low Germanic dialect, which became Anglo-Saxon, and the French, which the Norman conquerers brought with them in the eleventh century? And what are French and the other Romance languages, but "corruptions" of the Vulgar Latin which the Roman legions carried with them in their conquests?

In the essays of Maskilim like Isaac Baer Levinson and Abraham Baer Glottlober, Yiddish literature emerged from the primitive stage, and the folk tales of the prolific Isaac Meir Dick, which appeared in the sixties and seventies, proved that the language could be employed in belles-lettres also. In 1863 Alexander Zederbaum established the first Yiddish periodical, and in the eighties the chief works of the founder of modern Yiddish literature, Sholem Jacob Abramovitch, better known by his pen name Mendele Mocher Sforim (Mendele the Bookseller), had already been published. Among them were *The Puny Little Men*, *Fishke the Cripple*, *The Old Mare*, and other novels in which he laid bare with tender humor and merciless satire the follies, the sorrows and the abuses from which his people in Russia suffered.

Mendele was over eighty when he died in 1917, and he was affectionately called "the grandfather," but in the eighties his two principal "grandsons" were already building on the foundations he laid. They were the inimitable narrator and humorist Sholom Aleichem, whose first Yiddish stories appeared in 1883, and Isaac Leib Peretz, poet in verse and prose, who published his first Yiddish poem, *Monish*, four years later. And there were still other "grandsons" among them: Isaac Joel Linitzki, bold champion of Yiddish as a literary vehicle, who published his first story in the vernacular as early as 1865; Mordecai Spector, whose first novel appeared in 1883, and Jacob Dinesohn, whose novel, *The Dark Young Man*, appeared in 1877. The same year Abraham Goldfaden, the founder of the Yiddish theater, launched his first theatrical enterprise in Rumania.

The literary movement which these and other pioneers started continued among the immigrants from Eastern Europe, and many of the writers who had already achieved stature in the Old World joined their people in the New and, as we shall see, contributed to a literary, dra-

REFORM LEADERS

Union of American Hebrew Congregations

Isaac Mayer Wise

Union of American Hebrew Congregations

Kaufmann Kohler

CONSERVATIVE LEADERS

Courtesy of Congregation Mikveh Israel, Phila.

Isaac Leeser

Jewish Theological Seminary of America

Solomon Schechter

ORTHODOX LEADERS

Courtesy of Yeshiva University

Bernard Revel

"Kehot" Publication Society

Joseph Isaac Schneersohn

LABOR LEADERS

Blackstone Studios

Sidney Hillman

Harry Rubenstein, ILGWU

David Dubinsky

matic and journalistic efflorescence which, among the immigrant groups in America, stands unsurpassed for magnitude and quality.

6

Those, then, were the two major cultural possessions in the baggage of the Jewish immigrants from Eastern Europe: the ancient faith and the Yiddish language. With the first went, of course, an imposing corpus of sacred literature, most of it in Hebrew, and the age-old institutions that had molded their way of life. It was the conscious purpose of their people's life across the centuries, and the affirmative bond that united the diverse segments. For it their heroes had lived and their martyrs had died. But the other had also gathered strong loyalties. It mirrored their distinctive ethos, it had peculiar power to awaken nostalgia and soothe it at the same time, and it was producing a precious literature of its own. It was cherished especially by those among them in whom the religious bond had weakened and who wistfully hoped that a Jewish way of life could be built on secular foundations.

CHAPTER 11

Up from the Sweatshops

1

THEY FLED FROM PERSECUTION AND FOUND REFUGE IN THE land of liberty and opportunity, but for several decades of the mass influx, opportunity for the great majority of them was only a dream, and liberty meant freedom to toil like galley slaves or starve. In the mid-twentieth century the economic status of the Jews in America was one of dignity and competence, but most of them were perhaps unaware of the bitter struggle for subsistence which the immigrants of those early decades had to wage, and in their modern apartments in the cities and suburbs of the land, they rarely thought of the squalid tenements in the "ghettos" of the big cities to which their forebears were condemned. Filial piety, if nothing else, enjoins them to remember.

To understand the course of economic adjustment of these immigrant masses it must be seen against the background of the steady influx of new arrivals, impoverished and more or less bewildered. From the economic standpoint the constant flow meant a continuous process of replacement, the later arrivals taking the place of the earlier ones, many of whom had in the meantime graduated to higher economic status. The large majority of them, as we shall see, found employment in the needle trades, and the manufacture of wearing apparel came to be regarded as a "Jewish" industry, not only because the great bulk of the employers who owned it were Jews—that was still the case in 1950—but because most of the workers in it were also Jews. But by 1950 that was no longer the case: for many of the earlier arrivals, and certainly their children, no longer plied the needle, and the process of replenishment had come to an end.

A similar and concomitant rotation, it should be noted, proceeded in the "ghettos" of the large cities which these masses inhabited, especially New York, Philadelphia and Chicago. The outsider, whose vision was often blurred by prejudice, found those teeming concentrations not only crude and "clannish," but hopelessly static. But what he saw was an optical illusion. In reality there was a continuous exodus from the "ghettos" of those who had improved their lot and acquired familiarity with the language and ways of the land. But since their place was constantly taken by new arrivals, the illusion persisted, and it had not a little to do with shaping the attitude of the native towards the immigrant, particularly the Jewish immigrant.

2

One ideal which many of the newcomers cherished, although comparatively few took the drastic steps it called for and still fewer actually achieved it, was that of earning their bread by tilling the soil. It was a natural rebellion against the precarious occupations to which so many had been condemned in the Old World, and it was fed by the romanticized visions of life "in the bosom of nature," which the social theorists and the poets of Haskalah alike held up to the rootless denizens of the Pale. Peddlers at their pushcarts dreamed of orchards and grainfields, and men and women bent over their sewing machines hummed the song that celebrates the "carefree" life of the farmer, the words and music by the popular and prolific bard Eliakum Zunser, which begins with the lines:

Of plow and soil
*God speeds the toil.**

But there were some who were not content with dreaming dreams and seeing visions. First, there were those who, in addition to the ideal of returning to the soil, aimed also to establish a just social order, and formed into groups in order to achieve both goals. Second, there were individuals who turned their backs on the sewing machine and tenement and took to farming on their own. The groups established farm colonies all of which sooner or later disintegrated. One attempt of this sort, in fact, had been made even by the earlier immigrants; in 1837 a dozen Jewish families planted a farm colony in Ulster County, New York, which struggled on for ten years before it went out of existence. The individuals, on the other hand, invested their savings in farms of their own and a large number of them succeeded.

In January 1882 the first group of back-to-the-soilers, consisting of some sixty-five young people, arrived in New York, followed shortly afterwards by three more groups. They belonged to a movement which called itself *Am Olam* (Eternal People) and aimed to realize the

* Yiddish: *In der sokhe ligt die mazel brokhe.*

ideal of a collective life on the soil, very much like the BILU movement, but without making Palestine its objective. In the next few years nearly a score of joint farming projects were hopefully launched and sorrowfully abandoned. They, and others which followed them in later years, were assisted by the *Alliance Israélite Universelle*, the Baron de Hirsch Fund and the Hebrew Immigrant Aid Society.

In the earlier undertakings two men stand out for their dedication to these efforts. One was Herman Rosenthal, the leader of the *Am Olam* group, a man of many talents, poet, scholar, economist, and for the last twenty years of his life head of the Slavonic Department of the New York Public Library. He was the guiding spirit of the first farm colony, which the new immigrants established on Sicily Island in Louisiana. In the spring of 1882 the settlement was brought to an end by a flood of the Mississippi River, but in August of the same year Rosenthal led another attempt, this time on land in the present state of South Dakota. The colony, named Crémieux in honor of the president of the *Alliance*, was an impressive undertaking and made an auspicious start, but it lasted only three years, the victim of an assortment of natural calamities, including drought, hail, and insect pests. The other friend and ally, not only of the plow-and-soil enthusiasts but of all the needy whom persecution and poverty cast upon the shores of America, was the scholar and libertarian Michael Heilprin; him we have already met as the defender of the Bible against those who tried to make it bear witness in favor of slavery. Heilprin died in 1888, when the immigrant tide was still rising, but from the time it began he was a tower of strength to the Emigrant Aid Society, and in 1882 he led a group that established a farm settlement in southern New Jersey, which was named Carmel.

Among the ill-starred farm colonies in the eighties were eight that were attempted in Kansas and others in Virginia, North Dakota, Michigan, Colorado, Oregon and California. But Carmel was not one of them. New Jersey, in fact, became the scene of the most successful Jewish agricultural ventures, and for two reasons. First, although the farmers settled in groups, they renounced collectivist methods, each farmer cultivating his own holding. Second, they were close to Philadelphia and New York with their massive communities from which, when the need arose, they received readier help. Their proximity to those cities enabled them also to specialize in truck and poultry farming, for which they were better suited, and made it profitable for some of the settlements to introduce industrial enterprises to supplement their basic agriculture.

In addition to Carmel, Rosenhayn was established in New Jersey in 1887 and Woodbine in 1891. The latter developed into a sizable rural and industrial community, with synagogues, religious schools and other communal institutions. It was fathered by the Baron de Hirsch Fund, and until 1917 the Baron de Hirsch Agricultural School was the colony's best known institution; the training of Jewish youths in practical agriculture was continued by the National Farm School, established by the Reform rabbi Joseph Krauskopf at Doylestown, Pennsylvania, in 1896.* The school in Woodbine, as well as the colony itself, was directed by Hirsch Leib Sabsovich, who possessed a rare combination of social idealism and expert knowledge of agriculture and colonization. Woodbine became an incorporated borough in 1903 and Sabsovich was its first mayor; its subsequent mayors and nearly all of its other officials have also been Jews.

The urge to establish collective farm settlements did not, despite its failures, exhaust itself in the last two decades of the nineteenth century; it begot more failures in the first three of the twentieth: in Maryland, Wisconsin, Illinois, Alabama, Texas and other states. A settlement near Geneva, Ohio, devoted to viticulture had a more promising career until prohibition dealt it a crippling blow. Nevertheless the Jewish agricultural population, consisting of families each cultivating its own holding, grew steadily. In 1900 it was about 1,000, in 1954 it was estimated at over 100,000 with approximately 20,000 farming units. The largest concentrations were in the vicinity of Vineland and Lakewood, both in New Jersey. An important contribution to this result was made by the Jewish Agricultural Society, an offshoot of the Baron de Hirsch Fund, by means of loans, training, expert advice and cooperative organization. Many of the society's services were instituted by its manager, Gabriel Davidson.

Nor have Jews been absent from the field of agricultural science, which has so greatly advanced American agriculture in general. Among the leading scientists in the field were Jacob G. Lipman, who was considered the foremost authority on soil chemistry, and the agronomist Joseph A. Rosen, who, among his other activities, directed colonization projects for Jews in Russia and the Dominican Republic. And perhaps the world's best known agricultural reformer and organizer was David Lubin, who brought about the establishment in 1905 of the International Institute of Agriculture in Rome; it included seventy member countries and was headed by Lubin until his death in 1919.

* The National Farm School is now called National Agricultural College.

3

Only a tiny fraction, of course, ventured out to settle on the soil: centuries of forced separation from it could not be easily overcome. A small number trickled into trades, like cigar and cigarette making, that were new to them, but most of them turned to the two occupations they had practiced in the Pale: petty trade and tailoring. In the New World the first took the form of peddling small household needs from house to house or trundling heavier stocks of food and other wares on pushcarts, and might be succeeded by the more dignified occupation of "custom peddling," or selling costlier wares on the installment plan, and even by "opening" a small shop or store. But tailoring absorbed a much larger number, including a great many who had practiced other crafts in the Old World or whose ventures into peddling or "business" had proved unsuccessful.

What explains the virtual absence of these immigrants from the basic or heavy industries, like mining, railroading and building construction, and their concentration in the lighter crafts, devoted to the production of consumer goods? The answer often given is that the Jewish worker is not physically fit for the hard labor which the primary industries call for—an oversimplified answer that ignores important historic, economic and psychologic factors, and is challenged by the record of Jewish labor in agriculture, quarrying, roadbuilding and other rugged occupations in Palestine. It is a matter of history that for many centuries Jews dwelling in Christian lands were generally barred by law from owning and cultivating the soil, and their concentration in the cities and towns was also the result of legalized discrimination. There was, however, an additional circumstance that operated to exclude Jewish workers from the primary industries: Jewish capital and enterprise played hardly any role in them and the Jewish worker found no welcome in them.

A survey made by the magazine *Fortune* as late as 1936 disclosed that in the United States the share of Jewish capital in basic industries like steel, coal, oil, rubber and chemicals was still negligible. In many of the lighter or consumer-goods industries, on the other hand, the survey showed Jewish capital impressively represented, with 40 per cent in footwear, 50 per cent in furniture, and 50 per cent in liquor; and it played an important part in cotton conversion, motion pictures, printing, bookbinding and tobacco. But in wearing apparel the share of Jewish capital was preponderant, with 85 per cent in men's clothing, 95 per cent in women's dresses and 95 per cent in furs. In the eighties of the nineteenth century, when Jews did not dominate the apparel industry to the same degree, many of the workers and manufacturers were German Jews, and the new arrivals flocked to it not only because nearly half of them had plied the needle in the Old World, but because they counted on their coreligionists for help and understanding.

4

The demand for ready-made garments, on which the industry is based, had grown considerably since the early decades of the nineteenth century, when it was nonexistent and garments were either made at home or cut to measure and sewn by custom tailors. Even as late as 1880 only some 40 per cent of the clothes worn by men was bought ready-made and a much smaller proportion of those worn by women: the latter persisted much longer in wearing what they made themselves or had made for them by dressmakers. After 1880, however, the needle industry grew fast, New York City becoming the principal producing center of the cheaper grades of men's clothing and Chicago and Rochester of the better grades. In women's apparel the early vogue of cloaks and suits gave place to dresses, shirtwaists, and coats, and in the manufacture of these items New York City, with its famous Garment Center in mid-Manhattan, also became the leader, although the tendency among manufacturers to "escape" to locations where production costs were cheaper had grown. But the needle industry includes the manufacture of many other articles of wear: headgear and neckwear, shirts and pajamas, overalls and work clothes, millinery, underwear and furs. In 1950 women made up some 70 per cent of its labor force.

The industry as a whole, and its women's branch in particular, is bedeviled by continual changes in style, and from the standpoint of the labor force its principal evil is the seasonal nature of the employment: "busy seasons" that make excessive demands on workers are followed by "slack seasons" when they are practically idle. Even in the more stabilized men's clothing industry the workers have little more than thirty weeks of full employment in the year. The industry has suffered also from cutthroat competition. The average manufacturing unit is small, the temptation to venture and "be your own boss" is great, business experience is often scant, business practices unsound, and the mortality rate among the units has been very high. But in the eighties and the two decades that followed, the principal evil was the "contract" system and the foul sweatshops to which it gave rise.

5

During those decades comparatively few of the needle workers obtained employment directly from the manufacturers. The latter found it more profitable to employ cutters only, the most skilled workers in the industry, usually native-born of German or Irish stock, who considered themselves a superior caste, and the cuttings were bundled and delivered to contractors, who made them up into garments in shops of their own. This apparently innocent arrangement between manufacturers and contractors produced an industrial miasma which blighted the lives of untold thousands of the fugitives who had found asylum in the "golden land."

Numerous contractors arose who competed for the bundles, lowering the bids and depending on one thing only for profit: exploiting the workers they employed by lowering wages and raising the hours of work. In the slums of the large cities where the immigrants concentrated—in Chicago, Philadelphia, Boston and especially New York—the contractors multiplied and as a rule used their own wretched living quarters as the shops where the bundles were worked into garments. The sewing machine operators, basters and finishers worked in the "front room," and in the kitchen the irons were heated on the stove and the pressers performed their backbreaking labor. At the same time the crowded and fetid tenement continued as the home of the contractor and his family, and sometimes he even found room for boarders. He was not always the ogre or vampire the poets and socialist spellbinders of the ghettos saw in him; he was himself the victim of economic pressures and the callousness of the public at large, which reacted to the sweatshop evil only when it was revealed as a menace to the public health. The fire which trapped the workers of the Triangle Waist Company of New York in March 1911, taking the lives of 146 of them, brought home to the public the bitter lot of the needle workers generally.

The sanitary conditions in the sweatshops were appalling. The first victims, of course, were the workers themselves, among whom the incidence of tuberculosis and other diseases became exceptionally high. The number of hours they worked was incredible; they often began at four in the morning and continued till ten at night, with wages of men between $6 and $10 a week and those of women between $3 and $5. Workers had often to provide their own sewing machines, and when electric power was installed to pay for it themselves. They were subject to a variety of fines which reduced their miserable earnings, and the ingenious device of the daily task reduced them still more. The "task" called for the completion of a specified number of garments a day, with a fixed wage for the day's work. But the number of garments was constantly increased with the result that six days of labor produced no more than three or four "tasks," and earnings came down in proportion. Workers were often discharged and were always welcome to leave; the contractor had no anxiety about finding others. "Take your hurdy-gurdy and be off!" was the standing invitation to malcontents: the hurdy-gurdy was the sewing machine. Ships were always coming to port with new cargoes of starving "greenhorns." In New York City they swarmed on the "labor exchange" on Essex near Hester Streets, which became known as the *Chazer Mark* or "Pig Market."

Such were the infamous sweatshops in which great numbers of those who came in the last decades of the nineteenth century and in the first of the twentieth were doomed to toil; such the life to which they who flocked to the "golden land" with golden dreams in their hearts were condemned. Nor did this life of toil and exploitation fail to produce its inevitable quota of crime and vice.

The sweatshops persisted well into the twentieth century, and even after they were thought dead they had a startling way of raising their head, especially in times of industrial crisis and depression. They have been called the sweatshop system; Dante's Inferno was also a system.

6

The overthrow of the system was accomplished not by public agencies, indignant clergymen or idealistic settlement workers, helpful as all of them might have been, but by its victims themselves. After more than three decades of trial and error, advance and retreat, they organized themselves into stable and powerful labor unions, which proved strong enough to impose decent standards on the needle industries. And these unions not only achieved better working conditions, shorter hours and higher wages, the goals which all labor unions pursue, but pioneered boldly into new methods of maintaining constructive relations between management and workers and into a variety of novel services and benefits for their members. They served as a model and stimulus to the American labor movement as a whole.

At its inception, however, and for many years afterwards there was at least one outstanding difference between the labor movement among the Jewish immigrants from Eastern Europe and the American labor movement under the leadership of men like Samuel Gompers. What labor should insist upon, Gompers maintained, was its right to a larger share of the national income; it should, of course, "reward its friends and punish its enemies," but avoid committing itself to any political party or social philosophy. The Jewish labor movement followed a different course. From its start in the eighties and on into the first decades of the new century its leaders were ardent advocates of radical social programs and universal panaceas. The labor movement as an instrument for hastening the redemption of mankind was at least as important to them as its function in securing an immediate improvement in the lot of the workers. Along with the rest of the faith of their fathers they rejected the belief in a Messiah; nevertheless they were ruled by a genuine messianic passion. Nothing less than total and universal salvation at the earliest possible moment would satisfy them.

Despite their doctrinaire approach, however, these socialist zealots, with a strong admixture of philosophical anarchists among them, performed an important service by preaching the gospel of unionism. The sweatshop toilers of those decades were not ideal pupils: they became quickly enthused and just as quickly apathetic. When a strike was called they flocked to join the union, and continued the struggle with grim determination, often at the cost of great privation and suffering. But when the strike was over, and whether it was won or lost, the ranks of the union became depleted, the leaders were left without followers. Outsiders ascribed this sporadic attachment and detachment to the "volatile" Jewish temperament; it was due rather to the hope which these former independent artisans and traders nourished that their status as "wage slaves" was only temporary, that soon they would rise to a higher social level. They lacked "class consciousness," but their radical mentors persisted, and by word of mouth and in writing, kept alive the goal of strong and disciplined labor unions.

At least as much of their energy, however, was claimed by the sharp ideological dissensions that developed among them. Daniel De Leon, born of Sephardic parents in Curaçao, was the leader of the extreme Socialist Labor Party, which stood for an American labor movement based on revolutionary industrial unions. In 1895 he organized the Socialist Trade and Labor Alliance to replace the once powerful but already moribund Knights of Labor, as well as the conservative craft unions of the American Federation of Labor. The Federation, organized nine years earlier, was led by Samuel Gompers who, except for one year, served as its president until his death in 1924. This diminutive Jewish immigrant from London, who began his career in America as a cigar maker in a New York tenement when he was thirteen years old, became the giant of the American labor movement.

In 1897, two years after De Leon launched his Alliance, the right wing of his party seceded, and in 1901 formed the Socialist Party, which became the guardian and mentor of the Jewish labor movement. The revolt against De Leon was led by the twenty-six-year-old Morris Hillquit who, until his death in 1933 was one of the dominant figures in American Socialism, but in the Jewish labor movement the greatest personal influence was exerted by Abraham Cahan, gifted journalist, novelist and leader who, from 1902 until his death fifty years later, was editor in chief of the *Jewish Daily Forward.* Abe Cahan, as he was affectionately called, was not only an ardent champion of labor but a resourceful editor; he knew how to build up a huge circulation for his paper, though he was sometimes accused of stooping to yellow journalism.

7

The Jewish labor movement was not, of course, confined to the needle crafts. The United Hebrew Trades, which came into existence as early as 1888 to promote unionism among the Jewish immigrants in New York City and its environs, numbered among its affiliates not only organizations of needle workers, but of bakers, butchers, waiters, printers, teamsters, musicians, actors and others. But the two giant unions which the movement created were both in the apparel industry, one of them, the International Ladies Garment Workers Union, in the women's branch of it, the other, the Amalgamated Clothing Workers of America, in the men's branch. The struggles by which the sweatshop system was ended and decent wages and working conditions were won, not only for hundreds of thousands of Jewish workers, but for even larger numbers who belonged to other ethnic groups, are associated in the main with those two bodies. By the middle of the twentieth century, and even earlier, most of their members were non-Jews, but their largest single ethnic group was still Jewish, and their leadership was almost wholly Jewish.

By 1950 the International, launched in 1900 with 2,000 members, had some 400,000 on its rolls. The union began in the sweatshop era, when men and women worked sixteen and seventeen hours a day, and it brought the workweek down to thirty-two and a half hours, with impressive increases in wages. Its central organization was that of an industrial union, with its component craft unions in the various branches and localities of the industry under the control of bodies called joint boards, under whose leadership the workers bargained with employers and waged their strikes.

An outstanding episode in the history of the International was the general strike of the waist- and dressmakers, the great majority of them young girls, which took place in New York in 1909. This "Uprising of the Twenty Thousand" stirred the entire community, calling attention to the abuses from which all the needle workers suffered. But the struggle that marked the turning point in the career of the International was the strike in New York of 60,000 cloak makers which began in July 1910. The "Great Revolt" is the name by which this crucial strike is known in the history of the Jewish labor movement. It lasted two months, inflicted cruel suffering on the workers and severe losses on the manufacturers, and was concluded by a famous agreement known as the Protocol of Peace, of which a Boston lawyer named Louis Dembitz Brandeis, who had already achieved a national reputation for commanding ability combined with social vision, was the chief architect. The demand of the union had been for the "closed shop," against which the Employers Association was immovably opposed. Brandeis proposed the "preferential shop," which the union leaders finally accepted. The Protocol set up a permanent Board of Arbitration to deal with important issues, a Committee on Grievances for minor disputes and a Joint Board of Sanitary Control. In the years that followed, the Protocol was the cause of serious internal conflict, but it held firm and served as a model for similar agreements in other branches of the industry and in other industries as well.

The other giant union in the needle trades, the Amalgamated Clothing Workers of America, was launched in 1914 as the result of a split with the conservative United Garment Workers of America, organized nearly a quarter-century earlier. Numerous strikes had afflicted the men's clothing industry in New York, Chicago and other centers, the strike in Chicago in 1910 resulting in an agreement for collective bargaining with the firm of Hart, Schaffner and Marx, which proved to be an important stabilizing influence. The industrial upsurge during the First World War enabled the Amalgamated to launch a successful drive on the sweatshops and reduce the workweek to forty-eight hours and then to forty-four; by the middle of the century the prevailing workweek was forty hours. For a decade after the war the union fought off a series of lockouts by employers aimed at undermining its power, and by 1930 it had become firmly established in New York, Chicago, Philadelphia, Boston, Rochester, Cincinnati and other manufacturing centers.

During the twenties, when Communism rode high under the inspiration of Moscow, both unions, and especially the International, were bedeviled by Communist attempts to seize the leadership of their different units and joint boards by the technique of "boring from within," or by establishing rival unions. The entire labor movement of the country, in fact, was the target of these attempts, to which, among the important Jewish unions, only the International Fur and Leather Workers Union succumbed. In the following decade a new conflict arose which tore the entire American labor movement apart: the issue of industrial unionism versus craft unionism, the former represented by the Committee for Industrial Organization created in 1935, the latter by the American Federation of Labor. The same year the International threw in its lot with the Committee, which in 1938 changed its name to Congress of Industrial Organizations (CIO), but returned in 1940 to the Federation. The Amalgamated, which had only been admitted to the Federation in 1933, joined the CIO from its start and stayed in it.

In the matter of strikes and internal conflicts, the two leading Jewish labor bodies and their many little brothers in the "ghettos" of the great cities, were not different from other American labor unions and, especially in periods of depression when strikes were longer and more bitter, there were times when hoodlums were employed by both sides in the contests. But the Jewish unions became trail blazers for the labor movement as a whole in two important fields: auxiliary services to their members, and the introduction of new constructive relations with employers. The Amalgamated launched a solid educational program with courses in labor unionism and related subjects. It built cooperative apartment houses and low rental housing, and it instituted unemployment insurance before the Federal Government entered the field. It established a bank in New York and another in Chicago to promote its projects and serve the special needs of its members. It maintained health centers in New York and Philadelphia and a pension system for superannuated members. The educational program of the International was even more elaborate, embracing recreational activities, a labor theater, and a large vacation resort with moderate rates for union members. Its Health Center provided medical and dental services to its members at reduced cost. Both bodies contributed large sums to labor and to general relief and emergency funds.

But even more striking have been the innovations these unions introduced in their relations with employers. They have not only made the greatest progress in collective bargaining and the maintenance of machinery for adjusting differences, with permanent arbitration boards under full time impartial chairmen, they have also done the wholly unexpected by "invading" the business operations of manufacturers to promote their efficiency and stability. They were the only labor bodies in America that welcomed the advent of scientific management, sometimes called "the second industrial revolution," and the International even set up a management engineering department of its own. They were no doubt driven to this course in order to make their agreements with employers mean something; the excessive competition that plagued the industry and the bungling practices of many of its units jeopardized not only the manufacturers, but the jobs on which the workers depended. But the irony of this course was only too apparent: these unions, whose pioneers had been inspired by the vision of a socialist commonwealth, were helping to stabilize capitalist enterprise! The leaders who pursued this policy were a far cry from the rigid doctrinaires of the first few decades of mass immigration from Eastern Europe. It is commonly agreed, in fact, that the Jewish labor movement has been remarkably fortunate in the caliber of its leadership, more so, indeed, than the labor movement in general. Nearly all the leaders, it should be noted, began by plying the needle themselves. In the early period one of its most popular figures was the eloquent Joseph Barondess, organizer and strike leader, who devoted his later years to Zionism and civic affairs. The forceful and persuasive Rose Schneiderman, the foremost woman labor leader in America, began her notable career with membership in the United Cloth Hats and Cap Makers' Union. Benjamin Schlesinger, at different times president of the International, stood out as a skilful organizer and negotiator. In the United Hatters, Cap and Millinery Workers International Union Max Zaritsky rose to be president in 1919 and proved a dynamic leader.

Joseph Schlossberg was secretary-treasurer of the Amalgamated from its start in 1914 until his retirement in 1940; he was a prominent editor and journalist as well, and a member of the Board of Higher Education of the City of New York. Schlossberg was succeeded by

Jacob S. Potofsky, also active in civic and philanthropic affairs, who was chosen president of the Amalgamated on the death of Sidney Hillman. Abraham Shiplacoff, whose personal qualities won him wide popularity, was the first Socialist to be elected to the Assembly of New York State; he led strikes, served in a number of unions and was secretary of the United Hebrew Trades. Max Pine was also secretary of that body and played an important part in organizing relief for Jews in Europe during and after the First World War. Baruch Charney Vladeck, who died in New York in 1938 at the age of 52, possessed unusual versatility and brilliance. He left his mark not only on the labor movement, but on the civic affairs of New York City, especially in public housing.

But the two most distinguished leaders of Jewish labor were Sidney Hillman and David Dubinsky. The first was president of the Amalgamated from 1915 to his death in 1946. He initiated most of its auxiliary projects, including banking and cooperative housing, was one of the founders of the CIO, and achieved national prominence as director of the labor section of the War Production Board in the administration of Franklin Roosevelt and as one of his principal advisers. Through the CIO Political Action Committee, which he headed, Hillman became an important factor in national politics. Dubinsky began his career in America in 1911 at the age of nineteen as a cloak cutter; twenty-one years later he was president of the International, and the Union thrived under his keen and resourceful leadership. He too became a force in politics as a founder of the American Labor Party in New York, and in 1944, when the party fell under Communist influence, he took a leading part in launching the Liberal Party.

8

In the argot that punctuated the writings and speeches of the radical theorists of the mass immigration decades, and bewildered most of their readers and listeners, the peculiar word "proletarization" had an honored place. It was, in a real sense, a Jewish word because it had in view primarily the large number of rootless Jewish workers, the *luftmenschen*, or "up-in-the-air people," as the social philosopher and Zionist leader Max Nordau designated them. They were not firmly attached to a specific handicraft, and were difficult to mobilize for the labor movement, their thinking and ambitions being controlled by "bourgeois" standards. The great need, therefore, was to "proletarize" them, that is to transform them into proper proletarians, economically and psychologically. The socialists who were also Zionists pointed triumphantly to the Jewish workers in Palestine who had become authentic proletarians, and some of them even contended that only in that land could this happy consummation take place, a claim which was, of course, stoutly denied by their "cosmopolitan" opponents.

With regard to the Jewish workers in America, it must be set down that this hope of "proletarization" proved an illusion. It failed conspicuously with the immigrants who came before the abortive Russian Revolution of 1905, among whom the proportion of craftsmen was relatively small and the proportion of socialist zealots still smaller; the workers of that period made up the elusive membership of what may be called the "hit-and-run" unions, which grew like Jonah's gourd in time of a strike and went dry like "the streams of the south" when the strike was over. They were not "class-conscious," sought the first opportunity to become contractors or "bosses," became custom peddlers or candy-store keepers, and they certainly had no wish to see their children go into the sweatshops. But the process of "proletarization" was in the end equally unsuccessful with the more promising material that made up the even larger influx after the Revolution and pogroms of 1905 and 1906. The new arrivals, it is true, included a larger proportion of skilled craftsmen, and those who came from Russia had had a solid apprenticeship in "class consciousness" and labor unionism. Many of them had been conditioned by participation in the Russian revolutionary movement, or in the Jewish sector of it, the *Bund*.

The *Bund*, moreover, followed them to America, trying hard to preserve their socialist ardor and protecting them fiercely against capture by the communists. It was they who in 1912 organized the Jewish Socialist Federation as the Jewish section of the Socialist Party, and mobilized electoral support for the candidates of that party in the days before Franklin Roosevelt's New Deal stole its thunder and raison d'être. In 1914 the party elected Meyer London to the House of Representatives as the second Socialist Congressman, the first having been Victor Berger of Milwaukee, a Jewish immigrant from Austria, who was elected in 1910. In 1917 it scored an impressive vote for Morris Hillquit when he ran for mayor of New York on a platform opposing entry of the United States into the First World War.

As early as 1900 the socialist guardians of the Jewish labor movement had adopted another means for maintaining their tutelage over it. They created the *Arbeiter Ring*, or Workmen's Circle which, in addition to providing the benefits of a fraternal order, conducted a program of educational, social and recreation activities for its members and a network of Yiddish afternoon schools for their children, all of it, of course, in a spirit of socialist idealism. Yiddish, to which its members were deeply attached, represented the cultural atmosphere in which the program operated. In later decades, however, a sizable portion of the Circle's membership could no longer be classified as wage earners, and to recruit new members it had to form "English-speaking" branches, whose members lacked the socialist élan of their predecessors. By the middle of the century 10,000 of the 70,000 members claimed by the Circle belonged to those branches, and their ratio to the total continued to grow.

So the immigrants of both streams disappointed the expectations and—what was even more provoking—the theories of their radical leaders. They were quickened by the spirit that animated the entire country, where economic classes were not fixed but fluid, and every Cinderella could dream of her prince. They discovered that America was a land of opportunity after all, if not for themselves then for their children. Steadily the Jews yielded their preponderance in the needle trades to other ethnic groups, and if until the First World War they still made up more than 50 per cent of the membership of the Amalgamated and the International, it was not because there were no departures from its ranks, but because the "deserters" were being constantly replaced by new arrivals from the Old World. By 1923 their Jewish membership had dropped to 41 per cent, and that despite the fact that Jewish immigration since the end of the war was breaking all records. In the decade that followed, when the immigration law of 1924 was in force, the drop was more precipitate, and by the mid-century, when the two unions, approximately equal in size, had a total membership of 775,000, not more than 215,000, or less then 28 per cent, were estimated to be Jewish. Their places were being taken by Italians, Poles, Negroes, Puerto Ricans, and other ethnic groups. And along with their departure from the ranks of wageworkers, the political allegiance of the great majority of them went to one or the other of the two major political parties.

9

The basic occupational shifts in the past half-century among the Jews of America are obvious enough to all observers and they have been confirmed by statistical studies made in New York City, where in 1953 some 40 per cent of the Jews in America were believed to be concentrated, and in a number of smaller Jewish communities, like those in Buffalo, Detroit, Baltimore and Trenton. As compared to the foreign-born, a substantially smaller proportion of native-born Jews were found to be engaged in trade, manufacturing, and especially the handicrafts, and a much larger proportion in clerking, salesmanship and the professions. The ardent wish of the immigrant parent was to see his children follow a less toilsome occupation than he did and reach a higher rung on the social ladder, and spurred by a reverence for learning which is imbedded in his heritage, his highest ambition was to see them successful members of one of the learned professions. It is not surprising, therefore, that in 1954, when the Jews in America were about 3 per cent of the population, Jewish students in American colleges were estimated at 7 per cent of the total enrollment, and in the postgraduate professional schools the proportion was believed to be considerably higher.

The occupational structure of American Jewry has been subjected to the hostile scrutiny of anti-Semites, as well as to the anxious analysis of Jewish economists. The first, of course, found what they looked for: that the economy of the country was held in pawn by the Jews who occupied its most lucrative and strategic positions, with their "international bankers" controlling the destiny of all Christendom. The phantoms they conjured up were not without effect even on certain Jews, who offered their coreligionists a variety of advice: that more of them should go into agriculture and the handicrafts, shun the commercial and professional callings, curtail their participation in government service and forgo positions of conspicuous honor and public trust. The advice, well-meant of course, reflected the hope that, if followed, it would make the Jews less "visible." Others held that attempts to mollify the anti-Semite by changing the pattern of Jewish life were doomed to failure; he was sure to build up whatever image of the Jew served his purpose, and in the absence of facts he would resort to fancy.

But some Jewish economists, poring over the statistical tables, also found cause for concern. The rural population of the country at large was about 12 per cent of the total, but for the Jews, it was less than 2 per cent. About half of them were engaged in commerce and the professions, while in the population at large only about one-fifth were so engaged. But even in those fields too many were to be found in some sectors and too few in others. In manufacturing, for example, the Jews were concentrated in consumer goods, especially in the garment and leather-goods industries, and some regarded the so-called

Jewish economic sectors as the most vulnerable in times of depression. The veteran economist and statistician Jacob Lestschinsky, whose field of study included Jewish life in Europe as well as in America, found the economic health of the Jews in the United States threatened by two developments. One was the "descent" of "Nordic" groups to commercial and other positions which, until the calamitous depression that began in 1929, they were willing to leave to the Jews, and the other the "rise" to the same positions of ethnic groups from Southern and Eastern Europe.

There were other experts, however, whose appraisal of the Jewish economic position and prospects in America were not so gloomy. To expect the Jewish group to constitute a balanced economic unit was, in their view, neither realistic nor necessary. No other ethnic group was in such an "autarchic" position, nor for that matter was any local community in the country, large or small. Moreover, the occupations in which the Jews were highly represented were the very ones which, since 1870, had undergone the most marked expansion for the population at large. In utilizing the special economic bents and skills with which centuries of conditioning had equipped the Jews in the Old World, they found themselves in step with the economic development of America as a whole. It was, of course, natural to deplore the small proportion of Jews in agriculture, but it was not reasonable to expect that at a time when so many from rural America were flocking to the urban centers a sizable movement in the opposite direction could be started among the Jews. Whatever occupational adjustments—in commerce, manufacturing, the professions or other fields—changing conditions might require, the Jews in America, said the optimists, would make in obedience to economic pressure and with the adaptiveness for which they were noted.

10

Nevertheless, even the optimists recognized the threat to the economic welfare of large numbers of American Jews that lay in the practice of anti-Jewish discrimination in employment. The threat became more serious with the decline in opportunities for self-employment as a result of the trend towards big industrial units and the rise of large networks of chain stores, particularly in food, drugs and tobacco. Racial and religious discrimination in employment, of which Jews were not, of course, the only victims, was denounced by liberal groups and individuals as a violation of democratic principles and an obstruction to the economic progress of the country. Some demanded that the practice be banned by law, others maintained that fairness and tolerance could not be legislated into existence, and that only an aroused public opinion could correct the evil.

In 1941 the position of the first was strengthened when President Franklin Roosevelt created the Committee on Fair Employment Practices, which sought to insure the fullest utilization of the country's manpower by preventing discrimination in the execution of government contracts. But in 1946 Congress starved the Committee out of existence, and President Truman's efforts for a permanent Federal Fair Employment Practices Committee (FEPC) were balked in Congress by the Southern Democratic bloc. The opposition was led in the Senate by Theodore G. Bilbo of Mississippi and in the House by John E. Rankin of the same state, both dedicated champions of white supremacy, who established solid reputations as anti-Semites also.

But the principle of enforcing fairness in employment, promoted by a National Council for a Permanent FEPC, gained ground. The prevailing view of its advocates appeared to be that while an alert public opinion was an essential, the legally empowered FEPC could, in most cases without actually using its powers, be an effective instrument for minimizing an evil in the economic life of the country, which violated the rights and threatened the well-being of large segments of the American people.

11

By the mid-century the Jewish immigrants from Eastern Europe and their offspring had made an enormous advance in their economic status. They had wiped out the foul sweatshop system and established labor unions which, in important respects, were serving as pathfinders for the labor movement of the country as a whole. Many had risen from the stage of wage earners to become large or small entrepreneurs and employers of labor. Their children and grandchildren were occupying dignified positions in the commercial, industrial and professional life of the country, besides making notable contributions to its scientific, cultural and artistic progress. They were not, as the anti-Semites saw fit to represent them, crowding the highest rungs of the economic ladder, but the fundamental democracy of America had enabled them to find the level to which their abilities entitled them. And, in the last analysis, they were prosperous because America as a whole was prosperous.

The economic health they enjoyed was, of course, essential to them as individuals; it was essential also for their institutional and communal growth. And, as we shall see, it proved of vast importance to their less fortunate coreligionists in other lands, and especially to those who were making a supreme effort to restore the national life of their people in the ancient homeland.

CHAPTER 12

New Century

1

THE TWENTIETH CENTURY HAD DAWNED ON A PEACEFUL AND hopeful world; the lamentable war between Britain and the Boers in South Africa, which was still being fought in 1900, seemed a remote and minor scuffle, and was hardly sufficient to disturb the prevailing optimism. And in America the turn of the century saw a nation, now numbering 76,000,000, lifted suddenly to the status of a world power by its swift and decisive victory in the war with Spain in 1898.

Hostilities began in April of that year and were practically over in July, when the Americans captured Santiago de Cuba. But the important victories were gained on the seas: on May 1 the Spanish Pacific fleet was destroyed in Manila harbor, and on July 3 the Spanish Atlantic fleet suffered the same fate off Cuba. By the Treaty of Paris, which was signed in December, Cuba, whose sufferings at the hands of her Spanish rulers had been the immediate cause of the war, was freed, Puerto Rico became an American possession, and Spain surrendered the Philippines and the island of Guam in the Pacific. Four centuries had now elapsed since Spain sent Columbus on his momentous voyage and simultaneously drove the Jews from her "sacred" soil, and the far-flung empire she had won and unconscionably exploited was a thing of the past.

Perhaps it was a desire to strike a blow at this ancient persecutor, whose remorseless Inquisition had become the supreme symbol of oppression and bigotry, that motivated many of the Jewish volunteers who enlisted in the fighting forces of America. There were now about a million Jews in the United States, some of whom had had training in the armies of Russia, Austria and Rumania. About 5,000 are estimated to have been under arms, representing a somewhat higher proportion of the Jewish community than the ratio of all men under arms to the population as a whole. Most of the Jewish soldiers and noncommissioned officers were in the units of the State Volunteers, but there were more than a score of Jewish commissioned officers in the regular army—majors, captains and lieutenants—who were graduates of West Point, and several hundred noncommissioned officers. They fought in Cuba, and they fought in the long and stubborn insurrection, led by the overambitious Emilio Aguinaldo, which broke out in the Philippines right after the war and was not put down until April 1902.

Most of the casualties, by far, occurred on land, with a woefully large portion of them caused by disease, and the Jews contributed their full share to the tragic and heroic list. Fifteen Jewish sailors went down with the battleship *Maine* when it was sunk by an explosion in Havana harbor in February 1898, the incident which did most to exasperate the country. And there were at least half a dozen Jews in the most famous regiment that fought in Cuba, the "Rough Riders," who stormed San Juan Hill east of Santiago under Lieutenant Colonel Theodore Roosevelt. Among the many Jewish medical officers was Colonel Joseph H. Heller, who served in the Philippines and was decorated for "gallantry in action against Insurgent forces . . . in attending the wounded under fire."

In the Navy there were also about a score of Jewish officers, graduates of Annapolis. Three of them were destined for distinguished careers. Edward D. Taussig retired in 1909 with the rank of rear admiral after notable service in the Pacific and later as commander of the Navy Yard in Pensacola, Florida. Joseph Strauss, who was a lieutenant during the war, won the rank of rear admiral in the First World War and in 1930 he was appointed admiral on the retired list; in 1921 and 1922 Strauss was commander in chief of the Asiatic Fleet. The third, also a rear admiral when he retired in 1910, was Adolph Marix. Shortly before the *Maine* was blown up, Lieutenant Commander Marix, who was the executive officer of the battleship, was transferred to another vessel, but he had previously served in the office of the advocate general and was recognized as a leading authority on naval and maritime law. When, therefore, a court of inquiry was set up to investigate the sinking, Marix was appointed its secretary and drew up its report, which held Spain responsible for the disaster. Marix returned to active service in the war and was cited for "eminent and conspicuous conduct in battle."

There were many across the land who, for political or idealistic reasons, deplored the new course on which the Republic had embarked, with overseas possessions and commitments, and denounced it as imperialism, and there were idealists in the growing Jewish aggregations in the large cities who echoed these views. But the great majority of Jews in America shared in the glow of victory which the country as a whole experienced, especially since it was the land of the Inquisition and the Great Expulsion that was humbled. Most of them had come with the immigrant flood which started two decades earlier, and were still engaged in an intense struggle to strike economic roots in the new land. But it was a good future they envisioned for themselves and their children; for them too the new century dawned with hope and promise.

2

For the Jews in Europe, however, there was nothing rosy in the dawn of the twentieth century. In Russia, where six millions of them bore the heavy yoke of Nicholas II, who had become czar in 1894, the old restrictions were rigidly enforced and new ones were imposed which added to the congestion and destitution in the closely guarded Pale of Settlement. The quarter million Jews in Rumania were legally still in the status of aliens. The million in Galicia were the target of a relentless economic boycott instigated by the rising Polish middle class, and in addition found themselves caught in the bitter national rivalries between the Poles and Ruthenians.

But even in "civilized" Western Europe, where the Jews had at long last won the arduous struggle for emancipation, a new brand of anti-Semitism, made in Germany and decked out in the trappings of science and metaphysics, had come to plague them. Science now sat enthroned over cultured Europe and anti-Semitism, too, had to be "scientific." The new anti-Semites created a jargon of their own, with solemn phrases like "Kultur" and "blood and soil," which their Nazi successors were to sum up in the sacred word "Aryan." Historians like Heinrich von Treitschke and the renegade Briton, Houston Stewart Chamberlain, joined hands with rabble rousers like the court preacher Adolph Stoecker and scurrilous forgers like August Roehling, just as in the Second World War German philosophers and scientists were to collaborate with the mass murderers in the concentration camps.

From Berlin the poison spread east and west. In Austria it prepared the ground for the demagogue and proto-Nazi Karl Lueger; in 1897 he was chosen mayor of Vienna, and the gay and debonair capital of Francis Joseph's empire became worm-eaten with anti-Semitism. In England it played its part in the long and clamorous agitation that led the drastic Aliens Bill, it being an open secret that "aliens" stood for immigrant Jews. And strangely enough, in France, the cradle of liberty and enlightenment, where Jews were first granted legal equality, the new phobia, promoted by French apostles like Count Joseph Gobineau and Edmond Drumont, set the stage for the momentous Dreyfus Affair, which brought the Third Republic to the brink of civil war and filled Jews the world over with anxiety and dismay.

In 1894 Alfred Dreyfus, a captain of artillery attached to the French general staff, was convicted by a closed court-martial of having divulged military secrets to a foreign power, understood to be Germany, and sentenced to life imprisonment on the pestilential Devil's Island off the coast of French Guiana. Five years of intense and bitter controversy ensued, in which the forces of French liberalism and decency, headed by the novelist Emile Zola, were pitted against the clericals, the army and the monarchists, who hated the Republic and hoped to overthrow it by identifying it with Jews and treason. The first demanded a new trial for Dreyfus, the second opposed it—whether they believed him guilty or not, he and his people were too precious a scapegoat to be surrendered. In the meantime the real traitor, a Major Esterhazy, had fled to England, after the man who had shielded him, caught in the meshes of his own forgeries, committed suicide. So in September 1899 Dreyfus faced a new and open court-martial, and in a trial, which the London *Times* declared to have been "foul with forgeries, lies, contradictions and puerilities," was again found guilty—"with extenuating circumstances." Ten days later he was pardoned by President Emile Loubet, but it was not until July 1906 that the highest tribunal of France annulled the verdict of the second court-martial and declared Dreyfus innocent.

3

Naturally the events of this portentous Affair, covering more than a decade, were followed by Jews the world over with agonized interest. Nor, despite their distance from the scene, did the Jews of America feel immune from its sinister implications. But having no power to influence the judicial processes of a great sister republic, they could only pray for the eventual triumph of justice, and they found a measure of consolation in the sympathy of American public opinion for the victim of the dark conspiracy.

Not that the country was entirely free from anti-Jewish manifestations. There was as yet no widespread and organized hue and cry against the Jews, promoted by professional fomenters of prejudice; a movement of that sort was not to spring up until after the First World War and did not, as we shall see, assume ominous proportions until after the Nazis became the masters of Germany. But the spirit of Know-Nothingism, which abominated all "foreigners," was not dead, and the ancient animosity, which singled out the Jew for special aversion, came now and then to the surface.

In the first decade of the new century both antipathies merged in a mounting clamor against the immigrant "hordes" that were "overrunning" the country and a demand for drastic curbs on immigration—an outcry in which the anti-Jewish motif was clearly audible. While nothing so sensational as General Grant's Order No. 11 occurred in the period between the Civil War and the First World War, there were nevertheless a number of anti-Semitic incidents which stirred not only the Jews, but large sectors of American public opinion as well. In 1877, for example, a candidate for admission to the New York City Bar Association was rejected solely because he was a Jew; in 1891 appeared the charge by a writer in the *North American Review*, the most influential magazine in America, that the Jews had been absent from the armed forces in the Civil War; and in the same decade Goldwin Smith, a prominent British and Canadian historian, published magazine articles in which he hewed close to the line of the "scientific" anti-Semite Houston Stewart Chamberlain and his German and French disciples. But the two incidents during those years which produced the widest repercussions were first. the refusal in 1877 by a fashionable hotel in Saratoga, New York, to admit a prominent Jewish banker as a guest, and second, the false charge made in 1908 by a police commissioner of New York City that a disproportionately large share of New York's criminals were Jews.

Ostracism of Jews by fashionable resorts, clubs and college fraternities was, of course, an ordinary occurrence, but Joseph Seligman was not an ordinary man. He had been perhaps the foremost financier of the North in the Civil War, a friend of Lincoln and an intimate of Grant; the latter, in fact, had offered him the post of Secretary of the Treasury, which he declined. Seligman had also achieved some standing in politics, having served on the distinguished committee which was responsible for the elimination of the notorious Tweed ring from the municipal affairs of New York, and among his coreligionists he was regarded as the leading layman of the community. Now in June 1877 the Grand Union Hotel in Saratoga, managed by the former Tweed politician Henry Hilton as executor of the estate of the New York merchant A. T. Stewart, informed Seligman, who came to register there, that "no Israelite shall be permitted in the future to stop in the hotel." The news "made" the front pages of the New York metropolitan papers and echoed over the country, and the agitation that followed provoked a good deal of latent anti-Semitism into the open. It also provoked not a little indignation and is believed to have been the cause of the decline of A. T. Stewart & Company of New York and the eventual absorption of its retail business by John Wanamaker.

The impoverished Jews who came to America in the three decades after that incident were not interested in fashionable resorts or clubs and fraternities from which their people were excluded. But the teeming quarters they established in the large cities produced their quota of nativist resentment, and the jaundiced eyes of hostile observers magnified the effects of congestion and poverty. In September 1908 *The North American Review* published an article by Theodore A. Bingham, police commissioner of New York City, which contained the startling allegation that while the "alien" Jews of the city, or "Russians" as they were often called, were only 25 per cent of the city's population, they furnished 50 per cent of its criminals. There was excitement and dismay among the Jews as the charge was repeated by the newspapers with extensive and unfavorable comment.

There were, no doubt, Jewish homes where the swift and radical change of social and spiritual milieu, accompanied by the hardships and temptations which a keen struggle for existence always engenders, had undermined some of the ancient Jewish virtues. To a large extent the evil flowed from the unavoidable difference in tempo in the process of Americanization as between parents and children, giving rise to an attitude of deprecation in many of the young towards their elders, and aggravating the tension between the new generation and the old which, for that matter, seems to be the lot of humanity at all times and in all places. It was true that Jewish names were appearing in the rosters of crime, including even crimes of violence, in which such names had been singularly rare. Nevertheless the police official's charge was a flagrant falsehood, and when the newly formed American Jewish Committee confronted him with certain data in its possession he admitted he had no facts or statistics to support it. In its issue of November 1908 *The North American Review* published his complete and unqualified retraction, and the injury he inflicted was, to an extent, repaired. But to an extent only, for a denial and even a retraction, as is well known, fails to catch up with a slander.

Apparently the commissioner fell victim to the same distortion of vision which made the framers of General Grant's Order No. 11 see a smuggler in every Jew. The record revealed that of the 175,370 persons who were arraigned before New York City police magistrates in 1908, only 12,192, or about 7 per cent, were "Russians." And there can be no doubt that a considerable proportion of the "crimes" for which the "Russians" were arraigned were infractions of city ordinances with regard to peddling, picketing or Sunday observance—offenses which do not involve moral turpitude.

4

As late as the middle of the new century the stringent Sunday laws, which were still on the statute books of most of the States—laws which prohibited trade on Sunday as well as manual labor—led to numerous arrests of Jews in the larger cities of the country, who observed their own Sabbath and were seriously handicapped by being forced to remain idle on Sundays also. The Jewish Sabbath Alliance of America, launched in 1905 by Bernard Drachman, a distinguished Orthodox rabbi and scholar, to promote the traditional observance of the Sabbath, found itself compelled to devote a considerable portion of its resources to the legal defense of these transgressors of the "blue laws" which, it should be noted, were unpopular with a great many non-Jews also.

For the rest, the available statistical data reveal that the incidence of crime among the Jews in America has been strikingly low. In New York State, for example, where in 1941 Jews were estimated to constitute 17 per cent of the population, the proportion of Jews committed to penitentiaries and reformatories between 1930 and that year averaged 8.4 per cent of the total. For the country at large the same ratio prevailed: in the penal institutions the Jews had half the number of inmates to which they were "entitled" by their ratio to the general population. And this finding gained additional significance in light of the fact that while 90 per cent of the Jews in America were concentrated in cities with populations of 100,000 and over, only 30 per cent of the general population lived in such centers, for the incidence of crime is proportionately greater in cities than in small towns and rural districts.

Especially marked has been the decline of delinquency among Jewish children. Between 1909 and 1916 Jewish juvenile delinquents in New York City made up 22.6 per cent of the total; in 1941, when Jews formed 25 per cent of the city's population, they furnished only 7 per cent of such delinquents. In other places—Ohio, for example—the statistics revealed an even smaller ratio. The ratio of recidivism among Jewish children was also much lower: a large proportion of them were guilty not of housebreaking, assault or vandalism, but of peddling or begging. And this decline in juvenile delinquency was no doubt to a large degree a reflection of the growing cultural rapprochement between parents and children.

5

But the Jews in America, unlike their coreligionists in Germany and other lands of the Old World, found champions against their traducers in some of the foremost leaders of American thought and action. Among them were prominent clergymen like Henry Ward Beecher and Charles Henry Parkhurst, the philosopher Josiah Royce, the eminent scientist Nathaniel S. Shaler, the celebrated agnostic Robert Ingersoll, and literary notables like George William Curtis, Oliver Wendell Holmes and Mark Twain. American writers, in fact, have been singularly untainted by anti-Semitism, the only important exceptions being the eccentric and unintelligible poet Edward E. Cummings and the novelist Thomas Wolfe. Two other American poets whom the virus did not spare found it congenial to change their habitats: Ezra Pound preferred fascist Italy and Thomas S. Eliot chose England where he could number among his fellow-citizens such anti-Semitic colleagues as Hilaire Belloc and Gilbert K. Chesterton.

In the public life of America there were even more defenders of the Jews against their detractors. In 1892, for example, Zebulon B. Vance, the distinguished Southern statesman and Senator from North Carolina, who was one of the country's leading orators, delivered a notable address in their defense, which was widely circulated under the title *The Scattered Nation.* And shortly before the turn of the century a dramatic incident occurred in New York, which attracted nation-wide attention. From Germany in 1895 had come Pastor Hermann Ahlwardt, the successor of Adolph Stoecker as the arch anti-Semite of the Fatherland, to preach his gospel to the people of America. He launched his mission with a large public meeting in New York, and asked for special police protection in view of the possibility of hostile demonstrations by the Jews of the city. The police commissioner granted the request, and to guard Ahlwardt and his meeting he assigned policemen who were all Jews! The commissioner's name was Theodore Roosevelt.

Ahlwardt's mission was an eminent failure. But the Old World apostles of his creed, who were resolved to achieve its universal acceptance, never lost sight of the great Republic of the West, and a generation later their emissaries were destined to be more successful.

6

Three years before the advent of the new century, the daring enterprise known as political Zionism had been launched, and in the next half century it was to be a controversial issue in every Jewish aggregation and ultimately to demand a major decision from the nations of the world. In the affairs of American Jewry the issue, in the early decades of the century, grew to overshadowing proportions, giving rise to division and strife which, however, as the hour of decision approached, gave place, as we shall see, to an accord of sentiment and action such as the community had rarely evinced.

How did this unexampled movement, so obvious and inevitable to its adherents, so fantastic to its opponents, begin? On January 5, 1895, when the official degradation of Alfred Dreyfus took place in Paris before his fellow officers and 5,000 troops drawn up in stiff array, one of those who witnessed the imposing and appalling ceremony was a Jewish journalist from Vienna named Theodor Herzl. He heard the spectators give vent to their patriotic fervor with cries of "Death to the traitor! Death to the Jews!" and Herzl, who had become convinced that Dreyfus was innocent, was profoundly shocked by the spectacle. He had learned to know, moreover, how hopelessly infected the nations of Europe had become with the virus of anti-Semitism. So before many months he wrote and published a small book entitled *Der Judenstaat* (The Jewish State), in which he proposed what he thought was a new solution to the Jewish problem, the establishment of a Jewish state. And that, according to some accounts, was the way it all began.

But that was not the way it all began. The ingathering and national redemption of the scattered people—their restoration to the land of their ancient glory—was a hope that required no modern prophet to proclaim. It had been born the day when the Jewish commonwealth in Palestine was destroyed by the Romans in the year 70 and had never been abandoned in the more than eighteen centuries of dispersal and affliction. It had become the constant refrain of their prayers and the theme around which gathered a web of mystic fancies, associated with the advent of the Messianic age and the redemption of all mankind.

During those somber centuries, moreover, the hope had not confined itself to dreams and longings. From time to time individuals and groups had braved the hazards of the journey and the perils that awaited them in the ancient and ruined land, and gone there to live, or to die and be laid in its sacred earth. And we have already seen that a decade and a half before Herzl had his illumination, a movement was under way among the Jews in Eastern Europe calling itself Love of Zion, and although its immediate aim was to plant farm settlements in Palestine, it was impelled by the dynamics of the ancient hope of national restoration. Theodor Herzl had no knowledge of Leon Pinsker's *Auto-Emancipation*, in which the Odessa physician had declared the only remedy for his people's plight to be "the creation of a Jewish nationality . . . living on its own soil;" he did not read it until shortly after the appearance of his *Judenstaat*. "It was better," he recorded in his *Diaries*, "that I was unacquainted with it. I might perhaps have dropped what I was doing."

It appears, moreover, that Herzl, who had had little contact with actual Jewish life and none with that of Eastern Europe, was equally unaware of what this Love of Zion movement had already accomplished in Palestine and in Jewish communities across the world. In Palestine it had spurred and aided the establishment of some fifteen farm settlements, among them Rishon Lezion (First in Zion), Ekron, Ness Ziona, and Gederah in Judea, Zichron Yaakov in Samaria, Rosh Pinah in Upper Galilee, and Yesod Hamaalah in the far north near Lake Huleh. It had propelled the First Aliyah,* or immigration wave, into Palestine, estimated at about 25,000. Its network of societies had gathered a fairly large number of enthusiasts in Eastern Europe, and it had its outposts in Central and Western Europe and, as we shall see, in America. It had given birth to the dedicated BILU fraternity in Russia, and brought to the fore a number of commanding personalities, who were to play a leading role in the larger movement that followed and in the growth of the Jewish establishment in Palestine.

It is certain, therefore, that neither as an aspiration nor as a practical project operating with men, money, and machinery can the publication of Herzl's summons in 1896 be regarded as the beginning of the Zionist movement. Nevertheless that summons was supremely important; it had an electrifying effect on the further growth and fortunes of the effort, giving it a world arena and making it a world issue. The Love of Zion movement had sunk into the doldrums. The farm settlements in Palestine were not prospering and were only saved from failure by the princely patronage of Baron Edmond de Rothschild of Paris, a great-hearted philanthropist who was also a great lover of Zion. Those colonies, moreover, had no legal security; they were at the mercy of the whims and cupidity of a corrupt Turkish officialdom. In Odessa, where the headquarters of the movement was located, the

* The Hebrew word *Aliyah* (plural, *Aliyot*) means "a going up."

leadership was not only staggering under heavy financial burdens, but was torn with dissensions. It had all the appearance of a small-scale philanthropic enterprise, without power to stir the imagination or to command the moral and material resources required by the great goal and great need. Now from the glittering and emancipated West there sounded a call of extraordinary sweep and authority. The establishment of a Jewish state should be placed on the agenda of the nations. It should rest securely on an open charter of guaranteed rights. It should proceed with the tempo of mass colonization, operating not with mites but with millions. It should stand before the world as a deed of long due indemnification and an act of international statesmanship.

And who was this prophet or Messiah from whom came this bold summons? Nothing was known about him in the East and little enough in the West. He was the Paris correspondent of a Vienna newspaper, a maker of sparkling feuilletons, a writer of more or less successful dramas. But by the time the new century arrived three international Zionist Congresses had been held, all of them dominated by this newcomer, and he was not only known in every nook and corner of the Jewish world, but had already become something of a legend. His appearance was regal, his gifts of mind and character drew men like a magnet.

Not that he and his cause were hailed with universal approbation. Such, indeed, was far from being the case. From the very start he stood up to a staggering flood of opposition, mingled with that most corrosive form of it: ridicule. It came from the emancipated Jews of the West, who feared that the agitation for a Jewish state would bring their patriotism into question and undermine their new won equality. It came from the leaders of Reform Judaism, who saw the proposed ingathering of the Jewish people and its political reestablishment as a challenge to their doctrine that the dispersion was divinely ordained to be permanent. It came also from Orthodox leaders who rejected the notion that the redemption could be accomplished by human effort. It came from philanthropists, including Maurice de Hirsch and Edmond de Rothschild, deeply concerned for the plight of their persecuted people, but convinced that public agitation and political demands would only impede their efforts to help them. And it came even from the leaders of the Love of Zion movement, who looked upon Herzl's political démarches with profound skepticism, fearing they boded ill for their colonization efforts in Palestine.

Nevertheless Zionism kept on growing and Herzl, putting his trust in its hosts of humble followers, both organized and unorganized, was dismayed neither by his opponents nor by the many other obstacles he encountered.

7

Besides Leon Pinsker, there had been other heralds of Zionism, both Jewish and Christian, of whom Herzl had no knowledge when he wrote his *Judenstaat.* In 1876 the great English novelist George Eliot had pleaded the same cause with majestic eloquence in her *Daniel Deronda.* Before her, in 1862, Moses Hess had published his *Rome and Jerusalem,* a remarkably persuasive and profound plea for the national restoration of his people by an ardent socialist. And in 1825, Mordecai Manuel Noah, as we saw, had performed his grandiose gesture of restoration in distant America.

In the seven decades which followed that gesture, the Jews in America were not indifferent to the weal of their coreligionists in Palestine, but their interest was wholly philanthropic and found expression in efforts, like those promoted by Isaac Leeser and Judah Touro, to assist the many among them who were indigent. During the same decades, however, there proceeded from America three attempts to plant farm colonies in the Holy Land, but strangely enough, they were not made by Jews but Christians. In 1852 Warder Cresson, born fifty-four years earlier of Quaker parents in Philadelphia, sought to establish a colony near Jerusalem as part of a plan "to plant a new Palestine, where the Jewish nation may live by industry, congregate and prosper." But Cresson's attempt should perhaps be called Jewish, for his name was now Michael Boaz Israel, Cresson having become a convert to Judaism. He obtained support from prominent Jews in America and Europe, but his colony proved a failure.

About the same time Clorinda S. Minor, the wife of a rich Philadelphia merchant, led a group of Christian enthusiasts who settled on a tract of land near present-day Tel Aviv, which they named Mount Hope. It was their hope that if they lived the simple agricultural life of the early Christians in the Holy Land, their Savior would come again. For a few years the settlement prospered, but lack of funds, disease and Arab hostility combined against it, and by 1857 Mount Hope was deserted. A similar fate befell the third enterprise. It was launched in 1866 by more than 150 American pilgrims, most of them from Maine, led by a clergyman named Adams. They cherished the same hope as the followers of Mrs. Minor and settled on a tract in the same neighborhood, but disease and Arab forays on their crops compelled them to abandon the project.

8

For the rest of that century no real attempt at colonization in Palestine proceeded from America, and those that came in the new century were made under the stimulus of Zionism. But the cause of Jewish restoration had its apostles during that period in America also, and two of them gained a wide hearing.

One was Emma Lazarus, whom we have already seen leaving her ivory tower of poetry to bring help and cheer to the immigrants of the early eighties. But in those newcomers she saw not only pitiful fugitives, but the descendants of a great and heroic nation, destined not for perpetual asylums and shelters, but for a restored national life. "I am fully persuaded," she wrote in 1883, "that all suggested solutions other than this of the Jewish problem are but temporary palliatives." The same year appeared her *Songs of a Semite*, in which she lashed out at her people's enemies and called for a revival of the spirit of the ancient heroes of Israel. In her song "The Banner of the Jew," which later became a popular Zionist anthem, the martial note is especially striking.

O for Jerusalem's trumpet now
To blow a blast of shattering power,
To wake the sleepers high and low
And rouse them to the urgent hour!
No hand for vengeance—but to save
A million naked swords should wave

In 1891, four years after Emma Lazarus' untimely death, and five years before Herzl's epoch making *Judenstaat* appeared in Vienna, William E. Blackstone, a minister of the gospel from Illinois, sounded the same call in less poetic and more statesmanlike terms. He presented a Memorial to Benjamin Harrison, President of the United States, and James G. Blaine, his Secretary of State, which called upon them to exert their influence with the powers of Europe "to secure the holding, at an early date, of an international conference to consider the condition of the Israelites and their claims to Palestine as their ancient home." Blackstone, who had visited Palestine and seen the plight of the Jews in Europe, acted on behalf of a conference of Christians and Jews held in Chicago earlier that year, but his bold gesture was Christian in inspiration and endorsement. The Memorial bore the signatures of the country's foremost citizens, including the chief executives of the six largest cities, the editors of their principal newspapers, the leading clergymen of all faiths, jurists, educators and industrial magnates. Among the latter were the giants of that age of expansion: J. Pierpont Morgan, John D. Rockefeller, Cyrus W. Field, Russell Sage, William E. Dodge, Philip D. Armour, and others.

Blackstone's Memorial, of course, remained only a gesture: it is not the habit of governments to undertake major actions from motives of abstract justice, or to enter upon controversial courses unless their own interests are involved. But if nothing more, those impressive signatures attested that the American people, as in fact the Christian world as a whole, was still conscious of the historic connection between the Jews and the land of the Bible.

9

By that time the Love of Zion movement had been in progress for more than a decade, and although its appeal to the Jews in America was remote and feeble, it did not leave them untouched. Love of Zion societies, recruited from the more recent immigrants, made their appearance in the eighties in New York, Boston, Philadelphia, Baltimore, and Montreal, Canada. Orthodox rabbis condemned them for trying to force the hand of the Messiah, and radicals for diverting energy from the struggle for the socialist millennium. But the growing Yiddish press generally supported them, and they found some friends among the earlier arrivals also: the prominent rabbis Benjamin Szold, Sabato Morais, Henry Pereira Mendes of the Spanish and Portuguese Synagogue, and Aaron Wise of Rodeph Shalom, the last two in New York, and Aaron Friedenwald, a distinguished physician in Baltimore. The active promoters of the cause were, however, the "Easterners," chief among them the New York physician Joseph Isaac Bluestone. He numbered among his associates the merchant and manufacturer Joseph H. Cohen and the Hebrew and Yiddish lexicographer Alexander Harkavy, whose dictionaries helped thousands of immigrants to learn the language of their new country.

By 1890, members of the society in New York, not satisfied to be only platonic lovers of Zion, formed into a group which they named *Shovei Zion* (Returners to Zion), and some years later two of them went to Palestine and bought land for a settlement which, however, never came into being. But in August 1897 Adam Rosenberg, one of the emissaries, on his way back from Palestine stopped in Basel, Switzerland, where he witnessed the most remarkable gathering of Jews in two millennia.

It was the First Zionist Congress, convoked by Theodor Herzl and a group of associates, which launched the world-wide Zionist movement.

CHAPTER 13

English, Yiddish, Hebrew

1

THREE LANGUAGES—SPANISH, GERMAN AND YIDDISH—accompanied the Jews to the New World, and a fourth, Hebrew, was cherished by all of them, though its use was confined to prayer and scholarship, and a practical mastery of it never extended beyond a fraction of them. Gradually the first two disappeared from their schools and pulpits, where they held out longest, but in neither of them did the Jews of America create significant cultural values before the dominant vernacular submerged them. Not so, however, in the case of Yiddish and Hebrew. In the first quarter of the new century Yiddish was probably spoken and read by a majority of them, and even in the second its strength was far from spent, and a remarkable cultural surge welled up in that language and yielded a rich harvest in a vigorous press, literature and theater. And under the impact of the revival of Hebrew in the ancient homeland, the later decades of the period saw a new burgeoning among the Jews in America of that language also, resulting in a notable contribution to the literature that was being created in the ancient tongue.

It was inevitable that Yiddish should steadily give ground to the dominant idiom, and with immigration from Eastern Europe virtually ended by the edict of 1924, the process was bound to accelerate. Organized attempts to stem or retard it had little effect, the most important effort of the sort being represented by the Yiddish afternoon schools. The Yiddish Scientific Institute (YIVO) also labored valiantly in the field; launched in Vilna in 1925 and at the outbreak of the Second World War centered in New York, YIVO conducted a program that embraced not only Yiddish literature and linguistics, but Jewish history and sociology. Nor were the eloquent exhortations of the Yiddish enthusiasts any more effective.

Inexorably the Jews of America were drawn into the main stream of American cultural life and their contributions to it will be noted in a later chapter.* At the moment our concern is with the fruits of their labors in English, which they produced primarily for themselves.

2

By the end of the second decade of the new century the two most important undertakings of Jewish scholarship in the English language, the Jewish Encyclopedia and a new translation of the Hebrew Scriptures, had been completed. In all lands where they spoke and read a language other than Hebrew the Jews were not satisfied with translations of the Bible offered them by others. In ancient times they made translations of the Bible into Aramaic and the famous one into Greek, known as the Septuagint. Later came the Arabic translation by the illustrious tenth-century sage Saadia Gaon, the German by Moses Mendelssohn and his disciples, the English by Isaac Leeser. For a translation is not just a rendering of one set of words into another; more important is the delivery intact of the ideational structure and authentic spirit of the original. Besides, a goodly number of passages were translated by Christians—and in Jewish opinion, of course, mistranslated—to make them allude to the Nazarene.

Leeser's translation, which appeared in 1854, was widely used, but a new one was felt to be necessary. It was published in 1917, work on it having been started as early as 1892 with Marcus Jastrow, Kaufmann Kohler and Frederick de Sola Mendes, a leading New York rabbi and scholar, as the editors. In 1908 a larger board of editors was formed with Cyrus Adler as chairman and Max E. Margolis, a towering Bible scholar and linguist, as editor in chief. The other members of the new board were also men of first rank in Jewish learning: Kohler, Solomon Schechter, David Philipson, Samuel Schulman and Joseph Jacobs, a man of erudition in many fields. Thus, unlike Leeser's, this translation, which in the matter of style leaned heavily on the matchless King James version, was a collective enterprise and has been generally accepted as the standard Jewish version in English.

A decade earlier the last of the twelve massive volumes of the Jewish Encyclopedia had been published. It was a huge undertaking, the first of its kind in any language to be completed, embracing contributions by more than 600 scholars and specialists. Its projector and chief editor was Isidore Singer, who died in New York City in 1939 at the age of eighty, physically a little man who, among other labors, had been a valiant defender of Dreyfus in Paris and dreamed of establishing the

* Page 327.

ideals of the Hebrew prophets among the nations. His associates were the versatile and ubiquitous Cyrus Adler, Gotthard Deutsch, whom many considered the leading Jewish historian in America, Louis Ginzberg who when he died in 1953 was acknowledged as the ranking Talmudic scholar, Richard Gottheil, an Orientalist and professor of Semitics at Columbia University, Marcus Jastrow and his son Morris, the latter holding the chair of Semitic languages at the University of Pennsylvania, Kaufmann Kohler, Frederick de Sola Mendes, Joseph Jacobs and Crawford H. Toy, a Christian Orientalist of Harvard University.

The aim of this imposing compendium, as defined by the editorial board, was to "cast light upon the successive phases of Judaism, furnish precise information concerning the activities of the Jews in all branches of human endeavor, register their influence upon the manifold development of human intelligence, and describe their mutual relations to surrounding creeds and peoples." It was an aim which the work amply accomplished, but as the decades passed the emendations and amplifications which, like all works of the sort, the Encyclopedia required, were not carried out. In 1941 a new work in the field, the Universal Jewish Encyclopedia, appeared in ten volumes under the general editorship of Isaac Landman, a New York rabbi and leader in the interfaith movement, but it failed to command the authority of its predecessor.

The translation of the Scriptures bore the imprint of the Jewish Publication Society of America, a nonprofit community enterprise, launched in Philadelphia in 1888, the initiative having been taken by Joseph Krauskopf and Solomon Solis-Cohen, a prominent physician who attained distinction as a communal leader and poet also. Hundreds of titles have been published by the Society since its foundation, most of them in history, biography and religion, with a good sprinkling of fiction, especially for children. Some of the other notable volumes bearing its imprint include a series of post-biblical classics and the *American Jewish Year Book*, which began to appear in 1899. Millions of books were distributed by the Society to its members and others, and it earned a high place among the cultural agencies of the Jews in America. A number of commercial book publishers were also specializing in Jewish books, among them the Bloch Publishing Company, Behrman House, Schocken Books, and the Hebrew Publishing Company; and scores of books on Jewish themes were issued by the general trade publishers.

Four years after the founding of the Publication Society, and in response to a call issued by Cyrus Adler, the American Jewish Historical Society was launched "to collect and publish material bearing on the history of the Jews in America." Numerous monographs and studies have been published by it dealing with the Jewish past on both continents of the New World. Among those prominently identified with the Society were Oscar S. Straus, the noted book connoisseur Abraham S. W. Rosenbach, and Max J. Kohler.

3

Books in English by and about American Jews, novels especially, began to multiply in the last decade of the nineteenth century. Their number and quality grew as writers discovered what a rich vein of literary ore the immigrants in the "ghettos" offered, and gifted novelists who were dealing with the general American and human scene, like Fannie Hurst, Ludwig Lewisohn, Waldo Frank, Edna Ferber, Ben Hecht and others, turned to it for material and inspiration. The leading themes in the fictional portrayals of the Jews in America were the trials of the men and women who toiled in the sweatshops and swarmed in the tenements; the qualms and conflicts, especially the conflict between parents and children, which arose as old beliefs and standards were sapped by the new environment; the struggle of social and personal ideals to preserve their integrity, and, in later decades, the strains and heartaches of intermarriage. In nonfiction a type of literature appeared consisting of tributes of admiration and gratitude by the immigrant to the land of freedom and equality, of which *The Promised Land* by Mary Antin was the most popular example.

Prominent among the early novelists were the New York editor and Socialist leader Abraham Cahan and the Cleveland lawyer Ezra Brudno; Cahan's *The Rise of David Levinsky*, which appeared in 1917, won lasting popularity. The starkly realistic stories of Anzia Yezierska attracted considerable attention, and the novels of Samuel Ornitz and Michael Gold stood out for their unrelieved and brutal naturalism. There were writers—the prolific John Cournos, Elias Tobenkin who accompanied the Jews as they expanded westward, Myron Brinig, James Oppenheim, Paul Rosenfeld, Meyer Levin and others—whose work was not without depth and tenderness, and the humor in Jewish middle-class life, which appealed especially to the non-Jew, was dispensed pleasantly by Montague Glass and acridly by Jerome Weidman. Maurice Samuel wrote challenging expositions of the hard lot of his people in soi-disant Christian society, and Ludwig Lewisohn employed his eloquent style to sound a call to his people to return to their own fount in the ancient faith.

4

Periodicals in English also increased and multiplied across the land. In the middle decades of the nineteenth century most of them, as we saw, were published and edited by rabbis in English or German or both. The most distinguished was Isaac Leeser's monthly *The Occident and Jewish Advocate*, but in longevity it was far surpassed by Isaac M. Wise's weekly *The Israelite*, later called *The American Israelite*, which began its career in 1854 and was still being published a hundred years later.

As communities across the land grew and became integrated, scores of weeklies appeared, directed in the main to local affairs, with most of the publishers, if not the editors, now laymen and the language wholly English. Of broader scope was the *Congress Weekly*, published by the American Jewish Congress, and the *Jewish Post*. The weeklies were business ventures, bidding for maximum local circulation and depending for news and articles of wider interest on the Jewish Telegraphic Agency, founded in The Hague in 1917 by Jacob Landau, with Boris Smolar for many years its editor in chief. The Agency was world-wide and disseminated Jewish news to the secular press also.

There were also monthlies and quarterlies of merit, among them *Commentary*, published by the American Jewish Committee; *The Menorah Journal*, established and edited by Henry Hurwitz for the Intercollegiate Menorah Association; *The Jewish Quarterly Review*, published by Dropsie College for Hebrew and Cognate Learning, a post-graduate school of Jewish studies in Philadelphia founded in 1907 with a large bequest left by Moses Aaron Dropsie; and *Jewish Social Studies*, edited by the historian Salo W. Baron and published by the Conference on Jewish Relations, a body of scholars devoted to economic and sociologic research. In addition there were numerous organs of labor unions and other bodies, journals devoted to promoting Zionism, like *The American Zionist*, *The Jewish Frontier*, *The Hadassah Newsletter*, and *The Jewish Outlook*, and others that spoke for the different religious trends: *Liberal Judaism*, *Conservative Judaism*, the Orthodox *Jewish Life* and *The Reconstructionist*, organ of a new movement that sprang from Conservatism.

German was not heard again from the pulpits of synagogues until the victims of Nazi terror began arriving in America, when that language appeared also in journalism and literature. The weekly *Aufbau* (Reconstruction), under the editorship of Manfred George, was an outstanding publication, and among the prominent men of letters whom the ill wind brought to America from Germany and Austria and who continued writing in their new abode, were the novelists Lion Feuchtwanger and Franz Werfel, the essayists Erich Kahler and Alfred Polgar, and the poets Richard Beer-Hoffmann, Ernst Waldinger and Walter Mehring.

5

But the language in which journalism flourished with a range and exuberance unequaled by the press of any other minority group in America was Yiddish. As early as 1872 two ventures in the field, both weeklies and both quickly abandoned, were made in the New World. But two years later Kasriel Sarasohn, the promoter of one of them, tried again; he issued another weekly, *Die Yiddishe Gazetten*, which took root and prospered; and in 1885, when the influx from Eastern Europe was in full swing, he took the bold step of launching a daily. His *Tageblatt*, or *Jewish Daily News*, published of course in New York, is believed to have been the first Yiddish daily in the world. It was Orthodox and Zionist and its social and political views were conservative. Its rival was the socialist *Forward*, but in 1901 another Orthodox daily, *The Morning Journal*, began a career which lasted more than half a century; Jacob Saphirstein, its founder and publisher, and Peter Wiernik, its scholarly editor, disdained the devices of "yellow journalism," and their paper was dignified, sedate and Republican. In 1918 came a fourth daily, *The Day*, founded by Herman Bernstein, a bold and resourceful journalist, who in 1930 moved into diplomacy when President Herbert Hoover appointed him minister to Albania. *The Day* was Zionist without being Orthodox.

Still other dailies appeared and disappeared. Even Canada had enough Yiddish readers to support a daily, *The Canadian Eagle*, published in Montreal. The dailies published in New York made their way over the country, the "province," as it was condescendingly designated, but at different times the larger cities—Philadelphia, Cleveland, Chicago—had their own dailies. The Chicago *Jewish Courier*, for example, under the editorship of Leon Zolotkoff, could hold its own with its New York rivals.

Sometimes new papers were launched as the result of a clash of personalities, as when in 1905 the irrepressible Louis E. Miller established *Die Warheit* to compete with Abe Cahan's *Forward.* Sometimes they followed a party split, as when in 1922 the communist minority among the radicals established its own daily, the *Freiheit.* Throngs of Yiddish readers were constantly arriving, and the power and prestige of publishing or editing a newspaper was a great temptation. In 1925, however, the circulation reservoir began to drop. The first victim was the *Tageblatt*; in 1928, after a career of forty-three years during which it had become a familiar in scores of thousands of Jewish homes across the land, it gave up the struggle and was absorbed by the *Morning Journal*; and in 1953, after a desperate last stand, the *Morning Journal* was merged with *The Day.*

It was clear that only continued immigration could keep the circulation of the dailies at a viable level: most of the children and nearly all the grandchildren of those who spoke and read Yiddish no longer spoke or read it. In 1916, when the circulation of the Yiddish dailies stood at peak, it was well over half a million; by 1952 it had dropped to 37 per cent of that figure. Nevertheless, the persistence of the Yiddish press has proved greater than even the optimists among the prophets predicted.

Yiddish journalism in America was not, of course, confined to dailies. Weeklies and monthlies promoting social and literary movements and even humorous weeklies appeared from time to time, some of them displaying great vitality. The weekly *Freie Arbeiter Stimme* began in 1899 as a champion of anarchism, but in time became an apostle of democratic socialism. *Dos Yiddishe Folk* advocated the Zionist cause, *Der Yiddisher Kempfer* fought the battles of Labor Zionism, *Der Mizrachi Veg* (Way) spoke for religious Zionism. In 1954, after more than sixty years of struggle and a number of lapses, the literary monthly *Die Tzukunft* was still appearing. In the mid-century there were still more than sixty weeklies, monthlies, quarterlies and annuals printed wholly or partly in Yiddish.

The Yiddish press in America reflected the intellectual exuberance of the metropolitan "ghettos" of America. It resounded with the clash of ideologies, and at times the polemics of the opposing champions became raucous, descending to personalities, and adding to the relish the readers found in them. Most of the controversies stemmed from conflicting social panaceas; and with the upsurge of Zionism in the first two decades of the new century the debates between "nationalists" and "cosmopolitans" became loud and bitter. The revival of Hebrew as the vernacular of the Jewish community in Palestine led to an interminable wrangle between "Hebraists" and "Yiddishists," which was not yet silenced a half-century later. It would, in fact, be hard to say if the Yiddish dailies were primarily purveyors of news or forums of discussions; articles dealing with social, political, literary and scientific questions occupied at least as much space as news. And as an instrument of education, the Yiddish press inducted the immigrant masses into a knowledge of the history and institutions of their adopted country in the only language they understood. It taught them the meaning of American democracy and helped them to become naturalized. It did not, as was sometimes charged, retard their Americanization, but actually promoted it.

6

Still another important function was performed by the Yiddish press: it encouraged a flowering of Yiddish literature in the New World that vied in richness with the literature in that language which flourished in its native home in Eastern Europe. The readers of the dailies had a keen appetite for belles-lettres, and scores of poets and storytellers not only served their apprenticeship in their columns, but found them an important outlet for their mature work as well. This was especially true of the poets; and the writers of fiction, to meet the limitations imposed by the medium, developed the short-short story, or "sketch," into a highly flexible genre. The dailies and weeklies took the vocation of literary and dramatic criticism seriously, and held aspiring poets, novelists and playwrights to high artistic standards.

The flowering of Yiddish literature in America cannot, of course, be dissociated from its European fountainhead. In both hemispheres the classic triad: Mendele, Peretz, and Sholem Aleichem, were revered as the great masters. The third, uprooted by the War of 1914, spent the last two years of his life in New York, and was able to focus his brilliant satire on the foibles of his people in the New World. In 1951, the hundredth anniversary of Peretz's birth, a square on the lower East Side of New York, officially named Peretz Square, was dedicated by his devoted admirers. A goodly number of the outstanding figures of Yiddish literature in America, moreover, had begun their careers in the Old World. Nor can Yiddish literature in America or elsewhere be divorced from the movements and fashions in world literature in the nineteenth and twentieth centuries.

The Yiddish literary scene in America was a crowded and kaleidoscopic firmament, peopled with greater and lesser luminaries, but only the commanding figures can be admitted within the precincts of this brief narrative. The outstanding poets were Morris Rosenfeld, Solomon Bloomgarden, better known as Yehoash, Abraham Reisin and H. Leivick, as Leivick Halper chose to call himself. Rosenfeld's themes were varied; they embraced his people's ancient glories and new hopes, the balms of nature and the pangs of love, but his dominant theme was the dreary burden of the toilers in the sweatshops. The note of protest and exhortation pervaded the song of other poets also —David Edelstadt, Morris Winchevsky, Abraham Liessin—but in Rosenfeld it sounded with exceptionally poignant force. Yehoash's poetic canvas was even more varied: he found inspiration in the Bible and Talmud, in folklore and nature, in the eternal questions that challenge the mind and soul of man. His lyricism was tender and strong, his love for his people and its genius boundless: in the last ten years of his life he translated the Bible into Yiddish.

Abraham Reisin made his home in America in 1914 when he was thirty-eight, his reputation as a master of the lyric and short story already established. He was a prolific writer, but all his work had a cameo perfection, distinguished for purity and simplicity. Like Rosenfeld, he became enormously popular; some of his poems were set to music and achieved the status of folk songs. H. Leivick, who in 1912 was exiled to Siberia for life and escaped to America a year later, was distinguished for his depth and mystic élan. The social implications of his poetry are incidental, he was primarily a lyricist who sang with religious fervor. They formed a large and brilliant assemblage, the Yiddish poets in America, and other names clamor for mention: David Einhorn, Joseph Bovshover, Zisha Landau, Mani Leib, I. I. Schwartz, Ephraim Auerbach, Nochum Yud, A. Lutzky, Menahem Boraisha, Kadya Maladowsky, N. B. Minkoff and numerous others.

7

If the poet of the sweatshop was Rosenfeld, the man who depicted it in moving prose was Zalman Libin, master of the short-short story. Thousands of those "sketches" flowed from his prolific pen. He knew the life he portrayed, having spent years of his early manhood at the sewing machine. "My muse," he wrote, "was born in the dreary sweatshop . . . my muse was nurtured in the dark tenement graves."

Another prose artist in the naturalistic tradition was Leon Kobrin. He wrote short stories and full length novels, and most of his themes were derived from the life of his people in the New World "ghettos." Occasionally his fancy reverted to his early life in the land of his birth, one of his most popular works being *Yankel Boile*, the story of a Jewish fisherman in Russia; Yankel is the "natur mentsh," the child of nature, who stands in implied antithesis to the cramped and artificial life of the "ghettos." Other storytellers dealt with the lighter aspects of "ghetto" life, among them Israel Zevin, better known by his pen name Tashrak.

Israel Joshua Singer, author of *Yoshe Kalb*, *The Brothers Ashkenazi*, and other outstanding novels, came to America in 1939 when he was in his early forties. His themes were not drawn from the New World; he dealt with the social and spiritual crises of Jewish life in Poland, but he won wide popularity among Yiddish readers in America. And the Yiddish writer who was best known in the world at large was Sholem Asch. He made his home in the United States in 1914 and won recognition as one of the foremost American novelists, although all his works required translation into English. His late works included portrayals of Bible characters as well as novels of American Jewish life, but he was best known for his series on the central figures in the genesis and theology of Christianity, which, however, alienated many of his Jewish admirers. They accused him of espousing the fundamentalist Christian standpoint and even of playing the role of a missionary.

Zalman Schneur, one of the giants of Yiddish and Hebrew literature, found refuge in America when the Nazis invaded France. For forty years, beginning in 1900 when he was only thirteen, his restless spirit had kept him moving over Europe and Palestine, and he poured out a volcanic flood of poetry and fiction in both languages, which placed him with the few who stood on the summit of the two literatures. But perhaps the most typical Yiddish novelist in America was Joseph Opatoshu. America became his home in 1907 when he was twenty, and he renounced a career in engineering for literature. His works dealt with the life of his people in both worlds and in different epochs. Best known is his trilogy on Jewish life in Poland: *In Poilishe Velder* (In Polish Woods), *1863*, and *Der Roman fun a Vald Maidel* (Romance of a Forest Maid). Jacob Glatstein has also written impressive novels of Jewish life in Poland, and he has a place among the poets and essayists as well. Nor do those mentioned by any means exhaust the list of Yiddish writers of fiction in America.

8

The essay fell below the level attained by poetry and fiction. Its practitioners, in fact, were not primarily literary artists, but preceptors and propagandists, dealing with the questions of the day, and their writings were more in the category of journalism than literature. High among them stood Chaim Zhitlowsky, whose keen analysis of general and Jewish problems from the standpoint of his socialist premises, won him a large following; today, after events have refused to reckon with his assumptions and predictions, his logic sounds strangely unreal and sterile. Abraham Coralnik also won a large following; his style was distinguished for grace and clarity, his approach to Jewish problems was Zionist. Nahum Syrkin and Chaim Greenberg were the most eloquent exponents of labor Zionism, Greenberg writing also on questions of more general import. There was a large coterie of commentators in the columns of the dailies whose writings, trenchant though they were, proved as ephemeral as the issues they dealt with—men like Jacob Fishman, B. Hoffman, Samuel M. Melamed, Abraham Goldberg and Vladimir Jabotinsky, the last two of whom made a more permanent mark in the leadership of the Zionist movement. Unique among the essayists was Samuel Henry Setzer, who arrived in America from Russia in 1912 when he was thirty. Setzer renounced the temporary for the eternal; he wrote on the basic questions of philosophy, religion and morals and found illumination in the Chassidic tradition to which he was heir.

Literary criticism, however, reached a higher artistic plane than the essay. The foremost critic was Samuel Niger. He came to the United States in 1919 after nearly two decades as editor and writer in Poland and Russia. In the acrimonious debates between Yiddishists and Hebraists, Niger strove to justify both mediums, but the weight of his influence was for Yiddish. Among other noted critics were A. Mukdoni, B. Rivkin, for whom Yiddish literature became a quasi-religion; Hillel Rogoff, who succeeded Abraham Cahan as editor in chief of the *Forward*; Aaron Glancz, better known by his pen name A. Laieles, who had standing as essayist and poet also, and Samuel Listchinsky, an engineer who made criticism an avocation and labor of love.

9

At the very start of the mass influx from Eastern Europe the Yiddish theater made its appearance in America, and in the decades that followed it expanded and rose to a high literary and dramaturgic level. Into the drab life of hosts of men and women the operettas of Abraham Goldfadden—*Shulamis, Judah Maccabee, Bar Kochba* and others—brought the glow of romance and heroism, and many of his songs, like *Rozhinkes mit Mandlen* (Raisins and Almonds), attained the popularity and stature of folk songs. This versatile playwright, composer, poet and journalist died in New York in 1908, and by that time the star of Jacob Gordin, who gave the Yiddish theater serious dramas on modern themes, was already in the ascendant. Gordin, who began by adapting the work of outstanding European dramatists, wrote scores of plays of uneven merit, but the best of them, including such plays as *Mirele Efros, Gott, Mentsh un Teivel* and *Kreutzer Sonata*, made up an impressive repertory. The Yiddish theater, not only in New York but in the other large cities, flourished and prospered. Jews and others who were strangers to the language sometimes came in the spirit of the condescending slummer to patronize and be amused by this "exotic growth," and remained to admire.

In the decades that followed a galaxy of new Yiddish dramatists came to the fore. Not that they all adhered to the highest canons of art and good taste. Some of the fare they offered was trashy, and the critics were busy exhorting "the public" to boycott the lurid and vulgar. But the Yiddish theater attracted men of letters who also achieved stature as poets and novelists, and they enriched it with dramatic material of good and sometimes distinguished quality. Among them were Leon Kobrin, Zalman Libin, Sholem Asch and H. Leivick whose powerful poetic drama, *The Golem,* based on the legends of the fabricated automaton of Jewish folklore, was translated into Hebrew and English. Harry Sacher wrote polished fiction in Yiddish, Hebrew and English and excellent plays in the first two languages. Aaron Zeitlin, a distinguished Hebrew and Yiddish poet, novelist and essayist, also wrote plays in Yiddish.

But three writers must be noted—Perez Hirshbein, David Pinski and Ossip Dymov—who were primarily dramatists. Dymov, whose real name was Joseph Perelman, was a successful Russian playwright and novelist before turning to Yiddish when he got to New York in 1914; his best known play was *Bronx Express.* David Pinski, who came to America at the turn of the century, began by making his dramas a vehicle for his social ideals, then turned to Jewish historical themes and characters in dramas like *Sabbatai Zevi, Shlomo Molcho* and *The Eternal Jew.* Some of his plays, including *The Treasure,* were produced on the English stage also. Perez Hirshbein gave the Yiddish stage in

America a group of folk idyls of rare poignancy and beauty: *The Empty Tavern, The Blacksmith's Daughters, Green Fields* and others. An exceptionally deep impression was made in America and in other lands by the weird symbolic folk play *Der Dybbuk* (The Incubus) by Solomon Rapaport, better known by his pen name S. An-sky, and the repertory of the Yiddish theater was further enriched by translations of the great Europeans—Shakespeare, Ibsen, Shaw, Strindberg, Chekhov—and by dramatizations of the works of Peretz and Sholem Aleichem.

10

The Yiddish theater owed its success at least as much to its performers as to its playwrights. Most of the outstanding actors arrived before the turn of the century, and a striking number of them had begun their careers in synagogue choirs. As early as 1881 fifteen-year-old Boris Thomashefsky came with his father, an *Am Olam* idealist, both finding work in a cigarette factory when their dream of life "in the bosom of nature" proved an illusion. Eventually Boris became a colorful actor and excelled in heroic roles; he was also a tireless producer, nor did he, in spite of his dubious literary gifts, refrain from writing and "doctoring" plays. He was followed by others: Sigmund Mogilescu, one of the most delightful comics to appear on any stage, Jacob P. Adler, who remained the lion of the Yiddish stage for decades and headed a family of talented performers that included his wife Sarah, his son Luther and his daughters Stella, Frances, Celia and Julia; David Kessler, also a performer of commanding talent, Maurice Moscovitch, who achieved stardom on the British stage also; Bina Abramowitz and Jennie Moscovitz, both of whom created superb portrayals of the Jewish mother; Kenny Lipzin and Bertha Kalich, tragediennes in the grand and classic manner, and many others.

In the early decades of the new century many more performers of distinction made their appearance, among them the gifted comedian and singer Ludwig Satz; Jacob Ben-Ami, who made his mark on the American stage also; Menashe Skulnik, character actor and talented comic; Muni Weisenfreund, who as Paul Muni became a top-ranking cinema star; Rudolf Schildkraut, who had already played leading roles under Max Reinhardt's direction in Europe; the exuberant Molly Picon, who combined the verve of American vaudeville with the unique quaintness of the Yiddish idiom; and Maurice Schwartz who literally rose from rags—in his early teens he had been a ragpicker's helper in London—to artistic riches as a versatile actor and valiant producer. In 1918 Schwartz assembled a group of distinguished histrions and launched the Yiddish Art Theater, dedicated to the production of plays of outstanding merit only, and for a quarter century he overcame the trials that attend such ventures and achieved a notable degree of success.

But by 1945 the sun of the Yiddish theater had passed its zenith and was declining; as in the case of the press the stemming of the flow from Eastern Europe had shut off the reserves on which it depended. There were hosts of Jewish theatergoers, but they headed not for lower Second Avenue in New York, the Yiddish theater center, but for Broadway. There were many gifted Jewish playwrights, actors, producers and dramaturgists, but their lodestar was Broadway or Hollywood. The writers who watched their army of readers dwindle found crumbs of consolation in the thought that their work would at least endure between the covers of books. But by the middle of the century the once blazing torch of the Yiddish theater was only flickering here and there in sporadic attempts at revival.

11

The literature of the Jews in America spoke in the tongue of the Bible also. In 1916 a group of enthusiasts, most of them educators, founded *The Histadruth Ivrith* (Federation for Hebrew Culture). Five years later it began publishing the weekly *Hadoar* (The Post), which in 1951 celebrated three decades of continuous publication under the editorship of the essayist and critic, Menahem Ribalow. Still other Hebrew periodicals were appearing at the time, among them the monthly *Bitzaron* (Citadel), edited by the Talmudic scholar Chaim Tchernowitz. But those were not the first ventures in Hebrew journalism in America. As early as 1870 a Hebrew weekly had made its appearance and managed to survive for six years, and in the succeeding decades others came and went. The literary monthly *Hatoren* (The Mast), at one time edited by the eminent essayist Reuben Brainin, lasted a dozen years beginning in 1913. An attempt was even made in 1909 to publish a Hebrew daily, but after several months had to be abandoned.

The center of the Hebrew revival lay, of course, in Palestine, but it had its outposts wherever sizable Jewish communities existed, and the contribution made in America to all its branches—poetry, fiction, the essay, scholarship—was impressive both in quantity and quality. There were Hebrew writers in America even before the large influx of the eighties, and in 1892 came the two leading poets of the early period, Menachem Mendel Dolitzki and Naphtali Herz Imber, of whom the second won lasting fame as the author of the official Zionist anthem *Hatikvah* (The Hope). The early decades of the new century saw the rise of a group of young Hebrew lyric and epic poets, who drew their themes from their adopted country also, including the American Negro and the Indian aborigines. Among them were Simon Halkin, Hillel Bavli, Abraham Nahum Silkiner, Israel Efros, Ephraim Lisitzki, Isaac Zilbershlag, Moses Feinstein, and other gifted lyricists and narrators.

In prose fiction the leading Hebrew writers in America were Isaac Dov Berkowitz, Reuben Wallenrod, Johanan Twersky and Samuel Loeb Blank, their themes ranging over many lands and epochs, with Wallenrod perhaps the keenest observer of the American scene. The essayists, critics and scholars were even more numerous. Among the critics were Meyer Waxman, Simon Bernstein, Abraham Epstein, Shalom Spiegel and A. R. Malachi; the essayists included Nissan Touroff, S. D. Maximon, Kalman Whiteman, Zevi Scharfstein, and Daniel Persky; and there were men devoted to historical inquiry like Simon Federbusch and Pinkhos Churgin.

Numerous books in Hebrew, nearly all of them by Orthodox rabbis, continued to appear in line with Old World tradition. They were pious works of homiletics and biblical and Talmudic exegesis, in which the authors displayed new interpretations of the text and new discoveries in the ancient and inexhaustible fount.

12

Most of the subscribers to Hebrew periodicals and readers of Hebrew books were the teachers in the Jewish schools. In the first decades of the new century these men and women made up a dedicated band of zealots, who accepted privation and social subordination to serve the ideal of making the children of the immigrants informed and loyal Jews.

The obstacles they faced were formidable, and Jewish education continued to be an overriding problem. The ubiquitous and efficient public school took possession of the children, providing them with basic knowledge and skills, and inspiring them with devotion to America. All that, of course, was welcomed as good and essential. But these children were not cultural gypsies or upstarts. They were heirs to an ancient and majestic tradition, and were they to grow up strangers to this heritage? In the *shtetl* the environment had been the teacher's ally; in the New World it was in the main an enemy. And parents were too harassed by immediate cares to grapple with a problem whose implications were comparatively remote.

The Old World *cheder* made its appearance in the New World, but the soil was not congenial to it: it failed to win the respect of either parents or pupils. New instruments of Jewish education, better suited to the new environment, had to be devised, and the communal or neighborhood Hebrew school, with classes that met after the public school hours, came into existence. It took the name of Talmud Torah, as the Old World institution where orphans and children of the destitute were educated at the expense of the community, was called. In the New World, however, the Talmud Torah was not free, and the fees for tuition excluded many of the children of the poor. Talmud Torahs, however, multiplied and flourished across the country, giving a more or less adequate Jewish education to hosts of children, the teachers making up in zeal for what they lacked in pedagogic training. The later decades confronted the Talmud Torah with a crisis: the population of the neighborhoods in which they were built at so much pains and cost changed their ethnic character. Many of the schools languished and some had to be abandoned.

By that time, however, the congregational schools had arisen and spread throughout the country. They too were afternoon schools, supplementary to the public schools. They were open to all children, but each of them was attached to a definite synagogue or temple. The congregational unions, which the three religious divisions set up, assumed important responsibilities in meeting their pedagogic and administrative problems, while the three rabbinical seminaries established special schools to train teachers for them. The congregational schools generally began by setting up the same standards as the Talmud Torahs, but gradually they reduced the days and hours of attendance, while a great many contented themselves with Sunday schools only.

This process of attenuation brought anxiety for the future not only to educators but communal leaders, and even more alarm was created by the fact, which studies made in different communities revealed, that only 40 per cent of the children of school age were at any given time enrolled in Jewish schools, although over the eight-year period of elementary school age, some 80 per cent of the children were, at one time or another, receiving Jewish instruction.

In 1922 the Jewish Education Association was organized in New

York City by a group of laymen headed by Bernard Semel and Israel Unterberg, and it wrestled with the problem in that city and its environs, assisting in the erection of new Talmud Torahs, providing tuition for children of the poor, and striving to awaken parents and communal agencies to their responsibility for its solution. In 1939 the Association merged with a newly formed Jewish Education Committee, which commanded more ample means and became the central educational agency for the huge community in New York. Agencies with the same functions, usually named Bureaus of Jewish Education, arose in the larger cities all over the land, and to stimulate the formation of such bodies and promote Jewish educational effort in other directions the American Association for Jewish Education was established in 1940.

13

Three decades earlier a resolute attempt had been made to deal with the intrinsic aspects of the problem—the aims, content, tools and methods of Jewish education—by Samson Benderly. He was a Baltimore physician who left his city and career, and with the support of the newly formed Kehillah of New York, which sought to embrace all segments of the community in an overall communal program, he set up a Bureau of Jewish Education and labored at the task until the Bureau too was absorbed by the New York Committee established in 1939. Benderly was exceptionally persuasive, resourceful and tenacious, but he failed to win the confidence of the entire community. The Orthodox found his basic approach to be secular rather than religious, and the radicals objected to it as Zionist and Hebraist: such were the divisions among the Jews of America as reflected in the vital problem of education. Benderly did, however, achieve one significant result: he inspired a group of young men to make Jewish education their mission and career. It was they—Israel Chipkin, Alexander Dushkin, Emanuel Gamoran, Leo Honor, Albert Schoolman, and others—who manned many of the important posts in the Bureaus over the country. And one of the important gains the Bureaus made was the support they obtained from the numerous local Federations, Welfare Funds, or Community Councils, a recognition by the community as a whole that it shared in the responsibility for the religious education of its young.

In the fourth decade of the century Orthodox leaders introduced a new and bold departure, committed to the principle of a maximum

Jewish education. They established all-day schools where the pupils, boys and girls, were given a thorough Jewish education, as well as instruction in the three r's and the other subjects in the public school curriculum. They called these elementary schools "yeshivahs" or "small yeshivahs," using the name which in the Old World was reserved for Talmudic academies, or institutions of higher Jewish learning. In spite of the heavy financial burdens they imposed on the parents, the new schools took root. To foster their growth the American Mizrachi Organization, the religious wing of the Zionist movement, set up a "Commission for Orthodox Education," and a National Society for Hebrew Day Schools, better known as "Torah Umesorah" (Torah and Tradition), was established in 1944 for the same purpose. The schools grew rapidly, and all over the country. In 1935 there were 17 of them of which only one was not in New York City; in 1953 there were 156, and 89 were outside that city. The enrolment in 1935 was 3,000; in 1953 it was 30,000.

There had, no doubt, been progress in improving and extending the processes of Jewish education, but too many children were still receiving no instruction in their faith and traditions, and too many of those who were, received only a fraction of what was essential to insure their attachment to the faith. Of the children in the United States who were attending Jewish schools of all categories in 1952-53, the number enrolled in the Sunday schools was estimated at 53 per cent of the total, and there was general agreement that the one session of two to three hours a week which these schools provided was woefully insufficient. Basically the problem of inculcating the millennial heritage in the children of the community, upon which depended its continuity and ultimate survival, remained unsolved.

CHAPTER 14

Trends and Leaders

1

By the turn of the century the social configuration of American Jewry, which determined its eventual attitude to the daring project launched by Herzl and his colleagues and to other projects and issues, was rapidly taking shape. Of the million Jews in the United States at the time, some 600,000 are believed to have been part of the influx from Eastern Europe, which was still proceeding with undiminished volume. The others belonged to the two previous strata, with those that hailed from Germany, or their descendants, by far more numerous and influential. Poverty no longer oppressed or haunted them, and many of them had risen to ease and affluence. In every sizable center of the country they were the leaders in Jewish philanthropy and the unchallenged spokesmen of their coreligionists. More and more of them made their appearance, and some made their mark, in the civic and political life of their communities, to the great enhancement of their prestige among their fellow Jews. For what more natural than that the poor and humble newcomers from the lands of oppression should feel a glow of pride when one of their faith rose to a position of public trust and distinction?

The ranking Jew in America at the time was Oscar Solomon Straus, whom President Grover Cleveland appointed in 1887 envoy extraordinary and minister plenipotentiary to Turkey, his selection being intended by Cleveland as an indirect rebuke to the government of Austria-Hungary, which had refused to accept an appointee as United States minister because his wife was Jewish. Straus performed his difficult and trying mission in Constantinople with such success that in 1890, 1897 and 1909, when affairs in Turkey were in a critical state, three succeeding Presidents drafted him for the same post. And it is noteworthy that the ambassadorship to Turkey was later also held by Jews: Henry Morgenthau Sr. who was appointed to the post by

Woodrow Wilson in 1913, and Abram I. Elkus who succeeded Morgenthau in 1916.

In 1902 President Theodore Roosevelt appointed Straus American member of the Permanent Court of Arbitration at The Hague, and four years later Straus became his Secretary of Commerce and Labor, the first Jew to be elevated to a cabinet post, if we except Judah Benjamin, the Secretary of State in the government of the Confederacy. "I want to show Russia and some other countries what we think of the Jews in this country," said Roosevelt to Straus, when he told him why he wanted him in his cabinet. In Jewish affairs Straus played a leading part in educational enterprises and in efforts to protect Jewish rights abroad, in which we shall see American Jewry increasingly concerned.

In 1887 Oscar's two brothers, Nathan and Isidor, had become the owners of R. H. Macy and Company in New York. Isidor Straus held a number of civic, political and philanthropic posts in his city and state, served a term in Congress, and from 1893 to 1912 was president of the Educational Alliance in New York, the best-known Americanization center in the country. In 1912 Isidor and his wife Ida were on the *Titanic* when the liner struck an iceberg and sank; Ida Straus refused the rescue which was offered her, preferring to die with her husband. By 1900 Nathan had already achieved recognition as one of America's foremost philanthropists, his most important contribution being in the field of public health. For more than two decades he waged an unrelenting campaign for the removal of disease germs from milk by pasteurization, a campaign which brought a marked reduction in the death rate among infants and small children. His triumph came in 1914 when New York City made the pasteurization of milk compulsory. In later years his philanthropy centered largely on Palestine.

For sheer magnitude the benefactions of Nathan Straus were surpassed by those of Julius Rosenwald of Chicago. The Negro people of America, especially in the South, in whose education and progress Rosenwald was deeply interested, were probably his principal beneficiaries; in numerous Negro homes his photograph hung beside that of Lincoln. His great wealth came to him from his association with the mail-order merchandising firm of Sears, Roebuck and Company, of which he was president from 1909 to 1925. His benefactions included many Jewish causes at home and abroad, and his views on Jewish issues naturally carried considerable weight.

The roster of eminence at the turn of the century is far from exhausted. Mayer Sulzberger, brilliant jurist and original Hebrew scholar, who in 1895 was elected Judge of the Court of Common Pleas in Philadelphia, was one of the founders of the Jewish Theological Seminary of America. His cousin Cyrus L. Sulzberger, prominent merchant and civic leader in New York, was president of the Industrial Removal Office and the Jewish Agricultural Society. Jacob Henry Schiff had become head of the banking house of Kuhn, Loeb and Company in 1885 when he was only thirty-eight, and by the beginning of the new century had achieved a position as one of the country's leading financiers, philanthropists and patrons of learning. His son-in-law, Felix M. Warburg, emulated Schiff's career in general and Jewish philanthropy, as well as in finance. The versatile Cyrus Adler, who was to perform numerous important tasks as a scholar and communal leader, was a founder of the Jewish Publication Society in 1888 and of the American Jewish Historical Society four years later. In 1900 Louis Marshall, who was destined to play a commanding role in American Jewry, was forty-four, a member of the New York law firm of Guggenheimer, Untermyer and Marshall and one of the country's foremost Constitutional lawyers. The same year Stephen Samuel Wise, who was to clash with Marshall on many issues, was a rabbi in Portland, Oregon; six years later he declined a call to Temple Emanu-El in New York because its president, who was none other than Marshall, insisted that in controversial matters the pulpit must yield to the vestry.

In New York at the turn of the century the three Lehman brothers, Arthur, Irving and Herbert, were still in their twenties and preparing for distinguished careers in the service of their country and the Jewish community. Irving Lehman was to rise to the highest judicial post of his state, and Herbert was to be three times elected its governor and then chosen to represent it in the United States Senate.

2

With the exception of Cyrus Adler, those notables were all identified with the Reform wing of American Jewry. Nourished by the philanthropy of its laymen and the militant vigor of its religious leaders, Reform Judaism continued to prosper. Its temples added stateliness to the architecture of the cities across the country, and its philosophy, worship and educational apparatus moved rapidly towards integration. Isaac M. Wise died in 1900, sated with works, years and honors, and until 1903 the head of the Hebrew Union College in Cincinnati was Joseph Mielziner, whose *Slavery Among the Ancient Hebrews*, it will be recalled, rendered valuable service to the abolitionist cause. He was followed by Kaufmann Kohler, who convoked the famous Rabbinical Conference in Pittsburgh in 1885 and whom Samuel Schulman, himself a leading rabbi and exponent of Reform, called "the most powerful intellectual force in Reform Judaism in America." Kohler, who was president of the college for eighteen years, was a prodigious scholar and combined a critical, even radical, approach to tradition with a devout religious faith. Among his numerous writings his *Jewish Theology Systematically and Historically Considered* has exerted the greatest influence.

There were, of course, other bright stars in the Reform galaxy at the turn of the century. In Chicago Emil Gustav Hirsch, son of Samuel Hirsch, had become rabbi of Sinai Congregation in 1880 and occupied its pulpit until his death forty-three years later. He was a doughty champion of radical reform in the social as well as religious sphere; other Reform rabbis had conducted additional services on Sunday, he was the first actually to change the Jewish Sabbath from the seventh day to the first. In Cincinnati his colleague, David Philipson, was equally distinguished and militant. Philipson, who was chosen president of the Central Conference of American Rabbis in 1907, had been one of the first four graduates of the Hebrew Union College in 1883, and in Philadelphia his fellow graduate, Henry Berkowitz, was rabbi of Rodeph Shalom and planted that century-old congregation firmly in the Reform camp; in 1893 Berkowitz founded the Jewish Chautauqua Society for "the dissemination of knowledge of the Jewish religion." In New York the most prominent Reform rabbi was Joseph Silverman, who occupied the pulpit of Emanu-El from 1903 to 1922; in 1900 he had succeeded Isaac Wise as president of the Central Conference.

In the South the most distinguished figures in the Reform rabbinate were Maximilian Heller of New Orleans, who was president of that body in 1907, and Henry Cohen of Galveston, Texas. For forty years Heller was rabbi of Temple Sinai in New Orleans, and for more than fifty years his colleague in Galveston officiated in Temple B'nai Israel. Henry Cohen, who held numerous civic posts in his city and state, especially in the cause of prison reform, commanded to a remarkable degree the admiration and affection of the entire population; Woodrow Wilson called him "the first citizen of Texas."

Among the lay leaders of Reform a place of prominence for three generations was held by the Freibergs of Cincinnati. From its foundation in 1889 until 1903, the industrialist and civic leader Julius Freiberg was president of the Union of American Hebrew Congregations, and his sons J. Walter and Maurice J., as well as his grandson Julius Walter Freiberg, were also active in the affairs of that body.

3

Reform was definitely in the ascendant and Conservatism, which in later decades was to claim the title of "authentic American Judaism," had not yet by the turn of the century come of age either in its philosophy or organization. But its primary instrument, The Jewish Theological Seminary of America, which had its timid beginnings in 1886, was now a firm institution, and in 1902 Solomon Schechter, a scholar and religious teacher of exceptional force, arrived from England to become its president. Schechter occupied the post until his death thirteen years later, and it was he who gave Conservative Judaism in America its direction and impulse. His scholarly achievements were imposing. In the *Genizah*, or storeroom, of a synagogue in Cairo, Egypt, he discovered a huge mass of manuscripts which proved an invaluable source for the reconstruction of ancient Jewish books, including the important Apocryphal book of *Ecclesiasticus*, or *The Wisdom of Ben Sira*, and for the interpretation of significant periods in ancient Jewish history. His *Studies in Judaism*, a work distinguished as much for literary grace as for content, has furnished knowledge and inspiration to non-Jews as well as Jews. He paid his due to what was known as the "Science of Judaism," but he questioned the findings of the higher critics of the Bible, to which champions of Reform, including Kaufmann Kohler, were devoted, and he attached as much importance of the mystical as to the rational. The influence of his genial and exuberant personality on his students at the Seminary was deep and enduring: he was one of those rare teachers who accomplish more by what they are than what they say. And as, over the years, his students multiplied and dispersed to occupy more and more pulpits in the synagogues of America, his influence reached out to ever wider segments of American Jewry.

Schechter was fortunate also with the men who worked with him as teachers in the Seminary: the peerless Talmudic scholar, Louis Ginzberg; the historian and bibliographer, Alexander Marx; the pathfinder and illuminator in the realm of Medieval Hebrew literature, Israel Davidson; the Biblical scholar and essayist, Israel Friedlaender, and others. In 1901 the graduates of the Seminary had formed an association, which before long admitted others also; and the group, calling itself Rabbinical Assembly of America, became the Conservative counterpart of the Central Conference of Reform Rabbis.

Conservatism was, of course, a reaction against the "excesses" of which it accused its rival; nevertheless, its synagogues adopted some of the innovations of the Reform temples, especially mixed choirs and family pews, and some of them even introduced the organ. But the creedal differences between the two became more explicit. They found expression in the constitution of the United Synagogue of America, an organization founded by Schechter in 1913 on the model of the Union of American Hebrew Congregations. Among the aims adopted by the new group were the following:

> To assert and establish loyalty to the Torah and its historical exposition;
>
> To further the observance of the Sabbath and dietary laws;
>
> To preserve in the service the reference to Israel's past and the hopes for Israel's restoration;
>
> To maintain the traditional character of the liturgy with Hebrew as the language of prayer.

The first accepts the validity of the Talmud, "the historical exposition of Torah," which Reform rejected. The second repudiates the compromises made by Reform with the traditional Sabbath and the laws of *Kashruth*. The fourth is a protest against its tendency to assign Hebrew a secondary place in the liturgy. Most important from the standpoint of community life, was the third, for by 1913 the Zionist movement, which sought to accomplish "Israel's restoration," had become a formidable issue on which the two religious trends were thus brought squarely in opposition to each other.

4

The group to which the influx from Eastern Europe added most strength was, of course, the Orthodox. In 1877, according to figures compiled by the Statistical Bureau of the Synagogue Council of America, a body embracing all three religious trends, there were 227 congregations in the United States; in 1900 there were 850. During that period of nearly a quarter century new Reform and Conservative congregations were, of course, established, but the bulk of the increase may be safely credited to the Orthodox from Eastern Europe.

A strong propensity to form societies asserted itself promptly among the newcomers. As a group they remained unorganized, but organizations they had in abundance, nearly all of them small and self-sufficient. The young set up societies for cultural and social purposes, and they found encouragement in the Settlement Houses that sprang up in the "ghettos," sponsored by Jews and non-Jews eager to Americanize them. And of course they also formed societies to promote the various social panaceas with which the hectic revolutionary atmosphere in Russia had inoculated them. But more numerous than the others were the "Young Men's Benevolent Associations," which had their impulse in the nostalgic need of those who hailed from the same town in the Old World to continue associations freighted with cherished memories and human warmth. And to this initial and elementary impulse the Associations added a program of mutual aid in times of need.

Thus arose the so-called *landsmanshaften*, which have stood out as one of the salient features of the social landscape of American Jewry. They multiplied profusely, every city and *shtetl* of Eastern Europe being at one time or another represented. Most of them were short lived, but some became lodges of one or another of the large fraternal orders and were thus assured of a longer life span. A number, representing the larger Old World centers, like Warsaw, Vilna, Bialystok and Lomza, grew and prospered and enlarged their program of mutual help to their members, in time adding homes for the aged, for the "young men" had become old.

The *landsmanshaft* societies also became more social-minded, and in New York in particular where, of course, most of them were concentrated, they became valuable aids to important communal projects, like philanthropic federations and fund-raising efforts for the reclamation of Palestine. They went further and formed federations representing their countries of origin for the purpose of aiding their coreligionists in those lands and protecting their rights. Thus the Federation of Polish Jews in America, formed in 1908, mobilized its societies to provide relief to their pauperized people in Poland in the years between the World Wars. In 1930 it called itself the American Federation of Polish Jews, and it was particularly active under the leadership of Benjamin Winter and Joseph Tenenbaum. A similar program was followed by the Federation of Hungarian Jews in America; and the Federation of Galician and Bucovinian Jews, better known as the "Galizianer Farband," aided not only their coreligionists abroad but immigrants from Galicia in the United States.

By 1950 the federations had become extinct or dormant: their raison d'être had been swept away with the Old World communities whom the Nazi murder mills annihilated. The "Galizianer Farband," now calling itself The United Galician Jews of America, was a vigorous exception. It still embraced 150 *landsmanshaft* groups, but the projects they promoted were now centered in the State of Israel, where many from their land of origin had found refuge.

5

But more numerous than the benevolent societies were the congregations, all of them Orthodox. Many began by worshipping in ill-furnished quarters often located in buildings occupied by sweatshops and they too started with groups of *landsleit*. But they were more prompt to offer membership to others also, and their life span was much longer.

So, by the turn of the century, Orthodoxy had become numerically the strongest of the three religious divisions. But numerically only. With regard to the other attributes that make a group socially important—wealth, leadership, discipline and influence—it trailed its rivals far into the new century. To the peddlers, storekeepers and sweatshop toilers wealth was of course a stranger, and for decades to come to their children also. Leadership in a minority group tends to gravitate toward those of its members who achieve prominence—especially public office—in the majority, and the newcomers will require a long period of cultural acclimation before making a successful bid for such preferment. And social influence is, as a rule, a product of wealth and distinction. Each congregation, moreover, satisfied all the religious needs of its members and owed no allegiance to a superior authority: in Judaism such an authority, the Great Sanhedrin, had ceased with the destruction of the Jewish state in the year 70. And for a long time this lack of integration and discipline, added to its other handicaps, deprived the Orthodox group in America of the place to which its numbers entitled it.

In New York and Chicago, the two largest centers in the country, attempts were made early to establish a measure of unity and authority among the Orthodox congregations. In 1888 Jacob Joseph of Vilna, a renowned preacher and Talmudic scholar, accepted an invitation from fifteen of the leading Orthodox congregations in New York to come to their city and serve as chief rabbi of their community. But the venture failed. The congregations did not hold together, some of the other Orthodox leaders challenged the authority of the newcomer, and the levy on kosher meat, which was expected to finance the innovation, could not be raised: there was no power to enforce such a tax as there was in the communities of the Old World. Jacob Joseph was held in reverent esteem by the Orthodox; when he died four years after his arrival there were 20,000 mourners in the funeral procession which, as it passed a large factory, was the target of a scandalous anti-Semitic attack by the workers. In Chicago an attempt made in 1903 to rally the Orthodox congregations around Jacob David Wilowski as chief rabbi also failed, and essentially for the same reasons.

From time to time rabbis of exceptional caliber and influence stood out in different cities, men like Bernard Louis Levinthal in Philadelphia, Aaron Mordecai Ashinsky in Pittsburgh, Eliezer Silver in Cincinnati, Jacob Konvitz in Newark, and in New York the wise and witty Chaim Jacob Vidrevitz, known as the "Moscover Rov," Moses Z. Margolies, Israel Rosenberg and others; and some of them were called chief rabbis. But the title was only complimentary; it carried no official authority. There was no hierarchy in Orthodoxy, any more than there was in the other branches of Judaism in America.

Outstanding in Sephardic Orthodoxy was Henry Pereira Mendes who, from 1877 until his death sixty years later, was *hazan* and preacher of the Spanish and Portuguese Synagogue in New York. Mendes was a prolific and sometimes inspired writer, and took part in numerous philanthropic and civic enterprises. He was one of the founders of the Jewish Theological Seminary, and in 1898 he launched the Union of Orthodox Jewish Congregations of the United States and Canada. His colleague and successor in the venerable Sephardic congregation was David de Sola Pool. He also took part in civic affairs and was looked upon, in the non-Jewish world at least, as the leading spokesman of Orthodox Judaism in America.

6

Orthodox rabbis were not disposed to recognize a formal authority, but in 1902 they organized the Union of Orthodox Rabbis (Agudas Harabonim) of the United States and Canada to "place Orthodox Judaism in America on a firm basis" by furthering religious instruction, promoting the observance of the Sabbath and dietary laws, and regulating the religious aspects of marriage and divorce. In both World Wars this body extended valiant aid to academies of learning and their students and teachers in the ravaged lands.

One of the institutions which the Agudas Harabonim approved and supported was the Rabbi Isaac Elchanan Theological Seminary, a school for the training of Orthodox rabbis, which served as the initial unit of Yeshiva College. Under the imaginative leadership of Bernard Revel this college, which in 1945 was raised to the status of a university, became the key institution of Orthodoxy in America. Revel was a man of great heart and mind, and a firm believer in the compatibility between Orthodoxy and science; curiously enough, he began his career in America as an oil operator in Oklahoma. In 1928 he added a School of Arts and Science to the institution which, under the leadership of his successor Samuel Belkin, embarked shortly after the middle of the century on the establishment of its Albert Einstein Medical School and Center. Thus had the Orthodox wing achieved a degree of organization comparable to that of the other two trends, embracing a union of congregations, a rabbinical body, and schools for the training of rabbis and teachers.

Before long, however, it became apparent that the rabbinical graduates of Yeshiva University, for all their respect for the eminent members of the Agudas Harabonim, their preceptors and mentors, diverged from them too much, not in religious outlook, but in cultural background. The language of those graduates was English, the language of the others was Yiddish. The first, in addition to their ordination as rabbis, held baccalaureate degrees also; the education of the second had been obtained in the Talmudic academies of Eastern Europe, and rarely included the secular disciplines. By 1930 a new Orthodox rabbinical body, the Rabbinical Council of America, had come into existence, consisting in the main of graduates of the Yeshiva seminary in New York. Later it included also graduates of the Yeshiva Torah Ve'Daath in Brooklyn, the Ner Israel Yeshiva in Baltimore and the Hebrew Theological Seminary in Chicago. Leo Jung, writer, educator and leader in a variety of communal enterprises, was the first president of the Council, and among others who held the post were the teacher and organizer Herbert Samuel Goldstein and the eloquent Joseph Hyman Lookstein. The younger group, moreover, was the official rabbinic authority of the organized Orthodox laity, the Union of Orthodox Jewish Congregations.

Reflecting this division in the Orthodox rabbinate was the movement known as Young Israel in the laity. It had its start in New York City in 1912 and in 1954 it included 70 congregations with a membership of 50,000. Through its National Council Young Israel conducted a variety of activities, including an employment bureau for Sabbath observers and courses in Jewish knowledge, but its principal activity was the promotion of "model" synagogues for the young.

Thus over the decades Orthodoxy became acclimated and "Americanized." The process was slow, fumbling and beset with numerous problems and tensions. The venerable patriarchs of the first generation were bound to recede slowly and sadly into the shadows, and some of them saw their sons in the pulpits of Conservative and Reform temples, which they held to be travesties of the faith. But the future, for better or worse, belongs to the young, and he who deals with the past must leave speculation as to its shape and content to others.

7

But the Jews in America were confronted also with secular problems. It will be recalled that from the day of their first appearance in the harbor of New Amsterdam in 1654 they had to overcome opposition against their admittance and were denied certain basic civil and political rights. Complete legal equality in most of the states was won, as we saw, only after a more or less protracted struggle, and General Grant's Order No. 11 of 1863 proved that the victory was not wholly secure. This ethnic and religious minority, moreover, found itself, as the decades rolled on, the target of a xenophobia more deep-seated than that which the different brands of Know-Nothingism in America directed against other minorities, an antagonism summed up in the word anti-Semitism, which presented the Jews in America with an endless procession of problems. And as the new century advanced the immigration question moved ominously into the foreground. The foes of the open door became more numerous and vocal at a time when the future and even the lives of more and more of the Jews in the Old World depended on the extent to which it remained open.

Nor were those the only nonreligious problems that faced the Jews in America. They were growing rapidly in numbers and influence, but their people in other parts of the world were suffering persecution and defamation. Indifference to their plight was impossible. Not only did common humanity forbid it and the call of blood and faith demand it, but the degradation of their coreligionists anywhere in the world stigmatized them also. Official malevolence and mob savagery against their fellow Jews in the Old World made continuous demands upon them, requiring not only intervention and protest, but often enough large-scale measures of relief and succor. Indeed, no other ethnic group in America was confronted with formidable tasks like those which, owing to the precarious situation of their people across the world, the Jews in America were called upon to perform.

The need for a permanent and representative body in American Jewry to protect Jewish rights at home and abroad was felt as early as 1840 when the Damascus Affair cast its shadow over the Jews of the world, but it led to no action. The Board of Delegates of American Israelites, however, which came into being in 1859 shortly after the Mortara scandal, was, as we saw, a worthy attempt to constitute such an organ. But the Board, as well as the gestures towards union which preceded it, rested on a congregational or religious basis; in 1878 its functions were taken over by the newly formed Union of American Hebrew Congregations. The feeling, however, grew that since the tasks with which such a body was charged were not religious, it could and should embrace all Jews regardless of their religious orientation.

In 1891 an ambitious attempt to form such a union was launched and resulted in the Jewish Alliance of America, its immediate aim being to deal with the problems that flowed from the influx of immigrants from Eastern Europe. The Alliance was born at a convention that took place in Philadelphia in February of that year, in which a score of cities across the country were represented. Among the delegates were notables like Simon Wolf, Solomon Solis-Cohen, the physician and communal leader Charles D. Spivak, and the educators and social workers Henry M. Leipziger and David Blaustein. But the Alliance died in its infancy: a year after its formation it was absorbed by a relief agency, which also vanished promptly from the scene. Its disappearance was something of a mystery; apparently its policy of admitting representatives of the new arrivals to positions of responsibility was not agreeable to the older arrivals or their descendants.

8

In the fifteen years that followed this promising but abortive effort the need for such an instrument became more pressing, and the American Jewish Committee, which achieved more authority in the field than any other group had been able to command, came into existence. The birth pangs of the Committee were severe and prolonged, lasting from February 1906, when some sixty leading American Jews met in New York to consider the project, to November of that year when the first meeting of the Committee met in the same city, adopted a constitution and elected its first set of officers. The initiative for calling the first gathering had been taken by five men: Louis Marshall, Cyrus L. Sulzberger, Samuel Greenbaum, a Justice of the New York State Supreme Court; Nathan Bijur, a prominent lawyer who became a member of the same court three years later; and Joseph Jacobs, a scholar in many fields of learning, who was editor of the *American Hebrew*.

There were two principal issues which nearly wrecked the enterprise before it was launched. The first was the fear, which disturbed the leaders of the Union of American Hebrew Congregations and B'nai B'rith, two organizations which had acted from time to time to protect Jewish rights, that the new body would "pull the rug from under them." The second, which provoked heated debate, concerned the method by which the proposed Committee should be constituted. The clash was between the "democrats" and "oligarchs." The first, led by Louis Marshall and the New York rabbi Judah L. Magnes, urged that the members of the Committee should be elected by the congregations across the country. The second, whose leading spokesmen were Oscar Straus and Adolf Kraus, president of B'nai B'rith, insisted in effect that the Committee should be self-appointed and self-perpetuating. The ground of their insistence was no secret: it was fear and distrust of their coreligionists from Eastern Europe. A number of them, including Simon Wolf and Adolf Kraus, stated it with exemplary candor in a letter they addressed to Mayer Sulzberger, who had presided over the conference in February:

> The danger must be clear to any unbiased observer of the situation that unless this proposed new corporation . . . be composed of the most conservative men, the standing of the Jews in the American nation will be seriously affected for the worse. With the machinery for election as outlined, the probabilities are that conservative elements . . . will be crowded to the rear, and the new organization will fall into the hands of radical theorists whose vagaries will then be accepted by the American nation as expressive of the views and the intentions of the whole Jewish community.

"The machinery for election as outlined" was not adopted. Instead, a Committee of Fifteen was named and authorized to co-opt thirty-five additional members. The fears of B'nai B'rith and the Union of American Hebrew Congregations for their "vested interests" were also allayed: it was voted that the new Committee was "to cooperate with the different national bodies in the country." The two road blocks having been removed, the first meeting of the full Committee of fifty met and chose Mayer Sulzberger president, Julian W. Mack, a Chicago jurist and civic leader, and Isidor Newman, a New Orleans merchant and banker, vice-presidents; and an Executive Committee of nine was entrusted with the conduct of the affairs of the new agency.

The large and vital tasks the Committee assumed are defined in the Act of the New York Legislature by which it was incorporated:

> The objects of this corporation shall be, to prevent the infraction of the civil and religious rights of the Jews, in any part of the world; to render all lawful assistance and to take appropriate remedial action in the event of threatened or actual invasion or restriction of such rights, or of unfavorable discrimination with respect thereto; to secure for Jews equality of economic, social and educational opportunity; alleviate the consequence of persecution, and to afford relief from calamities affecting Jews, wherever they may occur.

9

The oligarchic composition of the Committee certainly insured a preponderance of "the most conservative men" who, as it happened, nearly all belonged to the previous, or "German," stratum of the community, as against the "radical theorists," whose "vagaries" engendered so much uneasiness, and who belonged to the later, or "Russian," stratum. It must be pointed out, however, that the "theorists" in question were not only—in fact, not even principally—those who preached radical social gospels, but the advocates of political Zionism who urged the establishment of a Jewish state. Indeed, in the course of time, the "most conservative men" of the Committee and the radical leaders who claimed to speak for Jewish labor, both of whom held Zionism in aversion, joined hands to thwart attempts that were being made to claim the hegemony for the Zionist viewpoint in American Jewry.

The barrage of criticism to which the American Jewish Committee was subjected came, therefore, principally from Zionists. The critics compared it to the Old World *shtadlanim*, or back-door diplomats and petitioners, who acted on their own authority, owing no accounting to those for whom they interceded. Nor were the members of the Committee indifferent to these strictures, especially when their opponents, with stinging irony, invoked the democratic spirit and institutions of

America against those who were fond of preaching American patriotism to them—the "200 per cent Americans," as they called them.

Nevertheless, as the decades passed the criticism lost its force, and by the middle of the century had become less than a whisper. And for three reasons. First, was the high caliber of the men who made up the Committee, and the impressive results which their labors produced. They were the unchallenged leaders of their respective communities; their devotion to the welfare of their people was unimpeachable, and they proved their capacity to conduct important affairs, which often required delicate handling. Second, was the policy of broadening its base, or "democratizing" itself, which the Committee pursued, by inviting delegates from important national organizations and setting up local advisory councils, so that as the years passed, more of its members came from the East European stratum. Finally, the Committee's attitude toward Zionism gradually changed from hostility to qualified sympathy, and in the end to support. The change did not come from indoctrination or inner illumination; it was, as we shall see, imposed by cataclysmic events that accompanied or followed two global wars. But come it did, confirming the words of an ancient Jewish sage who said: "What can be accomplished by time cannot be accomplished by reason."

10

Three years after its formation the American Jewish Committee gave its blessing to a bold experiment to assemble the *disjecta membra* of the largest Jewish aggregation in America—the largest, indeed, in the entire world—which had arisen in the City of New York, and forge it into a real community with power to regulate its common interests. In that city and in the others across the country there were, as we saw, Jewish organizations galore—congregations, fraternal lodges, *landsmanshaft* societies, trade unions, philanthropic agencies of all sorts and sizes, educational and cultural institutions. But none of these centers was really organized, no recognized authority existed to speak and act for it in matters that touched the honor and welfare of all its members. In 1909 the conflux in New York was estimated to number 1,500,000 souls, or some 50 per cent of the total number of Jews in the country, and if the experiment succeeded, the concentrations in the other cities would be sure to follow suit; and eventually they would federate, and American Jewry would emerge from chaos to order, from division to union. It was all so simple. If only free men could be moved and mustered like tin soldiers! But the only other large community which followed suit was the one in Philadelphia, and the experiment there met with even less success than in New York. In the small community of Denver the Central Jewish Council, established in 1912, had a more fruitful career.

In February 1909 a convention representing well over 200 organizations in New York gave birth to a new entity which named itself Kehillah (Jewish Community) of New York City, and its Executive Board of twenty-five was accepted by the American Jewish Committee as its New York chapter or district. On the part of the Committee this was no small step towards democratization, although it reserved to itself "exclusive jurisdiction over all questions affecting the Jews generally, not of a purely local character." The name *kehillah* was chosen because it harked back to the *kahals*, or local authorities in the Old World, which had effective power in the inner affairs of Jewish communities.

The New York Kehillah embarked on a large program, with a Board of Rabbis to regulate the religious aspects of marriage and divorce and the sale of kosher food; a Court of Arbitration, or *Bet Din*, to adjudicate religious disputes; a Bureau of Industry to settle differences between Jewish employers and workers; a Welfare Committee to cooperate with the municipal authorities in matters involving Jews that required police action; an Employment Bureau for the Handicapped; and a Bureau of Jewish Education to which reference has been made in a previous chapter. In all of those fields and especially the last, the Kehillah, of which the popular rabbi and orator, Judah L. Magnes, was the chairman, registered gains, but it also encountered serious obstacles. Some of them stemmed from ideological differences, others from vested economic interests, with which some of the Kehillah's activities, like the regulation of *Kashruth*, clashed.

The active period in the life of the New York Kehillah lasted about a decade. It became increasingly clear that the great aggregation in the metropolis was not receptive even to the limited program for permanent unification which the Kehillah undertook, and what with new and overshadowing problems imposed by a global war, the experiment languished and came to an end.

CHAPTER 15

Big Brother

1

IN GROWING MEASURE AS THE JEWS IN AMERICA BECAME stronger numerically and economically, their kin in other parts of the world, especially those who lived in poverty and insecurity in Eastern Europe, looked to them for help in times of need and crisis. Such times, alas, were not rare, and they became less so in the first half of the twentieth century, with its global wars and domestic upheavals. And the aid which the Jews in America furnished was not only material, but moral and political. The country of which they were part and parcel moved steadily towards world leadership, and as they became more closely interwoven with the manifold aspects of its life, their stature and influence grew and they were able to enlist its public opinion and the good will of its governments on behalf of their people in other lands. With respect to the attitude of American governments it may be affirmed that the statement made in 1879 by William Evarts, Secretary of State under President Rutherford B. Hayes, that "this government has ever felt a deep interest in the welfare of the Hebrew race in foreign countries," was generally borne out by the historic facts. Steadily, therefore, the Jews of America assumed the role of big brother to the Jewish communities across the world, and if at times the big brother, not without a touch of scorn, was called the rich uncle, his role was not less effective and beneficent.

2

The statement by William Evarts occurs in a directive he dispatched to John A. Kasson, the American minister in Vienna, who was conducting negotiations for the establishment of official relations between the United States and Rumania, and the particular portion of the "Hebrew race" with which the directive was immediately concerned was the Jewish community of that Balkan country. The persecutions to which the Jews in Rumania were subjected had already received attention from the American government on previous occasions. In 1870 President Grant, as we saw, appointed Benjamin Peixotto, head of B'nai B'rith, as consul-general of the United States to Rumania in the hope that he might succeed in mitigating the persecutions, but with all his industry and diplomatic skill, Peixotto, who spent six years in Bucharest, could make no real dent in the hardened anti-Semitism of Rumanian officialdom. In 1872 the American government again evinced its concern for the plight of the Jews in Rumania when the American representative in Paris informed the Foreign Minister of France that "the government of the United States would receive with the utmost satisfaction whatever the French republican government may do to put an end to the unrelenting persecutions which are a disgrace to Christian civilization." The same year Peixotto attended a conference in Brussels where, at the call of the *Alliance Israélite Universelle* and the Anglo-Jewish Association, the leading Jews of France, Britain and Germany assembled in a vain effort to bring pressure on Rumania to moderate her anti-Jewish policy.

Then came the year 1878, crucial in the history of Rumania, and it seemed to present a providential opportunity for the Jews of that benighted land. Until that year, although she had a free hand in her internal affairs, Rumania was a principality of Turkey, but having fought with Russia in a victorious war against her suzerain, she demanded complete independence. In 1878 the leading European statesmen met in the Congress of Berlin, and Rumania obtained her demand, but on condition that all her inhabitants, regardless of religious beliefs, should be granted equal civil and political rights. Rumania accepted the condition, and it was embodied in Article 44 of the Treaty of Berlin, but the Article became famous for the success with which the Rumanians made a complete mockery of it. The Article, of course, intended that the Jews of Rumania, who were in the legal status of aliens, should all be granted citizenship, but every application for naturalization had to be decided by the Parliament, and from 1880 to 1900 the Parliament approved only 85 applications.

In 1900 Rumania was hit by an economic crisis, and its more than a quarter million Jews who, as a result of repressions, lived on the verge of pauperism even in normal times, were reduced to appalling destitution. Thousands of them, men, women, and children, set out on foot for the ports of Western Europe where they embarked for the United States; between 1900 and 1906 some 70,000 of them left the country. The stampede created a sensation in Europe; and in America neither the Jews nor the government, which found the country at the receiving end of so much misery, could remain indifferent to it.

In 1902 John Hay, the scholarly Secretary of State in the cabinet of President Theodore Roosevelt, took diplomatic action of an unprecedented character. On August 11 of that year he dispatched a long note to the representatives of the United States in France, Germany, Great Britain, Italy, Russia and Turkey, the signatories to the Treaty of Berlin, for the attention of the governments of those countries. The note did not mince words; it was a scathing indictment of Rumania's policy which made paupers and fugitives of those whom she had promised in a solemn international undertaking to emancipate and protect. The United States, the note claimed, had the right to denounce that policy because it forced upon her shores a great many "outcasts, made doubly paupers by physical and moral oppression in their native land," whose immigration lacked "the essential conditions which made alien immigration either acceptable or beneficial." That, however, was not the only ground for protest. The note went on:

> Whether consciously and of purpose or not, these helpless people, burdened and spurned by their native land, are forced by the sovereign power of Rumania upon the charity of the United States. This Government cannot be a tacit party to such an international wrong. It is constrained to protest against the treatment to which the Jews of Rumania are subjected, not alone because it has unimpeachable rights to remonstrate against the resultant injury to itself, but in the name of humanity.

And the note took occasion to recount in some detail the numerous and disastrous disabilities which reduced the Jews in Rumania "to a state of wretched misery." It cited "their exclusion from the public service and the learned professions, the limitation of their civil rights and the imposition upon them of exceptional taxes," and it stressed the fact that they "are prohibited from owning land, or even from cultivating it as common laborers." Barred from the rural districts, they find that "many branches of petty trade and manual production are closed to them in the overcrowded cities where they are forced to dwell and engage, against fearful odds, in the desperate struggle for existence."

In the annals of diplomacy, except in time of war or on the eve of war, there is perhaps no other arraignment of one government by another so devastating as this one. Hay's note made a deep impression throughout Europe, and the Jews in America were gratified by the castigation administered by the great Republic of the West to the persecutors of their coreligionists in Rumania: their leaders had no doubt played no small part in the event. But the note proved a barren victory. It brought no amelioration to the lot of the Jews in Rumania, nor is there any indication that the governments to whom it was addressed bestirred themselves on their behalf. Such action by Russia was out of the question: her zeal in persecuting the Jews was no less keen than that of her neighbor; and the other signatories to the Treaty of Berlin discovered that their economic and political interests in Rumania made it unwise for them to risk the displeasure of her government. Hay's note of 1902 which, of course, had the unqualified approval of his chief in the White House, was no doubt a chivalrous gesture, but it remained only that.

A decade later, after the two Balkan wars which served as curtain raisers for the First World War, the Treaty of Bucharest of 1913 awarded Rumania a sizable portion of Dobruja at the expense of Bulgaria. The Jews of America helped to relieve the sufferings which the wars inflicted on their coreligionists in the Balkan countries and sought to safeguard their rights. Rumania promised that the Jews in her new possession would "be accorded the same rights and privileges as are given to persons of other races and religions," but again the promise was nonchalantly ignored.

3

Greater sorrows tend to eclipse lesser ones, and new blows that fell on their kin in Russia in the first decades of the new century nearly effaced from the thoughts of the Jews in America the trials of their people in Rumania. In Russia the ferment of revolution in the first lustrum of the twentieth century kept steadily mounting, and the government of Czar Nicholas II adopted the pogrom as the main instrument to suppress it. The pogrom would have two important uses: it would provide an outlet for the discontent of the Russian people, serving as a lightning rod to divert their wrath from their rulers, and the unleashed fury could be transformed into patriotic fervor by charging the Jews with responsibility for the revolutionary movement. It was the scapegoat technique which has been employed against the Jews many times and in many places.

In April 1903 Kishinev, capital of the province of Bessarabia, became the scene of a two-day onslaught of unprecedented bestiality upon the

Jews. Planned and organized by the authorities, it was preceded by a period of open fomentation, which included a charge of ritual murder, and the only action the police took during the outbreak was to disarm a group of Jews who were trying to defend themselves. The mob murdered, raped and looted without check. Forty-seven Jews were slain, hundreds wounded, 1,300 houses and shops were plundered and wrecked, and 2,000 families made homeless. On the evening of the second day—it was the Monday after Easter Sunday—the governor of the province received a telegram, for which he was apparently waiting, from Vyacheslav Von Plehve, the ferocious anti-Semite who was Minister of the Interior, and the violence was promptly suppressed.

The repercussions across the world were too formidable and Von Plehve called an intermission, but in September of the same year, the policy was resumed with an outbreak in the White Russian city of Homel. By that time young men and women throughout the Pale had organized for self-defense and the rabble in Homel was held in check, suffering almost as many casualties as it inflicted despite the cordon of troops that shielded it. Five months later—in February 1904—Russia embarked on her disastrous war with Japan, and as she suffered one humiliating defeat after another the revolutionary temper in Russia rose higher. Towards the end of that year there were again assaults on the Jews in South Russia, the bloodiest of them on Yom Kippur in the city of Kherson.

But the method by which the shaking autocracy hoped to stifle the revolutionary surge won its greatest "victories" in the two years that followed. The dregs of the Russian people were organized into the infamous Black Hundreds, and in the spring and summer of 1905 they staged a series of anti-Jewish riots, which were generally thrown back by the self-defense groups. In a number of localities, however, including the large industrial centers of Lodz and Bialystok, the attacks were made by armed soldiers and Cossacks.

But those affrays in the first half of 1905 were only rehearsals. The real performance began on the last day of October of that year. It was the day after the Czar had yielded to the demonstrations and strikes which paralyzed the country, by proclaiming civil, political and religious liberty and ordering elections to a representative parliament, or Duma. The proclamation was a dodge; the machinery that stood ready to uphold the autocracy and render the concessions nugatory, went into action. In towns and cities throughout the land the Black Hundreds, shielded by police and soldiery, against whom the self-defense groups were almost powerless, fell upon the Jews. Large numbers were killed—in Odessa alone there were 300 dead—thousands were maimed and scores of thousands made destitute.

The pogrom wave of October 1905 served its purpose. The Revolution was thrown into chaos, and the Duma, which convened in May 1906, was dispersed by imperial decree three months after it opened. And even while this ill-starred body was in session a second and more sanguinary assault took place in Bialystok. The chief role was played by the police and garrison of the city, and a new refinement was introduced in the art of pogrom making: the outbreak was set off by a shot fired by an *agent provocateur* on a religious procession. The Revolution of 1905 had inspired glowing hopes, which were shared by all America and especially by the American Jews, and their extinction added to the gloom into which the woes of their people in Russia had plunged them.

4

The first five decades of the twentieth century brought the Jews of America tidings of numerous outrages committed against their people in Europe and elsewhere, but it is doubtful if any of them produced such an outburst of indignation as the Kishinev pogrom of April 1903. Nor were they alone to be shocked by the massacre: there were denunciations by foremost Christian spokesmen of the western countries, and relief measures were launched for the wounded and homeless to which men of all faiths contributed. There were protests in Russia itself, the boldest by the great writer and moralist Leo Tolstoy, which the censors, of course, suppressed. In the first decade of the century civilized men had not yet become inured to such horrors.

But the reaction was strongest in the United States. In pulpits and newspapers throughout the land public opinion expressed itself plainly and scores of meetings were held across the country. The principal speaker at the demonstration in New York City was former President Grover Cleveland, and the chairman was the mayor of the city, Seth Low. A considerable sum was raised for the victims, the appeals for relief underscored by a song, heard often in the years that followed and ending with the refrain:

Give for shrouds to bury the dead,
Give to bring the living bread.

But the feeling of helplessness, which pervaded the community, itself needed relief, and the government was besought to take diplomatic action. A petition addressed to the Czar was prepared by B'nai B'rith, and President Roosevelt agreed to transmit it if the Czar would consent to receive it. It was signed by many thousands, leaders in every field of American life, including jurists, governors of states, members of Congress, clergymen, educators and the mayors of 150 cities. But the petition was laid to rest in the archives of the State Department. Von Plehve let it be known that His Imperial Majesty would not deign to receive it.

When tidings of the new pogroms, climaxed by the orgy that swept the whole of Russia from October 1905, reached the world there were again mass demonstrations throughout the United States. Platforms and pulpits resounded with denunciations, editors wrote angry editorials, and both houses of Congress, without a dissenting vote, adopted a resolution expressing horror and sympathy. A committee headed by Oscar Straus, with Jacob Schiff as treasurer, raised over a million dollars for relief, and on December 4, 1905 an imposing procession, with nearly 100,000 in line, paraded their sorrow through the streets of New York, the bells of Christian churches tolling as they passed.

It was all the big brother in America could do. But America herself could do more. America, the City of Refuge and asylum of the oppressed, could, if she would, keep her doors open for those who might escape from the terror.

5

Shortly before the outbreak of the World War in 1914 another anti-Jewish plot was hatched by the Czar's camarilla, directed this time not only against the Jews in Russia but the world over. It was a resurrection of the medieval libel of ritual murder, and a show trial was staged in the holy city of Kiev, designed to convict the entire Jewish people in the person of its immediate victim, one Mendel Beilis.

In March 1911 the body of a boy was found not far from a brickyard near Kiev, and Beilis, who was employed as a watchman in the brickyard, was arrested and charged with ritual murder. For two and a half years the case dragged on, with an elaborate structure of perjury, distortion, and anti-Semitic incitement built up by the government in St. Petersburg to secure the conviction of Beilis. But the evidence against him at the trial would not stand up and Beilis was acquitted. Nevertheless, the ignorant jurors were persuaded to add to the acquittal the statement that a ritual murder had been committed! The government appeared to have triumphed, but not long afterwards a notorious woman criminal confessed that it was she and her gang who had murdered the boy.

Again, as so often in previous centuries, the Jews of the world were placed in the grotesque and tragic position of having to deny the hideous accusation which, it may be noted, had been made by the pagans against the early Christians. In America, as in other countries, they enlisted the churches in the cause, and again a petition was addressed to "His Imperial Majesty, Nicholas II, Czar of All the Russias," bearing the signatures of the highest Protestant and Catholic prelates, headed by David H. Greer, Episcopal bishop of New York, William T. Manning, at the time the rector of Trinity Church, and John Cardinal Farley, the Catholic archbishop of New York. "In the name of our sacred faith," they prayed that the charge of ritual murder against Beilis be withdrawn, and expressed full confidence that "this appeal will be favorably received." This petition also obtained wide notice in the press of the country, but accomplished nothing more.

6

In the meantime the Jews of America watched with growing anxiety the steady increase of anti-immigration sentiment in the country. The first federal immigration law, which was enacted in 1882, and those that followed over the next quarter century, were not seriously restrictive. They imposed a moderate poll tax on immigrants and excluded contract laborers, mental defectives and others likely to become public charges, as well as persons convicted of serious, but not political, offenses. But during those years there were numerous reports on immigration by Congressional committees, and in 1910 came a forty-volume report by a special Immigration Commission, which demanded more drastic restrictions. Their special targets were the immigrants from Eastern and Southern Europe, and the principal device they advocated was a literacy test by which they expected a great many of them to be barred. And as the years wore on, the anti-Jewish overtones in the agitation became more pronounced.

The first attempt to enact a literacy test was made in 1897; it was included in a bill which passed both houses but was vetoed by President Cleveland, who took occasion to comment in the following words on the strictures that were current against the latest immigrants: "The time is quite within recent memory when the same thing was said of immigrants who, with their descendants, are now numbered among our best citizens." Cleveland's veto was sustained when the Senate failed to act on it after the House overrode it. But in the first and second decades of the new century, especially after the pogroms in Russia had swelled the influx from that country, more bills were introduced in Congress containing a variety of restrictions, with the literacy test still heading the list. In January 1913 the most formidable bill of the sort passed both Houses, but was vetoed by Taft. The veto was sustained by an extremely narrow margin, and the following year a veto by Woodrow Wilson of a similar bill was sustained by an even narrower one. Finally in 1917 another veto by Wilson was overridden, and the Immigration Act of that year, embodying a literacy test, became law.

Jewish immigration had reached its peak in 1906 when the number of arrivals was well over 150,000, and in 1914, before the World War could dam the flood, the number was nearly 140,000. In 1917, when the new immigration law was enacted, the war brought it down to 17,000 and in the three years that followed it went even lower. But the Jews in America were well aware that the cataclysm in Europe was preparing a mighty surge of their kin towards America as soon as the highways on land and sea should be opened, and they did their utmost to hold their country to its traditional open-door policy.

In the forefront of the struggle against restrictive legislation stood the American Jewish Committee whose spokesmen appeared at Congressional hearings, refuting the slanders against the recent immigrants that were bandied about by the sworn restrictionists, and fighting valiantly to avert or mitigate the blows against free immigration which appeared to be inevitable. With regard to the literacy test the ability to read Yiddish or Hebrew, which practically all Jewish immigrants possessed, was accepted as sufficient, and those able to show that they were fugitives from religious persecution were not required to submit to it. In the forefront on the other side stood the forces of organized labor, fearful of the competition of alien workers accustomed to a low standard of living, and for many years the country saw the curious spectacle of an immigrant Jew named Samuel Gompers leading the movement against free immigration, and a native Jew named Louis Marshall, who in 1912 became president of the American Jewish Committee, leading the cause of the "huddled masses yearning to breathe free," whom the giant statue in New York harbor had once appeared to welcome to the land of liberty and opportunity.

7

We must, finally, take note of a struggle which the Jews of America waged over many years, and with mounting intensity during the first decade of the new century, to safeguard not the rights of their people in other lands, but their own. The struggle centered around a Treaty of Commerce and Navigation which had been concluded as far back as 1832 between the United States and Russia, and its aim was to compel their own government to protect their equality as citizens of the Republic. The struggle ended in 1911 when a reluctant administration in Washington was forced to abrogate the treaty, and the last brief phase of it taught the community some useful lessons as to the methods a minority may properly employ to vindicate its rights in a democratic society.

The first article of that treaty contained the usual provisions granting the citizens of each country the right "to sojourn and reside in all parts whatsoever" of the other, but it added the apparently innocuous words "on condition of their submitting to the laws and ordinances there prevailing, and particularly to the regulations in force concerning commerce." Now Russia, taking her stand on that proviso, claimed the right to extend to American citizens of the Jewish faith who might find themselves within her borders the same restrictions that she imposed on her own Jewish subjects. Would the United States acquiesce in the Russian interpretation of the proviso?

It was not until 1866 that a case arose of actual discrimination against an American citizen of Jewish faith sojourning in Russia. He was Theodore Rosenstraus, who was denied the right to acquire real estate in the city of Kharkov because he was a Jew. His appeal for diplomatic aid, and the appeal of another American citizen who was banished from St. Petersburg in 1880 because he was a Jew, led to an interminable and dreary round of exchanges between the two governments. The United States took the position that she could not, as James G. Blaine, the Secretary of State in 1881, put it, "accept any construction of our existing treaty which shall discriminate against any class of American citizens on account of their religious faith." The Russian diplomats hedged and purred, gave assurances that they understood the American position, that "it was the desire of the Emperor to show all possible consideration to American citizens," but new cases of discrimination continued to crop up. And in 1893 it came to light that Russian consulates in the United States were denying visas to American citizens who were Jews.

Coincident with the futile diplomatic exchanges, resolutions were introduced in Congress, calling upon the Presidents to put an end to religious discrimination against American citizens in Russia, and since the introduction of such resolutions by Congressmen is rarely a spontaneous act, it may be assumed that Jewish leaders in America were not idle. Two of the resolutions were sponsored by Jewish legislators, one in 1894 by Congressman Isidor Raynor of Maryland, who later represented his state in the United States Senate, the other in 1902 by Congressman Henry Mayer Goldfogle of New York, who represented New York City's "ghetto." But resolutions were just as ineffectual as diplomatic representations. Most of them were buried in committee, and those which, like Goldfogle's, passed in one house failed to reach the other.

Finally, in May 1907, came a strange development. The Secretary of State, the distinguished and highly esteemed Elihu Root, issued a "Notice to American Citizens formerly Subjects of Russia who Contemplate Returning to that Country," in which, to all intents and purposes, he acquiesced in the Russian policy of discrimination. "An American citizen formerly a subject of Russia who returns to that country," said the Notice, "places himself within the jurisdiction of Russian law and cannot expect immunity from its operation and," the Notice continued, "this department will not issue passports to former Russian subjects or to Jews who intend going to Russian territory, unless it has assurance that the Russian government will consent to their admission."

This pronouncement by the Secretary of State involved even more than the issue of religious discrimination; the words "former Russian subjects" seemed also to countenance Russia's denial of the right of voluntary expatriation: once a subject of the czar, was the Russian stand, always a subject of the czar. That stand, which had been taken by other governments also, had been rejected by the United States as far back as 1868, when Congress declared voluntary expatriation to be "a natural and inherent right of all people" and the government announced its intention to extend protection to naturalized citizens in the lands of their birth also. Thus the Notice issued by Root made American citizens of Russian origin who happened to be Jews doubly vulnerable: as former Russian subjects and as members of a race that Russia proscribed.

There was a vigorous outcry by Jewish newspapers and leaders, and the American Jewish Committee stepped into the struggle. Its intervention brought a revision of the offensive document, but it became clear that more drastic action was necessary to remove all ambiguity as to the complete equality of American citizens of Jewish faith: the Treaty of 1832 must be terminated and replaced by a new one. Such was the bold demand which in the early months of 1908 Mayer Sulzberger, the president of the Committee, laid before Theodore Roosevelt.

In Washington there was no inclination to accede: the Far Eastern trade with Russia was held to be more important. A presidential election took place that year, and the politicians who drafted the party platforms did not have to be pressed hard to include a plank calling for "the just and equal protection of all our citizens abroad," but when the election was over the new administration proved indisposed to take effective steps to extend such protection to its Jewish citizens in Russia. For nearly three more years the "Russian passport question" continued to disturb the Jews of America, but in Washington the wall of indifference stood firm.

Gradually, however, the Jewish leaders changed their tactics. The genteel method of quiet intervention had failed, and the only recourse left was to rouse American public opinion to a wrong that impugned the honor and dignity of the entire nation. There were those who doubted that the "grandees" of the American Jewish Committee would stoop to public agitation, but the doubters were mistaken. The new note was sounded by Louis Marshall in January 1911. "It may be argued," said he in an address to the Union of American Hebrew Congregations, "that the suspension of commercial relations between the two countries may hurt our trade. I have a higher opinion of the American people than to believe that they are so destitute of idealism, so devoid of a sense of honor, as to regard a matter of this supreme importance with the eyes and souls of mere shopkeepers." It was the opening gun in a campaign that became steadily louder and in which prominent Christians took an increasingly important part. A National Citizens Committee was formed, headed by Andrew D. White, an eminent educator and former ambassador to Russia, with William G. McAdoo, already a prominent lawyer and rising political leader, as chairman of the executive committee. State legislatures passed resolutions, most of them demanding the abrogation of the treaty, protests against the treaty poured in on President Taft from individuals and organizations, and new resolutions were introduced in both houses of Congress.

In February 1911, when the campaign had not yet reached its crescendo, Taft invited representatives of the American Jewish Committee, B'nai B'rith and the Union of American Hebrew Congregations to confer with him on the "Russian passport question." The President's attitude at the conference suggested he was anxious that the agitation should be called off. To abrogate the treaty, he explained would be unwise; large American investments in Russia would be endangered; it might even lead to war; and besides, he had been informed by his ambassador that in Russian government circles all Jews were looked upon as dangerous radicals. The "dangerous radicals" who conferred with him left the President determined to step up the agitation against the treaty.

The campaign continued all through 1911 and was climaxed by an imposing meeting in Carnegie Hall, New York, which was addressed by Woodrow Wilson, then governor of New Jersey; Champ Clark, the Speaker of the House; Jacob G. Schurman, the president of Cornell University; William Randolph Hearst and other top-ranking Americans. In December of that year a resolution was brought into the House by Congressman William Sulzer of New York, calling for the abrogation of the treaty, and was passed by a vote of 300 to 1. The administration realized it was useless to hold out against the tide. The same month, before a resolution to the same effect could be acted upon by the Senate, Philander Knox, the new Secretary of State, formally denounced the treaty, and on January 1, 1913, in accordance with its provisions, it was no longer in force. The fight was won. It was a good fight, fought with the weapons of democracy to vindicate a basic democratic principle, and the victory added to the prestige of the Jewish community in America and, in particular, of the American Jewish Committee which spearheaded the struggle.

In Russia the year 1913, as we saw, was marked by the attempt of the Czar's government to fasten the blood libel on the Jewish people: the time was not propitious for negotiating a new treaty. And not many months after Beilis was acquitted, Russia plunged into the maelstrom of the First World War, which eventually brought czarism to an end. A new treaty of commerce with Russia remained indefinitely in abeyance.

CHAPTER 16

Alignments

1

THE REEMERGENCE OF A SOVEREIGN JEWISH NATION MAY be evaluated one way or another, but it was certainly the most spectacular event in nearly two millennia of Jewish history. For any sizable Jewish aggregation to stand aloof from the world-wide movement that brought it about was impossible, and as the decades between the First Zionist Congress in Basel and the proclamation of the State of Israel advanced, it was inevitable that the Jews of America should play an increasingly important role in the consummation. For already in 1914, when the nations were swept into a world war and the political horizons of the movement suddenly widened, the community in America was estimated to number nearly 3,500,000, the second largest under a single jurisdiction in the world. The first was the community of 6,000,000 that lay under the scepter of Nicholas II, but since that scepter would shortly be broken and nearly 50 per cent of those millions would fall under the sovereignty of a reconstituted Poland, the American community may be accorded first place even from the standpoint of numbers, and from other significant standpoints—freedom of action, material wealth, social and political influence—it was far ahead of any other.

Not that the Jews in America came promptly forward and offered all their advantages to the bold aim the Zionist Congress proclaimed in what became known as the Basel Program, the aim of creating "a publicly recognized, legally secured home for the Jewish people in Palestine." In the two decades that followed, the part American Jewry bore in the movement fell far below its size and resources. Instead, Zionism acted as a precipitant which crystallized the major tensions that divided the different segments of the community, for the new issue brought into sharp relief alignments which may be conveniently, though not with complete accuracy, be called the Right, the Left and the Center.

The Right consisted in the main of the "German" stratum of the community, the children and grandchildren of the forty-eighters, those who had risen to affluence and influence, eager to be undifferentiated from the majority, Reform in their religious orientation, with special attachment to the tenet which rejected national restoration for the Jewish people and expunged all allusions to the redemption of Zion and Jerusalem from the prayers. What is this peculiar ferment that has seized upon the Jews in Europe? they asked, and who is this Viennese messiah who confers with ministers and magnates, and is received in audience by the Emperor of Germany, the Sultan of Turkey, the King of Italy, and the Pope in Rome? A Jewish state? Fantastic and dangerous! It will undermine the position of all Jews who are citizens of the lands in which they live. Their patriotism will be questioned, their loyalty impugned, they will be charged with dual allegiance and the anti-Semites will be furnished with fresh ammunition. And some indulged in pleasantries. "If Palestine becomes a Jewish state," they said, paraphrasing a famous quip by a German anti-Zionist, "I want to be appointed its ambassador for life to Washington." It was fortunate, they felt, that in America the response was so feeble and confined to recent immigrants in the "ghettos." Neither the government nor the people of the country could possibly accept its adherents as representing the Jews of America. And they felt even more secure when the American Jewish Committee came into existence. No one could successfully challenge its right to speak for the Jews of America, and the Committee was adamant against Zionism and made no secret of its antagonism.

The Left was, if possible, even more adamant and certainly more vocal. It embraced the labor leaders, the apostles of socialism who preached its gospel by tongue and pen, and the large numbers who sat at their feet. Zionism must be fought as a sinister deviation from the true path. It was a mirage, compounded of religious romanticism and chauvinism. It was obscurantist and bourgeois: the innocent French word had become charged with dark meaning and capable of blasting anything at which it was thrown. The Left had a powerful weapon in the *Forward*, which lost no opportunity to belabor the "reactionary menace." There was no love lost between the Left and Right; the Right, in fact, was even more than bourgeois: it was upper bourgeois. But it had the great merit of being hostile to Zionism, so on occasion the two joined forces against it. Rarely did politics make stranger bedfellows.

And now for the Center. It was a huge but amorphous mass: the members of the thousands of Orthodox congregations in the cities of the country, the storekeepers and peddlers, the vast numbers of sweatshop and factory workers upon whom the exhortations of the social idealists made little impression. They had vivid memories of the bitter lot of their people in Eastern Europe, and in their consciousness the age-old hope of national restoration persisted, even if vaguely and impersonally. But a mighty effort was now afoot to realize it. Why not? they asked. Must their people wander forever over the face of the earth? Why shouldn't they too have a land of their own? And what other land could it be but the one where David sang his psalms, and Solomon built the Temple? So they read the reports about the splendid Congresses and Herzl's diplomatic "triumphs" with growing wonder and excitement. The ancient hope seemed on the verge of fulfillment.

But there is a lag between hoping and acting. These recent arrivals were still seeking their bearings in the New World. Their energies were absorbed by the economic struggle, their capacity for the kind of action the movement demanded was severely limited by their lack of social and political influence. True enough, the movement drew its strength primarily from the multitudes, but without leaders multitudes are helpless, and nearly a quarter century was to elapse before the Center would produce from its own midst leaders of stature and authority. For two decades, therefore, the great reservoir of strength for Zionism which lay in the Center remained largely untapped.

An important segment of the Center was made up of the growing number of those who became affiliated with the Conservative wing of Judaism in America. The Hebrew Union College in Cincinnati, which furnished rabbis for Reform congregations, had, under the presidency of Kaufmann Kohler, become the powerhouse of anti-Zionism, and it continued in that role under Julian Morgenstern, who succeeded Kohler in 1921. The Jewish Theological Seminary in New York, on the other hand, promptly became one of its chief bulwarks. Its president, Solomon Schechter, saw in Zionism the promise of a revitalized Judaism, and although he deplored its tendency towards secularism, he entered the lists as one of its boldest champions. Schechter inspired his students with his own convictions, which they in turn carried to the fast growing Conservative congregations across the country.

2

Some reservations must, however, be made with respect to each of the three alignments, for none of them presented a monolithic front. From the start there were individuals in both the Right and Left who refused to fall in with the majorities in their hostility to Zionism, and as time went on the number of dissidents increased. For many years, in fact, the Right provided the principal leaders of the movement in America. In their own milieu these "renegades" were stared at coldly, but the enthusiasts on the East Side of New York and the West Side of Chicago gave them a warm welcome. They had poise and social prestige, these "westerners," their English was impeccable, and they were invaluable for refuting the charge that Zionism was a foreign product, capable of appealing only to the un-Americanized.

The Left was dented when Socialist Zionism appeared on the scene. The first group of Poale Zion (Workers of Zion) was organized in New York in 1903; soon afterwards groups appeared in a number of other cities also, and at a convention in Chicago in 1909 they became the "Jewish Socialist Labor Party Poale Zion." The party became affiliated with a world federation of Socialist Zionists which had come into existence two years earlier at The Hague and was subsequently accepted as an autonomous body within the World Zionist Organization. In America the Poale Zion set up in 1912 the Jewish National Workers' Alliance, a Zionist version of the Workmen's Circle, which grew more rapidly than the party itself, providing the usual fraternal benefits and, like the Circle, conducting afternoon schools where children were instructed in Yiddish and other subjects and inspired with zeal for Zionism and socialism alike. The Poale Zion fought valiantly against the "cosmopolitans" who dominated the Left with promises of universal salvation, and Socialist Zionism managed to win a sturdy if not large following among those who were skeptical about ready-made nostrums for all ailments and who, it is sad to reflect, are always a minority.

Nor did the Center present a solid front of allegiance to Zionism. Apart from the indifferent and lukewarm, there were strong dissenters among the pious, who held that the redemption of Israel must be left to the Lord and His anointed, and their hostility was confirmed when they saw the leadership of the movement, at home and abroad, in the hands of men who had thrown off "the yoke of Torah" and no longer adhered to the sanctified rituals of the faith. Were they to accept these "renegades" as redeemers?

But there were also many among the pious, in the New World as well as the Old, who believed that human effort was not incompatible with the divine purpose. They would not, they felt, be true to the traditional way of life if they forfeited the right to safeguard its interests by absenting themselves from the movement. So in 1902 a group of them met in Vilna and launched the Mizrachi* party which, like the Poale Zion, was accepted as an autonomous federation within the World Organization. A year later Mizrachi societies began to appear in America. The leader of the party in Europe was the courageous and brilliant Isaac Jacob Reines of Lida, and in America, it was stimulated to fresh vitality by Meyer Berlin, a resolute and resourceful leader, who arrived from Germany in 1913 and for more than a decade served as president of the American Mizrachi.

The party drew large numbers of the pious into the movement, but others in both parts of the world remained intransigent, and in 1912 their leaders met in Kattowitz, Silesia, and organized the Agudas Israel, which for many years did its best to impede the political progress of the movement. In the United States the Agudah did not gain a foothold until 1939, but by that time Zionist sentiment in America was too firmly intrenched for the dissidents to impair it, and the Agudah itself, which had in the meantime established settlements and schools of its own in Palestine, had to a large extent banked the fires of its hostility against it.

3

The scene of the first organized effort in America in response to Herzl's call was not New York, but Chicago, and it came early in 1896, more than a year before the First Zionist Congress convened in Basel. Those who launched it were "Russians," their leaders the brothers Harris and Bernard Horvich, with the writer and journalist Leon Zolotkoff, whom they sent to Basel to represent them, their "intellectual" and mentor. But among them there was one lone "German." He was Bernhard Felsenthal, now in his seventy-fifth year, whom we have already met as a militant Reform rabbi and equally militant abolitionist. How he came to reject one of the basic credos of Reform, "the

* The word is a contraction of the two Hebrew words meaning "spiritual center."

mission of Israel," is not to be easily explained, but he must have dismayed the "missionaries" when he declared that "we as individual Jews have no special message to deliver to mankind. From Palestine, from a Jewish *Musterstaat* (model state), our so-called mission can best be fulfilled." But Felsenthal, as already indicated, was not the only "deviationist" in the Reform rabbinate. Among the others who stood out promptly were Gustav Gottheil in New York and Maximilian Heller in New Orleans.

The name which those first followers of Herzl in America chose for their group was "Chicago Zionist Organization Number One," the numeral proclaiming their confidence that other groups would spring up in their wake. But soon they changed the name to Knights of Zion, and the units that affiliated with the Knights were called "Gates" —portals, that is, leading to Zion. The change was in emulation of other organizations in America, like the Knights of Labor and the Knights of Columbus, and they emulated also their mysteries and rituals which, to the despair of rigid rationalists, seem to exercise a fascination even on the minds of the sophisticated.

The Knights of Zion made rapid progress. Its most effective leader was Max Shulman, and Chicago furnished other men who made important contributions to Zionism in America, among them the jurists Julian W. Mack, Hugo Pam and Harry M. Fisher; the rabbis and scholars Gerson B. Levi, Solomon Freehof and Solomon Goldman; Nathan D. Kaplan, who was among the first American Jews to settle in Palestine; and the chemist and industrialist Abraham K. Epstein. But for years the Knights of Zion, with the stubbornness that clings to organizations even more than to individuals, refused to surrender its independence, and not until 1913 did it become part of the national body of the movement, the Federation of American Zionists.

4

The Federation was born in New York in July 1898 at a national conference at which nearly 100 societies, 36 of them with a membership of some 5,000 in New York alone, were represented. In a career of nearly two decades the Federation had ample opportunity to reveal the defects from which it suffered. The unit of membership was the group, and the primary responsibility of the individual was not to the national body, but to his society. Many of the societies were small and short-lived, and the support they gave the Federation was meager and uncertain. The defects were not cured until 1917 when the Federation was replaced by the Zionist Organization of America, in which the unit of membership was not the group but the individual.

Until the outbreak of the World War in 1914, the Federation was an "East Side affair," a scornful epithet flung at it by its foes and signifying that it was an alien product without prestige or influence. But its outstanding leaders were not East Siders. From 1898 to 1904 its president was the Orientalist and Columbia professor, Richard Gottheil, son of Rabbi Gustav Gottheil of Emanu-El, and he was succeeded by the prominent Baltimore physician Harry Friedenwald. The first secretary was the youthful Stephen S. Wise, already noted for the matchless oratorical power, courage and zest for combat, which before many years raised him to leadership not only in Jewish affairs, but in the general life of the country; when Wise rejected the offer of the pulpit of Emanu-El in New York, branding it as "muzzled," the startling adjective referred chiefly to the unwillingness of the worshippers to listen to Zionist sermons. A successor of Wise in the office of secretary was his colleague and rival Judah L. Magnes, also an impressive orator and leader of initiative and courage; he was a brother-in-law of Louis Marshall and the darling and despair of his social "equals." But the leaders were like British officers in an army of "natives"; in their own milieu they could win no recruits to join them in their "descent."

The others who came to the fore in those early years of travail for Zionism in America were men who could not even hope to extend their influence beyond the masses from Eastern Europe. There was Zevi Hirsch Masliansky, for example, who had been active for years in the movement in Russia, an orator of extraordinary power who kept his large audiences spellbound. There was Joseph Barondess, the first prominent labor leader to free himself from the fetters of doctrinaire socialism and embrace the Zionist cause, also a persuasive orator and in addition a skillful organizer. In 1902 Jacob de Haas, a man of bold ideas and dynamic temperament, came from England at Herzl's behest to become secretary of the Federation of American Zionists. The sparkling Abraham Goldberg was a gifted writer and brilliant speaker, who knew how to enthuse his audiences, while his antithesis, Senior Abel, was a competent administrator who commanded respect with his quiet but cogent logic. And there was Louis Lipsky. He was born in Rochester, New York; his language was English, not Yiddish; his cultural background Western. Nevertheless, he was essentially an East European; if nothing else, a strong admixture of the literary artist made him partial to the exuberance and color in the life of the immigrants from the East. Lipsky became the outstanding figure in this early period of American Zionism, and eventually rose to a position of leadership in the movement on the international level also. He held many posts and performed many tasks, his first assignment being that of editor of the impecunious monthly organ of the Federation, *The Maccabean*, which began its brave and toilsome career in 1901. Lipsky was a forceful writer, a formidable debater and adroit parliamentarian; nearly always it fell to his lot to preside at the annual conventions, and he proved a past master in the art of controlling the storms that frequently swept over them.

5

To the American Jews, "German" or "Russian," who led the forces of Zionism in America must be added a number of brilliant emissaries from abroad who came at the behest of the world organization to extend and deepen the movement in the New World.

They began to arrive after the world movement had undergone two major crises: the untimely death of Theodor Herzl on July 3, 1904, and the rupture that occurred at the Seventh Zionist Congress a year later, when a minority of the delegates, led by the novelist Israel Zangwill of England, walked out and later established the Jewish Territorial Organization. The Congress was torn by the question of what to do with the offer of Uganda in East Africa, which Herzl had received from Britain; Zangwill and his followers refused to remain after the Congress, by an overwhelming majority, voted not to engage in colonization in countries other than Palestine and regions adjacent to it. Territorialism, as this defection from Zionism was named, also became a world movement, and until 1925, when the organization founded by Zangwill disbanded, it roamed the globe in futile efforts to find some region other than Palestine where Jews might establish an autonomous settlement. It even took a hand, for reasons that seemed unrelated to its objective, in the attempt to check the concentration of Jewish immigrants on the Atlantic seaboard by routing some of them to the port of Galveston. In the early years of its career Territorialism played hob in a number of lands with the movement from which it sprang, but in America its divisive influence created a problem only in its Socialist wing.

To the leaders in Europe the fast growing Jewish community in the New World was a bright hope but a present disappointment, and they sent some of their ablest apostles to propagandize it. The most persuasive among them were Nahum Sokolow and Shmaryah Levin, and their effectiveness, curiously enough, reached out to some of the notables whom Magnes, Wise and Gottheil tried in vain to influence. Sokolow and Levin succeeded in drawing the two foremost Jewish philanthropists in America, Jacob H. Schiff and Julius Rosenwald, into the orbit not, of course, of political Zionism, but of cultural work in Palestine: the establishment of a cultural center in the ancient land, where teachers, students and scholars would devote themselves quietly and serenely to Jewish learning, and even to the humanities and sciences, was a project to which even the most ardent anti-Zionist could be reconciled.

Nahum Sokolow was a man of exceptional gifts, a master of many languages, including English, and a distinguished Hebrew journalist, scholar and essayist. He was a brilliant speaker and even more brilliant conversationalist, astute and urbane—a diplomat to the manner born. Not many years afterwards, in fact, he was to be acknowledged as the diplomat par excellence of the Jewish people. But as an orator, with the rare ability to stir at once the heads and hearts of masses of people, he was surpassed by Shmaryah Levin. With his first appearance in America in 1906 Levin left his audiences dazzled and astonished. He was one of the most potent forces in the progress of Zionism in America, a rare synthesis of the teacher and orator, standing before his audiences like an ancient Hebrew prophet, castigating them and uplifting and comforting them at the same time.

6

In the fateful year 1914, when nations and political aspirations across the world confronted an overshadowing crisis, the alignments among the Jews of America towards this quasi-messianic enterprise held firm, and the alignments within the movement itself had taken definite shape. It, too, had its Right, the Orthodox Mizrachi, who stood for a Jewish commonwealth in Palestine based on Torah; the Left, or Poale Zion, whose aim was a cooperative or socialist commonwealth in Palestine; and the Center, or General Zionists, as they came to be called, who declined to commit themselves on religious and economic issues, but whose attitude was, on the whole, liberal and "bourgeois." It was the Center, the largest of the three, which stood forth as the spokesman of the cause to the Jewish community and the country at large.

By 1914, moreover, the Center had given birth to three auxiliary bodies, the Order Sons of Zion, Young Judea, and Hadassah, all of which, and especially the third, became important factors in the growth of the movement in America. The Order, which came into existence in 1907, aimed to attach the individual to the movement more firmly than the ephemeral Zionist societies were able to do, by providing its members with the customary benefits of a fraternal society. At the same time one of its primary aims was to labor for the fulfillment of the Basel Program. By 1914 the Order numbered several thousand members, grouped in "camps," as the local lodges were called.

That year, Young Judea, the youth branch of the movement, embraced 175 clubs of boys and girls between the ages of ten and eighteen with a total membership of 5,000. Young Judea, launched five years earlier, aimed to provide a future for Zionism in America by imbuing its members with "the high ideals and traditions of Judaism . . . a love for Palestine and a desire to participate in its rebuilding." Its first president was the educator, scholar and essayist Israel Friedlaender, who was to meet his death in 1920 at the hands of bandits while engaged on a mission of relief in Russia.

Hadassah, the Women's Zionist Organization of America, which began modestly in 1912 by federating a number of existing "Daughters of Zion" societies, was destined to become the largest Zionist body in the country. It set itself the double aim of "promoting Jewish institutions and enterprises in Palestine and fostering Zionist ideals in America,"and its principal task under the first was to promote the health of the people of Palestine, irrespective of race or creed. Early in 1913 two trained nurses dispatched by the new organization established a health center in Jerusalem, and thus began what became an imposing network of institutions for healing and health conservation throughout the neglected land. Hadassah grew rapidly and discarded the tutelage of the men's organization with which it began. From the Atlantic to the Pacific its chapters multiplied and flourished.

A sizable group of women came to the fore in Hadassah who proved able organizers and leaders, among them Rose Jacobs and Rose Halprin, who served on the Executive of the world movement, but the towering figure among them was Henrietta Szold. She was the organization's founder and inspiration, its mentor and pacemaker, and after numerous labors covering more than three decades, she achieved among her host of followers the status of a saint. Henrietta acquired her intense love for her faith and people in the home of her distinguished father, Rabbi Benjamin Szold of Baltimore, and after some years of service to the Jewish Publication Society, she devoted all her imaginative resourcefulness and meticulous industry to Zionism. She rose to a foremost place in the councils and executive functions of the world movement, and in Palestine, which she eventually made her home, she was revered as the "mother of the Yishuv."*

7

At the Eleventh Zionist Congress, which met in Vienna in September 1913, Nahum Sokolow read a letter of greeting from another American, a recent convert to the cause, who was shortly to be saddled with responsibility for the fortunes of the world movement and the fate of the expanding Yishuv. He was Louis Dembitz Brandeis, the Boston lawyer who has already appeared in this narrative as the chief designer in 1910 of the Protocol of Peace, which inaugurated a new era in the relations between workers and employers in the strife-torn garment industry. The position of authority to which Brandeis' exceptional gifts had raised him in American public life was so high, that a message from him to the Congress was considered significant. He was the most commanding personality the cause had attracted in America, and his attachment to it was profound and not likely to remain platonic.

There were forty delegates from the United States among the 500 from all over the world who assembled in Vienna. It was not a negligible contingent, and together with the twelve who came from Canada, attested that the movement was making headway in the New World. By 1914 the Jews in the Dominion numbered about 100,000, most of them, by far, having arrived after 1881, with the largest concentrations in Montreal, Toronto and Winnipeg. They were well represented in the public life of the land, and as pioneers, colonizers and entrepreneurs. Their communal institutions were generally modeled on those of their coreligionists in the United States, but Zionism had made proportionately much greater progress among them.

The delegation in Vienna, however, was certainly not commensurate with the size and importance of the community in the United States. But eight years were to pass before another Zionist Congress would convene, and during those critical years the chief burden of the world movement, as we shall see, would be borne by this outpost in the New World.

* The Hebrew word *Yishuv*, meaning "settlement," was specifically applied to the Jewish community in Palestine before the establishment of the State of Israel.

CHAPTER 17

World at War 1914-18

1

THE FIRST WORLD WAR HAD BEEN DECIMATING THE YOUNG manhood of Europe and ravaging its fairest regions for nearly three years before the giant Republic of the West entered the conflict, and it was another year before its might bore down to crush the first bid of the "master race" for world domination. Unlike the second, which Germany was to launch a quarter of a century later, the first gave rise to a long and acrid controversy over the degree of guilt of the different nations who were drawn into the vortex; and it may well be that none of them was blameless. But there can be no doubt as to where the immediate responsibility rested. Austria would not have declared war on little Serbia on July 28, 1914 without assurance of support from Germany in the dire consequences that were sure to follow. It was "the day" foreseen and desired by the anti-Semitic prophets of "German destiny," whose teachings had infected the entire nation.

The government of the United States began with a resolute effort to be scrupulously neutral. President Woodrow Wilson, whose lofty idealism led him at times to underrate the interests and instincts that control ordinary men, went so far as to exhort his countrymen to "be impartial in thought as well as in action." But his call fell on deaf ears. From the start the majority sympathized with the Allies. In spite of past differences, its sense of solidarity with England, rooted in language, culture and blood, came to the fore, nor could the presence of autocratic Russia among the foes of Germany overcome the conviction that the democratic civilization of the West was in danger of being submerged by the hordes of an arrogant and ruthless military despotism, the new "Huns," as they came to be called.

For most of the Jews in America, however, the presence of Russia could not be so easily brushed aside. Compared to the Russian brand of anti-Semitism, the German gave the illusion of being innocuous. Russia was the land of the Pale of Settlement, of mass pogroms, of the

Beilis blood libel. Countless thousands of Jews in America had felt the Russian knout, in one form or another, on their own skins; they could say with the Psalmist: "The plowers plowed upon my back; they made long their furrows." So the prevailing sentiment among them began with sympathy for the Central Powers, although there was one group in the community, the Zionists, whose attitude was almost from the first pro-Ally. For, several months after the war began, Turkey threw in her lot with the Central Powers, and the Zionists felt that an Allied victory would break up the stagnant Turkish empire and give their cause the opportunity which Herzl had sought in vain.

As the war went on and mounted in ferocity it gave rise to events which made it impossible for America to remain aloof and changed decisively the attitude of the entire Jewish community. American neutrality was destroyed chiefly by Germany's unrestricted submarine warfare, which took many American lives, and by the disclosure of her clumsy attempts to incite Mexico and Japan to make war on the United States. A sharp change in Jewish sentiment took place when, on March 15, 1917, a revolution drove Nicholas II from his throne and Russia became a constitutional democracy with civil, political and religious equality for all her people, including, of course, the Jews. And when, three weeks later, the Congress declared that a state of war existed between the United States and Germany, the Jews of America came forward to defend their country with a readiness exceeded by no other community in the land.

2

The reports which began reaching the Jews of America in the early fall of 1914 on the plight of their people in the eastern war zones were not calculated to diminish their detestation of the czarist regime. Those zones embraced the borderlands between Russia and the Central Powers, stretching from the Baltic to the Black Sea, in whose cities and towns lived some 75 per cent of the Jews of the world. Across those lands the embattled armies advanced and retreated. In August the Russians invaded East Prussia, and the same month they were hurled back in the Battle of Tannenberg. In September 1914 they captured Lemberg, the metropolis of Galicia, and drove on into the Carpathians; but the following Spring the Germans forced them out and pushed on until, by the fall of 1915, they had taken Warsaw and Vilna and were in possession of Russian Poland and Lithuania. In 1916 the Russians managed to reconquer a part of eastern Galicia, and in August of that year Rumania yielded to the temptation of plunging into the fray and joined the Allies, but before the year ended her capital had fallen and Rumania was a conquered land. Such was the series of disasters which the Central Powers inflicted on the huge armies of the Czar, crippling and demoralizing them, exposing the corruption and incompetence of the regime, and furnishing the fuel which flamed into revolution in March 1917.

In addition to the woes to which all the inhabitants in the borderlands were exposed, the Jews became the victims of special afflictions. They suffered even more at the hands of their "friends" than at those of the enemy. The Russian generals, defeated and disgraced, needed a scapegoat, and they found it as usual in the Jews, whom they accused of having commerce with the enemy. Whole communities were evacuated into the interior, some of them as far as Siberia. Women, children and old men were packed into boxcars or marched for hundreds of miles, and many of them perished on the way. When the Russians swept into Galicia and Bukowina—and six times in the course of the war they broke in and were driven back—the Jews in those provinces of Austria fled westward, but anti-Semitic Vienna did not welcome them, and they found small respite in the camps which were hastily improvised for them.

In Germany the Jews were not exposed to special physical hardships, but they were the victims of a studied insult by an anti-Semitic group in the Reichstag, on whose insistence a census was taken of the Jews in uniform, intended to prove that only a small proportion of them were serving at the front. The count disproved the slanders, but it served the purpose of humiliating the Jews and fomenting hostility against them.

The actual figures for all the belligerent countries, in fact, belied the defamations of anti-Semites everywhere. In Russia six to seven hundred thousand Jews fought in the armies of the Czar, all of them barred from officer's rank. They were not, however, barred from shedding their blood; the casualties among them numbered scores of thousands, and many received awards for conspicuous gallantry. In the armed forces of the other Allied powers there were thousands of Jewish commissioned officers, with Jewish generals in the French and Belgian armies. One of the most brilliant soldiers in the war was Lieutenant General Sir John Monash, the commander of the Australian divisions who fought in France. In Germany the 100,000 Jews who served in the armed forces and the 28,000 who gave their lives represented a larger proportion for the Jews in the country than did the corresponding figures for the population as a whole. In the Austro-Hungarian empire the number of

Jews in service is estimated to have exceeded 300,000. There were high-ranking officers, including generals, among them, and large numbers, in the Hungarian contingents in particular, were decorated for exceptional bravery in the field.

3

The woes which the war inflicted on their people in Europe made the Jews in America realize that they were confronted with a relief problem of unprecedented magnitude. The peacetime pressures that weighed upon the Jews in Eastern Europe had, to an extent, been relieved by emigration. The war put an end to that source of respite also: in the year preceding the war nearly 140,000 of them had entered the United States; in the year that followed, the number dropped to 26,000, and it went on declining until in 1919 it stood at only 3,000. The appeals from the war zones for immediate assistance and, later, for help in the task of reconstructing the shattered communities, could not be denied, and organized relief efforts were launched in neutral countries, as well as in Germany, Austria and Russia itself. But it goes without saying that the major response had to come from the big brother across the Atlantic.

It came promptly, but—such is the strength of faction in human affairs—each of the three groupings we have noted began by setting up a relief agency of its own. The first to act was the Center which, in October 1914, organized the Central Committee for the Relief of Jewish War Sufferers, with Leon Kamaiky, the publisher of the Orthodox *Daily News*, as chairman. Several weeks later the American Jewish Committee, the spearhead of the Right, established the American Jewish Relief Committee, with Louis Marshall, president of the first, as chairman of the second. The following year the Left entered the field with the People's Relief Committee, of which Alexander Kahn, a prominent member of the Socialist Party, became the chairman. All three applied themselves vigorously to the task of raising money and dispensing it for the relief of the war victims. They soon realized, however, that with regard to the second function, at least, joint action was essential, and in November 1914 the American Jewish Joint Distribution Committee was created, the new body starting with the first two agencies and being joined later by the third. Disaster at last united the disparate segments of the community, if only for the purpose of binding the wounds of the victims.

The Joint or JDC, as the new agency was briefly designated, became one of the conspicuous landmarks in the story of the Jews in America and even more in that of Jewish communities in many other parts of the world, wherever distress called for relief and the havoc wrought by war or persecution called for rehabilitation. As its name indicates, the Joint began by taking over the administration of the funds obtained by the three relief committees, but by the end of 1915 it took over the work of raising funds also, and for decades afterwards it performed both functions in a manner that commanded general admiration and gratitude. For its mission did not end with the termination of hostilities. Indeed, it faced its hardest and most important tasks when the war was over: finding homes for hundreds of thousands of refugees; checking epidemic outbreaks and bringing medical aid to the stricken; caring for the scores of thousands of orphaned children; restoring elementary schools and other educational and cultural institutions; and most important, promoting economic rehabilitation through free loan societies, credit cooperatives, farm settlement and other means.

The Joint rallied to its service the outstanding figures among the Jews in America in the hundreds of communities, large and small, across the country and in its central councils in New York. Its first chairman was Felix M. Warburg, with the leading members of the American Jewish Committee at his side: Louis Marshall, Cyrus Adler, Jacob H. Schiff, Herbert and Arthur Lehman, Cyrus Sulzberger and others. In 1932 Paul Baerwald, of the Lazard Frères banking firm, who had been its treasurer, became the chairman, and in 1941 Edward M. M. Warburg, son of the first chairman, was named to that post. Among the other prominent men on the Committee were William Rosenwald, son of the Chicago philanthropist; James N. Rosenberg, and Jonah B. Wise, son of the founder of Reform Judaism in America. The prominent Orthodox representatives on the Committee included Harry Fischel and the rabbis Meyer Berlin, Moses Z. Margolies, Leo Jung, and Aaron Teitelbaum, of whom the last carried out important missions overseas. The Joint was fortunate also with the other men to whom it entrusted its complex and arduous activities in the field, especially in Europe. They included Albert Lucas, its first secretary; Boris D. Bogen, its director-general; Joseph C. Hyman, Joseph J. Schwartz, Moses A. Leavitt, Isidore Coons, and many others. Its able European director for many years was Bernhard Kahn.

The work of the JDC was beset with numerous problems, which required the creation of specialized agencies and a far-flung network of activities in the Old World, as well as a nation-wide apparatus for raising the necessary funds in the New. By the end of 1916 some $6,000,000 had been raised; in 1917 alone the amount was $10,000,000, and in the years that followed it continued to mount. The Jews of America learned to give; they gave on a scale which no other voluntary effort by any group had ever attained. Nor should there be omitted from the tally of their total response the contributions of the many *landsmanshaft* societies and countless individuals who sent aid to communities, relatives and friends abroad. Those contributions are not easily calculated, but may be safely assumed to have amounted to a huge total.

4

But there was one community in a land not in the war zones of Europe, which also sent a call for help to the Jews of America. The settlement in Palestine—the Yishuv—was in distress.

By 1914 its population had grown to 85,000, and although the majority still depended on the *Chalukah*, the dole system replenished by funds that flowed in from communities across the world, the spirit of the Yishuv was now dominated by the sturdy and self-reliant farmers and workers, who came "to build and be rebuilt," as one of their songs expressed it. Some 12,000 of them were settled in nearly fifty farm colonies. They were refuting the skeptics who held that Jews could not become successful farmers, and they proved themselves able not only to fructify the neglected soil, but to defend their crops against brigands and spoilers. Another attainment, the revival of the Hebrew language as a living vernacular, which skeptics had likewise declared an impossible dream, was also a reality. And the Jews of the world, including the great conflux in America, had been watching the still tender growth with pride and solicitude. There were those—and they were comparatively few—who avowed themselves Zionists, and those who insisted they were not, but the Yishuv had a special place in the affections of all of them.

And now it was gravely menaced. The funds which sustained the *Chalukah* stopped flowing and its thousands of pensioners were faced with starvation. War and blockade shut off the overseas markets for the three export commodities—wines, oranges and almonds—on which the plantation colonies depended, and halted the importation of foodstuffs, on which the cities depended. Then came a locust plague of unusual severity and ravaged the vegetation of the country. To these economic afflictions were added others that stemmed from political causes. The Turkish officials, charging the Jews with planning to establish a government of their own, set out to destroy the Zionist institutions and arrested and exiled many of their leaders. Thousands of Jews who were Russian subjects and now enemy aliens, were expelled from Palestine, managing to find asylum in Egypt.

The war, moreover, enfeebled and disrupted what was basically the most important economic and political asset of the Yishuv, the world Zionist movement. The communities in East Europe, from which the movement derived most of its moral and material strength, were broken and helpless. The two most important branches of the world organization, the Russian and the German, were sundered. Could the movement in Europe be expected to cope with the perils that lowered over the Yishuv or seize the opportunities which the upheavals of a world war might produce? For it was apparent that this war would bring drastic political changes, and the goal for which Herzl had so desperately and vainly striven might be close at hand.

5

In this crisis, too, the New World stepped in to "redress the balance of the Old." On the eve of the war the organized forces of Zionism in America were still small and feeble; the convention of the Federation that met in Rochester, New York, in June 1914 represented less than 15,000 men and women who had subscribed to the Basel Program by paying the small coin in token of adherence called the "shekel," and the budget the delegates adopted amounted to the paltry sum of $12,000. Six weeks later the sudden emergency produced a transformation. On August 30, 1914 an "Extraordinary Conference" took place in New York, a Provisional Executive Committee for General Zionist Affairs was established, and a call was issued for an Emergency Fund of $200,000. Ten months later, the treasurer of the new Committee, E. W. Lewin-Epstein, reported that the fund had already transmitted $350,000 to Palestine, and before the succeeding convention the number of shekel-payers had more than doubled. American Zionism was sailing on broader waters with wider horizons, and the reason was apparent: a new captain stood on the bridge. Louis D. Brandeis had been elected chairman of the new Committee and in that capacity was now the leader of Zionism in America.

Brandeis was already fifty-eight years old, having been born in 1856 in Louisville, Kentucky, and his reputation as "the people's lawyer" and leader of the liberal forces in America was nation-wide. He had become a symbol of the cause of the common man, for whom he fought to keep open the avenues of opportunity against the greed of monopoly and what he called "the curse of bigness." It was all in the authentic American tradition as sung and preached by Emerson, Whitman and Theodore Parker, but Brandeis gave it expression not so much in words as in deeds. Towards any goal he chose, his intellect and will moved together with extraordinary skill and relentless resolution. He had, of course, gained many and distinguished enemies; when in 1916 Woodrow Wilson named him to the Supreme Court, the groan that went up from Wall Street was, in the words of one reporter, "like the echo of a great national disaster." And a drawn battle was fought out between the reactionary and progressive forces in America before the Senate confirmed the nomination.

The most important Jewish influence in the early life of Brandeis appears to have been his maternal uncle Lewis Naphtali Dembitz, whom we have already met as an ardent abolitionist and one of the nominators of Lincoln at the Republican Convention of 1860. Dembitz was a prominent lawyer and civic leader in Louisville, learned, deeply religious and a Zionist. In his contact with the garment workers in New York in 1910, Brandeis came to admire the intelligence and social idealism of the Jewish immigrants from Eastern Europe; they made him more keenly aware of his kinship with his people. And in Boston his full conversion to Zionism was accomplished by Jacob de Haas, one of Herzl's early disciples. Brandeis was allured by Herzl's vision of a Jewish state; it was, he felt, a noble ideal and possible of attainment also; in harmony, moreover, with the spirit of America. In 1907 Jacob H. Schiff had declared that one could not "at the same time be a true American and an honest adherent of the Zionist movement," a statement which had been vehemently denounced at a Zionist mass meeting called for the purpose. Brandeis held that "to be good Americans, we must be better Jews, and to be better Jews we must become Zionists." And as for the specter of dual allegiance, which was never completely laid, Brandeis removed it from the minds of a great many with the pithy statement: "Multiple loyalties are objectionable only if they are inconsistent." Brandeis wrote without attempts at elegance, he spoke without oratorical effects, but never was the cause presented with such simple cogency and, it goes without saying, by a voice of such commanding authority.

6

The new spirit with which American Zionism was infused found expression not only in the prompt and impressive increase in the number of its organized adherents and in the large sums raised by the

Emergency Fund, but in other significant ways. A group of men and women of distinction and influence joined the standard which was now held by Brandeis. Among them were Julian W. Mack, a judge of the United States Circuit Court; Felix Frankfurter, who in 1939 was to follow Brandeis on the United States Supreme Court; the philanthropists Nathan Straus of New York and Mary Fels of Philadelphia; Benjamin Victor Cohen, who was to figure as an important member of Franklin Roosevelt's "brain trust"; Louis E. Kirstein of Boston, one of the foremost New England merchants and communal leaders; Colonel Harry Cutler of Providence, Rhode Island, manufacturer, soldier and also a prominent civic leader; Eugene Meyer, Jr., one of the most brilliant financial experts in America, and others. The Provisional Executive Committee not only kept Zionist institutions alive, but by means of a Transfer Department made it possible for millions of dollars to be sent by individuals to Palestine and other parts of the Middle East, and to Russia and Rumania also. Its difficult operations were conducted with ingenuity and daring, and represented a major contribution to war relief.

Nor were the Zionists the only ones to come to the aid of stricken Palestine; one of the first sizable sums for relief came from the American Jewish Committee; it was sent to Henry Morgenthau, the American ambassador to Turkey and it was taken to Palestine on an American warship! Early in 1915 the American collier *Vulcan* arrived in Jaffa with 900 tons of food for the people of Palestine. Zionists and members of the American Jewish Committee had collaborated in the project, but there was some unpleasantness when the second partner refused to let the ship fly the flag of Zion beside the Stars and Stripes. That would have looked like "dual allegiance."

No such issue arose in an even more important enterprise for Palestine which had its origin in America: the American Zionist Medical Unit. Health conditions in Palestine had been steadily deteriorating, and the Provisional Committee charged Hadassah, established only three years earlier, with the task of organizing and dispatching a Medical Unit of physicians, nurses, social workers and administrators, together with the necessary supplies and equipment. The creation of the Unit involved not only organizational and financial problems, but diplomatic ones also, all of them borne by the tireless Henrietta Szold, who allowed no detail to escape her attention. The experience which she and her associates gained in this pioneer undertaking stood them in good stead in the years that followed, during which Hadassah built up its large network of health institutions in Palestine. The Medical

Unit, consisting of forty-five men and women, and headed by the noted economist, social worker and physician, Isaac M. Rubinow, arrived in Palestine in September 1918, when the British were already driving the Turks and Germans out of the country.

7

In every country groups and places wish to be looked upon as assets to the nation in peace and even more in war. Cities and towns, universities, churches and societies have their historians to preserve the names and deeds of their distinguished citizens and members, especially of those who fought and sacrificed in their country's battles, and the numerous Soldiers' and Sailors' Monuments bear further testimony to the strength and prevalence of this desire. It is strong, of course, in minority groups also, and particularly so in a conspicuous minority like the Jews, who have been endowed with an unusually large assortment of critics and maligners. For in times of stress and peril slander finds many open ears, and professional traducers reap large harvests.

The lesson of the Civil War, when defamation was rife and the Jews were falsely accused of evading service in the armed forces, was not lost on Jewish leaders. Before the end of 1917 an Office of War Records had been established by the American Jewish Committee, which performed a statistical labor of colossal magnitude, for if the number of Jews who bore arms for America in the War for Independence was counted in the scores or hundreds, and in the Civil War in the thousands, those in the First World War numbered hundreds of thousands. The labor bore fruit, not because it silenced the anti-Semites—prejudice and rancor are immune to facts—but because it fortified the self-respect of the Jews themselves, for the most precious asset of a community as of an individual is the sense of its own worth. It must, however, be set down that manifestations of anti-Semitism in America during the First World War appear to have been fewer and less serious than during the Civil War. Perhaps the most flagrant was the statement in a "Manual of Instructions for Medical Advisory Boards" that "the foreign born, especially Jews, are more apt to malinger than the native born." Woodrow Wilson ordered all copies of that manual to be destroyed.

8

The overall figures establish the fact that the Jews in America contributed more than their share of the fighting forces in the war and suffered more than their share of casualties. The computers do not all arrive at exactly the same figures, but all their findings bear out that conclusion. The total number of Jews in all branches of the service was approximately 225,000, or about 4.5 per cent of all Americans in uniform, while the number of Jews in the country was only 3 per cent of the total population. This higher ratio is explained first, by the large number of Jewish volunteers—thirty to forty thousands of them; second, by the greater efficiency with which the draft operated in the larger centers of population; and third, by the relatively fewer Jews engaged in agriculture and the metal industries, where many exemptions were granted. Jewish casualties were 3,500 dead, or 5 per cent of the entire American toll, and 12,000 wounded.

Of the 225,000 Jews in service 170,000 were in the Army, 23,000 in the Navy, 12,250 in the Marine Corps and the rest in the other branches. In the Army as a whole the infantry came to 27 per cent of the total; of the Jews in the Army the number who served in the infantry amounted to 48 per cent of the total. In the American Expeditionary Force the combatant branches—infantry, engineers, signal and aviation, and cavalry—were 60 per cent of the total; of the Jews in the A. E. F. the proportion in those branches was 75 per cent. A popular legend assigned an inordinately large number of Jews to the sheltered Quartermasters Corps, the business branch of the Army; in point of fact their ratio in the Corps was somewhat smaller than for the Army as a whole—5.9 per cent as against 6.2 per cent.

In all branches of the service there were over 9,000 commissioned officers who were Jews: over 8,000 in the Army, 900 in the Navy, and over 100 in the Marine Corps. The Jewish officers in the Army included 100 colonels and lieutenant colonels, 500 majors, 1,500 captains and 6,000 lieutenants. Colonel Abel Davis became a brigadier general, and Colonel Milton I. Foreman, who rose to the rank of lieutenant general, was the first National Commander of the American Legion. Both men had fought in the war against Spain. In the Navy the ranking Jewish officer was Rear Admiral Joseph Strauss, who commanded the mine laying operations in the North Sea; in the Marine Corps it was Brigadier General Charles H. Lauchheimer.

9

Statistics speak eloquently to minds gifted with imagination, but quantity alone can be a drab surface without the added dimension of quality, just as names and dates and facts, so indispensable to history, may leave the mind untouched by the travail of the human spirit, which is its essence. These hosts who now wore the brown and blue of the American armed forces belonged to a people to whom it was almost a fashion to deny the so-called martial virtues; most of them came from lands where they or their immediate forebears had been hounded and terrorized, and from civilian occupations that afforded no opportunity for the development of muscular prowess and physical endurance. What sort of soldiers would these "East Side boys," as they were called, make? Army officers assigned to train them began by being skeptical, but they soon discovered that in keenness and courage those youths were not behind the recruits from any other ethnic group, and in intelligence and resourcefulness they were outstanding.

They made excellent fighting men. Over 1,000 awards and citations for valor were bestowed on Jewish soldiers in the Army, 723 by the American Command, 287 by the French, and the rest by other Allied commands. Three were awarded the Congressional Medal of Honor and 147 the Distinguished Service Medal and Cross. Their names and deeds would crowd these pages to excess, but some of them should not be omitted. The three Congressional Medalists were Sergeants Sidney Gumpertz, Benjamin Kaufman and William Sawelson. Single-handed Gumpertz silenced a German machine-gun nest and took its crew prisoners. Kaufman, with one arm rendered useless by a bullet, performed a similar feat; in 1941, it may be added, Kaufman became National Commander of the Jewish War Veterans of the United States. Sawelson, who was awarded the Medal posthumously, was killed after he left his shelter in a rain of bullets and was assisting a wounded comrade. The winners of the Distinguished Service Cross included Louis Abend, Jack Hershkowitz, Abe Levenson, Jean Mathis, Alfred Meyerowitz, Hyman Silberman and Hyman Yarnis, to name at random only a few among a great many. The extraordinary heroism they displayed added to the luster of American arms in the titanic struggle through the towns, fields and forests of northern France, which broke the might of the German military machine, the most awesome the world had yet witnessed.

But the two Jewish heroes of the War whose deeds became almost legendary were Sam Dreben and Abraham Krotoshinsky. Dreben, who was known as "the fighting Jew," was that rara avis among modern Jews, a soldier of fortune. Before enlisting for service in France, he had fought in the war against Spain, in the Boxer Rebellion in China, and in a number of Latin American revolutions. Many were his exploits and decorations, but he performed his most spectacular feat when he rushed a German machine-gun nest and killed twenty-three of its crew. Krotoshinsky was the hero of one of the most heroic incidents of the American sweep through northern France, the stand of the "Lost Battalion." This unit of about 600 men of the 77th Division, under the command of Major Charles W. Whittlesey, was surrounded by the Germans in the Argonne Forest, refused to surrender, and for five days fought off the assaults of the enemy, lacking food, water and ammunition. It even found itself the target of American guns also. Its only hope was to bring word of its plight to the American lines. Singly or in small patrols, thirty-six men attempted it and were either killed or captured. Krotoshinsky volunteered to be the thirty-seventh, and after incredible escapes, gassed and wounded, he reached the American lines, and the "Lost Battalion," which by that time consisted of not more than 200 survivors, was saved.

The division to which that battalion belonged was 40 per cent Jewish. It was the only American division to reach the Aisne River, after penetrating further into the German lines than any other. In April 1919 Lieutenant Colonel Douglas Campbell, one of its officers, told an audience: "The Jewish boys of the 77th Division were the best soldiers on earth. They participated in the greatest battles and emerged sound." The 26th Division also contained a large proportion of Jews, of whom Major General Clarence R. Edwards said that they made an enviable record. "I remember instances of formerly intolerant gentiles," he added, "who asked that Jews be made officers in order that they might be their leaders." General John J. Pershing, the commander in chief of the American Expeditionary Force, wrote: "When the time came to serve their country under arms, no class of people served with more patriotism or with higher motives than the young Jews who volunteered or were drafted and who went overseas with our other young Americans."

10

In 1917 the Jewish community in America was aware at last of its responsibility for the religious welfare of its sons in the armed forces of the nation, and only a few days after the country entered the war emissaries from twenty-two national Jewish organizations established the agency which eventually called itself the National Jewish Welfare Board. In the training camps at home, as well as in centers behind the lines overseas, the Board conducted a variety of activities to meet the religious, recreational and personal needs of Jewish soldiers, sailors and marines, and together with similar agencies under the auspices of the other faiths, constituted the officially recognized United Service Organization for National Defense (USO). More national organizations became affiliated with the Welfare Board, and after the war it took under its wing The Young Men's and Young Women's Hebrew Associations, and Jewish Community Centers in the United States and Canada, providing them with expert guidance and educational material specially prepared to serve their needs. The designation of Jewish chaplains in the field was no longer the lamentable problem it had been in the Civil War.

On the home front Jews made an outstanding contribution to the war effort as members of government agencies responsible for the expansion and functioning of the country's gigantic war production machine. Foremost in this field was Bernard M. Baruch. In 1918 he became chairman of the War Industries Board, but even before that appointment he had begun a remarkable career of public service, which eventually brought him general recognition as the "elder statesman" of America. The War Industries Board had started as the Council of National Defense, and among its seven members, who were responsible for mobilizing the economic resources of the nation for defense production, there were in addition to Baruch, Samuel Gompers and Julius Rosenwald. In 1918 Eugene Meyer Jr. was appointed a director, then manager of the War Finance Corporation, an agency charged with the equally important task of financing business enterprise for the war effort. Shortly after the war Albert D. Lasker, whom President Warren G. Harding made chairman of the United States Shipping Board, reorganized the shipping industry and laid the foundations of the American merchant marine; he had already established his reputation as the leading advertising executive in America. And the Liberty Bond campaigns found American Jews in the first line of those who not only purchased shares of the issues, but promoted and sold them.

11

A contribution to the armed forces of the Allies, if not directly to those of the United States, was also made by American Jews to a military unit of singular historic interest. It was a Zionist enterprise, stemming from the conviction that the goal of the movement would be brought nearer if Jews played a part in wresting Palestine from the Turks, since only those who fight for victory may rightly claim a share in its fruits. The exertions of a group of zealots in America and other lands, who labored for the project were not in vain. For the first time since the Jews under Bar Kochba had risen up in arms against Rome more than eighteen centuries earlier, Jewish battalions, which came to be known as the Jewish Legion and included a large number of volunteers from America, fought in Palestine for the liberation of the ancient homeland.

The Legion had its genesis with the exiles from Palestine who had found shelter in Egypt, and its leading champions were Joseph Trumpeldor, one of the epic heroes of the Zionist saga, and Vladimir Jabotinsky, a brilliant writer and orator who later became the leader of the Revisionist or maximalist party of the movement. The British military authorities in Cairo were not receptive to their proposal that a Jewish fighting force be organized as a unit of the British army to participate in the conquest of Palestine. They offered instead to let the Jews form a body of muleteers to carry food and ammunition to the soldiers who manned the trenches in the ill-fated Gallipoli campaign. The offer was reluctantly accepted, and the Legion may be said to have begun with the 650 men who made up this Zion Mule Corps, as it was called. Its service, though auxiliary, was often performed under heavy fire; it sustained sixty-one casualties and some of its men were decorated for valor.

The Gallipoli campaign was abandoned in March 1916, the Mule Corps was disbanded, and the struggle for a Jewish unit to fight in Palestine was resumed, this time in London. Among the formidable obstacles it faced was the opposition of prominent British Jews who sensed danger to their civil status in an exclusively Jewish military force. Not until June 1917 did the War Office authorize its formation, but its first two battalions arrived in time to take part in the final phase of General Edmund Allenby's brilliant campaign in Palestine, which began September 19, 1918. Jabotinsky was a lieutenant in the first battalion, and among its volunteers was the world-famous and controversial sculptor Jacob Epstein, who had had his artistic apprenticeship on New York's lower East Side.

The second battalion consisted of volunteers from America. Its recruitment was difficult because citizens were subject to the general draft and only aliens could enlist in the Legion. Among those who spurred the effort were David Ben-Gurion and Isaac ben Zvi, two leaders of Jewish labor in Palestine who had been exiled and had made their way to America: three decades later they would be the leaders of a reborn Jewish state. The commander of the battalion was Colonel

Eliezer Margolin, a soldier from Australia who had lived in his youth in Palestine.

On September 22, 1918 the Jewish units drove the Turks from the ford of the Jordan at Um-esh-shert, opening the way for the Australian and New Zealand cavalry to break into Transjordania. "You helped in no small measure to win the great victory eventually gained in Damascus," the Jewish soldiers were told by Major General Edward Chaytor, commander of the British right wing. Allenby's campaign ended five weeks later with the rout of the Turkish and German forces in Palestine and the surrender of Turkey to the Allies.

A third battalion consisting of Palestinian Jews was also in service, the three battalions numbering some 5,000 men, and on Armistice Day 6,000 more volunteers were in training in Egypt, Canada and England. Most of the 6,000 were from the United States, a large proportion of them members of the liberal professions. The war was over before the Legion could make a substantial military contribution, but its symbolic significance was not lost on Jews and Christians throughout the world.

CHAPTER 18

The "Peace"

1

ON NOVEMBER 2, 1917, FIVE MONTHS AFTER THE AUTHORIZATION of the Jewish Legion, the British Government, headed by David Lloyd George as Prime Minister and Arthur James Balfour as Foreign Secretary, issued the momentous Balfour Declaration. It was a consummation in which the Jewish community in America had an essential role, both active and passive. The leaders of Zionism in America played an important part in the long and difficult negotiations that preceded the Declaration, and the approval of President Wilson, which at the request of Brandeis he conveyed to Lloyd George before the text was issued, tipped the scales in its favor against the powerful forces in London arrayed against it. Wilson's natural sympathy for the Zionist cause was fortified by his admiration for its leading proponent in America.

The passive role of the American Jewish community was equally significant. In the fall of 1917 the war presented a bleak picture for Britain and her Allies. The German submarines were playing havoc with British shipping, the French army was clinging to its trenches, the Italians had been disastrously defeated by the Austrians at Caporetto, and American manpower was not yet engaged in effective numbers. Most disturbing of all, Russia was no longer in the war, and the huge German armies on the eastern front were being shifted to deal the west a blow that might prove decisive. The British statesmen had always felt that the attitude of the Jews of the world, especially of America, was an important factor in the world situation. No doubt they exaggerated what one writer called "the incalculable and universal influence of Jewry," but years later Lloyd George made it clear that the prospect of rallying "Jewish sentiment and support throughout the world to the Allied cause" played no small part in prompting the Declaration. Nor were the British leaders alone in their appraisal. Hard upon the heels of the Declaration and with the official approval of

Germany, Turkey countered with promises of free Jewish immigration into Palestine and autonomous rights for its Jewish community.

What did the Balfour Declaration promise? Over the years that followed, the wording of the Declaration was conned and pondered by thousands of Jews in America, Palestine and other lands until it became as familiar to them as a passage in the daily prayers. The Declaration consisted of a single long sentence:

> His Majesty's Government view with favor the establishment in Palestine of a national home for the Jewish people, and will use their best endeavors to facilitate the achievement of this object, it being clearly understood that nothing shall be done which may prejudice the civil and religious rights of existing non-Jewish communities in Palestine, or the rights and political status enjoyed by Jews in any other country.

This rhythmic sentence was the consummation of three years of intense discussion and diplomatic activity centering in London and reaching out to Paris, Rome and Washington. The man who emerged as the dominant figure in these efforts was Chaim Weizmann, already prominent in Zionist affairs and a brilliant chemist, who was teaching in the University of Manchester. He made an important contribution to the output of munitions and thus gained access to the ears of British statesmen; he was destined to become a familiar figure to the Jews of America and gain access to the ears of American statesmen also.

But in the years that followed, the sentence was found to be suffering from tragic ambiguities and omissions. The boundaries of Palestine were left undefined, and the meaning of the term "national home" became the subject of endless dispute. The promise of a national home "in" Palestine led to British claims that the Declaration was fulfilled at a time when the Jews still owned but a small fraction of the land and were still a small minority of its population. Of the two "it-being-clearly-understoods," the second was, of course, intended to relieve the anxiety of Jewish anti-Zionists with respect to their status in the countries of which they were citizens. It failed to relieve them, but it was, at least, harmless. The first, however, proved to be the rock on which the Declaration ultimately foundered. It gave Britain ground for yielding more and more to Arab opposition and vetoing measures which the Jews deemed essential to a national home as they understood it and as, in fact, Lloyd George, Balfour, Churchill, Jan Smuts, Woodrow Wilson and other statesmen who had a part in framing the Declaration understood it. Wilson expressed the understanding clearly.

"I am persuaded," he wrote in March 1919, "that the Allied Nations, with the fullest concurrence of our own government and people, are agreed that in Palestine shall be laid the foundations of a Jewish Commonwealth." The Declaration, in other words, was understood as foreshadowing a Jewish Commonwealth.

And that was how Jews generally understood it when it was published. Who were they to question what the imposing statesmen, Jewish and non-Jewish, said about it? Great and loud was the exultation with which it was greeted. In America there were jubilant mass meetings in every sizable community across the country, and even the American Jewish Committee felt it necessary to take a stand.

The stand it took was a far cry from the Zionist position. In April 1918 it adopted a statement in which "the Committee welcomes the Balfour Declaration," but considers the two reservations to be of "prime importance." And the "home in the Holy Land for the Jewish people," as envisioned by the Committee, was to be a "center for Judaism, for the stimulation of our faith, for the pursuit and development of literature, science and art in a Jewish environment, and for the rehabilitation of the land." The Zionists found the statement unsatisfactory. Except for the last phrase, itself too elastic, no definition, in their view, could have been couched in language less realistic and more innocuous. The occupants of the "home" it envisaged seemed to be restricted to scholars, scientists, students and saints.

2

The tepid response of this powerful group to what was after all the most dramatic recognition the nations had ever accorded the age-old aspiration of the Jewish people, underscored the fundamental cleavage in American Jewry which, since the outbreak of the war, had brought increasing concern to the Zionist leaders. For if the war should present their cause with new opportunities, as it appeared likely to do, would not their realization depend in large measure on the position taken by the most important segment of the Jewish people, the community in America? And if the American government had a voice in resolving postwar issues, would not its policy on Jewish national aspirations in Palestine be determined, perhaps decisively, by the wishes of the same community? But as matters stood, the attitude of a hostile but highly influential group was likely to be accepted as that of the community as a whole.

Moreover, the matter of Jewish aspirations in Palestine was not the only issue at stake. The massive Jewish concentrations in Eastern Europe, whose future also lay in the balance, aspired in addition to what came to be designated as national or minority rights. They demanded, of course, civil, political and religious equality and the removal of all the disabilities and discriminations from which they suffered, and those demands had the full support of all sections of American Jewry, Right, Left and Center. But national rights meant more. They meant cultural autonomy for groups that differed with respect to race, language or religion from the dominant majority in the state. They meant the right to control their own charitable, religious, educational and social institutions, and even the right to proportional representation in the legislative chambers. They aimed, of course, to guarantee the survival of the groups against attempts by the majority to suppress and absorb them. Nor were the Jews of Eastern Europe alone in demanding national rights. Eastern Europe was a seething cauldron of minorities; their resistance to attempts to suppress their cultural distinctiveness was a source of endless friction and a constant threat to world peace. The Austro-Hungarian Empire was a crazy quilt of nationalities, and although an Allied victory was sure to transform it into sovereign national states, the boundaries of such states could not be drawn without including racial, linguistic or religious minorities.

The Center in the Jewish community of America, dominated by the Zionists, stood firm for supporting their people in Eastern Europe in their demand for minority rights, but the Right was opposed: they smacked too much of "a state within a state," and might encourage extremists to advocate them for Jews in America also. If then, as might well prove to be the case, the weight of American Jewry should tip the scales for or against the Jewish future in Palestine and the free development of Jewish life in Eastern Europe, could the Center permit the Right to figure as the spokesmen for the entire community? To the Zionist leaders, not only in America but in other lands, the answer was obvious.

Shortly after the beginning of the war, an effort was launched in the United States which was, in effect, a flank attack on the American Jewish Committee. It was the movement for a democratically elected American Jewish Congress to declare the will of the community on those two issues. Most of its initiators and early protagonists belonged to the large fraternity of the "illustrious obscure": the editor Gedaliah Bublick; the educator Simon Hirsdansky; the journalist and writer Bernard G. Richards; the Zionist publicists Charles A. Cowen and

Abraham Goldberg; the Poale Zion leaders Nahum Syrkin and Baruch Zuckerman, the Yiddish playwright Abraham S. Schomer, who had long advocated not only an American but a world Jewish congress. It was not long, however, before most of the Yiddish dailies espoused the cause, and the demand for a democratic Congress became so loud and determined that the American Jewish Committee could not ignore it.

There began a series of long and heated negotiations between the two wings with the object of producing a program that would unite the entire community. B'nai B'rith tried the role of intermediary but found the two sides too far apart and decided to have no part in the project. The role was attempted by the National Workmen's Committee on Jewish Rights, which had been set up by the Left, but its bias against the Center, especially on the question of Palestine, was too apparent and it could hardly be accepted as an impartial mediator. In 1917, it may be noted, the Workmen's Committee stepped out of the Congress movement, citing the revolution in Russia as the reason for its withdrawal; the revolution, they would have it, had solved the problem of the Jewish masses in Eastern Europe.

From October 1914 to October 1916 there was hardly a pause in the negotiations and the polemics that accompanied them. Besides the two basic issues, lesser ones came to the surface and heightened the clamor. The Right objected to the word Congress, insisting that the proposed assembly be called Conference: "Congress" might suggest that the Jews proposed to compete with the Congress in Washington! The Center demanded that the Congress be held at once; the Right took the position that the Conference should not meet until after the cessation of hostilities. The American Jewish Committee insisted, further, that the Conference should be an *ad hoc* gathering, dealing only with the postwar problems of Jewish rights, and not seek to become a permanent institution; the Congress advocates were not disposed to accept such a commitment.

3

During those two years of jockeying and agitation three episodes stand out as of special importance. The first was the Preliminary Conference called by the Congress advocates, which met in Philadelphia in March 1916. It brought together 367 delegates who represented some six thousand organizations across the country, and adopted a program for convening a Congress that would labor for "the attainment of full rights for Jews in all lands, for national rights wherever such are recognized, and for the furtherance of Jewish interests in Palestine." It concluded by electing a "Jewish Congress Organization Committee" with Louis D. Brandeis as chairman.

The second episode occurred four months later. The gathering in Philadelphia had made too strong an impression and the Right and Left combined to counter it. They called a meeting of delegates from national organizations which took place in New York in July. But the call to the meeting already revealed a long retreat by the Right. The word Congress was not tabooed, its holding prior to the termination of hostilities was not ruled out, and the sharp issue of national rights was practically conceded by defining them as "group rights wherever such are recognized and desired by the Jews themselves." Brandeis addressed the meeting as representative of the Congress Committee of which he was chairman. Eleven days earlier he had taken his seat on the bench of the United States Supreme Court, and to many he appeared to be defying the tradition which requires members of that august tribunal to avoid public involvement in controversial issues. He invited the meeting to unite with his own Committee, and was taken severely to task by Oscar Straus and the unpredictable Judah Magnes for declaring that the terms by which his Committee was bound for holding the Congress could not be altered. The venerable tradition had been offended: it became clear that Brandeis' leadership in Zionism and Jewish affairs would have to move to another plane.

Some three months later came the third important development, when the retreat became a virtual surrender. In October the two factions reached an agreement by which the Congress would be authorized to deal also with "the securing and protection of Jewish rights in Palestine." The phrase was vague and elastic, but it did recognize Palestine as having a special place in Jewish claims and hopes. A new committee, styling itself Executive Committee for an American Jewish Congress, its members named by each side in equal numbers, was now constituted and elected Nathan Straus as its chairman. The venerable philanthropist, who commanded universal affection and respect, was hailed as a symbol of the unity which, as far as appearances went, had at last been achieved.

4

But the American Jewish Congress did not, after all, convene before the fighting in Europe was over: when the United States became a belligerent, any other course was patently inadvisable. The place was

Philadelphia, the day December 15, 1918. But as early as May 1917 the delegates to this gathering, which, from the standpoint of communal solidarity was the most significant in the history of the Jews in America, had been chosen. They numbered 400, of whom 100 were named by the leading national organizations and the rest chosen in a popular election, in which 133,000 men and women voted. This number was on all sides regarded as an impressive demonstration of the strength which the movement had attained.

In Philadelphia the Congress chose Julian W. Mack president, and among the vice-presidents were Louis Marshall, Adolf Kraus, Harry Friedenwald and Henrietta Szold. And the warm-hearted Jacob H. Schiff, who had fared badly in the strife that raged around the Congress issue, laid aside his grievances and accepted the office of treasurer.

The Congress made three important decisions. The first was to send a delegation to Europe to cooperate with the representatives of Jews of other lands for the recognition of Jewish rights by the Peace Conference. The second was to instruct the delegation to cooperate specifically with the World Zionist Organization "to the end that the Peace Conference might recognize the aspirations and historic claims of the Jewish people in regard to Palestine" as set forth in the Balfour Declaration, and might declare that such conditions should be established in Palestine as would assure its development "into a Jewish commonwealth." The third decision bore on the question of Jewish rights "in the new or enlarged states," which the Peace Conference might call into being; and among the rights demanded were practically all those that were understood by the term national rights, nor was the term itself glossed over. Small wonder that Cyrus Adler, whose opposition to the Congress movement was unwavering, declared ruefully that the conclave in Philadelphia was "nothing but a Zionist convention."

But whatever the Congress was, its deliberations moved in an atmosphere of high optimism. The four-year nightmare of world war had ended with victory for the country they loved and for the cause of democracy, which they cherished as the chief bulwark of their equality and well-being. The hounded and oppressed masses of their people in Eastern Europe stood at last on the threshold of emancipation. And the ancient hope of national restoration was radiant with the promise of speedy fulfillment. There were, of course, some disturbing questions. What was happening to the millions of their people in Russia after the Bolshevik revolution with its policy of liquidating the bourgeoisie, to which the vast majority of them belonged? And what was the meaning of the arrogant and savage chauvinism which had so promptly seized the Poles? Only ten days after the Armistice they had broken into the city of Lemberg, where they staged a full-scale pogrom. And what of the reports that came from Palestine? When the officially authorized Zionist Commission, headed by Weizmann, had arrived there in April 1918, it found the attitude of the military administration anything but friendly.

But disquieting as they were, those questions could not dampen the high mood of the delegates, their hopes fortified by the confidence that the great statesman and even greater idealist in the White House would support their cause. It was the legions he commanded that had dealt the Germans the blows which had sent them reeling back to their borders, and his program for a new world order under a League of Nations the other victors were bound to accept. On March 2, 1919 Woodrow Wilson received a deputation from the American Jewish Congress and expressed his full accord with its objectives.

5

For seven months—from December 1918 to June of the following year—the Peace Conference held its sessions in Versailles, and to that fateful meeting Longfellow's lines might well have been applied:

Humanity with all its fears,
With all its hopes of future years,
Is hanging breathless on thy fate!

The idealism of Woodrow Wilson, though considerably battered by the cynical "realism" of the other three members of the Big Four—Lloyd George, Clemenceau, and Orlando—did nevertheless attain its major goal: the establishment of the League of Nations. But when the Senate of the United States rejected the Versailles Treaty, of which the Covenant of the League was a part, that noble creation was condemned to be a mere shadow of what its protagonist had envisioned. Simultaneously two other innovations, the mandate system and minority rights, which depended on the health and vigor of the League and in which the future of the Jewish people in Europe and Palestine was deeply involved, were also undermined. Indeed, the final breakdown of the peace of the world two decades later has been attributed by competent students of international affairs to the same cause.

6

The ten whom the American Jewish Congress chose as its delegation to the Conference have already been mentioned in these pages: Julian W. Mack, its chairman; Bernard G. Richards, its secretary; Louis Marshall, Stephen S. Wise, Harry Cutler, Bernard L. Levinthal, Nahum Syrkin, Joseph Barondess, Jacob de Haas and Morris Winchevsky. The Right, the Center and even the Left were represented in it, the latter by the Socialist poet and editor Winchevsky. The three factions had joined forces on previous occasions also, but they were occasions of alarm and distress, and the other group in which they were all included, the Joint Distribution Committee, was a philanthropic body, charged with raising and dispensing funds for relief. This delegation was the first and only body in the history of American Jewry that represented a union for political objectives.

In Paris the delegation found emissaries from Jewish communities of many other lands. On the two paramount issues of Palestine and minority rights, those that came from Canada and the countries of Eastern Europe saw eye to eye with the United States delegation, and in order to act in unison they set up the *Comité des Délégations Juives auprès de la Conférence de Paix* (Committee of Jewish Delegations at the Peace Conference), which in the three months it functioned was headed successively by Mack, Marshall and Nahum Sokolow. The emissaries from communities in England and France, on the other hand, refused to go beyond the demand that the Jews in all lands, including Palestine, should be granted civil equality as it was understood in the Western countries. They kept aloof from the *Comité*, but the two sides agreed to avoid the unseemly spectacle of decrying each other in public.

In accord with the instructions the American Jewish Congress had given its delegation, two memorandums were submitted by the *Comité* to the Peace Conference, one dealing with Palestine, the other with Jewish rights in the countries created or changed by the victors. But the task of safeguarding Zionist interests was left by the *Comité* to the representatives of the World Zionist Organization, headed by Weizmann, Sokolow and Menahem M. Ussishkin, the veteran leader of the movement in Russia.

The three immediate objectives of the Zionist leaders were to win the endorsement of the Balfour Declaration by the Peace Conference, secure the appointment of Great Britain as the Mandatory for Palestine, and safeguard Zionist aspirations in the text of the Mandate.

But a staggering array of difficulties and enemies converged upon the scene: the long standing rivalry between Britain and France for the control of the Near East; the ambition nourished by Arab potentates to establish one huge Arab state, from which Palestine, of course, must not be excluded; the aims of the Vatican in Palestine with which Zionism was held to conflict; the American Protestant missionaries and educators in the Near East, who saw eye to eye with the Arabs; and the hostility in certain Jewish quarters which not even the Balfour Declaration had laid at rest. In America, too, this antagonism was very much alive: in March 1919 the United States delegation to the Conference received a memorial signed by 299 Jews, described as "prominent," denouncing Zionism on the ground that it would saddle them with the painful problem of "dual allegiance."

In February 1919 the exalted Council of Ten, embracing the leading delegates from the United States, Britain, France and Japan, received a Zionist deputation which presented the claims of the Jewish people to Palestine. But no formal action was taken. The following month Arab opposition seemed to have vanished when the Emir Feisal, renowned son of the Sherif of Mecca, prospective monarch of the prospective Arab state, wrote an effusive letter in which he gave assurances that the Arabs "look with deepest sympathy on the Zionist movement" and "will wish the Jews a most hearty welcome home." The letter was addressed to Felix Frankfurter, one of the men who had followed Brandeis into the movement; he was in Versailles as legal adviser to the Zionist delegation. Feisal's billet-doux was hailed as a major diplomatic victory, and in the years that followed it was often cited against the charge that Zionism violated Arab rights. But the letter was only an example of the devious shifts of diplomacy in general and of its Levantine brand in particular. Feisal's assurances did not reflect Arab sentiment.

An American commission of inquiry went to the Near East to ascertain the wishes of the people with regard to their political future. It consisted of Henry C. King, educator and theologian, and Charles Crane, a wealthy Chicago manufacturer. The King-Crane Commission hewed close to the line of the American missionary educators in the Near East, and in August 1919 it came back with an anti-Zionist report, which added fuel to the fires of Arab hostility. Wilson had given his consent to the dispatch of the Commission: the best friends in the world are not uniformly helpful. The Commission, he hoped, would help to compose the rivalry between Britain and France.

In July, however, Lloyd George and Clemenceau had patched up their differences without benefit of the Commission's report, but in a manner that enflamed Arab nationalism to a new pitch. The military administration in Palestine was patently anti-Zionist and the Arab intransigents were emboldened to act. In March 1920 there was a treacherous attack on Tel Hai, an isolated Jewish settlement in the north, in which five of the defenders were killed and their leader, Joseph Trumpeldor, was mortally wounded. In April Arab riots in Jerusalem led to loss of life on both sides, the British forces directing their efforts chiefly against the Jewish self-defense groups.

But on the 24th of the same month the Supreme Council of European Powers, meeting in the town of San Remo on the Italian Riviera to dispose of the former provinces of the Turkish empire, put an end finally to the political vacuum in Palestine. In the peace treaty with Turkey, Palestine was declared a mandated territory, the Mandate awarded to Great Britain, and the Mandatory instructed to administer his trust under the terms of the Balfour Declaration. That was the celebrated San Remo Decision, and shortly afterwards, the military administration in Palestine was replaced by a civil government with Herbert Samuel at its head as High Commissioner. Samuel was a distinguished statesman who, besides other important posts, had been Secretary for Home Affairs in the cabinet of Herbert Asquith, and he was a Jew who was known to be friendly to Zionist aspirations.

Across the entire world Jews hailed the San Remo Decision and the appointment of Samuel with relief and rejoicing. In America they held grateful demonstrations all over the country. The road to speedy fulfillment of the age-old hope had, so it seemed to them, been finally cleared.

7

Their mood was heightened by the victory the *Comité des Délégations Juives* had won in Versailles in the struggle for national rights for the Jews in Eastern Europe, a victory which could hardly have been more complete. A new day appeared to have dawned for all racial, linguistic and religious minorities which found themselves incorporated into states controlled by dominant and usually hostile majorities. For the Peace Conference was not content to leave the implementation of minority rights to the tender mercies of those majorities. It incorporated them into the treaties which the states in question willingly or unwillingly accepted and, even more important, it placed them under the guarantee of the League of Nations. The treaty with Poland, signed at Versailles on June 28, 1919, on which those with Rumania, Czechoslovakia, Yugoslavia, Greece, Bulgaria, and Austria were patterned, provided that the rights guaranteed to minorities "constitute obligations of international concern and shall be placed under the League of Nations." Lithuania, in her concessions to her Jewish minority, even went beyond the stipulations in those treaties.

In the Jewish delegations from the United States, Canada and Eastern Europe there was great rejoicing. It was, of course, the triumph of a principle which had had many distinguished advocates, among them the eminent historian Simon Dubnow, and a group of humble zealots who had fought for it in America against powerful opponents. One of the men in Versailles who stood out for his practical wisdom and persistence in promoting it was Louis Marshall, and there was not a little irony in the fact that the president of the American Jewish Committee, which held the doctrine of national rights in aversion, had proved one of its ablest promoters. In America he, too, had begun by opposing it, but he came to realize that the minorities in Eastern Europe were in a different situation from those in France, Britain and the New World, where no official pressures bore down upon them and legal safeguards were unnecessary.

A statement issued by Mack, Marshall and Sokolow expressed the general satisfaction with restraint and dignity. The minority guarantees, it declared, "at last absolved the Jews of Eastern Europe from the serious disabilities from which they so long suffered, and will forever end the grave abuses of the past. They will enable the Jews as well as all other minorities to live their own lives and develop their own culture."

8

But the obligations those treaties imposed were bound to prove no stronger than their guarantor, the League of Nations, especially in reborn Poland and enlarged Rumania, whose representatives made no effort to conceal their resentment at being compelled to accept them. It was not long before those two countries, in which were concentrated 4,500,000 of the 6,000,000 Jews whom the treaties were designed to protect, flouted not only minority, but even more elementary human rights. Treaties proved powerless against the inveterate hostility of the majorities, which their new-found national grandeur only served to inflame.

The enthusiasm the victory in Versailles evoked was natural, but it was not vindicated. To the Jews in America it became quickly apparent that the only hope for their people in Eastern Europe was that the door which had been the portal to a better life for themselves and their children would remain open to the great numbers that would seek to pass through it.

CHAPTER 19

The Long Truce Abroad

1

THE DOOR DID NOT REMAIN OPEN. IT WAS NOT SHUT TIGHT, but through the chink that was left only about a tenth of the number who had found new life in America before the war was able to enter.

The clamor against the open door rose promptly when the war ended, and it was no longer content with so mild a device as the literacy test. As in previous years the agitation flowed from two quarters: the labor leaders and their followers who saw their jobs and living standards endangered by cheap immigrant labor, and the super-patriots who looked upon foreigners as a menace to American institutions and the American spirit. The first found support in the economic recession of 1920 and 1921 that brought a marked increase in the number of unemployed. The second played successfully on the uneasiness that settled on the country as a result of the Bolshevik revolution in Russia: immigrants from Eastern and Southern Europe were held up as carriers of the revolutionary germ to America. The first restrictive bill called for a moratorium on all immigration. It passed the House, but the Senate turned it down, replacing it with another which provided that the number to be admitted during the ensuing year from any country should not exceed 3 per cent of the natives of that country residing in the United States in 1910. The Senate bill passed both Houses and was vetoed by Woodrow Wilson, but was passed again and signed by Warren G. Harding, his successor. Finally, in 1924 came the Johnson Act, which reduced the annual quota from each country to 2 per cent and changed the basis of computation to the number of natives from that country residing in the United States in 1890. That Act remained the law until 1952 when it was replaced by the McCarran-Walter Immigration Act, in which, however, the National Origins Quota System was retained.

Here was a new principle of exclusion; and to injury it added insult.

For it was frankly racist in intent and effect. The Johnson Act resulted in a drastic reduction in the number of immigrants from Southern Europe, principally Italians and Greeks, and from Eastern Europe, principally Jews, and it favored Britain and the countries of Northern Europe. The McCarran-Walter Act hewed to the same line. It began by fixing the maximum annual immigration at 154,657, then assigned quotas to each European country based on the proportion which the natives of that country and their descendants in the United States bore to the total population of America in 1920. Under it the quota for Great Britain in 1953 was 65,361 and for Germany 25,814; for Italy it was 5,645 and for Greece 308. And it is important to add that while the pressure in the less favored countries to migrate was strong, it was otherwise in the more favored countries, who used only a fraction of their quotas.

In the propaganda that preceded the adoption of the Johnson Bill, the "Nordics," as the happy people of the more favored lands were called, were found to be a superior race, possessing every virtue, while the others were inferior and tainted with an assortment of vices, including the gravest of all: a leaning towards radicalism. The "Nordics" were the "Aryans" of those days, for in racism the fashion also appears to change. Perhaps Britons and Scandinavians did not take those encomiums too seriously, but it was otherwise with the Germans. The eulogies confirmed their conviction that they were the *Herrenvolk*—a conviction which before many years was to bring a new disaster upon mankind.

The effect of the Johnson Act on Jewish immigration may be gauged by the following figures: in the seven years before the First World War the number of Jewish immigrants admitted into the United States was 656,397; in the seven years that followed the adoption of the Act the number was 73,378. In terms of human hope and despair the figures mean that, given the same pressure upon the Jews of East Europe to migrate, only 11 were admitted into the haven of America where 100 had been admitted before.

But the pressure upon the Jews to migrate was not the same: in the twenty years of "peace" between the First World War and the Second it became increasingly more urgent. Until 1933 the hosts of Jews who looked desperately towards the haven of the New World were concentrated in the lands of East Europe: Poland, Rumania, Lithuania and Hungary. After 1933 they were joined by those in Germany, Austria and Czechoslovakia as these countries fell successively into the clutches of the Nazi monster.

2

The two and a half million Jews who found themselves after the war under the Bolshevik juggernaut of the Soviet Union were not permitted even to dream of escape. Until 1922 White Russia and the Ukraine, where two million of them dwelt, were swept by counter-revolutionary cohorts, who ravaged hundreds of Jewish communities, leaving hundreds of thousands of dead and maimed. Like the czars, their leaders found it profitable to hold the Jews accountable for the revolution, and the presence of a number of Jews in the Bolshevik hierarchy provided them with the necessary "proof." This falsehood, as we shall see, was seized upon by anti-Semites throughout the world, including America. The truth, however, was that even the Jewish workers, though Socialists, were anti-Bolshevik, let alone the merchants, small traders and independent artisans, who made up an abnormally large proportion of the Jewish population, and whom the new regime dislodged from their occupations and deprived of all civil and political rights. They joined the uprooted hosts of the "declassed" and rightless in the Soviet Union. In the 1920's nearly half the Jews in Russia were estimated to have no source of livelihood.

From the information that seeped out of Russia in the years that followed, it became clear to the Jews in America that the life which had sustained their people in Russia and which, despite persecution, kept them a spiritually rich and creative community, had been pulled up by the roots. Their religion was ruthlessly assaulted, more so probably than other religions, because the so-called Jewish Section, to whose tender mercies it was delivered, consisted of renegades and doctrinaire functionaries of more than ordinary ferocity and malice. The religious education of the young was practically outlawed, and the Hebrew language proscribed. Zionism was suppressed as a "tool of British imperialism," its leaders and workers were imprisoned or exiled, and many of them were in all likelihood liquidated. Yiddish, on the other hand, was unmolested and even subsidized, but after the Second World War it too was suppressed; the surviving Yiddish writers fell suddenly silent and all efforts made by their confreres in America to learn their fate proved futile. Unlike Nazi totalitarianism, the Communist variety did not apparently aim to destroy the Jews bodily and entirely, but all that had made them a distinctive nationality in Russia was erased, and the community appeared to be in a state of rapid liquidation.

The project launched in 1928 to develop a Jewish settlement in Biro-

Bidjan in eastern Siberia, for which substantial support was obtained from Jews in America, also languished and died. In the early fifties, moreover, a series of show trials and false accusations in the Soviet Union and her satellites, especially in Czechoslovakia, Rumania and Hungary, gave good ground for the fear that Communist totalitarianism had also embarked on a policy of open and official anti-Semitism. Those against whom the most preposterous accusations were leveled included leading Jewish physicians, the World Zionist Organization and, strangest of all, the American Jewish Joint Distribution Committee.

3

Between 1924 and 1938 this Committee had made a notable contribution to the economic rehabilitation of the "declassed" Jews. It established the Agro-Joint (American Jewish Joint Agricultural Corporation), which had the cooperation of the Jewish Colonization Association and the ORT (Organization for Rehabilitation and Training), an agency to train Jews in farming and handicrafts, which had been launched in Russia as far back as 1880 and had set up branches in other countries, including the United States. The aim of the Agro-Joint was to induct the declassed Russian Jews into industry and agriculture. The Soviet government supported its efforts, and in America its work was financed by a small group of philanthropists organized as the American Society for Jewish Farm Settlements in Russia. The Agro-Joint created a network of economic, educational and social service institutions in Russia, embracing farm settlements in the Ukraine and Crimea, cooperative workshops, loan societies, trade schools and medical societies all of which, as soon as they were in working order, were taken over by the government. The help of an outside agency was not unwelcome, but always more or less suspect, and a quarter century later it served the group in power as a convenient scapegoat.

4

As the dismal decades between the world wars advanced, the Jews of America became even more concerned over the plight of their people in the other East European countries and, after January 1933, when the senile Hindenburg called on Adolf Hitler to form a cabinet, over the shadow that began to darken the entire continent. A demonic force of unprecedented power and ferocity was unleashed against humanity, and since it openly challenged the God of justice and loving-kindness and called for a return to the ancient Teutonic deities and demons and the law of the jungle, it was natural that it should make the Jews, from whom Christendom had learned to worship that God, their primary target. But they needed more immediate reasons and invented them. The Jews were responsible for the defeat of Germany and for the "harsh" terms the victors imposed. It was they who set up the Weimar Republic and made other attempts to introduce democracy, which Nazism held in loathing. The Jews were alien to the blood and spirit of Germany, even as the anti-Semitic apostles of the previous generation had preached, and a drag on Germany in her struggle to achieve her "destiny."

The Nazis made no secret of their purpose to annihilate the Jews, but people in all lands either refused to believe anything so monstrous, or declined to be upset by it; the wild hue and cry against the Jews was only an outlet for the bitter frustrations of the German people, or at worst a sword that hung over the heads of the Jews alone. But secretly the Nazi program envisaged the destruction or enslavement of other peoples also, and the nations who were witnessing the progress of the virus without dismay were destined to pay a staggering price for their blindness or callousness.

The Nazi regime began with a ruthless campaign to wipe out the Jewish community of Germany, and by the outbreak of the new war had accomplished their purpose: the only Jews who remained in the Third Reich were in concentration camps or in hiding. Among the more important episodes in the seven-year orgy were the public burning of books by Jewish writers on May 10, 1933, and the enactment on September 15, 1935 of the Nuremberg Laws, which deprived all Jews of their citizenship and professions, compelled them to wear the medieval yellow patch, subjected them to forced labor and placed them under the jurisdiction of the Secret State Police, the Gestapo. The climax of the campaign came on November 10, 1938 shortly after Austria had been overrun and annexed, and France and England had betrayed Czechoslovakia by the ignominious pact of Munich. In a carefully organized pogrom of unparalleled dimensions the Germans demolished synagogues in hundreds of cities and towns throughout the land and wrecked and looted Jewish shops and homes. Thousands of men, women and children were maimed, hundreds were murdered and 30,000 of the well-to-do were shipped to concentration camps and their property confiscated.

This time the Western democracies were rather startled: for the first time many became aware that civilization stood face to face with something hideously strange and new. But the mass pogrom was still a "German internal affair," not subject to intervention by other governments. President Franklin Roosevelt was the only foreign statesman who acted: he recalled his ambassador from Berlin.

The following year events moved swiftly. In March 1939 the Nazis overran the Czechoslovak provinces of Bohemia and Moravia; in May they concluded a military alliance with Fascist Italy, and in August came the shocking pact between Germany and Soviet Russia, giving them a free hand against Poland. Finally on September 1, 1939 the mechanized Nazi hosts rolled across the Polish borders and the ruthless war Germany had been waging against the helpless Jews became the Second World War.

5

In the other states of Eastern and Central Europe, save Czechoslovakia, the fortunes of the Jewish communities, whose vicissitudes engaged the anxiety and exertions of the Jews in America, declined steadily after the First World War, but when the Nazis came to power in Germany the decline became precipitous and catastrophic. Now their leaders and populace were shown a swifter method of solving their Jewish problem. It came from a country which, unlike theirs, ranked among the leaders of world culture, and the indifference, certainly the inaction, of the other leading powers, persuaded them that they too could apply the method with impunity.

The largest of them was Poland; with the Austrian province of Galicia, which she obtained in Versailles, and with the depredations she committed on her neighbors, Poland had gathered within her borders three and a half of the six million Jews who inhabited those states. Her policy towards them was based on the premise that they were, as Polish leaders put it, a "superfluous element of the population." Economic boycotts seasoned with pogroms and other acts of terror, and special legislation which deprived them of their livelihood, reduced the Jews of Poland to an appalling state of poverty. In 1933 the temper of Polish anti-Semitism naturally rose higher, and pogroms became almost daily occurrences. It was especially savage in the universities; they resounded with riots and brawls as the Jewish students struck back at their assailants. In 1937 the government legalized "ghetto-benches" in the classrooms, a move that evoked vigorous protests from academic circles in America. But the anti-Jewish clamor in

Poland was only stilled in September 1939, when Nazi bombs began to rain down on her cities.

In Rumania the universities were also the scenes of violent anti-Semitic onslaughts, and the terrorist Iron Guard, the Rumanian version of the Nazi Storm Troopers, was openly encouraged by politicians and prelates of the Greek Orthodox Church. In Versailles Rumania had been greatly enlarged and nearly a half million Jews added to her population, bringing the total to some 900,000, but not only their minority rights, but their more basic rights of equal citizenship were violated. After 1933 the government proceeded to purge the Jews from the arts, the professions and even from commerce and the trades, and in 1937 a new law deprived over 200,000 of them of citizenship and with it of the right to earn a livelihood. Rumania swarmed with Nazi subversionists, her politics became a welter of conspiracy, treachery and assassination, and in 1940, with Ion Antonescu, the Rumanian Hitler, in control, Nazi troops occupied the country.

The same procedures brought ruin upon the proud Jewish community of Hungary, numbering some 700,000, with the Awakening Magyars emulating the role of the Iron Guard. The entire apparatus of boycott against Jewish trade was brought in from Poland, and in 1922 a *numerus clausus* was instituted in the universities. A more hopeful interval ensued, but the triumph of Nazism in Germany spurred the politicians and terrorists to fresh exertions. In 1939 a law was passed establishing rigid quotas for Jews in industry, commerce and the professions, which brought more than half of them face to face with extinction. In 1941 the country became a puppet of Nazi Germany.

The Jewish community of the impoverished little state of Austria, which was all that remained of the once proud and mighty Hapsburg Empire, was stamped out of existence overnight when in March 1938 Nazi hordes seized Vienna, where 90 per cent of the 200,000 Austrian Jews were concentrated. It is doubtful if an exhibition of sadism so brutal and cynical had ever before been put on open display. Men and women who stood in the vanguard of European culture were tortured, humiliated and thrown into concentration camps. The number of suicides alone was estimated at 2,000.

A year later the same fate befell the 350,000 Jews of Czechoslovakia, the one state created by the Versailles Conference which commanded the respect of decent men the world over: it was the only one where the principle of minority rights was not violated and the Jews were free from the scourge of official anti-Semitism. In March 1939, six months after the abject surrender at Munich, the Nazis occupied

Prague, the capital, and introduced the Nuremberg Laws as well as the complete apparatus of plunder, torture and concentration camps which the Gestapo had perfected.

6

After 1933 it became increasingly difficult, if not impossible, for the Jews of America to help their people in Eastern and Central Europe. But until the inroads of the Nazi scourge and later of the new World War compelled it to suspend its work, the Joint Distribution Committee enabled hundreds of thousands of them to survive the floods that raged around them. Nor was the help that sustained them merely eleemosynary; they were assisted to reconstruct their lives through productive labor. In addition, individuals sent help to friends and relatives and *landsmanshaft* societies remembered and aided the Old World communities from which they sprang.

In 1924 the JDC and ICA united in forming the American Joint Reconstruction Foundation, which took over the work of economic rehabilitation in all the countries of Eastern and Central Europe. The Foundation laid chief stress on the promotion of cooperatives, particularly credit cooperatives, or *kassas*, which helped the Jews to withstand the economic pressures that bore down on them. The *kassas* came to the rescue of traders, artisans and farmers, and in later years the Foundation also extended loans to refugees in Western Europe and America.

American Jews endeavored to help their people in the Old World through political action also. The numerous *landsmanshaft* societies joined forces in federations which attempted to exert influence through diplomatic channels, and the agencies that stood guard against infractions of Jewish rights acted to bring the persecutions to public attention and win the sympathy of American public opinion. It cannot, however, be said that these efforts brought positive results. The prevailing mood of the country after the First World War was isolationist, and concern in foreign affairs centered chiefly on what many people believed was the imminent threat which the success of the Communist revolution in Russia presented to the American way of life; the threat which Nazism presented was not discerned until years later. There were, moreover, many Jews in positions of leadership who felt uneasy about public agitation and political intervention; they feared that those methods would only exacerbate the hostility that surrounded the Jews in Eastern and Central Europe and aggravate their plight.

7

Three strong bodies had by this time come to the fore on the American Jewish scene that labored on the increasingly difficult task of protecting Jewish rights at home and abroad: the American Jewish Committee, the American Jewish Congress, and B'nai B'rith; and after 1934 a fourth group, the Jewish Labor Committee, entered the field. The Congress did not go out of existence with the fulfillment of the mission it entrusted to its delegation at Versailles: the apparent success of the mission only strengthened the conviction of Congress enthusiasts of the necessity of a permanent instrument of that sort, and it was not long before they urged its extension to a World Jewish Congress. And as for the provision, which the leaders had accepted in the agreement of October 1916, that "no resolution shall be introduced, considered or acted upon at the Congress, which . . . shall involve the perpetuation of such Congress," many of their followers took the position that no one could properly tie their hands in perpetuum as to what they might or might not do to further their people's welfare. Accordingly when, in May 1920, the Congress met again in Philadelphia, and after receiving the report of its delegation adjourned sine die, a group of delegates remained and reestablished it as a permanent body. Nathan Straus was its first president, but the man who set its pace and dynamics was Stephen S. Wise, who was chosen president in 1925 and with intermissions held that office until his death in 1949. The Congress spoke for the Zionist Center of the community; the American Jewish Committee, undiminished in strength and influence, continued to speak for the Right; and B'nai B'rith, identified at first with the Right, veered more and more towards the Center. The Jewish Labor Committee, led by the versatile Adolph Held and claiming to represent half a million Jewish workers, drew its chief support from the large needle-trades unions.

The triumph of Nazism in its native lair and the steady diffusion of its venom in every direction subordinated every other problem on the agenda of the four bodies. But joint action was balked by differences as to the methods to be employed. The Congress was in favor of demonstrations and an organized boycott of German-made goods; the Committee and B'nai B'rith maintained such methods would do more harm than good, and urged that the struggle against Nazism should become an all-American, nay an all-human, cause: men of all faiths should fight it with equal zeal as a challenge to the basic decencies of civilized life and a menace to the peace of the world. But it took a desperately long time for the others to become aware of the challenge and the menace.

On March 27, 1933 a huge demonstration called by the Congress took place in New York's Madison Square Garden, and similar demonstrations were held in some three thousand other cities over the land. On May 10 of the same year, when Germany rejoiced over the public burning of "non-Aryan" books, a protest parade was held in New York, and in March 1934 Nazism was "put on trial" at another demonstration in New York arranged by the Congress. The economic boycott of Germany and German dominated countries was promoted chiefly by the Non-Sectarian Anti-Nazi League to Champion Human Rights, founded in 1933 by Samuel Untermyer, one of the foremost lawyers of America, George Gordon Battle, also a distinguished lawyer and civic leader, James W. Gerard, a former ambassador to Germany, and other prominent Americans. Some two thousand organizations became affiliated with the League, and it established a World Council with branches in twenty-four countries. The League strove to mobilize all faiths in the struggle against Nazism, but its composition, support and active leadership remained preponderantly Jewish. The Congress and Labor Committee joined in the boycott, while the American Jewish Committee conducted a wide and intensive campaign of public education through the press, platform, radio, motion pictures and publications. The Anti-Defamation League of B'nai B'rith, launched as early as 1913 to expose anti-Semitic calumnies and combat anti-Jewish discrimination, girded itself to meet the new and more sinister challenge.

Attempts to bring about coordinated action, or at least prevent friction among the groups, continued. In June 1933 a Joint Consultative Council was established, through whose efforts the League of Nations appointed James G. McDonald, a former president of the Foreign Policy Association, as High Commissioner to aid refugees from Germany. But the American Jewish Committee and B'nai B'rith found themselves hopelessly at odds with the American Jewish Congress, the third partner of the Council, on its project to convoke a World Jewish Congress.

This project gave rise to basically the same pros and cons as the original plan for an American Jewish Congress and, long before that, to the calling of the first Zionist Congress. Those in favor maintained that Jews the world over faced needs and perils that required public and united action; those opposed argued that such assemblies, in the words of the American Jewish Committee, "furnished a pretext for spreading the false charge that the Jews are an international body with a divided allegiance."

In June 1938 another attempt to create a "united front," initiated by Edgar J. Kaufman, a Pittsburgh philanthropist, led to the formation of the General Jewish Council, in which the Labor Committee was also included. But the powers which the new Council should exercise became a matter of sharp dispute, the Congress favoring their extension, the others fearful for their autonomy and freedom of action. So three years later the Congress withdrew from the new Council.

8

The Nazi serpent, unchecked by the efforts of the Jews in America or, for that matter, of those who wielded vastly greater power, continued to wind its coils around lands and nations. The plight of the Jews in Eastern and Central Europe became more and more acute; in their own countries they were faced with imminent annihilation, while the Western democracies, even when aware of the danger that lowered over them also, hugged their precious immigration laws, which prevented the rescue of those who could have escaped from the monster. In July 1938 delegates from thirty-eight countries met at Evian, France, on the invitation of President Roosevelt to devise measures for speeding the rescue of the victims. The delegates made and listened to noble speeches, while thousands of unfortunates found themselves caught between the Nazis and those laws, and perished.

9

How in the meantime was the Yishuv in Palestine faring, and the National Home which the Balfour Declaration and the San Remo Decision promised to "facilitate," and which had stirred the imagination of the vast majority of the Jews in America? Did it provide the answer to the desperate need for an outlet for the Jews of Central and Eastern Europe?

Considered by itself as a work of economic, social and cultural upbuilding, the Yishuv in the two decades that separated the world wars made imposing progress. Between 1919 and 1939 its population grew from 55,000 to 475,000, and though still only 30 per cent of the entire population of the country, the Jews were paying 70 per cent of the taxes. Tel Aviv, now an all-Jewish city of 150,000, Jerusalem with new and modern suburbs around the walled Old City, and Haifa, one of the busiest ports on the Mediterranean, demonstrated the capacity of the Jews as city builders. By 1939 the farm settlements numbered more than 250, and Jewish labor had transformed many of the marshy and arid wastes into grain fields and groves, and covered bare hillsides with forests. The mineral wealth of the Dead Sea was being extracted, a hydroelectric system was providing the country with light and power, and factories and workshops, large and small, were employing scores of thousands of skilled craftsmen. The variety and quality of the Yishuv's industrial output was rising: it was producing textiles, agricultural machinery, building materials, clothing and shoes, chemicals and pharmaceuticals, and even optical and scientific instruments. And in agriculture as well as in industry, cooperative principles and methods in producing, marketing, purchasing and banking had enlisted a larger proportion of the population than in any other society in the world. The most important cooperatives were sponsored and nurtured by the *Histadrut*, the General Federation of Jewish Labor, which had become the dominant force in the community.

In the two decades the Yishuv also made dramatic progress in public health, especially in eradicating the two endemic diseases, malaria and trachoma. From 1923 to 1939 its death rate fell from 14.7 per 1,000 to 7.6, and the decline in infant mortality was even greater. In education, progress was equally impressive. The school system comprised hundreds of units: kindergartens, elementary and secondary schools, trade schools and teachers' seminaries; and capping the educational system were the Haifa Technical Institute, the Weizmann Scientific Institute at Rehovot and the Hebrew University at Jerusalem. Hebrew, of course, was the language of practically all the schools, as it was of the field, factory, office and market place. This unparalleled revival of an ancient tongue was now a fait accompli; it was one of the strongest factors welding the people of the Yishuv, regardless of origin or cultural background, into a single national group. And apart from the schools, the cultural efflorescence of this vibrant and picturesque community was the most luxuriant in the world. For its size it published more books, newspapers and other periodicals than any other; it painted more pictures, listened to more and better music and had a finer theater. And nowhere else were the gifted men and women who labored in the realm of the mind and spirit relatively so numerous and so highly regarded.

Such were the bright aspects of the National Home, such the progress it made between the world wars, and it commanded the pride and affection of the Jews in America. They were especially proud of the youthful pioneers, the *chalutzim*, most of them from Poland, who were restoring the ravaged soil and building the cities and colonies. Nor was this pride confined to those who subscribed to the Basel Program or belonged to a Zionist group. More and more in the camps of the Right and Left felt their dogmas, theories, and preconceptions fade before the throbbing reality. In the Right they called themselves non-Zionists and frowned on the idea of a Jewish nation, but how could they ignore the pioneering achievements of the Yishuv, which were raising the stature of all Jews in the sight of the gentiles? In the Left leaders of labor and their followers moved closer to reconciliation with Zionism as the American environment weaned them away from their doctrinaire commitments, the change of heart facilitated by the fact that the Histadrut was the dominant force in the Yishuv.

But during this period the need which the builders and dreamers of Zion hoped it would meet had grown immeasurably greater. Was that hope being fulfilled? True, more fugitives from Germany were finding asylum in it than anywhere else in the world; in July 1935 James G. McDonald, the League of Nations High Commissioner, reported that of 80,000 refugees 27,000 had found homes in Palestine and only 6,000 in the United States. In 1934 the new arrivals in Palestine from all countries reached the unprecedented total of 42,000 and the following year it jumped to 62,000; all except a few thousand of them came from Poland and Germany, the number from each about equal. Certainly the National Home was playing an important and heroic role as a haven for the homeless and proscribed, but those who clamored for admission far outnumbered those who were admitted. And the reason was not that the Yishuv refused to be burdened with them, but that the Mandatory Power refused to let them in.

As the years between the wars advanced, the political tribulations of the Yishuv multiplied. Its progress during the period was achieved in the face of stupendous obstacles, the most serious stemming not from the impediments of nature but the hostility of men. Arab antagonism mounted steadily and British vacillation and obstructionism kept pace with it. Indeed, the Yishuv was a source of anxiety also to the Jews of America, and in the first instance to the Zionist forces in the community.

10

In 1921 those forces went through a severe crisis. At the annual convention of their major component, the Zionist Organization of America, held that year in Cleveland, a large majority of the delegates voted to repudiate the leadership of Brandeis and his adherents, and a schism resulted which took nearly a decade to heal. The rift occurred after a year of intense agitation, in which the conflicting issues were epitomized by the two foremost leaders of the cause, Brandeis and Weizmann.

In July of the previous year the two men had clashed at a world conference which met in London to devise policies and instruments for the new era into which the movement had entered. On all questions of method and policy a broad and apparently unbridgable chasm rose up between them, which those who looked for pat formulas ascribed to the famous gulf between East and West. But basic conceptions also played their part: Brandeis was a methodical social engineer for whom Zionism was a majestic state-building enterprise to be brought to fruition primarily by sound economic measures. Weizmann was the Jewish zealot for whom Zionism as a work of cultural reclamation was equally important. Nor is it surprising that Weizmann, who had won a dominant position in the movement, should not have relished the prospect of relinquishing it to Brandeis or anyone else. The concrete measure on which all their differences came to a head was a new financial instrument, the Foundation Fund or *Keren Hayesod*, which the conference voted to establish. The new Fund was to include investments as well as gifts, a "commingling of funds," as Brandeis called it, and the majority of the American delegation refused to support it. Zionism in America, it appeared, would secede from the world movement and go its separate way.

But the convention in Cleveland ruled otherwise. Earlier in 1921 Weizmann, accompanied by a scientist of legendary fame named Albert Einstein and Menahem M. Ussishkin, the "iron man" of the movement, had come to America, where he set up a branch of the controversial *Keren Hayesod*. Samuel Untermyer became its president, and the youthful Emanuel Neumann, whose star was fast rising on the Zionist firmament, its director. It was Neumann whose organizing skill established the new instrument firmly across the country, and he was in the forefront of the group whose zeal swelled the ranks of the Opposition to the Brandeis regime in the hectic weeks that preceded the convention. And after the fateful vote in Cleveland Julian W. Mack, who was president of the organization, together with a majority of the Executive Committee announced their resignation, and Brandeis, who was honorary president, also resigned. The Brandeis era in American Zionism appeared to be over. The leadership now fell to a group among whom the ranking member was Louis Lipsky. In the political field their outstanding triumph occurred in 1922 when a Republican Congress adopted a Joint Resolution, which was signed by President Harding, "favoring the establishment in Palestine of a National Home for the Jewish people."

But the members of the Brandeis-Mack group, as they came to be called, did not retire from the battle and sulk in their tents. They concentrated on furthering the economic rehabilitation of Palestine and established the Palestine Economic Corporation, which eventually became the principal investment enterprise in the National Home, participating in its basic industries and setting up credit institutions that made loans to cooperatives, home owners, artisans and manufacturers. Among those who served as president of the Corporation were the economist Bernard Flexner, the Zionist leader and industrialist Julius Simon, and Robert Szold, one of the staunchest adherents of the Brandeis program. Brandeis himself continued to be a powerful force in the movement; his influence, in fact, even grew; his home in Washington became a shrine to which Zionists of all complexions turned for guidance and inspiration.

Before long, moreover, the "separatists" began to wing their way back to the main dovecote of the movement like homing pigeons, among the first to return being Stephen S. Wise and Abba Hillel Silver, both magnificent orators and bold leaders. By 1930 the old leadership was again in the ascendant; that year Robert Szold was chairman of the governing body of the Organization and Julian Mack the honorary chairman. And as the somber decade of the thirties drew on to its fateful close the two groups merged and became one again.

11

Shortly after the rift in American Zionism in 1921 Chaim Weizmann, now the unchallenged leader of the world movement, looked longingly toward the wealthy and influential Jewish bankers and magnates in America, non-Zionists all, whose princely generosity for all humane causes, including those on behalf of their own people, was almost proverbial. They were no longer the implacable foes of Zionism they had been before the Balfour Declaration, and some of them, including Jacob H. Schiff, Felix M. Warburg and Julius Rosenwald, were supporting Jewish projects in Palestine, especially in the field of education. If they all came in as equal and active partners in the enterprise, how much faster it could proceed! For Arab hostility and British obstructionism were not its only afflictions; it was plagued by a chronic lack of funds. And the way to a partnership was indicated by the Mandate itself, which in Article Four recognized the Zionist Organization as "an appropriate Jewish Agency" to represent the Jews of the world vis-à-vis the Mandatory Power, but required it to "take steps . . . to secure the cooperation of all Jews who are willing to assist in the establishment of the Jewish National Home." That should mean the non-Zionists, especially the non-Zionists of America.

From January 1924, when the first conference of American non-Zionists to consider the invitation to join the Jewish Agency took place in New York, to August 1929 when the enlarged Agency was actually constituted in Zurich, the extension of this body was one of the important questions in American Jewry and a major issue in the world Zionist movement. For Weizmann's proposal to give the non-Zionists an equal voice in the development of the National Home found numerous and resolute opponents, who feared that the new partners would dilute and even subvert its basic objectives. In America the leading opponent was Stephen Wise, but the great majority supported Weizmann; the prospect of a speedy remedy for the financial woes that afflicted the movement was too alluring. Among the non-Zionists Weizmann's principal ally was Louis Marshall; his stature in the community had grown; he was still president of the American Jewish Committee, and his participation, it was felt, insured the success of the longed-for partnership.

As a preliminary to the large development program on which the extended Agency was expected to embark, a Joint Palestine Survey Commission was named to carry out "a detailed survey of the economic resources and possibilities" of Palestine; two of its four members were Americans, the banker Felix M. Warburg and the economist and social worker Lee K. Frankel. In the summer of 1928 the Commission, which had had the assistance of a group of eminent experts, issued its report; and the Zionist Congress having adopted a number of stipulations to safeguard Zionist essentials, the way was cleared for the establishment of the partnership. The meeting in Zurich at which it took place was festive and impressive, among those who attended as non-Zionists being Louis Marshall, Albert Einstein, Herbert Samuel, the British industrialist Lord Melchett, formerly Sir Alfred Mond, and the French political leader Leon Blum.

But the high hopes to which the extended Agency gave rise proved illusory. Before long the participation of the non-Zionists dwindled to the vanishing point, the process hastened by the death of Louis Marshall, which occurred in Zurich shortly after that meeting. The Executive of the Agency again became identical with the Zionist Executive, though for formal reasons it was retained as a separate body.

12

During the twenty-year truce between the world wars the Jewish community of America, first not only in wealth and influence but in numbers, was the scene of the most significant growth the Zionist movement experienced across the world. The second of the two decades witnessed the more spectacular advance: in 1930 the total membership of all Zionist groups in the United States was 150,000; ten years later it was 400,000. No doubt the upsurge of anti-Semitism which, as we shall soon see, made alarming inroads into America also, helped to bring Zionism this large accretion of strength. A great many were rudely awakened to an awareness of their Jewish identity and chose to meet the challenge not with self-effacement but with self-assertion.

The energies of the movement in America were absorbed by two tasks: raising funds to meet the rising budgets of the Zionist Executive in Palestine and mobilizing American opinion to combat the dangers, physical and political, that lowered over the Yishuv. In 1925 the two principal fund-raising efforts for Palestine, the one for the Foundation Fund, the other for the Jewish National Fund, the land-purchasing agency of the movement, joined forces to form the United Palestine Appeal, and the sums that accrued to both continued to mount. The dangers, stemming from Arab intransigence and British vacillation, also continued to mount. In 1929 there was an attempt at a full-scale Arab uprising, and it was followed by a British White Paper, which in effect nullified the Balfour Declaration and the Mandate. But the Paper roused a storm of protest across the world, the American branch of the movement bringing the full weight of American public opinion to bear against it, and Prime Minister Ramsay MacDonald lost no time in writing Weizmann a letter in which he took the sting out of it.

By 1939, however, the British no longer vacillated; they surrendered completely to the Arabs. The surrender was embodied in another White Paper that was issued in May of that year, and was preceded by nearly three years of guerrilla terror conducted by armed Arab bands, most of them from across the boundaries of Palestine. Jews and Britons were attacked and slain impartially, as well as Arabs in Palestine who refused to pay the tribute the guerrillas levied. But the rebels did not depend entirely on their fellow Arabs; they received arms and money from German and Italian agents. For Nazis and Fascists the insurrection in Palestine had a double attraction: it was directed against Jews and it promised to shatter Britain's position in the Near East. So they combined to assist it just as they combined to insure the victory of

Fascism in Spain. The entire world was moving rapidly towards another abyss, and the Arab leaders felt the right moment had come to annihilate the Jewish community in Palestine.

But the Yishuv bore the long ordeal with remarkable fortitude and success. Not one of the many settlements that were attacked was lost, and during the three years some fifty new ones were added. There were gains in other directions also, with an increase of nearly 100,000 in the population, 80 per cent of it by immigration. The chief burden of protecting Jewish life and labor fell upon the Yishuv's own defense force, the Haganah, numbering some 25,000 volunteers. The fatal casualties for the three years were estimated at 140 Britons, 450 Jews and 2,300 Arabs.

And while Palestine was torn with violence the government of Neville Chamberlain was pondering the political aspects of the outbreak, especially its implications for the new war that stood on the horizon. In November 1936 a Royal Commission of inquiry, headed by Lord Peel, arrived in Palestine, the most important of the many British commissions that investigated the troubled land, and its report, which appeared in July of the following year, recommended "a surgical operation." Finding the Mandate "unworkable," it proposed partition of the country and the establishment of separate Arab and Jewish states. The Government began by favoring the proposal, but after another investigation in 1938 abandoned it, and tried to square the circle by calling an Arab-Jewish conference in London, in which the Arabs refused to confer with the Jews.

Then came the crushing blow, the White Paper of May 1939. The new edict announced that in the succeeding five years Jews would be allowed a maximum of 75,000 immigrants and none at all thereafter, and five years later, with the population still preponderantly Arab, the country would become a sovereign state. The Paper foreshadowed severe restrictions against the acquisition of land by Jews, and in February 1940 regulations were issued which made it practically impossible for Jews to purchase land in 95 per cent of the country. The overriding motive of the Chamberlain government was to avoid antagonizing the Arab world in face of the impending conflict, so the Balfour Declaration and the Mandate went by the board and racial laws were enacted against the Jews in their own National Home!

There was a loud outcry against the White Paper throughout the world—in Britain also, and even in Parliament; it was denounced as a repudiation of solemn obligations, an abject surrender and another Munich. It was, in the words of Herbert Morrison, who spoke for the

Labor Opposition, "a cynical breach of pledges given the Jews and the world, including America." In the United States the protest was not confined to the Zionists. In July 1939 the American Jewish Committee joined the American Jewish Congress and the leading Zionist bodies in a protest addressed to Neville Chamberlain, in which he was told that his government was attempting to solve the Palestine problem "by punishing the victims of ruthless oppression and by retaliation against the builders of the Jewish National Home."

13

Such, then, were the anxieties and labors of the Jews in America on behalf of their struggling kin in Europe and Palestine in the two decades between the world wars. No other group in the living fabric of America found itself challenged by similar tasks so numerous and so urgent, but the judgment of the generations will in all likelihood sustain the opinion that on the whole the Jews of America acquitted themselves with credit, if not always with success, of the obligations which the singular and fateful destiny of their people laid upon them.

CHAPTER 20

Rage of the Heathen

1

BUT THE JEWISH COMMUNITY IN THE UNITED STATES which, notwithstanding the virtual ban on immigration, grew in the two decades between the world wars from three and a half million to nearly five, was faced with tasks and problems directly related to its own welfare also. And those that engaged its deepest concern sprang from the same malevolence that blighted the lives of their coreligionists in Central and Eastern Europe. Did some of them in America, now that mass immigration was over, envisage a not-too-distant future when American Jewry will have evolved a destiny of its own, distinct and separate from that of other Jewish aggregations in the world? They reckoned without the forces of history, or as those of religious mind would put it, the Supreme Force in history, by Whose decree no segment of this people seemed able to divorce itself from the destiny of the whole.

During the first of the two decades there were two important carriers of the anti-Semitic virus in America. The first was the Ku Klux Klan, the order of sheeted and hooded nightriders of the South in the post-Civil War years, which was thought to have passed from the scene: it rose from the grave in a "reincarnation," and was no longer confined to the South. The second consisted of a coterie of sworn hatemongers grouped around, of all people, the most distinguished and admired tycoon in America, Henry Ford. Both of them were at least indigenous, authentic Americana as it were, although that fact gave the Jews no consolation. But the second decade witnessed a sharp rise in the epidemic, stimulated by its world center in Nazi Germany, and a rash of Fascist and Nazi groups erupted over America, with anti-Semitism the fever they all had in common.

At no time, of course, were anti-Semitic manifestations absent in America; many Jews, indeed, regarded them as a "normal" concomitant of Jewish existence. Just prior to the First World War the community was deeply disturbed by the case of Leo M. Frank, manager of a pencil factory in Atlanta, Georgia, who was arrested on the charge of having murdered a girl employe. Frank was convicted and sentenced to be hung in a trial that took place in an intensely hostile atmosphere: the defendant was a Northerner and a Jew. The only important evidence against him was the testimony of a former convict, also an employe of the factory, who was himself suspected of the crime. Appeals to higher courts were denied on technical grounds, but the governor of the state, who had come into possession of evidence which, owing to the state of popular feeling, he dared not divulge, commuted Frank's sentence to life imprisonment. There had been strong demonstrations of sympathy for Frank throughout the country, but they only exacerbated the bitter resentment in Georgia, and on August 16, 1915 an armed mob took Frank from his prison and lynched him. Ten years later an inmate of a Federal penitentiary confessed to the crime, implicating the man who had been the chief witness against Frank.

2

The "reincarnation" of the Ku Klux Klan took place the same year in the same state with William J. Simmons, a former minister of the gospel, as Imperial Wizard of the Invisible Empire, and an expanded program summed up in the slogan "native, white Protestant supremacy," which damned immigrants, Jews and Catholics along with Negroes. Until 1920 its progress was slow, but in the five years that followed, the postwar dislocations and frustrations, together with a shrewd campaign conducted by professional organizers, raised the Klan's membership from ten thousand to a colossal total estimated at four to five million. The Klan adopted the fiery cross as its chief symbol, and its masked riders, appointing themselves guardians of race purity and morality, committed numerous outrages, including murder, upon Negroes and whites whose conduct they disapproved. It was natural also that the Klan should go into politics, and its triumphs in that field, not only in the South but in other states of the Union, including Oregon, Indiana and Maine, were portentous. It elected or controlled members of Congress and state officials, including governors, and in the South nearly every political aspirant found it essential to join the Klan. Its anti-Semitism found expression not only in its literature, where the Jew was described as "an unblendable element," and in its anti-immigration propaganda, but in such exploits as breaking Jewish store windows and burning fiery crosses in front of synagogues.

But the Klan did not continue riding long on the crest of the wave. Although in 1928 it helped materially to defeat Alfred E. Smith, the

Democratic candidate for the presidency, who was a Catholic, its decline by the end of the decade was not less sensational than its rise. The two principal causes were the exposure of its leaders, who had enriched themselves at the expense of the members, and the crimes committed by its nightriders and politicians, some of whom, including the governor of Indiana, were convicted and imprisoned. Public opinion became aroused, laws were passed by state legislatures forbidding masks and secret proceedings, and the many thousands of decent people who had been swept into the Klan fell away from it. But during its heyday the reincarnated Klan gave the Jews of America "a bad quarter of an hour," historically speaking.

Towards the end of the second decade the Klan, aided and abetted by Nazi agents, attempted another "reincarnation," with greater emphasis on anti-Semitism in its official organ, *The Fiery Cross,* and a boycott campaign against Jewish merchants under the mystic symbol SYMWAO, contracted from the slogan "Spend Your Money With Americans Only." But its earlier momentum was gone, the sentiment against it growing stronger as its association with Nazism became more apparent. Nevertheless the Klan did not die, embers of it were still smoldering and flared up at times even after the Second World War, especially in Georgia. As late as 1945 the order was revived by its Grand Dragon Samuel Green, but suffered a decline when scores of its stalwarts were convicted by state and federal courts of crimes of violence and terror.

3

The "Seven Years War" waged against the Jews by Henry Ford was even more sensational than the antics of the Klan and gave the Jews of America even greater concern. Unlike the Klan's, the anti-Semitism of the Ford campaign was undiluted, and the vast resources of money and prestige of the country's foremost industrial magnate stood at its command. The war broke out in May 1920, when Ford's widely circulated *Dearborn Independent* began publishing a series of violent attacks against the Jews, and it ended abruptly in June 1927 when Ford issued an abject and public apology, addressed to Louis Marshall, the president of the American Jewish Committee, begging the Jews "as fellow men and brothers" to forgive him, and assuring them that "henceforth they may look to me for friendship and good will."

The inspiration and handbook of this crusade was even more grotesque and sinister than the crusade itself. It was *The Protocols of the Elders of Zion,* a fantastic forgery which first appeared in Russia at the beginning of the century. In 1905 an extended version of it was published in St. Petersburg by one Sergei Neilus, translations of it appeared in many languages, and it became the bible of international anti-Semitism. The *Protocols* protrays a vast conspiracy by the "elders of Zion," presumably the leaders of the Zionist movement, to bring about the downfall of all governments and set up a world empire with the "elders" as rulers. The result would be accomplished by means of terror, subornation, class strife and general demoralization, and with the help of corrupt politicians, Free Masons, liberals and atheists. In May 1935 a court in Berne, Switzerland, after hearing testimony by distinguished witnesses in a trial of two Swiss Nazis who had circulated the *Protocols,* pronounced it a forgery, but its fraudulent nature had already been exposed in the United States in the early twenties by Herman Bernstein, John Spargo, the Christian author and reformer, and others. Such was the screed that the *Dearborn Independent* made the basis of Ford's anti-Jewish campaign, and the articles it printed were assembled and published under the general title of *The International Jew.* And long after Ford's public penance, the ground swell of the waves he set in motion still persisted: the evil men do lives on even after they disown it. As late as 1941 *The International Jew* was reprinted and circulated by the Ku Klux Klan and Fascist groups, and in 1953 a large reprint of the *Protocols* was put in circulation by Conde McGinley, publisher of the anti-Semitic bi-weekly *Common Sense.*

Ford's mysterious excursion into anti-Semitism was explained by crediting him with a naïveté that made him the dupe of unscrupulous subordinates, and by his resentment against Rosika Schwimmer, a world renowned Jewish pacifist, with whom he became linked in a ludicrous attempt to end the First World War. His sudden change of heart was also variously explained: he became aware that he was being exploited by schemers; he found himself involved in libel suits, one of which, brought against him by Aaron Sapiro, a prominent lawyer and promoter of farmers' cooperatives, proved particularly irksome; he noted a decline in the sale of his vehicles as the result of a boycott by those who were repelled by his racial vendetta.

That the slanders of the anti-Jewish agitators of the twenties were not ineffective was demonstrated with startling vividness in September 1928 when the rabbi of the congregation in the small town of Massena in northern New York was brought to police headquarters by a state trooper for questioning by the mayor. A little girl had disappeared, and His Honor demanded to know if it was true that Jews offered a human sacrifice (sic) in connection with their Day of Atonement, which was approaching! The rabbi was cleared the following day when the little girl was found lost in the woods, alive and well.

4

In the second decade of the long truce between the world wars the anti-Jewish chorus became more strident; it fell silent only after the Japanese had bombed Pearl Harbor on December 7, 1941. Two new factors came upon the scene to feed the agitation. The first was the calamitous depression that smote the country in the fall of 1929 and held it in its grip for years afterwards. The second was the triumphal parade of Nazism in Europe and the systematic diffusion of its leading doctrine throughout the world.

The repercussions of the economic disaster of 1929 were world wide, the suffering it inflicted was acute, and its millions of victims became more inclined to listen to demagogues and charlatans. The depression played no small part in the progress of Nazism in Europe, and it fertilized the soil in America for a fungus growth of Fascist organizations, all of which made anti-Semitism the principal plank in their platforms.

The ground for charging the Jews with responsibility for the economic collapse was simple and startling, as all good slogans and catchwords should be: the Jews controlled American finance and the general economy of the country, and engineered the depression. Louis T. McFadden, a Congressman from Pennsylvania, explained it all in a speech he delivered in the House in May 1933, and in 1939 the House heard the same views from Congressman Jacob Thorkelson of Montana. Moreover, the Jews controlled international finance also; they were the international bankers and conspired against all Christendom. So often was the charge repeated that in the minds of many the term "international banker" became synonymous with Jew.

The wide currency achieved by the myth could not be ignored, and it led the editors of *Fortune* to publish their survey *The Jews in America,* which has already been noted in a previous chapter. The survey, which appeared in February 1936, revealed that Jews played a decidedly minor role in American commercial banking as well as in investment or international banking. With regard to the former it found that:

> Of the 420 listed directors of the nineteen members of the New York Clearing House in 1933 only 30 were Jews . . . There were none in the Bank of New York and Trust Co., National City,

> Guaranty Trust, Central Hanover, First National, Chase, Bankers Trust or New York Trust. Indeed, there are practically no Jewish employes of any kind in the largest commercial banks, and this in spite of the fact that many of their customers are Jews.

Two years later an investigation conducted by B'nai B'rith showed similar results for the country at large: of the 93,000 directors and higher-grade employes of commercial banks in the United States, some 600 or slightly more than one-half of one per cent, were found to be Jews.

But the "international bankers" whom the anti-Semites charged with the world's woes, were in the investment field, and how did the Jews figure there? The findings of the *Fortune* survey were as follows:

> In the investment field, although there are, of course, Jewish houses, of which Kuhn, Loeb and Co., Speyer and Co., J. & W. Seligman and Co., Ladenberg, Thalmann and Co., and Lehman Bros. are the best known, they do not compare in power with the great houses owned by non-Jews. . . . If these houses are ranked upon the amounts of foreign loans outstanding on March 1, 1935, J. P. Morgan with 19.87 per cent; National City Co. with 11.71; Dillon, Reed with 11.44; Chase-Harris Forbes with 8.45; Guaranty Co. with 6.67 per cent; Bancamerica-Blair with 6.19 per cent; and Lee, Higginson with 4.23 per cent, all rank above the highest Jewish house, which is Kuhn, Loeb with 2.88 per cent.

It goes without saying, of course, that the facts failed to kill the myth. From 1933, moreover, until the attack on Pearl Harbor the disreputable peddlers of anti-Semitism received aid and comfort from men of standing and influence, conservative isolationists who abominated Roosevelt's New Deal and his foreign policy. The New Deal was held up as a Jewish concoction, the presence of Jews among Roosevelt's advisers, among them Benjamin V. Cohen, Sidney Hillman and Samuel I. Rosenman, providing sufficient "proof" of the contention. It was also a simple matter to "prove" the Jewish genesis of his foreign policy: his support of the democracies against Nazi and Fascist aggression was not in the interests of America; it was just what the Jewish interventionists ordered. Among those who echoed these sentiments was the popular hero, Charles A. Lindbergh; he spoke of Nazism and Fascism as the "wave of the future," intimating that the wave was rolling towards America. In September 1940 respectable isolationism organized itself into the America First Committee, which did not try too hard to keep at a distance the anti-Semites of every stripe it attracted.

5

That the anti-Semitic clamor in the United States in the second decade of the long truce drew inspiration from Germany became apparent when the American apostles began to ape Nazi methods and mouth Nazi slogans. Secret Nazi agents with well-lined pockets came and coached the native *fuehrers*—William Dudley Pelley, who was later convicted of sedition and sentenced to prison for fifteen years; the Reverend Gerald Winrod, George Deatherage, Joe McWilliams, and numerous others—in the art of anti-Semitic propaganda. The German-American Bund appeared on the scene and served both as model and transmission belt to the native groups like The Silver Shirts, The Order of '76, The Black Legion, The Knights of the Camellia, and many others: there were, indeed, several hundred of them! The Bund, until its leader Fritz Kuhn was convicted of embezzlement and imprisoned, made ready for a Nazified America by drilling its young men in Storm Troop uniforms and training its youngsters to emulate the Hitler Youth in Germany. In May 1939 an attempt was made to overcome the principal weakness of these groups, their disunion. At a secret meeting in Jamaica, New York, George Van Horn Moseley, a retired army general, was presented as the man on horseback to lead all of them. The meeting, however, was not so secret after all; its proceedings were laid before the Congressional Committee on un-American Activities, the general was haled before it, and he left the hearing a thoroughly deflated *fuehrer*.

But the apostle of the anti-Semitic evangel à la Josef Goebbels who won the largest following during the hectic years before the attack on Pearl Harbor, was the Catholic priest Charles E. Coughlin. From his "shrine" in Detroit Coughlin disseminated his sanctimonious venom in a weekly radio broadcast to an audience that reached into the millions, and his incendiary *Social Justice*, which in its first two issues reprinted the *Protocols of the Elders of Zion*, was peddled with rowdy insolence in the busiest streets of America. The peddlers belonged to the priest's Christian Front, which became the largest and most sinister of the anti-Semitic fraternities. The Front was particularly active in New York and other Eastern cities, with noisy meetings on street corners and "Buy Christian" campaigns, and Coughlin's "crusade" was zealously promoted by Father Edward Lodge Curran, president of the

International Catholic Truth Society and editor of the Catholic weekly *The Tablet*, published in Brooklyn.

6

It was a recrudescence of the age-old religious antipathies, primitive passions and neurotic compensations that are normally held in check—the entire noisome brood that makes up the baffling phenomenon called anti-Semitism. And the resources of the three Jewish defense agencies, as they came to be called—the American Jewish Committee, the American Jewish Congress, and the Anti-Defamation League—were strained to the limit to deal with the problems and emergencies the throwback created. The first, with Cyrus Adler as president and Morris D. Waldman as executive vice-president, labored valiantly through a special Legal and Investigative Department to contain and expose the evil. A large group of able and distinguished men were active in the effort: Benjamin D. Buttenweiser, Samuel D. Leidesdorf, Solomon Lowenstein, William Rosenwald, Lewis L. Strauss and others. The American Jewish Congress was even bolder in its measures to alert public opinion to the menace. The Anti-Defamation League broadened its program, its work during the period headed by Sigmund Livingston and directed by Richard E. Gutstadt. B'nai B'rith, of which the League was an integral part, was headed by Alfred M. Cohen, who was succeeded in 1938 by Henry Monsky.

The efforts of these groups were considerably aided by the movement for better understanding among Protestants, Catholics and Jews, usually called the Interfaith movement. Under the championship of Isaac Landman, a Reform rabbi, who was the editor of the *American Hebrew,* the movement had its start in the early twenties, and obtained support from leading Christian clergymen, in particular from the Federal Council of the Churches of Christ in America, and from some of the foremost figures in American public life. In 1928 it took its longest step forward when the National Conference of Christians and Jews was established "to moderate—and finally to eliminate—a system of prejudices which disfigures and distorts our business, social and political relations." The first Protestant chairman of the Conference was Newton D. Baker, Woodrow Wilson's Secretary of War, who was succeeded in 1938 by Arthur H. Compton, a Nobel Prize physicist. Its Catholic and Jewish co-chairmen were, respectively, Carleton J. H. Hayes, a professor of history in Columbia University, and Roger Williams Straus, son of Oscar S. Straus and a prominent industrial and civic leader. Everett R. Clinchy, a Protestant clergyman, was named its director. From its headquarters in New York the Conference branched out to regional offices throughout the country, and in the early fifties it extended its activities on an international scale. A dramatic feature of its program was the sponsorship of Brotherhood Week, which since 1933 has been observed on a national scale during the week of Washington's Birthday. Among leading theologians of the three faiths the movement was actively promoted by Louis Finkelstein, a distinguished scholar and able administrator, who in 1940 succeeded Cyrus Adler as president of the Jewish Theological Seminary of America.

The Interfaith movement has naturally found its most ardent champions among Jews, with warm friends among Protestant clergymen and laymen, and some support among Catholics also. With all its limitations, which Jews have not hesitated to point out, it has been an important aid in upholding the basic decencies in interfaith relations. The main criticism directed against it was that it encouraged the tendency on the part of some Jews to suppress the differences between their faith and that of their neighbors; for what virtue is there in tolerance if it does not honor the right to be different?

7

But valuable as the work of the Jewish defense agencies and the Interfaith movement was, the principal bulwark in the struggle against the infiltration of the Nazi creed lay in the spirit and traditions of America. With all their tumult and shouting the Nazi eruptions represented only the "lunatic fringe" of the nation, the warped fraction which any sizable human aggregation is sure to include. Unlike Germany, Poland or Rumania, America as a whole stood firm against the clamor. With few exceptions the leaders in every sphere of thought and action, in organized labor and the Protestant churches in particular, turned their backs on the demagogues and bigots, and many of their foremost spokesmen joined in the efforts to combat them. And as Nazi Germany, with its network of fifth columns across the world, speeded its career of ruthless aggression, a feeling of apprehension was added to the aversion which the anti-Semitic hatemongers inspired.

CHAPTER 21

War and Postwar Trials

1

THE "WAR FOR SURVIVAL," IT WAS SUGGESTED BY PRESIDENT Roosevelt, should be the name of the war America fought against Nazi Germany and Imperialist Japan. If that war placed the survival of America in jeopardy, it placed the survival of the American Jewish community in double jeopardy: as a component of the American nation and as part of a people that Nazism had resolved to destroy physically and completely. It remains for this chronicle to take note of the efforts and sacrifices the Jews of America, together with Americans of all other creeds and national origins, made to overcome the common peril, and the special burdens and trials they bore as a result of the catastrophe that overwhelmed their people in Europe and the cataclysmic events that led to the rise of the State of Israel in Palestine.

2

In the three major conflicts since the establishment of the Republic—the Civil War, the First World War and the Second World War—the Jews of America served in the Armed Forces of their country in sizable numbers. In the first, the 150,000 or 200,000 Jews were still a tiny fraction of the population, but it will be recalled that even then the Board of Delegates of American Israelites made an attempt, which proved abortive, to assemble the data on the number of Jews who fought on both sides of the conflict, and that the publication of the facts thirty years after the surrender of Lee came in reply to an anti-Semitic slur that appeared in a public print.* In the half century between the Civil War and the First World War the American Jewish community had grown to nearly 3,500,000, or about 3 per cent of the total population, and its capacity to act for the protection of its good name had, in spite of inner divisions, grown considerably. The facts with regard to the 225,000 Jews who served in the Armed Forces of

* Page 97.

America in that war were, as we saw, assembled by a special Office of War Records established by the American Jewish Committee in 1917.

The work of compiling the corresponding facts with regard to the "War for Survival" was entrusted to the National Jewish Welfare Board, and was accomplished by its Bureau of War Records under the direction of Samuel C. Kohs, a prominent psychologist and social worker, and the noted statistician Louis I. Dublin. The Bureau was assisted in its colossal task by other experts and by volunteers in hundreds of American cities and towns. The results of its labors, published in 1947, make up two ample volumes entitled *American Jews in World War II: The Story of 550,000 Fighters for Freedom.* The first volume, the work of I. Kaufman, editor and war correspondent, may be called the "Book of Heroes"; it narrates the exploits of some of the many Jewish heroes of the war. The second may be called the "Book of Names," consisting as it does almost entirely of the names of Jews—men and women—"who received recognition for valor above the ordinary requirements of duty, and of those who suffered injury or death inflicted by the foe." The number who received awards, ranging from the Congressional Medal of Honor to Presidential Unit Citations and the Purple Heart, was 36,352. The casualties exceeded 35,000. Nearly 10,500—of whom 8,000 were killed in action—gave their lives; 18,000 were wounded, and the rest were about equally divided between those missing in action and those taken prisoner. But this Honor Roll of awards and casualties, we are told, "is far from complete. Thousands of names belong to it of Jewish service men and women who, for various reasons, were not identified."

As in the First World War the figures disclose that the proportion of Jews in the Armed Forces was higher than that of the total population. The fact stands out plainly from studies made in 1944 and 1945, in which all Jews in nineteen communities over the country were included, communities considered typical, like Boston, Allentown, Wilmington, Youngstown, Dallas, Denver, Oklahoma City, Spokane and others. In Boston, for example, the percentage of the total population in service was 9.3, that of the Jewish population was 12.1; in Denver the corresponding figures were 8.5 and 11.8; in Dallas 9.3 and 11.2; in Wilmington 8.6 and 11.7. The only exception was Galveston, where the figures were 11.6 and 10.6. The reasons offered for the higher proportion of Jews were first, that they were largely city dwellers, among whom the deferment rate was lower than in the rural areas; second, that they tended to marry at a higher age than non-Jews with a resulting decrease in the proportion of those who were eligible for deferment because of dependents; and third, that a large proportion of them were in occupations in which deferments were relatively few. But whatever the reasons, the overall figures indicate that while the proportion of the total population in the Armed Forces was approximately 8.8 per cent, that of the Jews was 11 per cent. In 1945 the Jews were about 3.6 per cent of the total population; in the Armed Forces of America at peak strength they were approximately 4.5 per cent.*

Nearly 60 per cent of Jewish physicians under forty-five years of age were in uniform, and a high proportion of rabbis served as chaplains. The Jewish chaplain who is best remembered is Abraham Goode; he went down with his three Christian colleagues when all four gave their life preservers to men on board the Army transport *Dorchester* when the ship was torpedoed and sunk in the Atlantic in June 1943. About 20 per cent of the Jews in service had officers' rank, with six major generals, thirteen brigadier generals, one admiral, two rear admirals, and one commodore. One of the officers killed in action was Major General Maurice Rose, commander of the Third Armored Division, who was the son of a rabbi in Denver.

Those, then, are the cold figures, and they can only be warmed by human blood, sweat and tears. A mere glance at the chapter headings of the "Book of Heroes" recalls the anguished and glorious road these men, together with their comrades of other faiths and ethnic origins, traveled, before the evil that threatened to possess the earth was finally crushed: "Pearl Harbor to Guadalcanal"; "Philippines to Okinawa"; "They Delivered the Atom"; "Battle of the Seven Seas"; "The Fight in North Africa"; "We Strike Through Italy"; "D-Day in Normandy"; "We Battle for France"; "Inside Germany." And how can their heroism be adequately told, their deeds in the deserts, jungles and mountains; in the clouds and skies; on the oceans and beneath them, amid the rubble of streets and cities?

If, arbitrarily, ten Jewish heroes of the war were to be chosen for mention the task of selection would be not only invidious but baffling. The ten might include Stanley Caplan, who took charge of a destroyer that fateful day at Pearl Harbor, and Ira Jeffery, who died "passing the ammunition" the same day on the battleship *California*, and for whom a destroyer was named. It could not omit the bombardier Meyer

* These percentages are based on the following statistics: estimated U. S. population, July 1, 1945 (Bureau of the Census): 139,934,000; peak strength of U. S. Armed Forces in Second World War (Department of the Army): 12,300,000; estimated number of Jews in U. S., 1945 (American Jewish Year Book, vol. 48, p. 599): 5,000,000; estimated number of Jews in U. S. Armed Forces in Second World War (National Jewish Welfare Board): 550,000.

Levin, whose deeds would require a separate scroll, nor Julius Kleinman the gunner who died on board his returning bomber after fighting off a squadron of enemy planes. We may well admit Hyman Epstein, who died binding the wounds of fallen comrades in New Guinea; David Hirsch, who kept his Flying Fortress on course while the blood oozed from a dozen wounds in his body, and Bernard Kessel, driver of a tank in Africa, who took on the task of an armored column. Two more to complete the *minyan*, and we mention, say, Abraham Todres, whose four-year fighting career as bombardier, gunner, engineer and paratrooper took him across the globe and brought him thirty decorations, and Lieutenant Raymond Zussman, who was awarded the Congressional Medal of Honor for a day of incredible tank exploits, in which he captured 92 Nazis, killed 17, and liberated a French town in the Rhone Valley. But more and more come thronging with those named: flyers and marines, soldiers and sailors, doctors and medical aides, officers and men in the ranks. And among them no doubt, will be those whose names and deeds, no matter how diligent the recorders, will be unknown and unsung.

It is a proud and splendid record, and the American Jewish community is indebted to the able and devoted men and women who gathered and published it. At the same time the massive and painstaking compilation induces some sober reflections. No other group in the ethnologic or religious structure of America has produced anything like it. Apparently no other minority group felt it necessary to place its war record on view for itself and others. What it was that impelled the Jewish group to do so can be easily surmised and is made explicitly clear by statements that appear in the two volumes. The first volume is recommended as "the best factual answer to the anti-Semite," and the Introduction to the second states that "the circumstances of the war period and of the events leading up to it compelled us to do this job and to produce a record that would convince through its reliability even those who would malign us."

3

In the twenty-seven months prior to that "day of infamy" at Pearl Harbor the progress of Nazi arms in Europe brought grave anxiety to the American people, and especially to the Jews. Few events in history foreboded such dire results for mankind as the fall of France in June 1940 and the Battle of Britain that followed. And the sweep of the Nazi legions through Russia from June 1941 to November 1942 confirmed, what appeared to have become a wide-spread conviction, that the German war machine was invincible. The nightmare of an imminent Nazified world was dispelled when America entered the war, but the three years that followed also had their weeks and months of anxiety, as when the fleets and cohorts of Japan swept through the western Pacific, including the Philippines, or when in the summer of 1942 Rommel's Afrika Korps stood deployed on the border of Egypt, or when the Germans counterattacked in the Ardennes Bulge in December 1944. But in May of the following year came the surrender of Germany, and three months later that of Japan: the cloud that darkened the earth for five years was lifted at last.

The Jews of America went through the emotional gamut of those years with all other Americans, just as they shared with them the toils and sacrifices the crisis demanded. For the Jews, however, the crisis was more acute: they knew that in a Nazified world there would be no room for them. But when the war was over they felt the full impact of a grief that was peculiarly their own: the destruction of European Jewry at the hands of the Germans stood revealed in all its enormity and savagery.

As early as the first years of the war rumors were in circulation of the murder mills the Germans established at Auschwitz, Treblinka, Maidanek, Dachau, Buchenwald, and numerous other places, but it took the Allies a long time to take note of the reports and a still longer time to believe them. It was only in December 1942 that the House of Commons in London was officially informed that the extermination of the Jews in Europe was in full swing. In America official and unofficial voices were raised in horror, Congress and state legislatures passed resolutions, there were public demonstrations, and days of prayer, fasting and compassion. But pitifully little was done for those whom it was still possible to save. In April 1943 a conference of delegates representing the American and British governments met in Bermuda to consider measures of rescue, but it resulted only, as did the conference in Evian in 1938, in expressions of lofty sentiments and profound regrets: lack of shipping and the immutable immigration laws prevented their admission into the United States, and the British White Paper of 1939 barred their admission into Palestine.

In January 1944 President Roosevelt, in response to pressure from Christian as well as Jewish sources, set up a War Refugee Board, with the Secretaries of State, War and the Treasury as members, "to forestall the plan of the Nazis to exterminate all the Jews and other persecuted minorities of Europe." In the summer of that year the

Board began operations from headquarters in Turkey, and under the direction of Ira A. Hirschmann, a New York business executive, and with the aid of the Joint Distribution Committee, the Jewish Agency for Palestine and other organizations, it was helpful in saving some hundreds of lives. By that time, however, the work of annihilation was nearly completed. The War Refugee Board only demonstrated what might have been accomplished by the democracies if the effort had not been so little and so late.

4

The salient features of the crime—the most stupendous in the blood-stained annals of mankind—should be here recalled, not only because vast numbers of its victims were relatives of American Jews, but because it formed the backdrop of anguish and desperation against which the bitter struggle of the Jews in Palestine for statehood was fought out, a struggle in which, as we shall see, the Jews in America also became inexorably involved. The physical dimensions of the crime are summed up in the following sentence of a summary of the verdict delivered September 30, 1946 by the International Military Tribunal, representing the United States, Britain, France and the Soviet Union, before which the major German war criminals were tried:

> Adolph Eichmann, who had been put in charge of the program to exterminate the Jews, has estimated that the policy pursued resulted in the killing of 6,000,000 Jews, of whom 4,000,000 were killed in the concentration camps and 2,000,000 were killed by the Einsatz Groups.*

The pattern of annihilation, which included psychological as well as physical devices, was prepared and executed with all the vaunted German thoroughness. The Jews of Poland, the first in the line of victims, were herded into squalid and congested ghettos where they were terrorized and starved. Under pretext of being taken elsewhere for employment they were then packed into boxcars and transported to "scientific" murder mills, equipped with gas chambers where they were asphyxiated and crematories where they were burned. And as the Nazis overran Western Europe and the Balkans, they deported countless thousands of Jews from those lands—France, Holland, Belgium, Greece, Jugoslavia, Hungary—to the concentration camps in Poland, where they too were done to death. Such was the main annihilation pat-

* Special units of the German army charged with "the duty of exterminating the Jews."

tern, but it had its variations. Thousands were shot down into mass graves which they had previously been forced to dig for themselves; others were systematically beaten, starved or worked to death; still others succumbed to experiments conducted upon them by German scientists. The lowest depth of depravity was reached by the Nazis in their destruction of babies and small children: of the six million victims the little ones are estimated to have numbered not less than a million. And it must be remembered that with the Jews of Eastern Europe not only a people was murdered, but an ancient culture and a noble way of life.

Most of the Christians, among whom the Jews had been living in Eastern Europe for centuries, looked upon the extirpation of the Jews with indifference or approval. Thousands of them collaborated with the Nazis in the work of destruction. There were, no doubt, instances of Jews, especially children, whom Christians, even at the risk of their own lives, saved from the toils of the Gestapo, but in Eastern Europe they were rare. They were not so rare in France, Belgium, Holland, Denmark and Italy. Thousands who escaped from France found refuge in Switzerland, and large numbers who, with the help of an underground organized and conducted by Christian Danes, fled across the channel from Denmark found refuge in Sweden. In America a plan was launched to admit refugees without offending the immigration laws by setting up camps for them as temporary homes; some 900 were admitted and lodged in a camp near Oswego, New York. It was a brave and ingenious plan, but it fell pitifully short of the high hopes it awakened.

One of the most imaginative and successful rescue undertakings was the Youth Aliya, inspired and led until her death in 1945 by Henrietta Szold. Its aim was to save Jewish children and bring them to Palestine. Beginning in 1934 with the rescue of children from Germany, it extended to the Nazi-occupied countries and even penetrated the concentration camps. By the end of 1945 some 17,000 children had been saved, but the work continued after the war and by 1954 the number had risen to 62,000. In America the leading promoter of the effort was Hadassah, with the women's branches of the labor and religious wings of Zionism also participating.

5

Many of the Christian homes and religious establishments in which Jewish children were given asylum weaned them away from their faith, and after the war insisted on retaining them, even when parents or relatives came forward to claim them, or when, in the absence of parents or relatives, they were claimed by Jewish communities. This situation, which brought heartbreak to a great many and stirred indignation among Jews the world over, was highlighted by the so-called Finaly Affair, which became a *cause célèbre*, involving the French Government, the Catholic Church and the Jewish community not only of France but of other countries, including America.

In 1944 the parents of Robert and Gerald Finaly, who had fled from Austria to France in 1938, were deported by the Nazis and never heard of again. But aware of the danger they faced, they had previously entrusted their two baby sons to a Catholic institution in the city of Grenoble, with the understanding that the children's religion would be respected. In July 1945 the boys' three aunts initiated a series of efforts to recover them, but it was not until eight years later that Hedwige Rossner, one of the aunts, succeeded in bringing them to her home in Israel. During those years, the court actions, negotiations, evasions, arrests, and finally the sensational abduction of the boys into Spain over the snow-piled Pyrenees in the winter of 1953 and their eventual return, were followed with tense interest throughout the world. Court orders were defied by the woman custodian of the boys, who had had them baptized, and by her aiders and abettors, among whom were not only laymen and priests, but important members of the hierarchy. The Affair carried echoes of the notorious Mortara abduction nearly a century earlier,* and it created tensions between the government of France and the Church that were reminiscent of the Dreyfus Affair. "No Jewish child," declared the Grand Rabbinate of France, "is any longer safe from a secretly administered baptism."

But in 1953 the Church could not defy world opinion as did Pius IX in 1858, and the Jews of the world were better equipped to assert their human rights. In the United States the American Jewish Committee made representations on the Finaly Affair to the State Department, conferred with the French and Spanish ambassadors in Washington, and its office in Paris shared in the long and intricate negotiations. The World Jewish Congress took a leading part in the labor of recovering the children, and the American Jewish Congress, its most important affiliate, was naturally involved in the effort; and the French Socialist and liberal press was enlisted for the cause by the Paris office of the Jewish Labor Committee.

---

* Page 85 ff.

6

There were, of course, numerous other "Finaly Affairs" in the bitter aftermath of the holocaust, but there were episodes in it that were not only tragic, but heroic and glorious. And the one that stands out most is the armed uprising in the spring of 1943 in the Warsaw ghetto, which evoked the amazement and admiration of the entire world.

Preparations for the uprising began more than a year earlier with the organization of twenty-two combatant units and the procurement of rifles, revolvers, hand grenades and a few machine guns. When the pitched battle between the pitifully armed Jewish units and the Nazi battalions, equipped with artillery, tanks, bombing planes and flame throwers, broke out on Passover 1943, only some 40,000 of the 450,000 people the Germans had herded into the walled enclosure were left; the others had been evacuated to the gas chambers and crematories of Treblinka. After more than a week of desperate fighting at close quarters the Nazis withdrew, finding the cost too high. They shelled the ghetto with heavy artillery and bombed it from the air, setting it on fire, and on April 28 launched a force of 6,000 men against the survivors. But it was not until two months later that the last flickers of resistance were extinguished.

Forty survivors, after crawling for twenty hours through the sewers of Warsaw, emerged on the "Aryan" side. They escaped in a captured truck to a forest outside the city, and a number of them, including Zivia Lubetkin, "the mother of the ghetto," lived to acquaint the world with this last gesture of pride and defiance. But it is often forgotten that there were uprisings in the ghettos of other cities also, in Vilna, Bialystok, Cracow, Bendin, Tarnopol and others, and there were even outbreaks in Treblinka, Sobibor and other annihilation centers.

The mood of the men and women who fought the subhuman enemy in the ghettos and forests of Poland, and of many of those who were taken to the death camps, found expression in songs that reached the ears of their people in America after the liberation. There was, for example, the *Song of the Vilna Partisans,* beginning with the lines:

Never say this journey is your last;
Golden days will come though skies are overcast.
The hour of our longing draws near:
Like a drum our tread will echo: "We are here!"

And the song that spread through the camps and was chanted by thousands before they died was *Ani Maamin,* "I Believe." The words

LEADERS IN GOVERNMENT

Courtesy of the National Archives

Judah P. Benjamin

Underwood—Stratton

Oscar S. Straus

Courtesy of the National Archives

Herbert H. Lehman

Courtesy of the National Archives

Henry Morgenthau, Jr.

AMERICAN JEWISH COMMITTEE LEADERS

Courtesy of the American Jewish Committee

Louis Marshall

American Jewish Historical Society

Cyrus Adler

B'NAI B'RITH LEADERS

Courtesy of B'nai B'rith

Alfred M. Cohen

Heinz Photo

Henry Monsky

are from the daily prayers asserting faith in the coming of the Messiah, when the world will be redeemed from evil; the haunting melody is a blend of resignation and triumphant faith.

I believe, I believe, I believe,
With perfect faith, with perfect faith,
In the coming of the Messiah!
And though he tarry,
None the less do I believe:
None the less do I believe.

In the years immediately following the war, survivors whom various hazards had saved from the gas chambers, or whom the American armies in their sweep through Germany had liberated from Buchenwald, Bergen-Belsen and other concentration camps, arrived in America. There were camp numerals tattooed on their forearms and stories of horror on their lips. With literal truth American Jews could say, "There, but for the grace of God, stood I," and many recalled also the words Joseph spoke to his brothers in Egypt after he made himself known to them: "For God did send me before you to preserve life."

7

It will be recalled that nearly four years after the end of the First World War the political future of Palestine officially became an international concern, when in July 1922 the Council of the League of Nations ratified the Palestine Mandate, in which the Zionist objective, as stated in the Balfour Declaration, was embodied. Large and influential segments of the Jewish community in America had been opposed to that objective, and although the Declaration and Mandate blunted their opposition, it nevertheless remained strong and asserted itself vigorously whenever an attempt was made to interpret the vague expression "a national home for the Jewish people" as meaning a Jewish commonwealth or state. On November 29, 1947, two-and-a-half years after the end of the Second World War in Europe, the Assembly of the United Nations voted that a sovereign Jewish state should be established in Palestine, and the Jews of America, including the great majority of the former opposition, hailed the decision and supported the Yishuv in its war to vindicate it.

The David-and-Goliath struggle, in which the Yishuv was pitted not only against the Arabs but also against the British government, began, as we saw, long before that decision. The hardest blow the Yishuv sustained at the hands of Britain had been the White Paper of May 1939, which sought to "freeze" the Jewish community in Palestine to a permanent minority of one-third, and restrict it to a small fraction of the country's area. With the world war that began three months later, the Yishuv declared a truce in the struggle, and placed all its resources —human, industrial, and scientific—at the disposal of Britain in the war against the enemy of mankind. In all these spheres—military personnel, food and war matériel, medical goods and services—the Yishuv made important contributions, although as in the First World War it was only after a long and hard effort, to which American Zionists lent their full weight, that a distinct Jewish Brigade was authorized as part of the British Army. The authorization was announced in September 1944 by Prime Minister Churchill; "it is indeed appropriate," he said, "that a special Jewish unit, a special unit of that race which has suffered indescribable torments from the Nazis, should be represented in a distinct formation among the forces gathered for their final overthrow." But as early as 1940 Jewish auxiliary units had served in North Africa, France, Italy and elsewhere, combat units of company strength had fought in Abyssinia and Eritrea, and Jewish commando units had performed gallant exploits on a number of fronts, including Syria.

8

But the truce was a one-sided affair: the British government did not suspend or relax the policy proclaimed in the White Paper, and as the months of war rolled into years and the reports of the mass murder of their kith and kin in Europe gathered volume, the men and women of the Yishuv realized that the Paper meant not alone the end of the Mandate, but a death warrant for many thousands of their people whom it kept out of the only land where they might have found safety. To this great wrong and desperate need they could not remain passive. It was from them that the most daring and effective efforts at rescue proceeded. Couriers from the Yishuv established rescue headquarters in Geneva, Budapest and Istanbul, and made contact with Jewish partisan groups in Nazi-occupied countries; they even pierced the vast slaughter-house of Poland, and those they saved were estimated at tens of thousands. The most spectacular rescue exploits were performed by a group of parachutists from the Yishuv who were dropped behind the enemy lines in Italy and the Balkans. Seven of those who jumped failed to return, among them Enzo Sereni, the leader of the group, and Hannah Senesch, both of whom died at the hands of the Nazis and became enshrined among the most cherished heroes of the Jewish redemption.

But those who were smuggled across borders and, after overcoming numerous other perils, were put on ships bound for Palestine, often failed to reach their goal. British destroyers and cruisers patrolled the Mediterranean to stop them, and many of those whose rickety ships managed to elude His Majesty's Navy were rounded up by the British garrison in Palestine and thrown into prisons and internment camps. Others were deported to the island of Mauritius in the Indian Ocean or to Cyprus. The British called them "illegals"; the Jews called them *maapilim*, "those who dared," and classified them as a new immigration "wave," which they designated cryptically as *Aliyah Bet*. And many of the *maapilim* perished on the high seas; their "coffin ships" met with various disasters, all traceable to the ruthless enforcement of the White Paper.

Three of the ships, the *Patria*, the *Struma* and the *Exodus 1947*, stand out in the long and lamentable roster. In November 1940 the *Patria*, with some 1,800 refugees who had arrived earlier that month on two crippled freighters, was in Haifa harbor, scheduled to sail to Mauritius. But some among them had resolved to end their tragic odyssey; they blew up the ship and 260 of her passengers perished. Even more shocking was the fate of the *Struma;* all but one of her 769 passengers went down with her when in February 1942 she sank in the Black Sea, after being denied entry into Palestine. And as late as the summer of 1947 the ship with the challenging name *Exodus 1947* went through a sensational odyssey, which held the attention of the entire world. Originally an American coastal steamer built to carry 700 passengers, the ship, with 4,500 refugees on board, was intercepted by a British squadron. At Haifa her passengers were huddled into three prison ships and five days later the ships anchored off Marseilles, expecting to land their human cargo in France, from which the refugees had sailed. Since the summer of the previous year intercepted refugees had been deported to Cyprus, but the internment camps on the island had become overcrowded and the London government determined to deport them instead to the country of their embarkation. But the refugees refused to land, and the French would not receive them unless they came uncoerced. For nearly a month the duel between the British Empire and the tormented fugitives continued, the entire world outraged by the grim spectacle. Finally the ships took them to the British Occupation Zone in Germany, where they found themselves again behind the barbed wire of concentration camps.

Those were only a few of the many spectacular encounters in the long and stubborn Battle of Immigration the Yishuv fought against Britain before and during the war years, and with growing intensity in the three years after the war. Nor can it be said that the battle went against the Yishuv. During the war years alone some 60,000 immigrants were added to its population, a considerable portion of them "illegals," and from the middle of 1945 to the end of 1946 about 25,000 more were added: apparently most of the ships that carried them defeated the vigilance of the British planes, warships and radar stations. Detachments of the Haganah, the Jewish underground militia, brought the passengers to land, sometimes wading out and carrying them to shore on their shoulders, and dispersed them swiftly among the settlements.

Two other crucial battles were being fought at the same time in this war against Britain, the Battle of Colonization and the Battle of Defense. Between 1939 and 1944, the Jewish National Fund, in spite of the drastic restrictions on land purchases, increased its holdings by nearly 250,000 dunams, and 50 new settlements were planted, half of them in the strategic Upper Galilee and Negev. The British, of course, did what they could to obstruct the extension of Jewish colonization, and there were some strange encounters between them and the settlers, like the one in Birya in March 1946, which the settlers won with passive resistance. On a single day in October 1946 eleven new settlements sprang up in the Negev. The feat was accomplished after long and secret preparations, and the British were caught by surprise.

The Battle of Defense was perhaps the most decisive of all. Bitter experience had taught the Yishuv that its physical safety depended primarily on itself, but the British found the Haganah a thorn in their side: the Haganah had created and was operating the network of activities involved in Aliyah Bet, and it stood guard over the establishment of every new settlement. So they pressed the battle with raids in search of arms, show trials against Jews accused of possessing arms, and direct attempts to disarm and disband the Haganah.

9

There was another and more ominous phase to this war against the British rulers of Palestine. A goodly portion of the Yishuv, but by far not the majority, became convinced that there was no hope for the Jews as long as the British stayed, and that only terror would make them go. The fighting men belonging to this minority had seceded from the Haganah as early as 1938 and named themselves *Irgun Zvai Leumi*

(National Military Organization), and a later schism in their own ranks resulted in the formation of the "Fighters for the Freedom of Israel," better known as the Stern Group, who went ever further in their implacable hostility against the British. In November 1944 two members of the Group assassinated Lord Moyne, the British Resident Minister in the Middle East, and for three years after the war the acts of terror committed by the dissidents, and the counter-terror, official and unofficial, with which the British tried in vain to stem them, kept the country in turmoil. Palestine became virtually a police state under martial law, and it was the British even more than the Jews who found themselves under siege. The responsible leaders of the Yishuv also made strenuous efforts to check and stamp out the terror; they declared it repugnant to the ethics and traditions of Judaism, and it besmirched the good name of the Yishuv and undermined its interests. But they refused to play the part of informers or to become embroiled in a civil war for the benefit of a regime which, in the opinion of the entire community, was, by its brutal and unlawful policy, itself responsible for the terror.

In July 1945 the Labor Party took over the government of Britain, but by the fall of the same year the Yishuv realized that the glowing hopes the change had inspired were a total illusion. The previous month Earl G. Harrison, the American member of the Inter-Governmental Committee on Refugees, had reported to President Harry S. Truman that "Palestine is definitely and preeminently the first choice" of the Jewish survivors still subsisting in the concentration camps, and the President urged the Labor government to admit 100,000 of them without delay. The request was ignored, and two months later the British Foreign Secretary announced that an Anglo-American Committee of Inquiry, consisting of six Britons and six Americans, would examine the situation in Palestine and in the concentration camps, and make recommendations. The Committee investigated and recommended unanimously that the 100,000 be admitted immediately, but the Labor government summarily rejected the recommendation. Ernest Bevin, the burly and splenetic Foreign Secretary, an up-to-date version of Peter Stuyvesant of old New Amsterdam, added to his pronouncements crude jibes against the Jews, accusing the survivors of the Nazi death mills of trying to "get to the head of the queue," and even charging that when President Truman urged the prompt admission of 100,000 of them to Palestine, he was yielding to the political pressure of "New York Jews."

So the acts of terror on both sides mounted in frequency and ferocity, while the little freighters crowded with refugees kept gliding towards the coast, many of them landing their human freight, others intercepted by British men-of-war and seized by boarding parties in the classic and bloody style of the pirates of former days. The spirit of the men and women they carried spoke even from the names the ships bore: *Ghetto Rebel, Four Freedoms, Enzo Sereni, Hannah Senesch, Unknown Illegal, To The Negev, Motherland.*

Finally, in February 1947 the British government announced its decision to refer the entire Palestine problem to the United Nations. It was a startling announcement, a public confession of failure and defeat. So Palestine became officially a world problem, and two months later the Assembly of the United Nations met in New York in special session to deal with it.

10

Those, then, were the two grim and overshadowing realities that dominated the cares and toils of the Jewish community in America after the triumph of their country over its enemies: the plight of the homeless survivors of the unparalleled disaster that had overwhelmed their people in Europe, and the desperate struggle of the Yishuv in Palestine. The community in America was now not only the most influential but also the largest in the world; the war made it a dominant factor in the destiny of the Jewish people as a whole, just as the vital part the United States played in the defeat of Germany and the supreme part it played in the defeat of Japan made America the world's leading power. To meet the double crisis the Jews in America could make at least two important contributions: provide the huge sums which the resettlement of the survivors required, and obtain the moral and political support of the American people and government for the aspirations of the Yishuv in Palestine. The first was the clear and immediate task of every segment of the community, the second devolved primarily on the Zionist organizations. But by the fall of 1947 it too, as we shall soon see, became the overriding concern of the entire community.

CHAPTER 22

New Pride, New Care

1

THE GRIM BUT STIRRING EVENTS IN PALESTINE AND ON THE sea lanes leading to it, coupled with the appalling fate of their people in Europe and the grievous lot of the survivors, brought the Jews of America to the Zionist standard by the hundreds of thousands. The world Zionist Congress, meeting, after a lapse of seven years, in Basel in December 1946, represented 2,100,000 shekel payers, more than half of them in America, and the American delegation of 120 was the largest in the assembly. By 1948 the organized strength of American Zionism had risen to nearly a million.

When the war broke out the Zionist bodies had formed a united front to assume the burdens of the world movement, as they had done in 1914 on the outbreak of the First World War. The American Zionist Emergency Council, its name after the war changed to American Zionist Council, became the spokesman of all the units, and applied itself to mobilize the public opinion of the country for its cause. Hundreds of local Emergency Councils were established, forty state legislatures adopted pro-Zionist resolutions and as many governors sent President Roosevelt a pro-Zionist petition. Over 15,000 Christian leaders of the nation in public life, industry, labor, education, science, and the arts united in an American Palestine Committee with Senator Robert F. Wagner of New York as chairman, and 2,500 clergymen of every denomination joined a Christian Council for Palestine headed by Henry A. Atkinson, leader of the Church Peace Union; in May 1946 the two combined and became the American Christian Palestine Committee.

In July 1944 the nominating conventions of the two major political parties had inserted pro-Zionist planks into their platforms, and in December of the following year both Houses of Congress adopted pro-Zionist resolutions. To support the "activist" program of the Irgun Zvai Leumi against the Mandatory, a Hebrew Committee of National Liberation came into existence as well as the American League for a Free Palestine, of which Senator Guy M. Gillette of Iowa became president, and which in 1948 claimed a membership of 150,000, with an impressive number of literary and stage celebrities among them. The Committee, headed by Peter Bergson, with the help of the publisher William Ziff, the writers Ben Hecht and Louis Bromfield, and other Jewish and non-Jewish notables, roused the public opinion of America against the anti-Jewish policy of the British in Palestine.

Foremost in the leadership of American Zionism in the forties were Stephen S. Wise and Abba Hillel Silver, who, at different times headed the Emergency Council, and Emanuel Neumann, who shaped and directed its program, all three identified with the General or Center section of the movement. But the importance of the American scene brought to the United States some of the leading figures in the world movement also: Chaim Weizmann, David Ben-Gurion, Moshe Sharett, Nahum Goldmann and others.

The Jews of America, moreover, rallied to the support of the embattled Yishuv not only by standing up and being counted; they gave of their substance on a scale unmatched in the field of voluntary giving by any other cause, Jewish or non-Jewish. In 1946 a quota of $100,000,000, set by the United Jewish Appeal for relief and reconstruction in Europe, North Africa and Palestine, was oversubscribed, and in 1947 the Appeal raised a total of $170,000,000, about half of it being allotted to Palestine.* At the same time groups were formed to supply the Yishuv directly with some of the instruments, especially ships and crews, which the struggle demanded. The *Exodus 1947* was not the only American ship that was purchased and remodeled to carry refugees to Palestine; among the others being the *Haganah,* the *Theodor Herzl,* the *Medinat Ha-yehudim* (Jewish State), the *Komemiut* (Resurgence), the *Chaim Arlosoroff,* named for a distinguished Zionist leader, the *Ben Hecht,* and the *Wedgwood,* named for Josiah Wedgwood, a prominent Briton, who never wavered in his zeal for Zionism. Some 250 Americans, including a number of Christians, were among those who manned the refugee ships. Arye Lashner, who had a leading part in recruiting the crews of the *Haganah* and the *Wedgwood,* fell in Israel's War of Independence, and William Bernstein, second mate of the *Exodus 1947,* was killed in the clash that followed when the ship was rammed and boarded by the British. The group in America en-

* In the five years that followed, the new state of Israel received $416,000,000 from American Jews, of which two-thirds came from the proceeds of the United Jewish Appeal.

gaged in procuring and remodeling ships and enlisting seamen for the Battle of Immigration was headed by Rudolf G. Sonneborn.

2

It was apparent that not only the preponderant majority of the Jews in America, but the public opinion of the nation as a whole upheld Jewish aspirations in Palestine. In government quarters, however, deeds did not always conform with words, nor did the government always move in all its parts in the same direction. In Zionist circles the opinion was freely voiced that on the question of Palestine the State Department stood at the bidding of the Foreign Office in London. The two major considerations controlling British postwar policy in Palestine seemed to guide the American State Department also. The first was the importance of having and holding the friendship of the Arabs in a world which, as soon as the Nazi peril was overcome, was confronted by the menace of Communist aggression. In the event of another war, it was held, the Near East might become a theater of crucial military operations. The second consideration arose from the rich oil resources of Saudi Arabia, Iraq and Transjordan, which Britain and the United States controlled. Arabian oil, it was alleged, was essential for the naval and air forces of both countries, and the Arab rulers would turn their oil fields over to Soviet Russia if their wishes with regard to Palestine were ignored.

In both considerations, however, competent critics found fallacies. The military potential of the Arab states, they affirmed, was no obstacle to a possible Russian incursion, and the oil installations would in the event of war be exposed in any case to attack and demolition. And they pronounced absurd the notion that the Arab rulers would willingly transfer their oil to Russia, dependent as they were on American and British oil royalties and having no illusions on what awaited them under Communist domination. But in the Pentagon as well as in the State Department there were officials who thought it folly to antagonize them for the sake of a quixotic and sentimental enterprise basing its claims on, of all things, the Bible! They were impressed by the blood-and-thunder manifestos of the Arab potentates, and even President Roosevelt, who received King Ibn Saud of Saudi Arabia on board his cruiser in the Mediterranean after the Yalta Conference, declared he had learned more about "the Moslem problem, the Jewish problem, by talking with Ibn Saud for five minutes, than I could have learned in exchange of two or three dozen letters." The picturesque old desert warrior, it was reported, had solemnly assured the President that "if Palestine is given to the Jews, I will never rest until I and all my sons have been killed in the defense of Palestine."

3

During the war years and after them, the American Jewish scene was punctuated with many demonstrations, conferences and conventions, among which two were of special significance. The first was a conference called by the Zionist Emergency Council and held in May 1942 at the Biltmore Hotel in New York. With every sector of the movement represented, it adopted a declaration crystallizing its new spirit and demands, which became known as the Biltmore Program. Denouncing the White Paper of 1939 as "cruel and indefensible" and without "moral or legal validity," the declaration demanded "that the gates of Palestine be opened, that the Jewish Agency be vested with . . . the necessary authority for upbuilding the country," and that Palestine be established as a "Jewish Commonwealth integrated in the structure of the new democratic world." The Biltmore Program became the rallying point of the movement not only in America but in Palestine and everywhere else.

If only the entire community could be mobilized behind the Program! An attempt to do so was made at the second important gathering during those years. It was the American Jewish Conference, held in New York in September 1943, its convocation prompted by basically the same motives that led to the American Jewish Congress of 1918. Directly and indirectly its delegates were estimated to represent some 2,250,000 men and women, and the high point of its deliberations was a declaration calling for the reestablishment of "Palestine as the Jewish Commonwealth." Of the 502 delegates 498 voted for the declaration, among them those of B'nai B'rith under the dynamic leadership of their president, Henry Monsky of Omaha. But among the few who dissented were the delegates of the powerful American Jewish Committee, led by its president, Joseph M. Proskauer. In 1943 the Committee was not yet prepared for a "Jewish Commonwealth." But history was marching with seven league boots, and in 1947 the Committee joined the Zionists in demanding not a Commonwealth, a term still affected with ambiguity, but a sovereign state.

That was the year when the United Nations made its momentous decision on Palestine, and the American Jewish community was practically united on the once divisive issue. One group, however, calling itself the American Council for Judaism, dissented. It consisted of a small minority of laymen and rabbis of the Reform wing, headed by the prominent Philadelphia merchant and civic leader Lessing Rosenwald, son of the noted philanthropist Julius Rosenwald, with Morris S. Lazaron of Baltimore its leading rabbinical spokesman. The Council appeared to be a concentrate of all the fears which Zionism once provoked, with the old specter of "dual allegiance" in the lead. During the three years after the war, when American Jews in rapidly growing numbers demonstrated their solidarity with the embattled Yishuv, the Council faced the rising tide and commanded the waves to roll back, nor did it seem able to reconcile itself to a Jewish state even after it was established.

4

The United Nations played an essential role in the rise of the state of Israel: its decision of November 29, 1947 served as the juridical foundation for the proclamation of statehood issued by the Yishuv on May 14 of the following year. To the extent that the Jews of America, spearheaded by the organized Zionist forces, overcame the formidable array that opposed the adoption of the decision, they may be credited with having made a vital contribution to the event. But it cannot be too strongly emphasized that when the decision was challenged by the armed forces of the surrounding Arab states, it was the Yishuv that enforced it with the blood of its young manhood and womanhood.

The only action taken by the Special Session on Palestine of the General Assembly which opened April 28, 1947, was to name a United Nations Special Committee on Palestine (UNSCOP) "to investigate all questions and issues relevant to the problem of Palestine." During the bitter debates that preceded the naming of the Committee, the Jews of America were puzzled and disturbed by the "neutral" attitude of the American delegation, resembling closely, as it did, that of the British; powerful forces in Washington were apparently supporting the British Foreign Office. The Russians, on the other hand, produced a surprise: they declared their readiness to support "the division of Palestine into two independent separate states, one Jewish and one Arab," a solution which, in principle, the Jews were prepared to accept. The Russians, of course, were not inspired by a passion for justice to the Jews; they were eager to see Britain dislodged from the Near East, nor was the prospect of tension and turmoil in that region unwelcome to them; some years later, in fact, the same motives led the Soviet Union to favor the

Arabs to the extent of using its veto power in the Security Council in disputes that involved the interests of Israel and the peace of the Near East. Nevertheless the Russian stand held out the immediate possibility of meeting a dangerous world problem without the implacable rivalry between the East and West that balked attempts to solve every other problem.

In June 1947 the UNSCOP, consisting of eleven members with the five major powers excluded, had its first meeting in Jerusalem, where they heard Jewish spokesmen, and went to Beirut, where the Arab case was laid before them. In August they visited Europe and saw the survivors of the holocaust who still waited for deliverance, and on the last day of that month the Committee published its report. Its members all agreed that Britain should surrender the Mandate "at the earliest practicable date," but on the political future of the country there was a majority and minority report. The essence of the majority report was that two independent states, a Jewish and an Arab, be established in Palestine, with an international regime under the authority of the United Nations for Jerusalem and its environs. The minority proposed a unitary federated state. The Arab leaders rejected both reports out of hand. The Jews accepted the majority report as the basis for a solution.

The regular session of the General Assembly opened in September 1947 at Flushing Meadows, New York, and two months later adopted the majority report. Those months of fierce debate and political jockeying were the most hectic the world organization had yet experienced. To be approved, the Partition Plan, as the majority report was designated, had to obtain a two-thirds vote in the General Assembly, but despite Russia's assent, there were a number of factors that held the outcome in suspense. The most serious was the vacillating attitude of the American delegation, an attitude which stood out despite its declaration in favor of the Plan, and made other delegations whose stand was normally determined by that of the United States, feel free to shift their support to the Arab side or abstain from supporting either side. All the influence, energy and skill the Jewish groups could muster was employed to change the lukewarmness of the American delegation to wholehearted support, and to woo and win other delegations to cast their vote in favor of the Plan.

5

In this struggle the Zionists no longer stood alone; the other segments of the community entered the battle, contributing to the final victory. But in view of the road travelled by the American Jewish community in the previous half-century, the two groups whose collaboration was most significant were the American Jewish Committee and the Jewish Labor Committee. They represented respectively the Right and Left of the community, who were once united in their adamant opposition to the Zionist program. Each of them, of course, had its own grounds of antagonism, which they expounded with zeal and eloquence as unalterable truths. But few are the "eternal verities" that abide against the onslaughts of time and change.

In a telegram to Secretary of State George C. Marshall, signed by its president, Joseph M. Proskauer, and the chairman of its executive committee, Jacob Blaustein, the Committee said: "After the most careful consideration by its Committee on Palestine of the reports submitted by the UNSCOP, the American Jewish Committee urges upon the United States Government that it vigorously and speedily endorse and support the report of the majority group." And in the grueling struggle that followed, the Committee as a whole, and its president in particular, spared no effort to secure the adoption of the Partition Plan.

The Jewish Labor Committee sought support for the Plan from the labor movements in America, France and Belgium and the labor governments in Britain, Denmark, Norway and Sweden. Except in Britain the response to its efforts was favorable, particularly in the Scandinavian countries. "Over many years we have been united by our common Socialist ideal," the Committee pleaded with the British Labor Party, urging that "the gates of Palestine be opened to Jewish immigration," a plea to which the Party turned a deaf ear. When the Partition Plan was approved by the General Assembly, Adolph Held, the president of the Committee, declared: "I am proud that throughout the deliberations on the Palestine problem in the United Nations the Jewish Labor Committee cooperated fully with the Jewish Agency."

6

The leadership in this crucial test fell to Abba Hillel Silver, whom the world Zionist Congress of the previous year had named Chairman of the American Section of the Jewish Agency, or Zionist Executive. He proved a bold, resourceful and effective leader. His matchless oratory lifted his pleas in the councils of the United Nations high above the general level, but they were not mere forensic performances; his words and strategy were governed by a realistic and almost ruthless appraisal of the interests that swarmed around the issue. Nor was he the only spokesman of the Jews before the United Nations to whom the delegates and the entire world listened with deference. Chaim Weizmann spoke with the wisdom and persuasiveness which thirty years of leadership of the world movement had ripened, and the words of Moshe Sharett and David Ben-Gurion carried echoes of the unshakable determination of the Yishuv to achieve the status of a sovereign state. The Arab case had its champions in the delegations of the six Arab states who were members of the United Nations, and in Jamal el Husseini, who represented the Arab Higher Committee of Palestine. Any partition boundaries that might be established, Jamal warned, would become "walls of blood and fire."

It was a fluctuating battle with sudden shifts by a number of delegations to one side or the other and the outcome in doubt almost to the end. When on November 29 the vote in the General Assembly was finally tabulated, it stood 33 for the Partition Plan, among them the United States, France and the Soviet Union, and 13 against, two more than the required two-thirds majority. There were 10 abstentions, with Britain among them: Bevin's "sulky boycott" of Israel, as Churchill called it, had begun.

So a Jewish state in Palestine was decreed by the United Nations, and Jews the world over rejoiced. In New York and other cities of America young men and women danced in the streets, and strangers greeted and embraced each other.

7

There was rejoicing in Palestine also, but the Yishuv had no illusions as to what lay ahead. The Arab-Jewish war broke out on the morrow of the decision, and except for cease-fires ordered by the Security Council, it continued through 1948. It did not formally end until the spring of the following year when the Arab states, their armed forces checked and humbled on every front, were forced to sign armistices with the newly created state of Israel. In May 1949 the General Assembly of the United Nations elected Israel a member of the world organization.

The conflict had two phases. The first, which lasted until May 15, 1948, was a guerrilla war against the Jews fought by bands of Palestine Arabs reinforced by large and numerous contingents from the neighboring Arab countries. They called themselves the Arab Army of Liberation, and their objectives were to paralyze the Yishuv by forcing

Jewish traffic off the roads, to cut it in two by seizing the strategic Valley of Jezreel and to destroy the outlying settlements. The second phase began May 15, 1948 when the armed forces of all the neighboring Arab states crossed their borders, their aim being to destroy the new state and throw the Jews into the Mediterranean.

During the first phase the British were still in Palestine, but their principal aim appeared to be to hamper the Jews in their efforts to defend themselves, and to make sure that the country would be in a state of administrative chaos when they left. Among the scores of clashes and attacks from ambush that took place during this period the most disastrous was the destruction in April of a convoy carrying supplies and personnel to the Hebrew University and the Hadassah Hospital on Mount Scopus, the British having previously pronounced the road safe. Among the 76 who perished was Dr. Chaim Yassky, who headed the Hadassah Medical Organization. But the decisive event in this phase of the war, which also occurred in April, was the Battle of Mishmar Ha-emek (the Emek Watch) in the Valley of Jezreel, where the Jewish settlers, reinforced by contingents of the Haganah, routed the Arab Army of Liberation.

Shortly afterwards the Jews seized Tiberias, Safed, Haifa and Jaffa, and in a sudden movement that had the appearance of a stampede the Arab inhabitants of those cities fled across the partition boundaries, and the lamentable Arab refugee problem came into existence. But the flight was primarily the result of the strategy and directives of the Arab leaders. The armies of the Arab states stood poised on the borders; soon they would march and hurl the Jews into the sea, and those who fled would come back and find abundant compensation for their brief absence.

8

But in the previous month the Jews had suffered a strange defeat, not in Palestine but in Flushing Meadows, New York. The government of the United States suddenly reversed its stand on the Partition Plan, and came forward with another from which a Jewish state was glaringly absent. The plan, which called for a "temporary trusteeship" over Palestine when the Mandate ended, was ascribed by American Jews to the pressure of Near East oil magnates and missionaries, and pro-British officials in the State Department and the Pentagon. Nor was it the first evidence of hostility in Washington. In December an embargo had been imposed on the shipment of arms from the United States to the Near East, a move which was impartial in appearance only. Actually it denied desperately needed arms to the Jews while their enemies were receiving ample supplies from the British.

The reversal by their government produced shock and indignation among the Jews of America. Special prayer services were held in synagogues across the country, and in New York 40,000 Jewish war veterans marched in a protest parade through Fifth Avenue, with a quarter-million spectators on the sidewalks. Public opinion was bewildered and antagonized. In April another special session of the General Assembly on Palestine convened at the desire of the United States to consider the new plan, but the delegates failed to be impressed by it. Its apparent purpose was to prevent the proclamation of a Jewish state on which the Jewish leaders were known to be determined.

On May 14 the delegates were still engaged in desultory debate on the American proposal when word arrived that the Proclamation had been issued. Then something even more startling than the reversal occurred: ten minutes after the issuance of the Proclamation, President Truman extended de facto recognition to the new state. The reversal was reversed!

9

By Friday, May 14, the British, except for those who had enlisted to fight with the Arabs, had left the country they had ruled for three decades. And in Tel Aviv, the first capital of the new state, the thirty-seven members of the National Council, representing the Yishuv and the Zionist movement, heard its Chairman, David Ben-Gurion, read the solemn Proclamation. It recalled the historic connection of the Jews with Palestine, the First Zionist Congress in 1897, the Balfour Declaration twenty years later, the Nazi holocaust which engulfed the Jews of Europe, and the decision of the General Assembly of the United Nations. The climactic declaration then followed:

> Accordingly we, the members of the National Council, representing the Jewish people in Palestine and the Zionist movement of the world, met together in solemn assembly today, the day of termination of the British Mandate for Palestine, by virtue of the natural and historic right of the Jewish people and of the Resolution of the General Assembly of the United Nations, hereby proclaim the establishment of the Jewish State in Palestine, to be called ISRAEL.

10

One minute after midnight of May 15 the army of Egypt crossed the frontiers and the same day the battalions of Syria and Lebanon came down from the north and the Iraqis irrupted from the east. The redoubtable Arab Legion of Transjordan, financed, trained and officered by the British, was already in Palestine, and contingents from Saudi Arabia joined the descent. They came with the weapons of modern warfare, including tanks, heavy artillery and planes, which the Jews could not match. "This will be a war of extermination," said the Secretary General of the Arab League, "and a momentous massacre." Nevertheless, the unequal contest resulted in a victory for the newborn state. The Jews fought for what appeared to them their own and their people's last chance, and in more than a figurative sense the six million who had died in the German death camps fought with them.

This second phase of the Arab-Jewish war, called Israel's War of Independence, lasted some eight months and was marked by periods of intense fighting, separated by cease-fires ordered by the Security Council. For the Jews it was, in the first two months, essentially a holding action. Its army had no weapons for an offensive, its navy and air force were almost non-existent. It was during this period that Jerusalem, unable to reply to the guns of the Arab Legion and cut off from the rest of the state, suffered its supreme ordeal. But the swift victory the Arab states expected failed to materialize.

The first cease-fire lasted from June 10 to July 9, and was followed by only ten days of renewed hostilities, but the short period produced a transformation. The Army of Israel, now much better equipped, took the offensive and won a series of victories: in the north against the re-formed Army of Liberation, in the center against the "invincible" Arab Legion, and in the south against the Egyptians. Jewish commando units, calling themselves "Samson's foxes,"* played havoc with Egyptian contingents in the Negev.

There came a second cease-fire, which was "ordered" to extend indefinitely. It was accepted by the Provisional Government of Israel against the advice of its army chiefs, who saw the imminent and total defeat of the invaders. But despite the cease-fire the Arab Legion continued to shell the New City of Jerusalem, which the Jews inhabited, the remnants of the Army of Liberation made incursions into Galilee, and the Egyptians harassed the Negev settlements in an attempt to cut them off from the rest of Israel.

* Judges, XV, 4-5.

There followed three brief campaigns by the Israel Army, two in October, the third in December, which sent the irregulars fleeing from Galilee into Lebanon, and drove the Egyptians out of the Negev. The Jews swept across the Egyptian border, and captured the airfield and outskirts of El-Arish on the coast: "Operation Ten Plagues" was the name they gave to this campaign. The strongest of the Arab states had been humbled and invaded.

The Foreign Office in London became alarmed and its fears were shared in Washington: in Egypt the internal situation was explosive and the invasion might set off an eruption that would disturb the entire Near East. Under pressure of the United Nations and once more against the advice of its General Staff, Israel accepted another cease-fire and its troops retired across their border. But it was now clear to the seven members of the Arab League, as it was to the entire world, that their attempt to strangle the infant state at its birth had been defeated. They were now ready for an armistice, if not for peace.

Efforts to bring about a peace made by a Palestine Conciliation Commission of the United Nations were balked by the insistence of the Arab states that Israel must permit all the Arab refugees to return, and that Jerusalem be internationalized, although on the second demand Jordan, whose Legion occupied the Old City of Jerusalem dissented: Jordan was the new name adopted by Transjordan after annexing those portions of Palestine which were to make up the Arab state as contemplated by the Partition Plan. Israel found both demands unacceptable. The hundreds of thousands of refugees would constitute a potential fifth column imperiling its existence, and the 100,000 Jews of Jerusalem had gone through a long and harrowing siege and could not now be torn from the state. The Arab governments, moreover, showed no disposition to recognize Israel, as by now practically the rest of the world, including Great Britain, had done.

The efforts to arrange armistices were more successful; whatever hopes for a "second round" the Arab states nourished, they were anxious to bring the present one to an end. The negotiations were conducted through Ralph J. Bunche, the Acting Mediator, appointed by the United Nations, the first Mediator, Count Folke Bernadotte of Sweden, who had lost the confidence of the Jews, having been assassinated the previous September by a group of Jewish terrorists, an act which shocked the world and not least the Jews of Palestine.

It took all of the first six months of 1949 to negotiate the armistices between Israel and her five active foes: Egypt, Lebanon, Jordan, Iraq, and Syria. But armistice lines seldom remain inviolate, and as the years passed and the Arab states persisted in their rejection of all overtures for a permanent peace and kept up an economic boycott and blockade against their new neighbor, the clashes along those lines, especially along the extended line between Israel and Jordan, grew in frequency and gravity.

11

Such, in swift outline, was the course of the War of Independence fought by Israel to vindicate her statehood, and incidentally the decree and prestige of the United Nations also. Naturally the events of those crowded months were followed by the Jews of America with the keenest concern, and the great majority of them were partners to the sorrows and triumphs they brought.

Nor did they remain mere spectators of the struggle. They furnished the political help of which the new state, in the unpredictable shifts of American policy, was always in need. And they furnished direct physical aid by providing crucial matériel, which Israel sorely lacked, and contributing volunteers and trained personnel, especially for its Air Force.

In political action the American Jewish Committee and the Jewish Labor Committee were not, of course, the only groups that collaborated with the Jewish Agency, others being the American Jewish Congress, B'nai B'rith, the Jewish War Veterans of the United States, the large fraternal orders, the rabbinical organizations and the congregational federations. The Christian friends of the cause, grouped in the influential American Christian Palestine Committee and the two branches of the American labor movement, vigorously supported Zionist objectives. And the thousands of Jews who were not affiliated with organizations were moved as never before to give of their means to help the new state in its supreme ordeal and, after the war, to promote the huge program of immigration and settlement which the Jewish Agency assumed on behalf of the state.

Naturally, the war accelerated the efforts in America, begun during the Battle of Immigration, to procure matériel for the poorly equipped fighting forces of Israel, the emphasis being now on aircraft. And owing to the embargo the government imposed on the shipment of military goods, those who promoted the effort took the risk of penalties from which some of them did not escape. But before hostilities ended the Israel Air Force had given a good account of itself, among the targets of its bombers being Cairo, Damascus, and Amman.

Finally, volunteers estimated to number 900 to 1,000 regulars and 100 to 150 technicians and pilots came from the United States and Canada for the Army and Air Force of Israel, and helped to repel the invaders in the hills of Galilee and the wastes of the Negev. Their value should not be judged by their number alone. At one time the Israel Air Force was manned almost entirely by overseas volunteers, the fighter pilots being largely South African, and the Americans, with a number of Christians among them, concentrated in the Air Transport Command. The Seventh Israel Brigade, commanded by the Canadian, Colonel Ben Dunkelman, included several hundred American and Canadian volunteers. About 70 Americans were among the fatal casualties, the most distinguished of them being Colonel David Marcus. A West Point graduate and a brilliant soldier, Marcus had become a tower of strength to the Army of Israel; he was in command of the crucial Jerusalem sector when he was killed.

12

To many Jews in America the victory of the infant state against a ring of enemies, a victory of 650,000 against a group of nations numbering 30 to 40 millions, had all the semblance of a miracle: all the explanations failed somehow to add up to the amazing result. And the new reality 5,000 miles away that emerged, scarred but victorious, from its test of blood and fire, belonged in a real sense to them also. Not, of course, in the political sense: their allegiance belonged without reservations to America. But this allegiance, they felt, did not require them to stifle a surge of heart and spirit which did not in any way diminish or impair it. A new pride came into their lives, and with it a new care and a new responsibility.

CHAPTER 23

In the Warp and Woof

1

BY THE MID-CENTURY THE JEWS OF AMERICA, WITH ALL their involvement in the fortunes of their coreligionists in other lands, had become intimately interwoven with all phases of their country's life. More and more of them rose to importance and distinction, augmenting the contribution of the community as a whole to the weal and greatness of America, not only in war, but also in peace. The preponderant majority of them were now native to the soil, more of them could sing without having to ascribe symbolism or courtesy to the words:

Land where my fathers died,
Land of the pilgrims' pride.

The roll of Jewish notables in the decades before the Civil War, whether they owed their distinction to what they achieved for their community, for the nation as a whole, or for both, could be called without serious risk of omitting any of them. To compile a similar roster for the mid-twentieth century would be a task of forbidding proportions. Only a work of encyclopedic magnitude could hope to encompass all the Jews in America who have risen high in government and public service, in industry, commerce and the professions, in science and invention, literature and the fine arts, in journalism, the theater and sports, in education and philanthropy, and still other spheres. This modest chronicle must forgo such an undertaking and, at the risk of dissent and demur, restrict itself to naming only a few of the many in each field whose contributions have enriched American life.

2

Their general place in the economic life of the country has already been indicated in a previous chapter. If at this point a few may be named who rose to a high level in American industrial enterprise, the list would have to include Meyer Guggenheim, who came to America from Switzerland in 1847 at the age of nineteen, and his seven sons, Isaac, Daniel, Murry, Solomon, Benjamin, Simon and William. They became leaders in the mining and refining of copper and lead, tin, nitrates, and other minerals, and were equally distinguished for public service and philanthropy, especially in the promotion of education, the arts and aeronautics. For six years Simon Guggenheim represented Colorado in the United States Senate, and the John Simon Guggenheim Foundation, which he established in memory of his first-born son, has aided numerous artists, scientists and scholars without regard to race or creed. Nor could the list omit Gerard Swope, who was chosen president of the General Electric Company in 1922; David Sarnoff, who became president of the Radio Corporation of America in 1930; Samuel Goldwyn and Louis B. Mayer, who have stood out in the long list of Jewish motion picture producers; Nelson Morris, a pioneer of the meat packing industry, whose son Ira was United States minister to Sweden during the First World War; and Lucius N. Littauer, a leading glove manufacturer, who was even more famous as a philanthropist, and served ten years in the House of Representatives. Jews rose high in large-scale merchandising, establishing many of the leading department stores over the country, with merchants like Edward A. Filene, Benjamin Altman, Michael Friedsam, Samuel J. Bloomingdale, Louis Bamberger, Michael Schaap, Felix Fuld, Bernard Gimbel and of course the Strauses, prominent also in philanthropy and public service. In the two decades many Jews, most of them of East European origin, won an important place in building construction also: Louis J. Horowitz was president of the Thompson Starret Construction Company for nearly a quarter century, and among the leading subway builders was Samuel Rosoff.

3

On all government levels, local, state and national, and to all three of its branches, legislative, executive and judicial, Jews were elected or appointed to office in growing numbers, and figured prominently in the less-defined areas of civic affairs and public service. In 1932 Benjamin Nathan Cardozo joined Louis D. Brandeis as an associate justice of the United States Supreme Court; he had previously been chief judge of the New York State Court of Appeals, the highest judicial post in the Empire State. In 1939, the year Cardozo died and Brandeis retired, Felix Frankfurter was appointed to the Federal Supreme Court. It is noteworthy that the three Jewish members of that august body, while they certainly were not the radicals they were sometimes accused of being, have been identified with its liberal wing: they viewed the law not as a hardened system of logic and precedent, but as a living organism designed to serve the needs of an evolving society. Jewish judges who have sat on the bench of the Federal Circuit and District Courts are too many to list in these pages, and in the state, county and municipal courts their number has, of course, been much greater. But two who, in addition to Cardozo, occupied the highest judicial posts in their states should not be omitted: Irving Lehman, who was elected chief judge of the New York State Court of Appeals in 1939, and Simon E. Sobeloff who in 1952 became chief judge of the Court of Appeals in Maryland: two years later President Eisenhower appointed Sobeloff Solicitor General of the United States.

Not only Brandeis and Frankfurter, but practically all other American Jews who have worn the judicial robe have been active in the affairs of the Jewish community. Cardozo was a life-long member of the Spanish and Portuguese Synagogue of New York, an honorary member of Zeta Beta Tau, one of the largest of the dozen Jewish college fraternities in America, and he supported the work of the Jewish Education Association of New York. Irving Lehman headed the Jewish Welfare Board for nearly a score of years, served in the highest councils of the American Jewish Committee and was prominently identified with other Jewish endeavors. Sobeloff took a leading part in Zionist affairs, in the American Jewish Congress and in the promotion of Jewish education.

The judiciary appears to have enlisted more American Jews than any other branch of government, but they have not been absent from the other two branches. They were elected to the state legislatures and were especially prominent, both in number and service, in those of New York, Illinois and Pennsylvania. In the Upper House of Congress a number of Jewish Senators—Judah P. Benjamin, Isidor Raynor, Simon Guggenheim—have already been mentioned, and to these should be added Benjamin F. Jonas of Illinois, Joseph Simon of Oregon and Herbert H. Lehman of New York. The number of Jewish Congressmen was, of course, very much larger, with perhaps the most distinguished among them Adolph J. Sabath of Illinois, who served from 1907 to his death in 1952, and Julius Kahn of California, whose wife was elected to fill his post when he died in 1924. Among other Jewish Congressmen of distinction were Sol Bloom, Samuel Dickstein, Nathan D. Perlman, Isaac Siegel, Emanuel Celler and Jacob K. Javits all of New York, and Herman P. Koppelman of Connecticut.

Jewish aides were prominent in official White House families, especially in those of Franklin D. Roosevelt and Harry S. Truman, but the most distinguished careers in the executive branch of the federal government were those of Bernard M. Baruch, whose place as the "elder statesman" of America was noted in a previous chapter, and Henry Morgenthau, Jr. The latter served as Secretary of the Treasury from 1934 to 1945, and on his retirement headed the United Jewish Appeal and the campaign for the sale of Government of Israel bonds. And among the many others who held important posts in Washington were David K. Niles, who was administrative assistant to both Roosevelt and Truman; Nathan Straus, Jr., who served as United States Housing Authority Administrator; and Anna M. Rosenberg who, as Assistant Secretary of Defense, dealt with problems of manpower and personnel. David E. Lilienthal was director of the Tennessee Valley Authority for thirteen years and in 1947 became the first chairman of the Atomic Energy Commission. In 1953 the Commission's chairman, appointed by President Eisenhower, was Lewis L. Strauss. Another outstanding career in public service was that of Robert Moses of New York who was recognized as the foremost creator of parks, highways, bridges, playgrounds and other civic improvements. And among the American Jews who represented their country abroad were Laurence A. Steinhardt, who was ambassador to Soviet Russia from 1939 to 1942, and Jesse Isidor Straus, who was ambassador to France from 1933 to 1936.

Besides Herbert H. Lehman of New York, other Jews were elected governors of their states. They included Moses Alexander of Idaho, Simon Bamberger of Utah, Michael Hahn of Louisiana, Henry Horner of Illinois, Julius L. Meier of Oregon, and Arthur Seligman of New Mexico. David Sholtz, who was governor of Florida, forsook the faith in which he was born and does not properly belong in our list.

4

Equally if not more striking was the large and growing participation of American Jews in every phase of the nation's cultural life. They kept pace with the quickened march of theoretical science and its technological applications to the needs of war and peace. They played an important part in the progress of American medicine both as science and art, and of public health. The social sciences were advanced by their scholars and teachers, and Jewish economists have been not only theorists and university professors, but men of affairs grappling with industrial and government problems.

In the plastic arts their fine painters, sculptors and architects made up sizable contingents in the classic as well as the newer modes of expression; and their Maecenases have been many and generous. They contributed important novelists, poets, playwrights, critics, and book publishers to American literature, and every phase of American journalism, from newspaper publishing to news reporting, has benefited from their enterprise and ingenuity. Their contribution to music has been particularly notable; they furnished many of the important American composers and most of the leading virtuosos and conductors. Equally important has been their share in the American cinema and theater, in radio and television entertainment, nor have they been absent from the different fields of American sports. The Jews of America entered into the warp and woof not only of their country's civilization, but also of its culture.

As early as 1907 Albert A. Michelson, who headed the department of physics in the University of Chicago, had raised the prestige of American science to a new plane when he became the first American to be awarded the Nobel Prize in Physics, the award being based on his successful experiments in optical interference and in measuring the velocity of light. But the science that loomed largest in the first half of the twentieth century was the so-called new physics, with which mathematics, astronomy and chemistry were more closely integrated than ever, and which revealed the breath-taking universes that constitute the structure of the atom. The new physics fascinated also the nonscientific mind, on the one hand by its quasireligious intimations, and on the other by the vista of incalculable power it opened to mankind. In its theoretic as well as its applied aspects American Jews made up a sizable group in the large number of brilliant American scientists who insured the preeminence of the United States in the field of nuclear physics. Albert Einstein, the undisputed monarch of the realm, who had won the Nobel Prize in Physics in 1921 became an American citizen in 1940, and among the others, this brief chronicle can only mention Isidor I. Rabi, who also won the Nobel Prize in Physics, and Harold C. Urey, who was awarded the Nobel Prize in Chemistry.

Their researches proved essential to the development of the atom or fission bomb, and later of the hydrogen or fusion bomb. The scientist who was universally acknowledged as having played the key role in the actual production of the first atom bomb, a weapon which shortened the war with Japan and saved the lives of many thousands of American troops, was J. Robert Oppenheimer, the director of the Los Alamos laboratory, where the bomb was developed. Edward Teller, known as "the father of the H-bomb," played a similar role with respect to that horrendous and apparently ultimate weapon. And two other crucial applications of atomic energy that added to the military potential of the country were achieved by American Jews. The first atomic-powered submarine became a reality through the imaginativeness and tenacity of Rear Admiral Hyman G. Rickover, and the formidable engineering and other problems involved in the production of the first atomic shell were conquered by a young engineer from the Bronx named Robert Schwartz. He was awarded the Army Medal for Exceptional Civilian Service, the citation affirming that "his initiative, ingenuity, judgment and perseverance in the basic design and development of the atomic shell, despite extremely short time schedules, have resulted in providing the Army a new weapon of critical importance."

Nevertheless, the pride American Jews felt in these contributions to the strength and security of their country could not mitigate their pain when Julius Rosenberg and his wife Ethel were convicted of engaging in atomic espionage for the benefit of Soviet Russia, and made to suffer the supreme penalty. The two belonged to the large contingent of American youth of all faiths, especially in the colleges and universities, whom the woes of the lingering depression of the thirties conditioned for the lures of Communism, and some Jews among them were impelled, in addition, by the enormous crimes against their people committed by Nazism, of which Communism gave them the illusion of being, in all respects, the antithesis.

5

Some of those who made their mark in other areas of science should be mentioned, though it must be again recalled that only a few of them can be named in these pages. An outstanding figure in biology was Jacques Loeb, famous for his tropism theory, who was head of the division of general physiology in the Rockefeller Institute for Medical Research. Abraham J. Goldforb was professor of biology at the College of the City of New York, and Nathan Fasten was one of America's leading zoologists. Morris Loeb was a noted chemist as well as a leader in communal work and philanthropy; his father was the banker Solomon Loeb and his brother James established the famous Loeb Classical Library. Julius Oscar Stieglitz was president of the

American Chemical Society and head of the chemistry department of the University of Chicago; his brother Alfred became internationally famous for his pioneer work in photography and as a promoter of art. Still another distinguished chemist was Carl L. Alsberg, who specialized in biochemistry and held important government and university posts.

In astronomy an important name is that of Frank Schlesinger; he was director of the Yale University Observatory and president of the American Astronomical Society and of the International Astronomical Union. Edward Israel was an astronomer who won even greater fame as an heroic Arctic explorer. The number of American Jews who gained distinction in pure mathematics is particularly large. Among them was Norbert Wiener, the prodigy son of Leo Wiener, a philologist who wrote the first important history of Yiddish literature in English. Norbert was professor at the Massachusetts Institute of Technology and noted for his work in the new science of cybernetics. Among other eminent Jewish mathematicians were Joseph B. Rosenbach, who was professor at the Carnegie Institute of Technology in Pittsburgh; Oscar Zariski, who was professor at Johns Hopkins University in Baltimore; and Jekuthiel Ginsburg, who headed the department of mathematics at Yeshiva University and edited its *Scripta Mathematica.*

In American invention a prominent name is that of Emile Berliner, the inventor of the microphone and gramophone who, it may be added, was also devoted to philanthropy, particularly in public health and education; and Elias E. Reis made many inventions, especially in electronics. An inventor and engineer of exceptional renown was the naval officer Edward Ellsberg who, among other dramatic feats, succeeded in raising a United States submarine from the bottom of the sea where she lay after colliding with a steamer in 1926.

6

An even larger number of Jews made important contributions to the progress of public health and medicine in America, and the number of distinguished names in those fields this limited chronicle must omit is therefore greater. And since progress in medicine, like scientific progress in general, is not confined by national boundaries, American medicine is indebted also to the phenomenal achievements of Jewish physicians in Europe, among them Sigmund Freud, Otto Meyerhoff, Paul Ehrlich, Otto Loewi, and numerous other pathfinders in the field.

Jews came to America with a tradition of reverence for the art of healing that went back to the Middle Ages; many of their greatest medieval scholars, philosophers and poets had been practitioners of the art. In the New World the tradition retained its vigor, and in the dreams of thousands of sweatshop toilers the first choice of a calling for their sons was that of physician. And the policy of anti-Jewish discrimination that medical schools in America adopted brought keen disappointment to many a parent, while others sent their sons to medical schools overseas. It is, of course, impossible to compute the loss this policy inflicted on the country, but some intimation of its extent may be gained from even a cursory examination of the contributions of American Jews in medical research and practice.

Better health in America owes much to Jewish philanthropists like Nathan Straus, but among the scientists who advanced the cause of public health Simon Flexner and his brother Abraham, Milton J. Rosenau, Joseph Goldberger and Sigismund S. Goldwater are entitled to special places of honor. Simon Flexner made many outstanding contributions to bacteriology; for more than thirty years he was director of laboratories of the Rockefeller Institute for Medical Research. His brother Abraham, who was primarily an educator, and one of the foremost in the country, was responsible for a thorough reorganization of medical education in America. Rosenau fought epidemics in Europe and America and served as professor at the Harvard School of Public Health. Joseph Goldberger discovered malnutrition to be the cause of pellagra and did notable work also in the control of malaria and yellow fever, using himself as a guinea pig in his experiments. Goldwater was Health Commissioner of New York City and perhaps the foremost authority on hospital administration in the country.

Among the other American Jewish scientists whose labors brought important advances in public health was Casimir Funk, the discoverer of vitamins; the pediatrician Bela Schick who devised the Schick test for susceptibility to diphtheria; Henry Koplik, also a pediatrician, the discoverer of "Koplik's spots" in measles; and the microbiologist Selman A. Waksman, who pioneered in the development of the antibiotics: in 1952 Waksman received the Nobel Prize in Medicine and Physiology.

The list of American Jewish physicians and surgeons who made important contributions to the science and art of healing is imposing. It includes surgeons like Albert A. Berg and Charles Elsberg; diagnosticians like Emanuel Liebman and David Riesman; cardiologists like Bernard S. Oppenheimer and Alfred Cohn; gastroenterologists like Max Einhorn and Burril Crohn; gynecologists like Joseph B. De Lee and Isidor C. Rubin; neurologists like Israel Spanier Wechsler and Bernard Sachs; psychiatrists like Abraham Brill and Abraham Myerson;

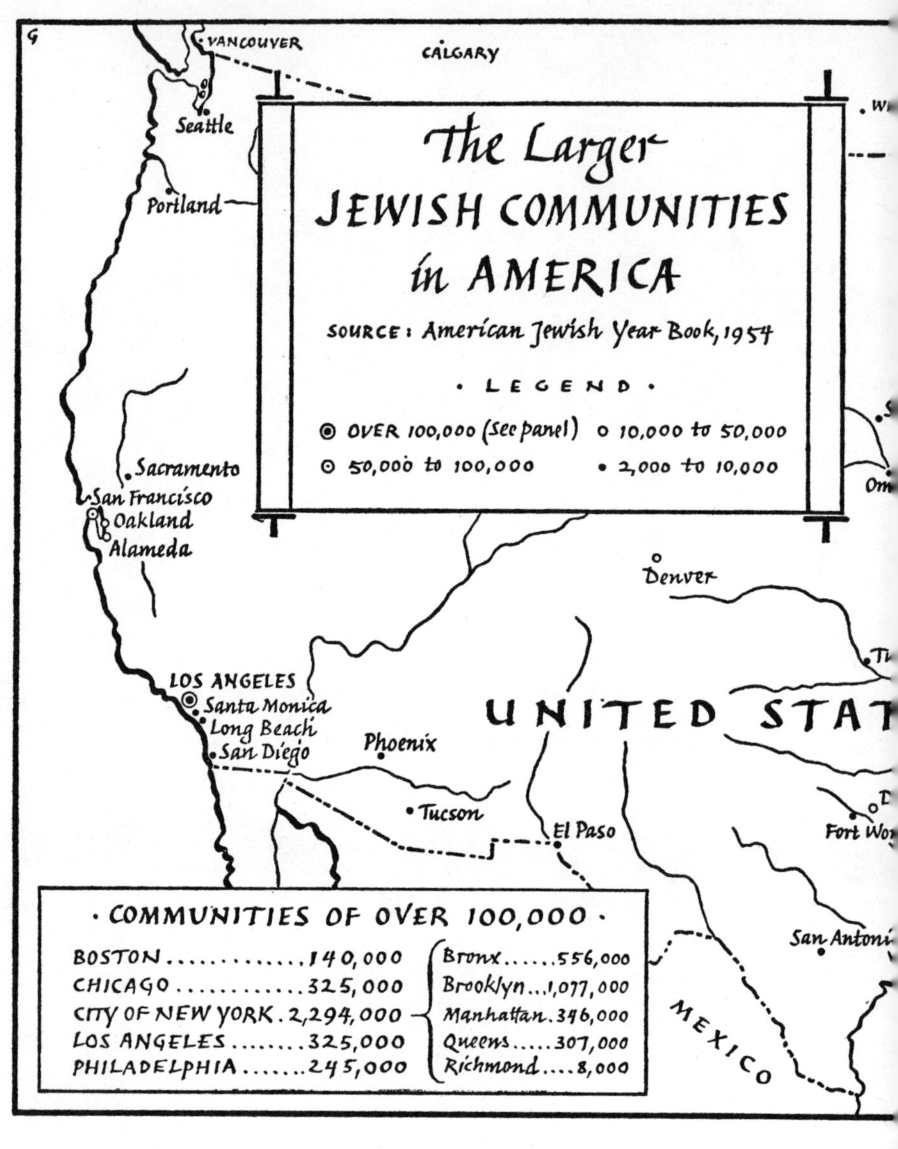
The Larger JEWISH COMMUNITIES in AMERICA
SOURCE: American Jewish Year Book, 1954
· LEGEND ·
OVER 100,000 (See panel)
10,000 to 50,000
50,000 to 100,000
2,000 to 10,000
VANCOUVER
CALGARY
Seattle
Portland
Sacramento
San Francisco
Oakland
Alameda
Denver
LOS ANGELES
Santa Monica
Long Beach
San Diego
Phoenix
Tucson
El Paso
UNITED STAT
MEXICO
· COMMUNITIES OF OVER 100,000 ·
BOSTON 140,000
CHICAGO 325,000
CITY OF NEW YORK . 2,294,000
LOS ANGELES 325,000
PHILADELPHIA 245,000
Bronx......556,000
Brooklyn...1,077,000
Manhattan.346,000
Queens.....307,000
Richmond....8,000

CANADA
QUEBEC
MONTREAL
OTTAWA
TORONTO
Portland
Haverhill
Lawrence
Lynn
Lowell
BOSTON
Syracuse
Hartford
Rochester
Utica
Providence
Flint
Buffalo
Albany
Milwaukee
Scranton
Wilkes-Barre
Madison
Detroit
Cleveland
Allentown
NEW YORK
CHICAGO
Youngstown
PHILADEPHIA
Toledo
Akron
Pittsburgh
Harrisburg
South Bend
Rock Island
Canton
Greensburg
Wilmington
McKeesport
Baltimore
Peoria
Dayton
Columbus
Washington, D.C.
Indianapolis
Cincinnati
Richmond
St. Louis
Charleston
Louisville
Norfolk
Nashville
Chattanooga
Memphis
Birmingham
Atlanta
Charleston
Savannah
Shreveport
Jacksonville
New Orleans
Tampa
St. Petersburg
West Palm Beach
Hollywood
Miami
MILES
100 200 300 400 500
1
Brockton
Fall River
New Bedford
Springfield
Worcester
2
Bridgeport
New Britain
New Haven
New London
Norwalk
Norwich
Stamford
Waterbury
3
Chester
Reading
Lancaster
4
Binghamton
Bronxville
Cedarhurst
Elmont
Freeport
Great Neck
Hempstead
Kingston
Larchmont
Long Beach
Lynnbrook
Mt. Vernon
Newburgh
New Hyde Park
New Rochelle
Portchester
Poughkeepsie
Rockville Center
Roslyn
Schenectady
Spring Valley
Troy
Valley Stream
White Plains
Yonkers
5
Asbury Park
Atlantic City
Bayonne
East Orange
Elizabeth
Englewood
Fairlawn
Hillside
Irvington
Jersey City
Lakewood
Linden
Long Branch
Maplewood
Newark
New Brunswick
Passaic
Paterson
Perth Amboy
Plainfield
South Orange
Teaneck
Trenton
Vineland

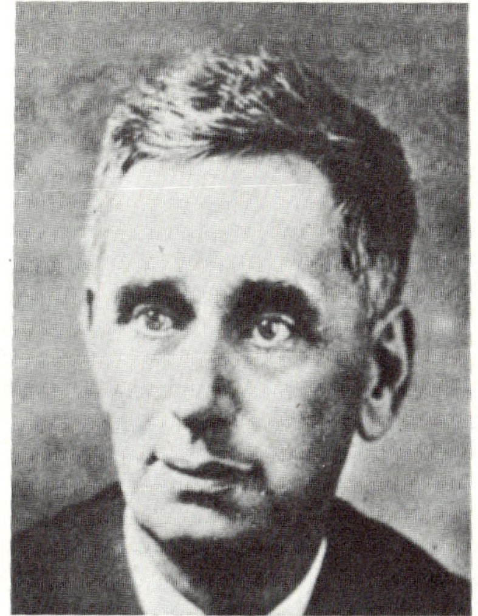

Zionist Archives and Library

Louis D. Brandeis

Hadassah

Henrietta Szold

Union of American Hebrew Congregations

Stephen S. Wise

Zionist Archives and Library

Louis Lipsky

U. S. SUPREME COURT JUSTICES

Courtesy of the National Archives

Benjamin Cardozo

Zionist Archives and Library

Felix Frankfurter

LEADERS IN PHILANTHROPY

Photograph by Pach Brothers

Jacob H. Schiff

Jewish Theological Seminary of America

Felix M. Warburg

ophthalmologists like Carl Koller and Jonas Friedenwald; haematologists like Nathan Rosenthal, and many other creative scientists and clinicians.

7

Besides Abraham Flexner there were other American Jews who were prominent in education, among them Isaac L. Kandel, Paul Klapper, Felix Adler, who founded the Ethical Culture movement, Julia Richman, and Abram L. Sachar, president of Brandeis University, established in 1948 in Waltham, Massachusetts, as the first secular and nonsectarian institution of higher learning in the United States under Jewish auspices. American Jews made important contributions to the social sciences, especially economics, with which they have dealt not only as writers and theorists but also as practitioners. Among leading American economists must be numbered Edwin R. A. Seligman, who was an expert on public finance; Mordecai Ezekiel, who served as economic adviser to the Secretary of Agriculture; Leon Kayserling, who headed the President's Council of Economic Advisers, Robert R. Nathan, and the brothers Jacob and Selig Perlman. No American stood higher in anthropology than Franz Boas, other important scholars in that field and in sociology being Paul Radin, Alexander Goldenweiser and Melville J. Herskovits. Jews ranked high also in the university faculties of political science, government and law. In archaeology notable work was done in the Near East by Nelson Glueck, who succeeded Julian Morgenstern as president of the Hebrew Union College in Cincinnati and headed also the Jewish Institute of Religion, established in New York in 1922 by Stephen S. Wise, which merged with the College in 1950.

Among important figures in American philosophy were Irwin Edman, Morris R. Cohen and Horace M. Kallen, of whom the last two, it may be noted, were active in Jewish community affairs. Harry A. Wolfson, David Neumark, and Isaac Husik were scholars who delved into the history of Jewish philosophy, while Abraham J. Heschel, Will Herberg and Milton Steinberg wrote eloquent restatements of the Jewish creed in the idiom of modern philosophic insights.

8

American Jews made significant contributions to the journalism, literature, music and the plastic arts of their country. In the roster of

American newspaper publishers, if high standards as well as success are taken as criteria, it is doubtful if any names would take precedence over those of Joseph Pulitzer of the *New York World* and Adolph S. Ochs of *The New York Times.* Pulitzer's life is an American epic; under his direction the *World* became a crusading paper, and although in 1931 his sons allowed it to merge with the *New York Telegram,* Pulitzer continued to exert a posthumous influence on American journalism through the Graduate School of Journalism at Columbia University and the Pulitzer Prizes in journalism and letters, both of which he endowed. Ochs, who began his journalistic career in 1878 in Chattanooga, made *The New York Times* the premier daily in America, and its eminence has been maintained by his son-in-law and successor Arthur Hays Sulzberger and its general manager Julius Ochs Adler. Other important newspaper publishers were Eugene Meyer of the *Washington Post;* Paul Block, who owned a chain of newspapers across the country; Julius David Stern, who also published dailies in a number of cities; and Dorothy Schiff of the *New York Post.* In the editorial and reportorial branches of American journalism names like Simeon Strunsky, Herbert Bayard Swope, Isaac Marcosson, George Seldes, and William L. Laurence may be mentioned, but they are only a few of the large number of American Jews who attained distinction in those fields.

In the literature of America, especially in the novel, the years since the First World War saw many Jews make their mark, some of whom, like the eccentric Gertrude Stein and the imaginative Robert Nathan, have already earned a permanent place in American fiction. Others who are often included among those whose work should endure are Dorothy Parker, Ben Hecht, Irving Fineman, Ludwig Lewisohn, Meyer Levin, Myron Brinig and Charles Angoff. In the mid-century a fairly large number of Jewish novelists were still in the first stage of their careers, but it may be noted that some of the most successful novels of the Second World War came from young Jewish writers: *The Caine Mutiny* by Herman Wouk, *The Naked and the Dead* by Norman Mailer, *Face of a Hero* by Louis Falstein, and *Battle Cry* by Leon Uris.

On the top rung of American poetry a place must be allowed to Karl Shapiro, who came to the fore in the early forties and whom some critics considered "the outstanding poetic spokesman of his generation." A fair number of other American Jews had by that time already earned their niche in American poetry: Babette Deutsch, Louis Untermeyer, Muriel Rukeyser and others. Among literary critics were Maxwell Geismar and Alfred Kazin, and among biographers Irving Stone and Matthew Josephson.

The plastic arts and music of America have been even more enriched by American Jews. Albert Kahn was one of the early distinguished American architects, and among those who followed him were Charles B. Mayer, Alfred S. Alschuler and Joseph H. Friedlander. David B. Steinman and Leon S. Moisseiff belong among the foremost bridge designers of America; the second was also a Yiddish writer and communal worker. A prominent figure among early American sculptors was Moses Ezekiel, who fought for the South in the Civil War, and in later years Jo Davidson, Jules Butensky, Enrico Glicenstein, William Zorach, Chaim Gross, and Max Kalish were among the Jews who added distinction to American sculpture. Among those who stood out in American painting were Leon Kroll, Max Weber, Abraham Manievich, Ben Shahn and the twin brothers Moses and Raphael Soyer. In creative art-criticism no one stood higher than Bernard Berenson, who was born in Vilna in 1865.

To American music Jews contributed composers of commanding originality like George Gershwin, Aaron Copland, Ernest Bloch, Louis Gruenberg, and Rubin Goldmark, and among those whom persecution brought to America were Kurt Weill and Arnold Schoenberg, the latter one of the foremost figures in world music. In the more popular sector of musical composition the outstanding creators were Jews, among them Jerome Kern, Sigmund Romberg, Irving Berlin, and Richard Rodgers. At the same time Jewish folk and liturgic music was cultivated by a group of talented composers: Joseph Achron, Abraham W. Binder, Lazare Saminsky, Jacob Weinberg, and others.

Even the critics who cry down American culture admit that Americans are a music-loving people, and to the musical elevation of their countrymen Jews have contributed even more through their patrons and distinguished performers than through their composers. Perhaps the most munificent patron of the art was Otto H. Kahn who, as chairman and president, headed the board of the Metropolitan Opera Association for nearly three decades. Another generous patron of music was Adolf Lewisohn, donor of the Lewisohn Stadium of the College of the City of New York; he, as well as his son Sam Adolf, were active also in other civic, artistic, and philanthropic fields. As for virtuosos and conductors, even those American Jews who hold first rank are too many to enumerate in this brief chronicle. The mention of only a number of them—Jascha Heifetz, Efrem Zimbalist, Mischa Elman, Yehudi Menuhin, Isaac Stern, Nathan Milstein, Bronislaw Hubermann, Vladimir Horowitz, Ossip Gabrilowitsch, Harold Bauer and Emanuel Feuermann among the instrumentalists; Walter Damrosch, Eugene Ormandy,

Leonard Bernstein, Serge Koussevitzky, Fritz Reiner and Bruno Walter among the conductors—is enough to indicate what Jews have meant for the musical delectation of America. Nor could Alma Gluck, Jan Peerce, Sophie Breslau, Regina Resnick and Richard Tucker be omitted from a list of the leading American vocalists.

What has been said with regard to American music applies in equal, if not greater measure to the drama as a literary art, to the stage, and to the lighter forms of entertainment—all that is embraced in the popular term "show business." As playwrights Jews began to contribute to the American stage in the early nineteenth century: Isaac Harby and Mordecai Manuel Noah have already figured in these pages. A hundred years later the work of scores of Jewish playwrights had been produced on Broadway, and the plays of many of them—Elmer Rice, Lillian Hellman, Sidney Kingsley, Clifford Odets, Irwin Shaw, Arthur Miller, and others—represented contributions not only to the stage but to the enduring dramatic literature of America. There were others who furnished plays in lighter vein—George S. Kaufman, Moss Hart, Samuel N. Behrman, and Arthur Kober—and in dramatic criticism the most important arbiter of the American theater was George Jean Nathan. As actors, too, Jews contributed an important contingent to the leading American histrions, with David Warfield, Louis Mann, Helen Menken, Sylvia Sidney, Joseph Schildkraut, and many others. Perhaps the most remarkable career in the American theater was that of David Belasco, who died in 1931. He was a leading producer and actor as well as playwright; his story has been called the story of the American stage.

In theatrical as in cinema production the contribution of American Jews can only be described as massive. Their ventures in this hazardous realm have been bold and imaginative. The expansion of the American theater would hardly have been possible without the ingenuity and daring of men like Oscar Hammerstein, Lee Schubert, Charles and Daniel Frohman, Sam H. Harris and Abraham L. Erlanger.

The sector of "show business" represented by light entertainment is important for a people like the Americans who are prone to live too tensely. Here the Jews who have stood out and delighted huge audiences on the stage, over radio and television, and on the screen—performers like the sensational magician and "escape artist" Harry Houdini, Fannie Brice, Sophie Tucker, Al Jolson, Eddie Cantor, Ed Wynn, Jack Benny, Milton Berle, Sam Levenson, the Marx brothers, Danny Kaye and many others—can only be compared in number and importance to the Jewish virtuosos and conductors in the field of music. Few will deny that the foremost comic of the silver screen was

Charles Spencer (Charlie) Chaplin. He was, indeed, its leading figure without qualification; his genius lifted him above ordinary comedy into the reaches of great art. Chaplin was born in London to a Jewish family named Thornstein that arrived in England from Eastern Europe about the middle of the nineteenth century.*

9

Finally, this all-too-rapid survey of the inweaving of the Jews in America with all phases of their country's life must not omit the area of sports and athletics, an area that holds no small place in the enthusiasms of the American people. It would have been a bold prophet who, in the eighties or nineties of the previous century, had predicted that the children and grandchildren of the shrinking fugitives from Eastern Europe would take their place among the leading athletes of America, that some of them would be the crowned champions of their country and add to its laurels at the Olympics and other international athletic competitions. But in a field where prejudice and discrimination have perhaps been less active than in others, they soon showed a prowess not behind that of any other group of Americans in running and jumping, skating and swimming, in boxing, fencing and wrestling, in wielding the bat, racket and hockey stick, in shooting the ball through the basket or carrying it across the goal line.

In the thirties, before the "manly art" became almost a monopoly of the splendid Negro boxers and Americans of Italian descent, Jewish pugilists played a leading role in the sport. Among those who fought their way to the highest place in their class were Abe Attell, who was world featherweight champion from 1908 to 1912; Battling Levinsky, who was light heavyweight champion from 1916 to 1920; Maxie Rosenbloom, who reigned in the same class from 1930 to 1934; and Barney Ross who in 1934 held the lightweight and welterweight championships. Perhaps the most popular Jewish ring idol was Benny Leonard, who was the world lightweight champion from 1917 to 1924. The two outstanding Jewish heavyweights were Joe Choynski, who "hung up his gloves" in 1904 after a notable ring career of twenty years, and Max Baer who reigned as champion of his class from June 1934 to June 1935.

American Jews have furnished outstanding "big league" baseball players like Johnny Kling, Moe Berg, "Buddy" Myer, "Hank" Greenberg, Al Rosen and numerous others. In 1935 Greenberg was voted

* *Juedisches Lexikon,* Berlin, Juedischer Verlag, 1927; vol. 1, col. 1329.

"the most valuable player of the year" in the American League, and the same distinction was awarded to Rosen in 1953. Among the renowned football players of the country were Benny Friedman and Henry Newman of Michigan, Marshall Goldberg of Pittsburgh, and Sid Luckman of Columbia, to mention only a few of them. But the game in which the Jews excelled most was basketball. The stars they contributed to college basketball teams are too many to choose from, but if one of them is to be named it would have to be Nat Holman, equally distinguished as player and coach.

In the thirties, forties and fifties American Jews became prominent as tennis players. Among the many who achieved stardom in the game were Julie Seligson of Lehigh University, E. W. Feibelman of Harvard, Joseph Fishback of St. Johns, and Julius Heldman of the University of California. In the latter decades Herb Flam and Richard Savitt were among the leading American tennis stars. There were also American Jews among the "great" in wrestling, fencing and hockey, and in ice skating one of the world's greatest was Irving Jaffee.

For reasons best known to themselves sports editors include chess in their columns. For centuries this "sport" has been almost a passion among Jews, and to compile a list of Jewish chessmasters in America is a task beyond the range of this chronicle. We may only note that Wilhelm Steinitz and Emanuel Lasker, whose successive reigns as world champions covered a period of fifty-five years, spent the later years of their lives in the United States, and the list of American champions includes Reuben Fine, Samuel Reshevsky and Larry Evans.

10

Thus, by the mid-twentieth century the interpenetration of American Jewry with every area of the nation's life had become the outstanding fact about the community. The vicissitudes of a two-millennium dispersion had brought sizable segments of this people into many other lands and civilizations, but no other Jewish aggregation had in so short a time become so thoroughly interwoven with the institutions, culture, and spirit of the nation of which it formed a part. It responded eagerly to the opportunities which, notwithstanding rebuffs and hostility in some quarters, democratic America held out to them.

CHAPTER 24

Of Today and Tomorrow

1

THE AMERICAN JEWISH COMMUNITY WAS CERTAINLY AMERican, but was it also Jewish? Did it cherish its own Great Tradition, which, in the words of the ancient benediction, "has kept us alive and preserved us and enabled us to reach this season?"

The answer will not be single or categorical; it will depend not only on objective facts but on individual criteria and demands. There were certainly important negative manifestations. The prolonged and savage assaults to which Jews as such were subjected the world over had its effects on a goodly number of them in America as elsewhere: the morbid phenomenon of self-doubt and even self-hate made its appearance among them. The proportion of Jewish illiteracy—ignorance of the ancient heritage—had grown alarmingly: the community was paying the penalty for its failure in the earlier decades of the century to provide adequate Jewish education for its young. And the process of total assimilation had widened, expressing itself most clearly in a growing number of marriages outside the faith, especially in the smaller centers of the country. In the American Jewish community, as in all others and in all times, there was no doubt a substantial amount of indifference, alienation and defection, and many observers contemplated the future with misgivings.

Others were able to find consolations. Some, whose basic outlook was religious or superrationalist, and who believed in the divine purposefulness of Jewish continuity, noted that all through history this continuity had been entrusted not to large masses but to "saving remnants." Others were satisfied that the ethics and fundamental credos of Judaism made so strong an appeal to human reason and experience, that they would endure and guarantee the survival of the group. Still others cited more down-to-earth reasons: the persistence of anti-Jewish hostility, "civilized" or savage, while it stimulated a good deal of defection, promoted also resistance and cohesion.

2

By the middle of the century the full-time anti-Semites of America had become less strident and more subtle than they were in the thunderous thirties. Their chief tactic was to attach themselves to the ultra-conservative and isolationist segment of the country, the element that frowned on the United Nations in general and its Educational, Scientific and Cultural Organization (UNESCO) in particular, opposed foreign aid, resented immigration, abhorred economic and social legislation that smacked of the "welfare state" and denounced modern education as atheistic and subversive. The standard bearers of this sizable segment were men and women of standing and reputation, some of whom disavowed racial and religious bigotry, and professional anti-Semites found it profitable to penetrate their councils, influence their policies and enjoy the cover of their respectability: it was a leaf out of the Communist textbook of infiltration and subversion which they adapted to their own ends.

Nor, more than the America First Committee of the thirties, did the respectable isolationists and conservatives of the fifties extend themselves to keep at a distance anti-Semites like W. Henry MacFarland, leader of the American Flag Committee, Andrew B. McAllister of the vicious "We, the Mothers" of Chicago, Allen A. Zoll of the National Council for American Education and certain henchmen of Gerald L. K. Smith, leader of the Christian Nationalist Party and publisher of the inflammatory *The Cross and the Flag,* who was the acknowledged high priest of anti-Semitism in America. In 1952 Smith's Party and the Constitution Party, the latter launched by conservative Republicans for whom Eisenhower was too liberal, and taken over by anti-Semites, nominated Douglas MacArthur for president. The popular hero neither accepted nor rejected the nomination and received some 20,000 votes, more than half of them in California and Washington State.

In 1954, however, isolationism and conservatism found a more impressive domicile in a group calling itself For America, with Robert E. Wood, who had once led the America First Committee, as one of the co-chairmen. Among the others prominently identified with For America were Robert R. McCormick, the editor and publisher of the *Chicago Tribune,* and Hamilton Fish, once a Republican Congressman from New York and, before the attack on Pearl Harbor, one of the leading sponsors of Nazi Germany in America. Its declared purpose was to combat "internationalism, interventionism and communism," but it required no exceptional gift of imagination to see the anti-Semitic miscellany across the country looking towards the new and apparently well-heeled group with avid anticipation.

3

In the social structure of the community as a whole the tendency, especially in the decades after 1930, was clearly towards greater consolidation. The virtual suspension of immigration by the Act of 1924 speeded the coalescence of the different strata: the lines between "Germans" and "East Europeans" began to blur. "Intermarriage" became more common: on the college campuses and in the Hillel establishments the sons and daughters of East European immigrants mingled with those of "German" parentage, and marriage, as is well known, is largely a result of propinquity. In growing numbers the pulpits of Reform temples were occupied by sons of parents who hailed from Poland and Russia. They also rose to high station in the councils of the leading national organizations, which in earlier decades appeared to be the exclusive domain of "Germans." Jacob Blaustein, who headed the American Jewish Committee from 1948 to 1954, was the son of an immigrant from Russia, and so was his successor, Irving M. Engel; in 1954 the chairman of its administrative committee, Simon H. Rifkind, was himself a native of Russia. The three men who held the office of president of B'nai B'rith from 1938 to 1954—Henry Monsky, Frank Goldman and Philip Klutznik—were also sons of immigrants from Eastern Europe.

As in the past, the leading bodies of the community joined hands on occasion for common counsel and action, the most important enterprise of the sort in the fifties being represented by the Conference on Jewish Material Claims Against Germany. By an agreement between the governments of West Germany and Israel signed in 1952, the first undertook to make restitution for material losses suffered by Jews at the hands of the Nazis. There was bitter opposition to the agreement by a minority in Israel and by Jews in America and other lands on the ground that the wrongs inflicted by the Germans upon the Jews were beyond negotiation or indemnification. But practical considerations prevailed, and it was emphasized that the restitution was for material claims only. The total sum in goods and credits to be paid over a number of years by the Bonn government was fixed at $822,000,000, of which $715,000,000 was allocated for Israel. The balance of $107,-000,000 was for Jewish victims of the Nazi regime throughout the world, and the Conference on Jewish Material Claims Against Germany was set up to receive and disburse this balance. In the Conference, which embraced twenty-two leading Jewish organizations over the world, seven were American: the American Jewish Committee, the American Jewish Congress, B'nai B'rith, the American Zionist Council, the Jewish Labor Committee, the Joint Distribution Committee and the Synagogue Council of America. The president of the Conference was Nahum Goldmann, who had played the major role in the negotiation of this agreement.

Nevertheless the hope, cherished for more than a century, of achieving a permanent single authority for the entire community was as remote as ever. The leading bodies jealously guarded their autonomy and longstanding areas of activity, and in 1952 even an attempt to allocate those areas with a view to eliminating duplication—and the competition and waste it entails—came to grief. The plan was based on a survey of the programs pursued by the different groups in the field of community relations made by the noted sociologist Robert M. MacIver, and the effort to implement it was promoted by the National Community Relations Advisory Council (NCRAC), a coordinating body set up in 1944 but, as its name indicates, restricted to advisory and recommendatory functions only. Eight bodies were envisaged in the plan: the American Jewish Committee, B'nai B'rith, the American Jewish Congress, the Jewish Labor Committee, the Jewish War Veterans of the United States of America, and the lay organizations of the religious groupings: the Union of American Hebrew Congregations, the United Synagogue of America, and the Union of Orthodox Jewish Congregations. But the first two refused to be "coordinated," and without them the plan was unable to go forward.

Considerable progress towards unity was made, however, in philanthropy. A marked reduction was effected in the number of fund-raising campaigns of national as well as local scope. The national appeals, of which the main objective was overseas relief and reconstruction, reached a high degree of integration when in 1939 the United Jewish Appeal (UJA) was established as the fund raising instrument for the JDC, the United Palestine Appeal, comprising the Palestine Foundation Fund and the Jewish National Fund, and the National Refugee Service, later called the United Service for New Americans, an agency to assist the adjustment of Jewish refugees who had found haven in America. Among the most prominent in the national leadership of the vast enterprise were William Rosenwald, Abba Hillel Silver, Jonah B. Wise, Edward M. M. Warburg, and Henry Morgenthau, Jr. In time other important agencies were made beneficiaries of UJA, still further reducing the number of "drives," with their inevitable competition, confusion and waste.

On the local level a movement of equal significance, represented by combines calling themselves Federations, Welfare Funds or Community Councils, had by the mid-century made enormous progress. They raised, allocated and distributed funds for local, national and overseas needs, and coordinated the programs of the charitable and educational agencies within their respective communities. In 1953 these local combinations, nearly all of them affiliated with a national body called the Council of Jewish Federations and Welfare Funds, were estimated to represent more than 95 per cent of the more than five million Jews in the United States and some 90 per cent of the 220,000 in Canada. Their counterpart in general American philanthropy was the Community Chest, and in many cities the establishment of Chests was stimulated by the example set by the Jewish welfare agencies.

4

A conspicuous development in Jewish communal life was the rise and spread of an institution generally called the Jewish Community Center. In essence it was not an American creation; it harked back to the traditional three-fold function of the Old World *Bet Hamidrash* as a house of prayer, a house of study or school, and a house of assembly or civic center. The American institution also integrated these functions, but included in the last two a much more expanded program of activities—recreational, social and cultural—that answered to the American environment and aimed to attract every individual in the community by appealing to all age groups and both sexes. And the scores of handsome structures that rose up over the land to house these activities would have made the frequenters of the Old World *Bet Hamidrash* stare with wonder and admiration, while some of their installations would no doubt have struck them as strange and irrelevant; they would have been puzzled, for example, by the gymnasiums and swimming pools.

Two earlier American institutions played their part in the rise of the Centers. The first was the Young Men's Hebrew Association which, as we saw, had its start in Baltimore in 1854 and was still flourishing in many communities a hundred years later. The second was the Settlement House, planted in the larger Jewish concentrations by benevolent Christians and wealthy Jews to "Americanize" the immigrant hosts from Eastern Europe. Neither the Y, as the first came to be called, nor the Settlement House was distinguished for the Jewish content of its program. The Y might include Purim and Chanukah entertainments among its social functions, but it was primarily a secular institution, providing its youthful members with opportunities for recreation and the pursuit of cultural interests. The Settlement House usually saw itself as an oasis in a cultural desert and made it its mission to speed the integration of the immigrant youth with American ways. In time, however, the more thoughtful leaders of both realized that the Americanization process was well qualified to take care of itself; the newspapers, the cinema, the street, and above all the public school were its faithful and efficient allies. It was rather the heritage of religion and learning which the immigrants brought with them that stood in jeopardy, to the detriment of their inner integrity, especially in the case of the young.

The Jewish Community Center placed the emphasis on the word Jewish in its name, and gradually the Y's fell in line with the new outlook. The trend became stronger after 1921 when the National Jewish Welfare Board took the Y's under its wing together with the Centers: in the middle of the century some 350 Y's and Centers in the United States and Canada were affiliated with the Board. The Settlement Houses, on the other hand, found it hard to modify their outlook and program, a notable exception being the Educational Alliance in New York. Their function as Americanization agencies became redundant; after the twenties, in fact, no new Settlements came into existence.

The new emphasis found strong advocates also among Christian leaders in America. In September 1922 Vice President Calvin Coolidge who, less than a year later, became the President, in a letter to Otto A. Rosalsky, a prominent jurist and lay leader in Jewish education, stated:

> One of the dangers to America is that those who came here will break with their past. . . . No person who is false to his own nationality can be true to America.
>
> Teach the ancient landmarks to the youth of the Jewish race. . . . That learning and wisdom which has been a sustaining influence to the Jewish race through all the centuries must be preserved for the benefit of mankind. The youth of your people can associate themselves for no more patriotic purpose.

5

In the sphere of religion two developments must be noted that stand out in striking contrast to each other and bear testimony to the polychrome composition of the Jewish religious spectrum in America. One is Reconstructionism, the other Chassidism. The temper and philosophy of the first may be described as rationalist and humanistic. The second is the mystic and ecstatic version of the ancient faith that sprang up in the eighteenth century and swept the Jewish masses of Eastern Europe. It won an important place in the American community when many of its leaders, forced to flee from persecution in Europe, found asylum in the United States.

Reconstructionism owes its teaching and leadership to Mordecai M. Kaplan, a professor of homiletics in the Jewish Theological Seminary of America, and has been generally associated with Conservatism, a goodly number of Conservative rabbis having been attracted by it. Reconstructionism speaks of Judaism as a "civilization," of which religion is the major but not the only component, others being Jewish literature, music and art. Like Reform, Reconstructionism made radical theological changes. It rejected the doctrine of the divine election of the Jewish people and the revelation at Sinai, and its concept of the Deity, though difficult to grasp and state, appears to be apersonal and impersonal: the Deity, that is, is conceived as a force, a principle or a tendency, rather than "an entity or a being." Unlike early Reform, however, Reconstructionism believes firmly in the national destiny of the Jewish people and has staunchly supported the Zionist movement. The new teaching had resolute foes not only among the Orthodox, but in the other two sectors of American Judaism also. They accused it of negating fundamental Jewish credos, and its God, they averred, was an abstraction, "not available for religious purposes." But Reconstructionism won many adherents also, especially among Zionists, who found secular nationalism incapable of nourishing their deeper spiritual wants.

The Old World Chassidic leaders or "rebbes," most of them scions of illustrious "dynasties," found devoted followers in the large communities of the country, especially in the Williamsburg section of Brooklyn, New York, which became the Orthodox stronghold of America. Distinguished among them was the rebbe of the intellectual branch of Chassidism, known as *Chabad,* the name being made up of the first letters of the Hebrew words meaning wisdom, understanding and knowledge.* He was Joseph Isaac Schneersohn, generally called the "Lubavitcher Rebbe," or simply the "Lubavitcher." He was a leader of heroic mold, having in the course of his career withstood Bolshevik pressures and Nazi air raids, and under his inspiration a network of elementary and higher schools was established, where the ancient faith was taught in the spirit of *Chabad.* Under his son-in-law and successor, Menachem Mendel Schneersohn, who had begun as an engineer and was as much at home in secular learning, including modern philosophy, as in the ancient lore, *Chabad* began to attract some Jewish intellectuals also.

The empiricism and relativism that go with the sway of the scientific method over men's minds took their toll in Judaism as in all other faiths. At the same time, however, a trend in the opposite direction was clearly discernible. In October 1953 Maurice N. Eisendrath, the president of the Union of American Hebrew Congregations, the lay body of the Reform segment, reported that in the decade ending that year the number of congregations affiliated with it had risen from about 300 to 461, with a growth in membership from approximately 50,000 to well over 150,000. In 1948 the congregations affiliated with the Conservative wing, the United Synagogue of America, numbered 265; in 1954 they numbered 473, and there were indications that their membership had also undergone considerable growth. For the Orthodox wing, the Union of Orthodox Jewish Congregations of America reported an increase of units affiliated with it from 450 in 1944 to 720 in 1954, with an increase in membership from 101,250 to 172,800. But only a minority of the Orthodox congregations in the country, estimated to total approximately 3,000 in 1954, were affiliated with the Union; the membership of all of them was placed at approximately 720,000.

Since nearly every congregant represents a family group, and with the figure 3.3 representing the size of the average Jewish family in America, it appeared that nearly 3,400,000 of the approximately 5,000,000 Jews in America were associated with a synagogue or temple. Nor could all of the remainder be written off from such an association. For a substantial portion of those who attended the houses of worship, especially in the Orthodox segment, were not dues-paying members. And while the urge impelling men and women to join a church or synagogue is often social rather than religious, such affiliation does bring them under religious influence, and in the case of Jews it testi-

* The words are *chachmah, binah, daath.*

fies, also, to a recognition, conscious or unconscious, of the primacy of the synagogue in Jewish communal life.

There were also significant religious developments that were not subject to statistical evaluation. In Reform, for example, there was a definite tendency to restore rituals and practices that had long been discarded. Among secularists of different complexions some form of observance of the Jewish festivals became almost a fashion. Chassidism was studied and admired, and attempts were made to utilize its spirit and teachings. The two foremost Jewish religious philosophers of those decades, Franz Rosenzweig and Martin Buber, found disciples in America also. The spiritual void which a rigid rationalism produces longed for redemption, and many found it in a return to the ancient sanctities.

6

The rise of Israel confronted the American Jewish community not only with a new and precious burden, but with the question of what should be its relationship to the Jewish state. It was an altogether novel question. In the 300 years of their history the Jews of America had on many occasions, as we saw, given concrete and vigorous expression of their concern for the fortunes of Jewish communities in other lands, obeying the command implied in the ancient dictum: "All Israel are responsible one for another," and no one thought of challenging their right and duty to be so concerned. But the community in Palestine, now called *Medinat Yisrael*, or State of Israel, was like no other of the previous two millennia. It was a political entity, a sovereign state, and it appeared to some American Jews that a special concern for it on their part might give rise to the accusation that they were compromising their loyalty to the land of which they were citizens. Assurances by leaders of American Jewry and by responsible spokesmen for Israel that the allegiance of American Jews belonged under all circumstances to America, failed to allay their misgivings. They were, of course, the die-hard anti-Zionist minority of the community, and they maintained that the attitude of American Jews towards Israel should not be different from their attitude towards, say, Chile or Afghanistan. How right they were by the test of formal reasoning; how wrong by the test of instinct and experience—by the test, that is, not of reasoning but of reason. For the great majority felt intuitively that the failure of Israel would be calamitous for Jewish communities the world over, and its success, on the other hand, would raise the stature of Jews the world over, and would, in a manner they found it hard to define, contribute a new dimension to their lives as individuals and as a community.

There were some who attempted to define it. They harked back to the theories and prognostications of Achad Ha'am (One of the People), as Asher Ginsburg, the most important philosopher of Zionism called himself: he spoke of an elite community in Palestine as a spiritual powerhouse or "center" that would recharge and vivify all other communities, whom he described as the "periphery." But after the Second World War his theories and predictions seemed stricken with the ills to which most philosophic "certainties" are heirs: the juggernaut of history refused to reckon with them. The large Jewish communities of Eastern and Central Europe were either annihilated or sealed off behind the iron curtain, and the free and powerful community in America, solicitous as it was for the security and progress of Israel, did not seem disposed to place itself under its spiritual tutelage. And the question was further complicated by the problems of social and cultural integration with which Israel itself was faced. For in the first five years of statehood the little country had admitted the colossal total of 700,000 immigrants, half of them from North Africa and the Middle East with a cultural and psychological background that differed in important respects from that of the rest.

So there was considerable speculation on the relations, present and future, of the two most significant Jewish communities in the world, and much of the discussion was windy and barren. But it was the Zionist sector of the American community that felt most deeply involved. To many Jews it seemed that the rise of the state had removed the raison d'être of the movement that inspired it, and some of the leaders in Israel appeared to be of the same mind. They insisted, of course, that the continued support of the American community was vital for Israel, but they looked for it—and found it, too—not among the Zionists alone but all Jews in America, many of whom still held aloof from the organized movement. But Zionism had become the major spiritual nutriment in the lives of a great many American Jews, who viewed the prospects of its imminent decay and demise with grave anxiety. The movement, moreover, had accumulated over the half-century a large corpus of institutions, procedures and functions—things that gather tradition and sentiment, and cling desperately to life.

But the threat turned out to be not so imminent after all. The relations between the movement, represented by the Jewish Agency or

Zionist Executive, and the state were undergoing definition, under which important responsibilities were assigned to the first. And in 1954 the American Zionist Council, embracing all the Zionist bodies in the country, reported a combined membership which, in spite of a decline of about 25 per cent from its peak in 1948, still stood at the impressive total of 750,000.

7

Blueprints with regard to the eventual relationship between the Jewish community in America and the Jewish state may be fatuous, but that some mode of mutuality will subsist between them is fairly certain. It is also certain, however, that neither community will endure if its existence, material or spiritual, depends chiefly on the other. American Jewry cannot live in spiritual dependence on Israel, just as Israel, if it is to survive, must become economically self-dependent.

In the anxious discussions that proceeded on the future of American Jewry, a prominent place was held by the word "survival." Will the Jews in America survive as a distinctive community? was the question that preoccupied religious and lay leaders and intellectuals. But the ability to survive is neither a virtue nor even a boon, unless the life it brings is wholesome and dignified. And while the hostility to which Jews have been peculiarly exposed cannot be ignored as a survival factor, it alone will certainly not engender a dignified and creative communal life. Other survival factors must be found, and they must be sought where, in the unique experience of the Jewish people across continents and millennia, they have always been found: in the realm of mind and spirit.

Of that the leaders and intellectuals have not, of course, been unmindful, so in the same discussions "Jewish culture" occupied an even more prominent place. Jews were urged to cultivate and promote Jewish culture. It is not a well-defined term, but it evokes certain modes of intellectual and aesthetic expression, including literature, the plastic arts, music, the drama and even the dance. And while in a number of areas—painting and sculpture, for example—the existence of a specific Jewish genre has been questioned, and the fact that an artist is of Jewish descent is no assurance that his work will have Jewish significance, it is nevertheless true that in all those areas there are works that have Jewish themes, moods and meanings. So in the name of group survival American Jews were exhorted to include such works in the sphere of their cultural interests. They were also urged to cling to, or acquire, the Yiddish or Hebrew language or both. Nor was the doctrine of "cultural pluralism" omitted from those appeals.

If, however, Jewish culture in America can find no other motive, and group survival no other sanction, the prospects for both do not appear bright. The expectation that any significant number would, in the name of group survival, exert the effort entailed in those demands is farfetched and has, in fact, proved an illusion. Nor is the ability to read Yiddish or Hebrew, or an appreciation of the towering Hebrew poet Saul Tchernikhovsky or the paintings of Marc Chagall a prophylactic against the forces that make for group dissolution—intermarriage, for example.

8

A deeper and more potent sanction of group survival has operated in the four millennia of Jewish history. Without it all others have sooner or later proved of no avail; with it all others fall into place as part and parcel of it. It is, of course, the religious sanction. For the Jews of America it also has the great merit of being in harmony with the spirit, traditions and institutions of their country. For religious pluralism is something all Americans understand and take for granted; "cultural pluralism" the average American does not understand, and he would probably be dubious about it, if he did.

If the past is to guide us, we may fairly affirm that the American Jewish community must be, as indeed it has been in the first 300 years of its career, essentially a religious community, or it will not be at all. If that is so, some will ruefully rejoin, it is doomed. But with all that may be adduced to support their pessimism, their verdict is premature. Religion in general is not to be dislodged from the human spirit, and Judaism will in all likelihood speak its ineluctable truths to the human heart and mind, as it has always done, through a people that has lived and endured by it and for it.

BIBLIOGRAPHICAL NOTE

FOR READERS WHO DESIRE ADDITIONAL MATERIAL

The following are the major reference works containing material on the history of the Jews in America:

The Jewish Encyclopedia. 12 vols., New York, Funk & Wagnalls, 1901-05 (KTAV reprint 1966).

The Universal Jewish Encyclopedia. 10 vols., New York, Universal Jewish Encyclopedia Co., 1939-43 (KTAV reprint 1968).

Publications of the American Jewish Historical Society. 60 vols., New York, 1893-1971.

The American Jewish Year Book. 72 vols., Philadelphia, The Jewish Publication Society of America, 1899-1971.

In addition books, monographs, articles, and pamphlets—too numerous to list here—have appeared dealing with particular localities, events, periods, historic figures, congregations, and other bodies. Even more numerous, perhaps, are the publications devoted to special themes, like immigration, Americanization, anti-Semitism, philanthropy, the labor movement, Zionism, etc., etc. For information as to available material on a particular subject in American Jewish history write to American Jewish Historical Society, 2 Thornton Road, Waltham, Mass. 02154.

EPILOGUE

AMERICAN JEWRY 1954-1971

ABRAHAM J. KARP

The almost six million Jews who comprise the American Jewish community in 1970 make it the single largest in the three millennial history of the Jewish people. The only comparable communities were the pre-World War I Russian Jewry of some five million souls and the Palestinian community before the rebellion against Rome, estimated at some four and one-half million.

It is a community possessed of great affluence and wide freedoms. Its members took full advantage of America's ever expanding economy. The sons of shop laborers and small storekeepers entered the free and salaried professions in continuously increasing numbers. They have become successful entrepreneurs and have made their mark and fortunes in soft-goods manufacturing, in merchandising, and in areas of the communications complex. True, the major industries which are the sinews of America—oil, steel, transportation, finance, and electronics—have maintained and retain their executive suites virtually *Judenrein.* Nevertheless, the economic rise of the Jew in post-World War II America is an authentic success story.

The freedom enjoyed by the American Jew is twofold. The law of the land extends to him fullest civic rights and unqualified political equality. His is also the right to choose whether to associate or affiliate with the Jewish community and to what degree. He is free as a citizen of the republic, and free in his relation to the Jewish community. His freedom is however tempered by societal usage and communal pressure. Barriers to educational institutions and employment opportunities have all but disappeared in present-day America. There remains, however, the "five o'clock shadow," which divides and separates associates and neighbors when the working day ends. Home and circle of friends, country club and resort retain exclusiveness and discrimination. His freedom in relation to the Jewish community is not absolute; Jews will pressure him to associate, affiliate, and participate. His non-Jewish neighbor will mark and call him Jew without rancor but with persistence. This extends even, on occasion, to Jews who have converted to Christianity and have become active members of a church. His Jewish associate will solicit his contribution to the U.J.A., and ministers have been quoted as informing rabbis, "We have some of your people in our church."

In the 1960's it was noted that American culture had taken on a distinct Jewish coloration. Not only were leading novelists, playwrights, and critics Jewish, but they wrote from Jewish perspectives and on Jewish themes. Jewish professors were leading members of the faculties of America's most prestigious universities; nor were college presidencies denied the American Jew—even two in the Ivy League.

Affluent, free, influential, the American Jew in this eighth decade of the twentieth century is in crisis. No longer a crisis of security, opportunity, or status, but a crisis of identity. He recognizes that he is at one and the same time a citizen of America and a member of the Jewish people. In the 1950's he thought he had the problem licked. He happily accepted the image of America as the home of the three great faiths and saw himself as an American Jew, a member of the American-Jewish religious community, as his neighbor was an American Protestant or an American Catholic. But in the late 60's, and even more so as we enter the 70's, there is an ongoing shift from religious to ethnic designation. The Six Day War brought strong and lasting peoplehood identity to many American Jews, the young in particular. The American Jew sees himself as a citizen of America and a member of a world people. He sees American Jewish community as a group within and in America, and at the same time as a segment of world Jewry. Something new has happened to the American Jew in the last decade and a half. It was caused in part by the Black Revolution, in part by the larger looming presence of the State of Israel in his life, and by the tensions, crises, and ferment in American life. He has an as yet unformed perception of himself as a person, as an American, as a Jew, in a world where yesterday's certainties are today's perplexities, and today's turmoil in life and thought is the only ready base on which to build for tomorrow.

There are those who see the crisis facing the American Jew not as one of identity but of survival. They point to a declining birthrate, a rapidly accelerating rate of intermarriage, a persistence of anti-Semitic sentiment, dormant in prosperity, but which may flare up in times of social turmoil and economic upheaval. As the American Jewish community approaches the last quarter of the twentieth century, it would be useful to turn to a historical and sociological overview of aspects of American Jewish life, a consideration not so much of persons and events as of groups, movements and trends.

1. *The Matter of Demography*

The estimated Jewish population of the United States rose from 5,000,000 in 1954 to 5,869,000 in 1968.[1] This records a significant growth of the post-World War II Jewish community. This seemingly large increase should give heart to all concerned with Jewish survival in America; but analysis and comparison of these figures would temper optimism and lead to a pessimistic prognosis.

The rate of growth of the Jewish population during this period averaged 1.15% a year. In the same period the average annual growth of the United States white population was 1.425%. More. The United States Census Bureau Report, March, 1957, disclosed that whereas the percentage of persons fourteen years and younger in the general community was 29.1%, the percentage of the Jewish population was 22.6%. It should be pointed out that these are self-perpetuating figures. A decade later there will be that many more in the general com-

[1] All population figures are taken from Volumes 56–71 of the *American Jewish Yearbook*.

munity to produce the next generation, and that many fewer in the Jewish community; hence fewer children; hence fewer adults to produce children, etc., etc. All indications point to a steadily decreasing Jewish birthrate since 1968. The lowest birthrate is in middle-class suburban communities and this is precisely where the American Jew lives. As we examine the Jewish population figures we find that the percentage of increase from 1955 to 1960 was over 10%, the increase from 1963 to 1968, less than 5%.

Small wonder that demographers and sociologists warn that the birthrate of the American Jew has fallen below the survival rate.

The same Census Bureau report indicated where Jews resided in 1957. Ninety-six percent of American Jews live in urban centers as against 64% of the general population. The larger the city the greater the concentration of Jews. Over 87% live in urban centers of 250,000 or more. More recent figures indicate that 70% of America's Jews live in the ten largest urban centers. The same areas contain but 15% of America's population. Over 40% live in the New York area and over 10% across the continent in Los Angeles.

The most dramatic growth of Jewish population in the last decade has been in Los Angeles, Miami, Washington, D.C., Phoenix; while the most persistent loss has been to communities of 200 or fewer families. Many small communities in the Northeast, Midwest and South seem to be inexorably heading for extinction.

Since World War II, an increasing number of communities have undertaken demographic studies. A recent survey of these studies[2] discloses that 75–80 percent of American Jews are native-born and claims:

> Generally, there is a high degree of stability—consequently little migration manifested with regard to living in or near one's birthplace or original settlement.

[2] Ronald Goldstein, "American Jewish Population Studies Since World War II" in *American Jewish Archives*, April 1970.

The claim would be disputed by most observers of the contemporary Jewish scene. It probably reflects the findings of studies which are already dated, for there is great and increasing mobility in the Jewish population.

American Jewry is becoming less and less a community of small or large businessmen and is becoming more and more a community of professionals, of the technically skilled and the managerially trained, a highly mobile group.

The number returning from college to the family business has decreased because a life of business pursuit has low priority in the desires of the new generation, because the number of businesses has decreased (a storekeeper in the inner city will often retire rather than relocate), and because many businesses have been joined to large corporations or amalgamations and ownership has passed out of the family. The free professional (i.e., doctor, lawyer, architect, accountant) once settled, generally remains. The salaried professional (i.e. chemist, engineer, physicist, academician) will go where his career takes him, and it generally takes him to more than one employer, or scattered installations of the giant corporations and conglomerates.

Some 85 to 90 percent of American Jews of college age go off to college. This in itself makes for mobility, for it is an actual uprooting of some and a change in life style. The end product of the educational system is an individual trained for a role in an economic system which is vast and impersonal. It sends the employee where it determines in accordance with its needs and moves him when it needs to do so. In this educational-industrial complex one seeks employment not in one's home town but on the campus where he meets company representatives and gets leads and recommendations from the placement service. Indeed, one's "home town" is his profession. Mobility is furthered by a decrease in the percentage of the self-employed and a growth in the percentage of the salaried professions. The economic strength of the community is changing from entrepreneural daring and merchandising acumen to technical skills and managerial expertise. Such a group is highly vulnerable in periods of economic stress. The implications of the new economic posture of the American Jew for the future stability and well-being of the Jewish community has not as yet been seriously considered.

In 1960 the Jewish community of Rochester, New York conducted a population study and published a report.[3] The population was reported as being 22,000. The figure has remained more or less constant during the past forty years. In the same period the general population of the area has doubled. Why the decrease in the percentage of the Jewish population? Why not a similar growth?

During the latter decades of the nineteenth and early decades of the twentieth centuries, the major industry of Rochester was men's clothing. This was an industry largely in the hands of Jews as employers and employees, in Rochester as nationally. There was therefore a high incidence of Jews in the labor force of Rochester because of the nature of its industry. Today men's clothing companies are only a small segment of Rochester industry. The few factories which remain have few Jewish employees. The sons and daughters of Rochester clothing-factory workers of yesterday who have remained in the area are today its doctors, lawyers, pharmacists, and are employed as physicists, chemists, and engineers at Kodak or Xerox. A large influx of new Jewish families have come from all sections of North America, Europe, and Israel to become the salaried professionals in Rochester's industries.

The median age of the Jews of Rochester was 38 compared to 32 for the general white population. The Jewish children below ten years of age were 20% less of the total Jewish population than non-Jewish children of their population group. The Jewish population is not keeping pace with the general population due to a perceptibly lower birthrate.

Seventy-nine percent of Rochester's Jews were born in the United States, 52% in Rochester. The 27% who were born elsewhere in the country and migrated to Rochester were generally in the younger groups.

The number of Jewish college graduates was considerably more than double that of non-Jews. It is no surprise, then,

[3] *The Jewish Population of Rochester, 1961.*

that the income level was markedly higher, especially in the above $25,000 group.

Almost three-quarters of the family heads were dues-paying members of a congregation and over 90% of the families contributed to the United Jewish Appeal.

Summary:

American Jewry today is 42% of world Jewry. In 1800 the percentage was 1/12 of 1%; in 1850, 1%; in 1900, 10%, and 1933, 28%. It comprises slightly less than 3% of the American population. It is concentrated in the suburbs of the urban centers of the Northeast, upper Midwest, and Southern California. Small-town Jewry is decreasing, almost to the point of disappearance. Economically the movement is from business and labor to the professions, free and salaried, and the managerial sectors. It is high in education and income. It resembles in almost all the above the suburban middle-class population of the United States of which it is part and among and with whom it lives.

2. *The Organized Community*

The American Jewish community of the post-war era was at one and the same time quantitatively highly organized and functionally disorganized. The American Jewish Year Book for 1970 lists as "National Jewish Organizations" twenty-three in the field of community relations; thirty-two cultural; eighteen dealing with overseas aid; one hundred twenty-nine religious and educational organizations and institutions; twenty in social, mutual benefit; twenty-nine in social welfare; and sixty-six Zionist and pro-Israel.

Over three hundred national organizations serve the various and varied needs and interests of American Jewry, yet there is no one over-all representative body mandated to plan for, to speak for, and to act for a united organized Jewish community. Within the sub-groupings there are coordinating bodies, but these are largely without power and are smaller in budget, staff, program, and influence than the independent organizations which they "co-ordinate." Thus in the field of community relations, the American Jewish Committee, the Anti-Defamation League of B'nai B'rith and the American Jewish Congress outstrip in power and program the National Jewish Community Relations Advisory Council. The American Zionist Council is the "coordinating and public relations arm of the twelve national organizations which comprise the American Zionist movement," but the twelve remain autonomous and the Council exists at their pleasure or sufferance. Similarly the Synagogue Council of America "acts as the overall Jewish religious representative body of Orthodox, Conservative, and Reform Judaism . . . ," but the national organizations of these religious movements have delegated no power and relegated no programs to the Synagogue Council. Each of the constituent bodies retains a veto on policy and pronouncement of the Council, thus rendering it ineffectual as a spokesman for American religious Jewry. It may be said that American Jewry is a community of organizations lacking organization. This reality is the product of the unique and unprecedented factors in American political, social, and religious life which were reflected in the American Jewish historical experience.

The American Jewish community is a voluntary community. In Europe a Jew was born into the community—*kehillah* or *gemeinde*—and was recognized as a member of the community by the government. This made for communal unity, strength and internal control. To dissociate oneself from one's community of birth, one had to undertake an active act of dissociation, generally religious conversion. In America the person is born a citizen of the nation. To become a member of an ethnic or religious community demands an act of affiliation through formal membership or association through will and activity. The American Jew then had the choice to affiliate or not, and through which institution, organization, or movement to express his association with the community. This made for a multiplicity of organizations and institutions expressing a variety of interests and commitments. It militated against one overall body, any part of whose policy or program would be counter to the views or beyond the interests of the individual, who had a full and free choice to join in or remain outside.

The form of organization of the American Jewish community was in response to the self-definition and image: "What is he?" or, more pressingly, "What am I, an American Jew or a Jewish American?" That is, am I a Jew who is by residence and citizenship an American or am I an American who is by faith or ethnic-cultural preference a Jew? In pre-Emancipation European countries, the Jew was a distinct part of the mosaic composition of the state divided into estates. He was neither nobleman, serf, nor clergy. He was Jew. The established church excluded the Jew as individual and the corporate body of Jews from the political-religious configuration of the state. Jacob, son of Isaac, was a Jew who resided in particular political entity, a member of a Jewish community apart and separate. In the United States there was neither division into class or estate, nor an established church. All white Americans were free and equal citizens. The self-definition which Jacob Isaacs (great-grandson of Jacob, son of Isaac) accepted was that he is an American who, ethnically or religiously, or both, is a Jew.

He was then, first and foremost, an American. The state did not demand or suggest that its Jewish citizens organize as a community. Many Jews felt that an organization which did not have its parallel in the Christian community would stand in the way of the full acceptance of the Jew into the American community, would hinder his Americanization, his integration in the American civilization.

The parallel institution which the Jew established was the synagogue. In the eighteenth and nineteenth centuries the church was an institution serving the spiritual, educational, charitable, fraternal, and benevolent needs and interests of its communicants. The synagogue was organized to parallel and mirror the church in its multiple program and varied activities. The growth of America and its secularization brought the government and the civic community into the everyday life of the people. Education was provided by the government; social care and welfare became a community responsibility. This was reflected in the Jewish community in the transfer of charitable and social-welfare activities to organizations and institutions established for a specific purpose—orphanage, hospital, charity societies, relief organizations for local and overseas needs.

The process of Americanization, the project of immigration, the stresses of hostility at home and abroad all gave rise to organizations. Often when the old need no longer obtained, the organization remained and sought out a new need to serve for a high priority of institutional and organizational life is self-perpetuation. The attempts to organize a representative body of American Jewry each came in response to a worldwide Jewish crisis which reminded the American Jews of their common Jewish destiny, and which demonstrated to them a shared community of interest. The Damascus Blood Libel of 1840 brought forth the first call for a Union of Israelites by Isaac Leeser. The activity surrounding the protest against the papal authorities for their role in the Mortara Affair resulted in the establishment of the Board of Delegates of American Israelites in 1859. The American Jewish Committee was organized in the wake of the Kishinev Massacre of 1903. Planning for the post-war needs of World War I made the American Jewish Congress; and World War II, the American Jewish Conference. In all cases, the unity was short lived. Leeser recalls that the Shearith Israel Congregation of New York refused to join because its Sefardi leaders were afraid that a Union would be dominated by the German Jews. The Reform Jews did not give support to the Board of Delegates because it was led by Traditionalists. The American Jewish Committee, composed of the more "prudent" element of American Jewry, refrained from supporting an effective Congress and Conference, because (whatever the reason officially stated) such an overall representative body did not conform with its view of the status, place, and function of the Jewish community in the community and civilization which is America.

In the past two decades there has been little talk and no attempt to establish an overall representative body. The Jewish institutions and organizations of America are jealous for their independence and zealous for their prerogatives. They are in no mood to surrender either a measure of power or a modicum of independence. There seems to be neither overriding need nor overpowering will to unify and organize. In time of special need, the Conference of Presidents of Major American Jewish Organizations acts as representative of American Jewry.

The past decades have seen the proliferation in number and growth of power of the local Jewish Community Councils and Welfare Funds. The great fund-raising efforts which have been the leading activity of American Jewry necessitated organized Jewish communal efforts. Within the individual Jewish communities the Councils or Welfare Funds wield vast power. They have expanded their activities beyond fund raising to community planning, community relations activities, and of late, into the fields of Jewish education and culture. There are today some 230, and their influence promises to continue and grow.

This growth of power and broadening of interest is true also of the Council of Jewish Federations and Welfare Funds. The stated purpose of this national body is to aid the local agencies in "fund raising, community organization, health and welfare planning, personnel recruitment and public relations." But because it brings together the effective leaders of the American Jewish community, and since it exercises considerable influence in allocation of funds, it has become the recognized address for decision making in American Jewish life. Special interest groups have learned that it is to be influenced, for the influence it bears is considerable. Thus in 1969 when a group of Jewish students wanted to effect a reordering in priorities of allocations, it came in protest before the Council at its annual meeting in Boston and received a platform to put forth its plea for Jewish education and culture.

In expanding its field of concern and interest, the Council was instrumental in the founding of the National Foundation for Jewish Culture in 1960. A decade later the Foundation began a program of "lump sum" budgeting, receiving from local welfare funds a "lump sum" allocation, which it in turn will distribute to its members' agencies in the field of Jewish culture. The Council has also inspired studies of Jewish education nationally and locally and is presently urging in-depth studies in Jewish identity. All indications point to the Council's becoming more and more effective, if not official, overall representative body of American Jewry. It is, however, technically a service agency, without ideology or program. But allocation of funds and choice of fields of interest and activities are in themselves an ideology, since they are expressive of a point of view, necessitate the setting up of a hierarchy of priorities, and thus constitute commitment to a system of values.

It seems likely that with the continued growth in power and program of the Council, with the new interest in ethnic identity, and with the increased commitment to the concept of community in America, the issue of an American Jewish democratic representative body will again come to the fore. Those who will argue for it will point to the strength which a posture of unity will bring in relationship to other bodies in America and abroad; to the efficiency which unity brings; to the ability for the total community to undertake self-study and carry on orderly planning; to the desirability that priorities in Jewish life be established by democratically elected representatives rather than by those who exercise the weight of wealth; that such a body, through local counterparts, would serve as a vehicle of affiliation, association, and identification for the individual Jew whether his Jewish allegiance be religious, cultural, national, or social. Those arguing against such a body would argue that one is a citizen of a state and a member of a civic entity. How can he be part of a political entity for which there is no parallel in the general community? Must a Jew be and continue to be "different"? They would argue that it would not be tactically wise for the Jews to speak in one voice. They would further state that it would be impossible, in practice, for all Jews to adhere to such a body. Can a committed anti-Zionist remain affiliated if the body adopts a pro-Zionist platform? Will it not militate against religious diversity and variety? Will it not be inimical to special or unpopular cultural and educational interests?

As the concerns of American Jewry turn inwards this issue will be joined, in a confrontation between those who value the order, strength, and efficiency which unity will bring, and those who esteem the freedom, variety, and creativity which a loose federation of independent bodies makes possible.

3. *American Jewry and the State of Israel*

No sooner had the celebrations marking the founding of the State of Israel come to an end when American Jewry was called upon to marshal its resources in aid of the new state fighting for its existence. The borders secure, the energies and resources of American Jews were placed in service of immigration of European, Near Eastern and North African Jews to Israel and their rehabilitation and settlement on the land. The effort required skilled organization, unprecedented philanthropic vision and commitment, energetic and ongoing campaigns, and political activity as well.

In the years 1939–1969 the American Jewish community raised in local, central community campaigns three billion, eight hundred and ninety-six and a half million dollars ($3,896,-500,000). The initial impetus was the plight of the displaced persons of Europe. A decade later the campaign appeal was resettlement in Israel of a large immigration of Jews from the Arab lands where life was gettting increasingly uncomfortable and the future was viewed with great foreboding.

The annual United Jewish Appeal campaign became the central activity of American Jewish communities. It unified the diverse social, economic, and religious groups into one organized enterprise. Ideological division and historical antagonism fell before an overriding unity which the cause demanded and which the campaign apparatus effected. Once joined in common effort, communities utilized structure and personnel (lay as well as professional) to address themselves, as well, to national and local problems and projects. There developed an acceptance of *communal* responsibility for community relations, education, communal planning, the Jewish student on the college campus, and the plight of Soviet Jewry. What began as campaign, pure and simple, developed into a corporate structure which increasingly undertakes those projects and activities which are the responsibilities of a viable organized community.

The "Campaign" has been a philanthropic accomplishment unprecedented and unequaled in scope and in results. In 1930, the total raised was a little less than twenty-nine million. The founding of the State of Israel and the War of Independence unloosed a generosity which was hoped for but hardly expected. The campaign of 1948 which raised over two hundred million set the tone and level for the subsequent years. In the 1950's and 1960's the amounts realized averaged some one hundred and thirty million per year.

The Six Day War in June, 1967, had a profound effect on the life of the American Jew. A great wave of Jewish consciousness, a sense of the oneness of Jewish destiny, a new commitment to a heightened priority for Jewish interests and welfare, and an outpouring of generosity, engulfed community after community. For the moment we speak only of the new-found generosity as expressed through the central Jewish community campaigns:

Estimates in millions of dollars:

Year			*Dollars*
1965			132.6
1966			137.3
1967	Regular	146.0	
	Emergency	173.0	
	Total		319.0
1968	Regular	153.2	
	Emergency	83.0	
	Total		236.2
1969	Regular	164.9	
	Emergency	103.0	
	Total		267.9

What is most noteworthy is that the regular campaign total continued to increase and the "Emergency Campaign" is becoming accepted as part of the ongoing "Regular" annual commitment. In the same three years (1967–8–9), $428,687,000 in State of Israel Bonds were sold in the United States. This constituted more than a third of a sale of $1,208,849,000 in the years 1951–69. The monies realized in the community campaigns were allocated not only for overseas relief, but for national and local institutions and organizations as well. The appeal was to the American Jews' interest in resettlement and rehabilitation abroad, and the bulk of the money was channeled to the United Jewish Appeal, but the Jewish defense agencies, Jewish education, Jewish health services, and cultural enterprises at home benefited from this joint philanthropic endeavor. The campaign process, with its program of educational rallies and meetings addressed by leaders of Israel and American Jewry, and with its missions to Israel served as a bridge and bond between the communities of Israel and America.

Tourism and education serve as an even stronger bond and "busier" bridge. Tourism had been growing to such a degree that during the peak seasons of 1971, the number of visitors outstripped Israel's hotel facilities. American Jewish organizations found that organizing tours of Israel is an activity both substantive and financially rewarding. The American visitor has become a commonplace in Israel. Generally the visit is of a two- or three-week duration, but an increasing number of American Jews are establishing their second home in Israel.

Of greater significance is the very large number of American Jews studying in Israel. Most spend a year at the Hebrew, Tel Aviv, or Bar Ilan Universities; a goodly number study in Israel's *yeshivot;* an American College has been established in Jerusalem. The *kibbutz,* as a new life style, is attracting a growing number of young Americans to a summer's, half-year's or year's residency. As in all matters pertaining to Israel, student interest increased dramatically in the period of the Six Day War and has not wavered but grown. The number of student visitors, the number of applications to Israeli universities, and the numbers settling in Israel increase year by year.

Grown, too, has *aliyah,* immigration of American Jews to Israel. Prior to 1967, *aliyah* was demanded only by Israeli leaders (and that in decreasing decibels and zeal) and lip homage was paid to it at Zionist conventions. No one really expected significant numbers of American Jews to leave affluence and security for uncertainty and deprivation. But in 1970, the bare figures tell of this new (and really unexpected) phenomenon in American Jewish life. In the years 1967–1970 as many American Jews settled in Israel as in the preceding twenty years.

In the 1920's American Zionists were joined in a debate on emphasis and priority: political activity or the practical labor of rebuilding; ideology or philanthropy? Movements are rooted in an ideology and demand political commitment of their adherents. Organizations deal with practical matters, with giving, with providing, with helping. It has been noted that movements may come to an end, but organizations tend to perpetuate themselves. In America, Zionism has expressed itself more through organizations than as a movement. This is due in part to the American temper which is more given to practicality than ideology, and in part to the role the American Jew needed to and was able to play in the Zionist program—philanthropy and influence.

The organizations of Zionism remain and function in America. They retain an ideological stance but their life is in their practical function. They are joined together in a loose confederation, the American Zionist Council. To the left is a constellation of Labor Zionist groups reflecting the party divisions in Israel. The Labor Zionist Organization of America, the Pioneer Women and its youth group, Habonim, is the largest. Smaller in number are the Progressive Zionist League and the United Labor Zionist Party. The centrist General Zionist are the Zionist Organization of America and Hadassah, the women's Zionist organization. The latter is the largest by far of the Zionist organizations. It has a great and enviable record of continuing service to its medical, public health, child welfare, and vocational education institutions in Israel. In America it carries on a program of education and publishes a magazine of quality, *The Hadassah Magazine*. To the right is the United Zionist-Revisionists. The religious Zionists of America are comprised of Mizrachi-Hapoel Mizrachi and Mizrachi Women. All have their youth groups and programs of activities in the United States and institutions and interests in Israel.

Opposition to Zionism in America is in the extreme left and right of Jewish religious life. The American Council for Judaism opposes Zionism for its nationalism, seeing it as a hindrance to national, civic, cultural, and social integration of the American Jew into American life. The followers of the Rebbe of Satmar oppose Zionism as an antireligious force which is usurping the role to be played by the Messiah and is thereby flouting God's will and placing God's people in jeopardy.

Since the Six Day War, strong anti-Zionist and anti-Israel sentiments have been expressed by the New Left. Much of it echoes the anti-Zionism of the Old Left. Israel is accused of imperialism, of being the vehicle of international capitalism in the subjugation and suppression of the peoples of the Near East. The contemporary restatement of this old accusation is that Israel is a state of white colonial settlers exploiting the indigenous population and suppressing it in its struggle for national liberation. Israel is labeled an outpost of American interests in its oppression of the Afro-Asian populations of the "Third World." The fact that some Jewish students are in the leadership of the New Left pains the pro-Israel American Jewish community and amazes and perplexes the Israeli.

The United States policy in the Near East has remained constant in principle and purpose during the last two decades, but has changed in its practical relations with the State of Israel. The Middle East is to serve as a bulwark against communist expansion and the United States seeks the reduction of tension between Israel and the Arab states. In terms of American national interests the latter is in service of the former. In 1954 the State Department declared "a policy of impartial friendship" to all countries in the area. In practical working out of policy, the nature of friendship and how it is expressed is dependent upon the fulfilment to the basic policy of Russian containment.

When in October 1956 the Israeli forces occupied the Sinai peninsula of Egypt, the Eisenhower administration pressed for Israeli withdrawal. American Jewry united in opposition to a return to the status quo and urged Washington to propose to the General Assembly of the United Nations that Israel and the Arab States be required to enter peace negotiations. American public opinion was successfully marshaled in opposition to any United States "sanctions" against Israel. Israel finally yielded to American insistence on withdrawal. President Eisenhower wrote to Premier Ben Gurion that "Israel will have no cause to regret . . ." its action.

Throughout this period of Israeli-American tension American Jewry remained constant in its support of the Israeli position, which it claimed was in the best American interests, despite Administration policy. The moral argument was that the United States, as the "leader" of the free democratic world, owes special friendship to the one free and democratic state in the Near East desiring peace and stability in that sector of the world. The practical reasoning was that a free and strong Israel was the best deterrent to Russian incursion into the Middle East. At all times American Jewry's political activity in friendship for Israel was resolute, skillful, and of consequence.

A perceptive observer of the American Jewish community writes:[4]

June 1967 marked a watershed in contemporary Jewish affairs—the climax of a generation, the sealing of an era and the culmination of a 1900-year cycle. The historical generation which began with the creation of the State of Israel in 1948 reached its climax in the liberation of Jerusalem after 1900 years of foreign rule. The six day war united the members of the generation that witnessed the founding of the state with those of a new generation, one that grew up accepting the existence of Israel as a matter of fact, only to encounter suddenly the harsh possibility of its destruction, making both generations deeply aware of the shared fate of all Jews, and the way that fate is now bound up with the political entity that is the State of Israel. . . . Even Jews farthest removed from Jewish associations "instinctively" realized how crucial the survival of Israel was to their own welfare as individuals. As one rather casual Jew put it, "it was not only a matter of *identifying* as Jews but of *being* Jews."

The changes in the psyche of the American Jew and his redefinition of his Jewishness wrought by the War is proving to be longer lasting and more decisive than most thought possible. The meaning of Jewish existence, the essential fact of Jewish peoplehood, the mutuality of Jewish welfare and destiny

[4] Daniel J. Elazar, "The Rediscovered Polity," *American Jewish Year Book*, Vol. 70, 1969, pp. 172ff.

have become central concerns in the life of the Jewish community.

The tie of the individual Jew to Zion, the bonds between the communities of the Diaspora and Israel are no longer a matter of Zionist ideological commitment, but a basic fact of Jewish existence. This was dramatically (and in a practical manner) expressed through the reconstitution of the Jewish Agency of Israel. The report on "The Historic First Assembly of the Reconstituted Jewish Agency of Israel," issued by the Council of Jewish Federations and Welfare Funds, July 1971, states:

> The historic first Assembly of the Reconstituted Jewish Agency for Israel which met in Jerusalem June 21–25 marked a turning point in the cooperation of Jewish communities throughout the world with each other and with the people of Israel. . . . The Agency is now a fully autonomous body—it was formerly integrated with the World Zionist Organization. . . . Leaders of the World Zionist Organization comprise one-half of the governing bodies of the Jewish Agency. The other half is now made up of leaders of the United Israel Appeal. . . .

Max Fisher, a leader of the United Israel Appeal of the United States, spoke the prevailing sentiments of American Jewry in its relationship to Israel at the final session of the First Assembly:

> Out of this land once came a great message to the world: justice, freedom and human dignity. And we Jews, we choose to believe that out of this land will yet come another such message, to be given a chance to make our contribution to that goal, to be able to do our part by re-establishing our people, to build for the peace that will surely come, to have a small share in creating that Israel that will shine again as a light unto the nations. All this is a privilege beyond price.

A young member of the "now" generation would also add in hope and in anticipation, "and a life style which can make life meaningful and living a joyous adventure."

4. *The Jew and His Neighbors*

Franklin Hamlin Littell reports in his *From State Church to Pluralism,* published in 1962:[5]

In a dramatic ceremony during National Brotherhood Week, February 1961, the non-fiction award of the year was granted to a book entitled, *An American Dialogue.* This book, written in collaboration between a brilliant Protestant theologian (Robert McAfee Brown) and a distinguished Catholic theologian (Gustave Weigl), with an introduction by one of the greatest contemporary Jewish scholars (Will Herberg) marked the high point to date of an expanding network of discussions between representatives of the three major faiths in the Republic. These discussions, sometimes spontaneously emerging on a local basis and sometimes fostered by national movements like the National Conference of Christians and Jews and the Association for the Co-ordination of University Religious Affairs, call for a maturity and self-understanding which all three faith groups have yet to gain in a setting of voluntarism and pluralism.

Less than a decade later it all sounds dated. "Brotherhood Week," "'Dialogue' Discussions," "The National Conference of Christians and Jews," had all departed the arena of intergroup relations. The "three major faiths" as a concept and as a force in American life is but a memory. The pluralism of America had become more an ethnic matter than a religious one. Seventy percent of Americans thought that the influence of religion was increasing, in 1957; in 1970, 75% thought it was decreasing.[6]

In the 1920's and 1930's anti-Jewish discrimination in business, education, and housing was an accepted reality in American life. From time to time overt acts of anti-Semitism recalled to the Jew his tenuous status. America's leading industrialist of the twenties supported anti-Jewish publications, and the best-known Catholic priest of the thirties spouted anti-Semitism on a coast-to-coast radio network.

The threat and reality of anti-Semitism brought men of noble sentiments together in an effort to legitimize differences and to accept one another. Interfaith activity in the United States

[5] Anchor Books, Garden City, New York, 1962, pp. 168–69.

[6] According to a Gallup poll taken in 1957 and again in 1970.

was the result of Christian goodwill and Jewish need for acceptance, status, and security.

Post-World War II America saw a virtual elimination of anti-Jewish quotas in industry, education, and housing. Jews found full employment opportunities in heretofore limited occupations, as for example, engineering. Not only did quotas limiting the percentage of Jewish students in colleges disappear, but college faculties became open to Jews who now entered in significant numbers. In 1970 such prestigious institutions of higher learning as the Universities of Chicago and Pennsylvania and Dartmouth College were headed by Jews. There were almost no areas restricted against Jewish residence. Anti-Semitic spouting in print or by mouth was limited to a small lunatic fringe with little support and acceptance. Even veiled anti-Semitic sentiments of a public or elected official could eliminate him from public life.

In the 1950's anti-Semitic slogans accused Jews of communism and depicted the Soviet Union as an instrumentality of an international "Zionist" conspiracy. Anti-Zionism began to become a cloak for anti-Semitism. In the late 50's southern desegregation and the situation in the Near East were utilized by the anti-Semites. On occasion overt acts gave pungency to the pronouncements. The anti-Catholicism which came to the fore during the John F. Kennedy campaign for the presidency spilled over into anti-Semitism as well. The pro-Arab propaganda which was stepped up after the Suez and Sinai battles also contributed to a marked increase in anti-Semitic activity in 1960, highlighted by the organization of an American Nazi Party. Seven synagogue-bombing incidents were reported, swastikas were daubed on Jewish institutions, and the press gave wide coverage to anti-Jewish activities.

Throughout this time the official and formal relationships among Jewish, Catholic, and Protestant groups remained firm, warm, and active. They not only labored to establish stronger ties between themselves and to foster bonds of understanding between their constituents, but also joined in a common endeavor in a great effort to erase racial discrimination. Leaders of the "three faiths" marched together in protest against bigotry and labored for racial integration in American life.

The 1960's saw a breakdown in interfaith relations and activities. At the same time a threat to Jewish security and well-being was seen to arise from a new source. Rising militancy and demands for Black Power led to a rejection by the Negro minority of white "paternalism" and liberal benevolence. Confrontations that ensued included attacks against Jews. The most highly publicized confrontation was during the strike of the largely Jewish United Federation of Teachers in New York City in 1968. Proponents of "community control" in Black school districts, mainly Ocean Hill-Brownsville, were accused of anti-Semitic pronouncements and acts.

Geoffrey Wigoder's report on the "Jewish Scene" in the *Jerusalem Post,* June 3, 1970, was headlined: "A Look at Black Anti-Semitism." He states:

> While it is extremely difficult to gauge black hostility toward the Jews, it can be said it is not something new. It goes back a few decades and is rooted in the unequal status, friction-generating urban encounters (of landlord-tenant, merchant-consumer, housewife-domestic).

His conclusion:

> Only a small minority of militants have stridently reproached the Jewish State and proclaimed their racial solidarity with the Arab world. And although those in the black community who are outspokenly pro-Arab are most likely to be nationalists, not even the majority of black nationalists are vocally anti-Zionist.

In a widely quoted and discussed article in *Commentary,* "The Black Revolution and the Jewish Question," Earl Raab speaks of the residue of anti-Semitic sentiment which remains in America, and points to the readiness with which it is used by the Black Revolution. Anti-Semitism may be, to be sure, merely an expression of anti-whiteism, but what difference does that make functionally? The Jew still suffers. Nor can the Jew take hope that white America, seeing it as an arrow armed against itself, would rise in opposition to it, for it was learned during World War II, that though Nazism was linked with anti-Semitism in the minds of most Americans, there was "increased hostility toward Nazism, without reducing hostility toward Jews."

Confronted with new and unexpected realities in American life, symbolized and characterized by the Black Revolution, the Jewish community, says Raab, is being spurred "into a renewed understanding of pluralistic politics. . . . There is a new tendency to ask seriously a question which has been asked jokingly for a number of decades: " 'Is it good for the Jews?' "

During the decade, the coalition of the "three great faiths" had come apart. This came dramatically to the fore in the spring of 1967. When the future of the State of Israel seemed in jeopardy, most American Jews sensed their own status and security tied to the fate of Israel. They found almost no understanding or appreciation of this on the part of the organized Christian community with whom they had ties of mutually expressed admiration and commonly shared enterprises. In the wake of the Six Day War, an assessment of the situation disclosed that most American Christian leaders and organizations had remained silent before the war and many turned cool after. There was great heart-searching among those who had made investments in building bridges to the Christian community and found that when they were needed the bridges collapsed.

Interfaith activity had been evaporating during the 60's. What happened in 1967 was only an attestation of what had been happening over a decade and more. Interfaith came to an end because the needs which established it came to an end and the energies which propelled it had turned to other interests and commitments. The Jews entered into interfaith activities with all their enthusiasm and zeal, for they saw in it a vehicle for the strengthening of their acceptance, status, and security in America. It would also serve as a dignified vehicle of integration into mainstream American life. Further, amity and goodwill is in the service of America, for it adds to national unity and stability, not to speak of such ideals as "brotherhood, equality, etc." Christians of goodwill entered with religious devoutness into an activity which was expressive of Christian love—particularly for a people long bereft of and therefore in need of "love". It was also an expression of traditional American hospitality to the newcomer and stranger.

As the Jew became integrated into American life and as he found ever wider acceptance in industry and culture, the need for "interfaith" decreased. Moreover, office, factory, campus, and neighborhood now served as more natural and effective vehicles for integration and acceptance. Jews began to cool to it because it no longer served a pressing need. At first organization and zeal were turned from "mutual admiration" fests into common endeavors in service of the nation in the race revolution. Commissions on religion and race did good and effective work, but soon the Black community rejected these as paternalistic and patronizing.

The Christian community now turned its missionary zeal inward to the inner city. Energies once used for interfaith were now utilized in the service of a greater felt need, inter-race. The sentiments of ecumenism, once expressed in Jewish-Christian interfaith activities, now found a more meaningful expression in Christian intrafaith projects made possible by a new openness in Catholicism engendered by the spirit and acts of Vatican II.

It should be noted also that the crisis besetting organized religion in the 70's caused each religious group to turn its concern, resources, and energies inward, to reassess its own situation and restructure itself towards a greater effectiveness which would assure its viability and survival.

A manifestation of this "inward turning" in the American Jewish community is its increasing concern for the welfare of the Jews of the Soviet Union.

As early as 1954, Abraham Joshua Heschel sounded the alarm, and called upon free American Jewry to use its voice and influence against the government-inspired "cultural genocide" which threatened Russian Jewish life with extinction. In the 60's, national organizations convened conferences and sponsored meetings. More vocal and more radical in their activity were Jewish student organizations. The post-1967 years saw a dramatic expression of Jewish national and cultural reawakening in the Soviet Union, and an increase in immigration to

Israel. Equally great was the interest of American Jews, old as well as young, dramatized by the emergence of the Jewish Defense League, with a militancy in word and deed unprecedented in Jewish life. Denounced by the organizations of the American Jewish establishment, it nevertheless gained considerable grassroots approval.

As the Jew prepares for his future in an America which has opened up to him its resources, campus, culture, and neighborhoods, he might well ponder two statements. One, by a seventeen year old black girl in an essay which appeared as an introduction to a catalogue of an exhibition, "Harlem On My Mind," at the Metropolitan Museum of Art in the winter of 1969:

> . . . psychologically Blacks may find that anti-Jewish sentiments place them, for once, within a majority. Thus, our contempt for the Jew makes us feel more completely American in sharing a national prejudice.

The other, by Earl Raab, in the abovementioned essay:

> . . . there is a liberal movement toward the public-funded privatization of the public school system . . . the consequences of such a development, with its potential for racial, ethnic and religious separation, may call for independent evaluation by the Jewish community . . . [it] may be required to act more politically as a community if it is to hold its own. . . .

The past quarter of a century turns out not to have been, as some envisioned, the passageway to some terminal American dream. It has been a staging ground for some as yet indistinct future American design. The Jews, somehow in trouble again, need to make their own particular sighting on that future.

5. *Religion, Education, Culture*

The American Jewish community is at one and the same time part of world Jewry and a component of the American nation. The spiritual life of this community has been shaped and is influenced by the demands and requirements of Judaism and by the realities which have been and are today the American environment. Two features above all others characterize American Jewish religious life: the tripartite division into Orthodox, Conservative, and Reform, and the centrality of the synagogue.

The first Jews arrived in New Amsterdam in the summer of 1654. The following March the minister of the Dutch Reformed Church wrote to his superiors in Amsterdam that he feared "that a lot would yet follow and then build here their synagogue." That his fears were based on the actual desires and plans of the Jewish arrivals is borne out by a letter of Governor Peter Stuyvesant to his superiors, dated June 10, 1656, in which he complains: ". . . they [the Jewish nation] have many times requested of us the free and public exercise of their abominable religion." A congregation was established in New Amsterdam. More followed and the synagogue became a part of the religious landscape of America.

Nineteenth-century visitors to America were surprised at the central role which religion played in the life of the people. The Italian Jesuit, Giovanni Antonio Grassi, who lived in America early in the century, writes with astonishment that "every religion and every sect is fully tolerated, is equally protected, and equally treated . . ." and that "there is . . . much show of piety." A later observer, Alexis De Tocqueville, reports that, "There is no country in the whole world in which the Christian religion retains a greater influence over the souls of men than in America," and that, "The sects which exist . . . are innumerable. They all differ in respect to worship which is due to man from his Creator, but they all agree in respect to the duties which are due from man to man." And he adds: "The Americans combine the notions of Christianity and of liberty so intimately in their minds that it is impossible to make them conceive the one without the other."

Grassi, the priest, is struck by the proliferation of sects which freedom permits. The layman, De Tocqueville, noting the same, understands that the freedom which permits division on matters of doctrine unites men in their esteem of religion as necessary for democracy and liberty.

Until the end of the nineteenth century, America was a land of the frontier (and in large measure many of the features of the frontier continue on into the twentieth century). On the frontier, religious life flourished for it served as a civilizing, culturizing, and stabilizing force, and it mitigated the perils of existence with the assurance of a kindly, watchful, ever-present Providence. Church and churchman were considered necessary ingredients in the unfolding of the American dream and the fulfillment of American destiny. The vast spaces of the expanding frontier and the variety of its population as well as its pioneering spirit in all matters—geographical, political, and spiritual—made for a proliferation of religious groups. But they were all accepted as legitimate and respected as useful.

Against this background of esteem for religion, the church and the churchman, and the ready acceptance of religious differences, organized Jewish religious life developed in America. The synagogue in America was a socializing, culturizing, civilizing, stabilizing force in the life of the immigrant community. It also provided a "tie with home" and served as a "surrogate family," for the recent arrivals. More, it was an "Americanizing" force, bringing the Jew into American life, for the synagogue was viewed by all not only as a Jewish institution but as an American institution as well. This accounts for the American phenomenon of Jews who, on the one hand, declared themselves "not religious" yet, on the other hand, were staunch supporters and often leaders of a synagogue.

The freedom of America permitted free choice in all matters and considered one choice as right and legitimate as another. Orthodox, Reform, or Conservative views could make for division and dissension, but American freedom and tolerance in matters of conscience, forced an acceptance of the legitimacy of dissent upon all but the most militant proponents of one or another religious outlook.

In the twentieth century religious affiliation increased in significant measure. In 1890, 22.2% of the population of the United States were reported as being members of churches. By 1950, the percentage had risen to 57% and, by 1967, it reached 63.2%, or one hundred and twenty-six million men, women, and children. Jewish affiliation increased in similar manner, at first slowly, but after World War II, in dramatic fashion.

In 1951, Will Herberg estimated that 3,400,000, some 68% of America's five million Jews were in some way associated with a synagogue or temple. He also claimed that beyond the "physical growth" of Jewish religious institutions, there was a discernible "interest in, and concern with religion, as manifested by the present student generation."[7] A less sanguine view was that of Abraham S. Halkin who observed, "the increase in the number of synagogues built can . . . be readily ascribed to geographic and social factors rather than to a religious revival."[8]

Whether the growth in the number of congregations in the percentage of affiliation and in the erection of synagogues was due to sociological forces or religious awakening was debated throughout the 1950's. But the physical growth in institutions and activities was apparent in the new suburbs which became the areas of Jewish residence in postwar America. The "cathedral synagogues" of the inner city built in the twenties were abandoned and new multi-purpose synagogues blending into the suburban landscape were erected and staffed and programmed to "meet the spiritual, cultural and social needs of every member of every family." The boast of justification was that at long last the synagogue was fulfilling the function which its names promised—*beth tefillah,* a house of worship; *beth hamidrash,* a house of study; and *beth haknesseth,* a house of assembly.

A survey article in *The New York Times,* in 1959[9] about the proliferation of congregations in the New York area disclosed that since 1947, ninety-nine new congregations had sprung up in the suburbs, thirty-one Reform, thirty-three Conservative, and thirty-five Orthodox.

Jewish life increasingly centered about the synagogue and expressed itself through its activities. As the Jewish home became more and more assimilated to the environment, and as the life style of the Jew became more and more like that of

[7] *Judaism,* Summer 1951.

[8] *Judaism,* Spring 1954.

[9] April 6, 1959.

his middle class neighbor, synagogue activities and projects became the chief, if not the sole expressions of Jewish living. There were indeed those who raised the alarm, warning that the synagogue cannot take the place of home, as the schoolhouse and arena of Jewish living, and that activities and projects cannot compensate for the loss of the Jewish way of life. But a feature of American religious life already noted in the nineteenth century would not be denied: religion in America functions more through institutions and their activities than through convictions which are expressed through a way of living.

A reaction to religion as leisure play-time activity was beginning to be discerned in the late fifties among thoughtful and serious religious leaders and scholars. Surveying the literature of the period, Jacob Neusner found that there were "strong signs of theological concern and seriousness about Jewish faith," and that the writings "stressed the compelling relevance of Judaism for contemporary man." The Jewish theological seminaries were finding a new breed of students applying for admission. Heretofore most of the students came to the Seminary out of the experience of Jewish living, coming from homes devoutly Jewish and backgrounds of Jewish learning. Now a significant number of young men, raised in homes tangentially Jewish, found Judaism in practice in summer camps, or in its promise in courses in religion in the university, and come for Seminary studies to prepare for a life of Jewish religious service and/or scholarship. Because of the changed nature of its student bodies (in 1957–58 more of its students were graduates of Harvard than of Yeshiva University) the Jewish Theological Seminary reorganized its curriculum in 1957, placing greater emphasis on traditional text studies and laying down more stringent demands for religious observance. The Isaac Elchanan Theological Seminary of Yeshiva University broadened and liberalized its *semiḥah* (ordination) program, and the Hebrew Union College-Jewish Institute of Religion increased emphasis on the study of these sacred texts and the Hebrew language.

The 1960's saw a rise in Jewish theological writing and interest. The trend toward the discovery of contemporary relevance in the tradition, which Neusner noted in the fifties, continued and grew. Jewish thought became a central concern of a small but influential group of Jewish scholars. The existentialist mood was evidenced in the popularity of the writings of Martin Buber, Franz Rosenzweig and Abraham Joshua Heschel, and in renewed interest in the ways of Ḥasidism. One met with serious theological interest and concern on the campus and saw it in the writings of "radical" Jewish students seeking a new view of God, world and self, and a new way of life.

The *American Jewish Year Book* reports:

During the Hebrew calendar year, 5722, that is from September 11, 1961 to September 28, 1962, press, periodicals, institutional bulletins and other literature continued to report on the flourishing state of the American Jewish communities' religious bodies. Attention was drawn to increased congregational membership, newly established congregations, higher enrollments in Sunday, part-time and all-day religious schools, and the growing number of adult study groups and student programs.[10]

A year later, the *Year Book* reports:

Organizationally, 1962-63 was a year of consolidation rather than expansion for the American synagogue.[11]

The next year the survey of religious life states that in the year 1964 and 1965:

There has been no decline in Jewish religious life, but the force of upsurge which characterized the American Jewish community immediately after World War II has abated.

It must be emphasized that organizations continued to maintain high levels of activity but there has been no sign of rethinking within any of the Jewish religious groups comparable to the major reformation that has taken place within Catholicism.[12]

[10] Freda Imrey, Volume 64, 1963, p. 145.

[11] Morris Kertzer, Volume 65, 1964, p. 75.

[12] Sefton Temkin, Volume 67, 1966, p. 176.

Much of the rethinking has taken place in Jewish religious life and many of the attempts at reformation in its institutions have taken place outside the religious establishments. Creative Jewish theological thinking and writing and innovative institutional experimentation (as, for example, the *ḥavurah* or religious commune) have generally not been institutionally sponsored or organizationally supported.

In the waning years of the sixties and in the early seventies there was a perceptible weakening in organized religious life. It was in part due to the general crisis in organized religious life in America. Church membership had dipped and church attendance had declined. The mainline Protestant bodies were experiencing a serious diminution in adherents, support, and influence. Aspects of Catholic life were in disarray. Only the Fundamentalist, Adventist churches were healthy and growing.

In the Jewish community the number of synagogues was diminishing. Some closed down because of neighborhood changes, others amalgamated. Synagogue membership seemed to be in decline while the median age of members had gone up. Reports from college campuses indicate that interest in and attendance at "services" per se was at a minimum. There was life and vitality and increase in right-wing orthodoxy in the large urban centers. The hasidic groups showed signs of spiritual well-being and *Habad hasidim* carried on missionary educational campaigns in communities and on campus which aroused interests and gained some "converts."

In the 1970's Jewish life in America continued to revolve about the synagogue. Healthy or ailing it remained the central institution of American Jewry. There were indications that individual synagogues, and belatedly the national synagogal bodies, were beginning to see and face up to the challenges of the growing secularization and polarization of America. Some indications and direction toward a solution may be found in some heartening phenomena in the life of a small but growing segment of young Jewish Americans.

Since 1967 in particular there has been great interest in the way of life of Israel's Jewish community. Some see the concept of the kibbutz as an attractive alternative to middle-class life. Some are attracted to the spirit of commitment, seriousness and purpose they sense in Israel. Some have "found religion" in the Holy Land. The idea and experience of *ḥavurah* living is gaining interest and adherents. There is a growing interest in religion on campus. The number of courses in Jewish studies has proliferated and the attendance has been beyond expectations. Some students have organized "free Jewish universities" for expanded Jewish studies, and kosher eating clubs are growing in number. There is some indication, then, that Judaism as a subject of serious study is gaining interest and that one or another form of Jewish living as an alternate life style may find adherents.

Young American Jews seem to be seeking what thoughtful young Americans seek—a faith worthy of one's interest and commitment, the experience of true communal living, and a set of values and way of living which raise the individual to significance, which make him feel wanted and loved in the world.

Spokesmen for Judaism will proclaim that Judaism offers all that and more. It remains to be seen whether organized Jewish religious life in America can restructure itself to offer what is sought, whether the next generation will find spiritual sustenance in or outside organized Jewish religion, or in some other faith or spiritual discipline.

6. *Education*

In the past half-century, the sponsorship of Jewish education changed radically from a preponderance of schools under communal organization to some eighty-five percent in the 1970's under congregational auspices. One of the effects of this has been to create a large number of school units. Of the two thousand or more schools, the great majority are too small to be a viable and effective school unit. There are, however, a significant number of large congregational schools, adequately funded and staffed with enrollments of above five hundred.

In the post-World War II years the most significant rise in school enrollment has been in the all-day schools. Previously they were almost all in the greater New York area and attracted students almost wholly from Orthodox families. A quarter of a century after the War, almost one of every seven students enrolled in any sort of Jewish school was in a day-school, over 60,000. The percentage was even higher in the large metropolitan areas where the motivation for day-school enrollment was not only religious or cultural but resulted also from the difficulties besetting the urban public school system.

Almost half of the Jewish school population was enrolled in Sunday School, deemed as inadequate by all three religious movements. The Conservative movement had all but eliminated the Sunday School for the middle grades in favor of a week-day supplementary school. The greatest strength for the Sunday School lay in the Reform movement. But more and more Reform congregations were adding week-day afternoon instruction to the Sunday School. Orthodox week-day afternoon education was weakened in its numbers by the loss of potential students to the day school.

The curricula of the weekday schools are remarkably similar be they Orthodox, Conservative, or Reform. The differences are more structural than ideological, the Conservative and Orthodox requiring more hours per week and more years of attendance than the Reform. In all schools there is considerable emphasis on the Hebrew language but achievement rarely matches goals. The achievement levels of the day-school in Hebrew language, literature, history, and Bible studies is notable, both because of the amount of time devoted to Jewish studies each week and because pupils react with more seriousness and greater motivation toward a school which is their total arena for formal education and not merely supplemental to their general schooling as are the weekday afternoon and Sunday schools.

From 1948 to 1954 student enrollment in Jewish schools rose from 240,000 to 400,000. Fifty-two percent attended Sunday schools, the rest week-day and all-day schools. The next two years witnessed a 22% increase to 488,000. A similar increase was achieved by Protestant and Catholic schools in these years. The increase continued to 1962 when the total enrollment was reported as 588,955. In the mid-60's a decline began. The 1966–67 census of Jewish schools estimates a total enrollment of 554,468. The decline continues as a result of a decreased Jewish birthrate and projections for the future see this an ongoing trend. The percentage of pupils attending Sunday school decreased from 53.9% in 1962 to 42.2% in 1967, while the percent in all-day schools rose from 8.8% to 13.4%. We thus see a decrease in numbers but an increase in intensity of education.

There are eleven accredited teacher-training institutions in the United States but it has been estimated that they graduate only one-tenth of the teachers needed to replace those leaving the profession.

A significant contribution to education has been made by educational summer camps such as Masad and the Ramah network of the Conservative movement. All three religious groups have growing programs of informal education in the summer months in Israel.

Jewish education is beset with the problems which have brought on a crisis in education in America. Added to these are the special problems of inadequate hours, too few years, and lack of motivation brought on by the knowledge that (save in the day schools) the Jewish school is supplemental to the public school. Despite these difficulties some significant progress has been made. A very large percentage of Jewish children are exposed to some form of Jewish education. A growing number is receiving an adequate (often excellent) Jewish education in the day schools.

7. *Culture*

In the late 1950's and the 1960's Jewish writers were widely considered to form the dominant "school" in literature and criticism. Any best-seller list throughout this period contained one or more books written by Jews and usually concerning Jews.

This eminence was achieved after the great mass of East European immigrants, or their children, had learned the language and found themselves at home in the new land; and after writers, publishers and the reading public, horrified by the Holocaust and enchanted by the establishment of Israel, found a new interest in the Jew as a subject.

The most brilliant of the analysts of the place of the Jew in the world, Maurice Samuel, continued as the "premier teacher" on the Jew, his fate and his faith, through book and lecture platform. Norman Mailer dazzled the literary scene with what many consider the finest war novel, *The Naked and the Dead,* and developed his own form of literary expression which weds fiction to historic event. Herman Wouk won wide readership for his portrayal of the shallowness of middle-class Jews of New York in his *Marjorie Morningstar,* and turned his talent to a "love paean" to traditional Judaism, *This Is My God.* The most comprehensive fictional study of American Jewry since the turn of the century are the novels of Charles Angoff.

Arthur Miller was one of the leading playwrights of the 1960's, and Karl Shapiro, the most noted Jewish poet. The leading arbiters of literary taste were mainly Jewish, the critics Norman Podhoretz (editor of *Commentary*), Leslie Fieldler, Irving Howe, and Alfred Kazin.

A strange but telling phenomenon is the popularity of the novels and short stories of Isaac Beshevis Singer. A Yiddish writer, living in New York, he writes about the *shtetl,* but peoples his Eastern European scene with grotesqueries, writing with an unfettered picaresque imagination. It is instructive, too, to note that the most popular stage production of the sixties (and continued so into the seventies) was *Fiddler On the Roof,* a musical production based on Sholom Aleichem's tales of *Tevya, The Milkman.*

It was a group of Jewish novelists who colored the American literary scene of the sixties "Jewish." Most notable were J. D. Salinger, whose novels of the "half-Jewish" Glass family captured the mood and affection of young America. Philip Roth soared to popularity through stories about Jews in *Goodby Columbus,* and *Portnoy's Complaint,* a literary sensation about the sex-obsessed son of his son-obsessed Jewish mother. A more sensitive and gifted writer is Bernard Malamud. His people are real, poignant, strugglers for survival, for whom survival is salvation, and who grow into heroes in their striving for integrity. *The* novelist of the period is Saul Bellow, a man of broad general and Jewish culture, possessed of a superior intellect and a gifted pen. His *Herzog* is the central statement of the theme of the times, alienation and search for identity.

The Jewish contribution to, and coloration of the American literary scene in the sixties is stated in the lead article in the *New York Times Book Review* (May 30, 1965), titled, "Some of Our Best Writers":

> There seems to be a dominant school at any given time in American fiction; in the 1920's it was realist-naturalist; in the 1930's it was proletarian; in the 1940's and early 1950's it was southern. We live now in the time of Bellow, Malamud, Mailer, Salinger, and Roth.

But, perhaps better known than any of the above as a purveyor of culture in America and as representative of the many Jews in musical creativity, was the talented Leonard Bernstein. Composer, director, pianist, he dominated, for a time, the cultural scene of the cultural capital of America, New York.

Of more lasting significance to the Jewish cultural enterprise is the emergence of a generation of American-trained Jewish scholars. The giants, Salo Baron in history, Harry A. Wolfson in philosophy, Saul Lieberman in rabbinics, H. L. Ginsberg in Bible, Abraham Joshua Heschel in theology, and Joseph B. Soloveitchik and Louis Finkelstein as religious teachers, continued in their creativity and influence.

We may add as products of American training such as have already put forth students and disciples, Jacob R. Marcus in American Jewish history and Robert Gordis and Harry Orlinsky in Bible. But what is most notable is the group of scholars who came to the fore in the 1960's. A too brief listing would remind us of Judah Goldin and David Weiss in rabbinics; Moshe Greenberg, Nahum Sarna and Yohanan Muffs in Bible; Jacob Neusner, Ellis Rivkin, Gerson D. Cohen, Joseph Yerushalmi, Lloyd Gartner, Isadore Twersky in various branches of historical study; Marshall Sklare and Charles S. Liebman in the sociology of the Jew; and Eugene Borowitz, Seymour Siegel, Jacob Petuchowski and Arthur A. Cohen in Jewish thought.

8. *On the Question of Survival*

One of the most knowledgeable and thoughtful students of the American Jewish scene, Marshall Sklare, writes in the March, 1970 issue of *Commentary:*

> American Jewry may be inordinately "problem"-ridden and "crisis"-beset, but its institutions, with all their attendant activities, continue to thrive. New synagogues and community centers are constantly being built. . . . Enrollment in Jewish day schools shows a steady growth. . . . Even the grave problem of the loss of Jewish identity among college youth is not entirely a one-sided proposition. There is a new enthusiasm for Jewish studies on the campus and it is now harder to find suitable instructors than it is to attract interested students.

Having said this, Dr. Sklare continues:

> But whatever significance one may attach to these developments, they are overshadowed by one persistent trend: the ever-increasing incidence of intermarriage between Jews and non-Jews. It is intermarriage which weighs more heavily than all the positive trends combined, and which calls into question the "creative survival," as the phrase has it, of the American Jewish community.

What raises Sklare's fears is the disclosure in a study of the Jewish population of Boston in 1965 that in marriages where the husband is between the ages of 31–50, the incidence of intermarriage is 7%, but where the husband is under 30, it is 20%. He extrapolates that if in 1965 the intermarriage incidence is one of five marriages, by 1970 it must have risen to one in four. He further argues that "if this is true in so conservative a city as Boston, it must mean that intermarriage has reached large-scale proportions throughout the country as a whole."

The dramatic increase in intermarriage in the United States and its threat to Jewish survival became a matter of central Jewish concern in the 1960's. It had been generally assumed that the rate hovered about six or seven percent. Indeed, the United States Census Bureau reported in March 1957 that the percentage of families in which *one* of the spouses is Jewish is 7.2%. A study of the Jewish population of Greater Washington, D. C., in 1956 disclosed that the rate of intermarriage in that community was 13.1%. It was also found that 70% of the children of intermarried couples were not Jewish. It was further disclosed that in Iowa the rate between 1953 and 1959 averaged 42.2%.

Erich Rosenthal delineated the problem in 1960:

> If we accept the findings of the 1957 survey of the United States Bureau of the Census of a national intermarriage rate (for Jews) of 7.2%, and if at the same time we assume that the statistics for Iowa and the San Francisco area (31%, 17.2%, 20% and 37%) are merely regional variations of an over-all rate, we can probably be justified in defending the current survival formula as adequate for the preservation of the Jewish group. If we assume, however, that the findings for Iowa and San Francisco are the first indications of the future over-all rate of intermarriage, then the efficacy of the survival formula must be seriously doubted.[13]

To be sure there were intimations and indications that the rate of intermarriage would increase as the American Jew became more integrated in American society. The Jews of the cities of Western Europe had become integrated before their American counterpart. The rate of intermarriage there in the 1920's and 1930's was: Vienna, 25%; Budapest, 28%; Berlin, 45%; Trieste, 71%.[14]

Indications of increase were unfolded by statistics. In the United States the incidence increased from 2% in 1912 to 7.2%

[13] Erich Rosenthal, "Acculturation Without Assimilation?" *American Journal of Sociology*, Volume LXVI, November 3, 1960.

[14] Aryeh Tartakower, *Ḥahevra Hayehudit*, p. 217.

in 1957. In San Francisco it grew from 6.9% in 1938 to 17.2% twenty years later.

Certainly someone should have raised the alarm of the impending problem and threat. Professor Mordecai Kaplan did so in *Judaism As A Civilization,* in 1934:

> Jews must be prepared to reckon frankly and intelligently with intermarriage as a growing tendency, which, if left uncontrolled, is bound to prove Judaism's undoing.

But other matters took priority on the Jewish communal agenda and nothing was done in anticipation and preparation.

Added to its rapid growth is its acceptance by the community and by some religious leaders as well. It does not stand in the way of a person's assuming national or local leadership of a Jewish organization or institution, nor in some instances even congregational leadership. The following announcement of a marriage in *The New York Times* is not unique:

> Miss J . . . R . . . S . . . was married yesterday to H . . . M . . . J . . . Rabbi L . . . B . . . performed the ceremony in his study at Central Synagogue, after which the Rev. T . . . B . . . blessed the marriage at St. Thomas Protestant Episcopal Church.

As one follows wedding reports one finds that more and more are solemnized by judges. "It was a Jewish judge," is offered as explanation for "Jewish" legitimization. In the above-quoted statement, Professor Kaplan continues:

> They [the Jews] must realize that the power and vitality of a civilization are put to test whenever the members of different civilizations come into social contact with each other. When that contact results in intermarriage and children are born, the more vigorous civilization will be the one to which the children will belong.

Professor Kaplan speaks of intermarriage but his analysis and caveat may be expanded to the whole question of continuity of a tradition and survival of a community. In the open and fluid American society, children born of Jewish (as well as intermarried) parents have the option to choose among the different civilizations which comprise the American scene. "The more vigorous civilization will be the one to which the children will belong."

The decades ahead will be a time of testing whether the "civilization" called American Judaism will have the vigor, vitality and ongoing promise to hold its own children.

We find in America a vibrancy in Jewish communal endeavor and a vitality in Jewish institutional life unmatched in any Diaspora community. There are those who are beginning to discern a new awakening to Jewish living and to the promise of Jewish creativity in the generation now emerging. Perhaps there is no more than a spark but traditional Jewish optimism already sees a bright flame.

Pessimistic concern and optimistic certainty mingle to make the mood of contemporary American Jewry. An ancient and perennial mood and belief, holding to this paradox as a philosophy of history and a commitment of life, speaking in fear: "We may be the last generation of Jews," and proclaiming in faith: "We are an eternal people."

Index